Models of Voting in Presidential Elections

MODELS OF VOTING
IN PRESIDENTIAL ELECTIONS

The 2000 U.S. Election

**Edited by Herbert F. Weisberg
and Clyde Wilcox**

STANFORD LAW AND POLITICS
An imprint of Stanford University Press
Stanford, California 2004

Stanford University Press
Stanford, California

Printed in the United States of America on acid-free, archival-quality paper

Library of Congress Cataloging-in-Publication Data
Models of voting in presidential elections : the 2000 U.S. election / edited by
Herbert F. Weisberg and Clyde Wilcox.
    p. cm.
    "Chapters in this book were originally commissioned for a conference . . . held at
the Mershon Center on the Ohio State University campus, March 7–10, 2002"—Pref.
    Includes bibliographical references and index.
    ISBN 0-8047-4855-1 (alk. paper)—ISBN 0-8047-4856-X (pbk. : alk. paper)
    1. Presidents—United States—Election—2000. I. Weisberg, Herbert F.
II. Wilcox, Clyde, date–
JK526 2000 .M63   2004
324.973'0929—dc22   2003015436
ISBN 978-0-8047-4855-1 ISBN 978-0-8047-4856-8
Original Printing 2004

Last figure below indicates year of this printing:
13 12 11 10 09 08 07 06 05 04

Typeset by G & S Typesetters, Inc. in 9.7/11 Sabon

Contents

Tables and Figures

Tables

Figures

Preface

The chapters in this book were originally commissioned for a conference, "Assessing the Vitality of Electoral Democracy in the U.S.: The 2000 Elections," which was held at the Mershon Center on the Ohio State University campus, March 7–10, 2002. (It was originally scheduled to be held September 21, 2001, but was postponed after the September 11 terrorist attacks.) The conference was sponsored by the Mershon Center along with the Department of Political Science and the College of Social and Behavioral Sciences of the Ohio State University.

The conference grew out of a concern about the health of America's electoral democracy, a concern that existed even before the outcome of the 2000 election produced a vote total that was too close to call. Low voter turnout and increased polarization were seen as potential challenges to government legitimacy. At the same time, increased political independence, stronger third-party movements, and divided government could also make it more difficult for either party to govern effectively. Thus, recent U.S. electoral trends were viewed as potentially threatening the legitimacy and governability that are essential to successful electoral democracy.

America's national security depends centrally on the maintenance of its democracy, and the health of America's democracy depends directly on the continued vitality of its electoral democracy. The 1980s and 1990s witnessed a wave of democratization across the world, but at the same time there were threats to the health of American democracy. Countries as diverse as Spain, Russia, and Chile now use free and meaningful elections to determine their leaders, while the electoral health of the United States weakened.

The unusual outcome of the 2000 election could have exacerbated these concerns, but instead the public accepted the results as legitimate. Surveys show that the closeness of the outcome did not delegitimize the election. The public did not even view the postelection situation as a crisis; a majority felt that the president should go ahead with his plans for the country regardless of the small margin of victory. Even though surveys found that many people believed that Bush had not won the election fairly, the overwhelming majority of the public accepted him as the legitimate president. As Paul Beck argued at the election conference at Ohio State, even supporters of losing candidates are not too troubled by election outcomes because the business of most Americans is not politics. People just wanted to get on with their business.

Three subsequent events beyond the president's control further diminished any lingering concerns about the legitimacy of the Bush presidency. First, the September 11 terrorist attacks on the United States caused the country to come together behind its leader. Second, Republican gains in the 2002 midterm election were widely interpreted as giving Bush the mandate that the 2000 election did not confer on him. Third, Al Gore's decision in late 2002 not to run again in 2004 assured the country that the 2004 election would not degenerate into the type of vicious rerun election that occurred in 1828 and 1892 when candidates who had won the popular vote but lost the electoral college in the preceding elections argued that the office had been stolen from them.

An election reform law was enacted in the wake of the 2000 vote count debacle in Florida. That reform notwithstanding, the election was less influential in setting the agenda of American politics than were postelection events, such as Sen. James Jeffords's departure from the Republican Party, the recession, September 11, the Enron scandal, and the wars in Afghanistan and Iraq. Contrary to some initial expectations, reform of the electoral college did not become part of the public agenda, possibly because that would challenge the legitimacy of the Bush presidency.

The 2000 election has deservedly become the most studied of U.S. presidential elections, but we believe the approach this collection takes is original. The authors were asked to analyze empirical data about voting in the 2000 election, and we are using their research to contribute to the larger topic of understanding the models that are used to study presidential voting.

We are very appreciative of the conference's sponsors and hosts, the Mershon Center, as well as the Ohio State University's Department of Political Science and College of Social and Behavioral Sciences. We wish to thank the other participants in the conference for sharing their insights about the election as well as their comments on the papers, including Herb Asher, Paul Allen Beck, Gregory Caldeira, Morris Fiorina, Ken Goldstein, John Green, Michael Hagen, Sunshine Hillygus, Jon Krosnick, Dean Lacy, Steve Mockabee, Kira Sanbonmatsu, Merrill Shanks, and Rich Timpone. Also, anonymous reviewers provided very useful suggestions for revisions.

Additionally, we wish to express our gratitude to the contributors for staying with us as the conference was postponed and through seemingly innumerable revision requests. And, on behalf of our contributors, we acknowledge the National Election Studies for their continuing efforts to pursue an essential electoral data collection and to the National Science Foundation, in the hope that they recognize the vital importance of maintaining this invaluable resource. We owe a special indebtedness to Margaret Williams for her wonderful assistance in the conference, doubly so since she prepared the September conference and then stayed with the project when the conference had to be postponed. Elizabeth Cook spent hours proofreading the manuscript and helping with the copy edits. Keiko Ono helped with the preparation of the manuscript. Also, special gratitude to Kenneth Strickland for preparing the final manuscript, even through the difficulties of modern computer communications, and to Erin McAdams for indexing the book. Finally, our thanks to Amanda Moran and the people at Stanford University Press who worked with us on this project.

Contributors

Janet M. Box-Steffensmeier is a professor of political science at the Ohio State University. Her forthcoming book with Bradford Jones, *Timing and Political Change: Event History Modeling in Political Science*, will be published by the University of Michigan Press. She has published on election and public opinion in the *American Political Science Review, American Journal of Political Science,* and the *Journal of Politics.*

Barry C. Burden is Associate Professor of Government at Harvard University. His research and teaching focus on American politics, with an emphasis on electoral politics, public opinion, representation, and the U.S. Congress. He is coauthor with David Kimball of *Why Americans Split Their Tickets: Campaigns, Competition, and Divided Government* (University of Michigan Press, 2003) and editor of *Uncertainty in American Politics* (Cambridge University Press). He has also published numerous articles in the *American Political Science Review, American Journal of Political Science, Legislative Studies Quarterly, Political Science Quarterly,* and elsewhere. He is the recipient of the Council of Graduate Schools' Distinguished Dissertation Award for the best social science dissertation completed between 1998 and 2000 in the United States.

Steven E. Finkel is Professor of Politics at the University of Virginia. He has published numerous articles on political participation, public opinion, and voting behavior in the United States and cross-nationally, including "Rational Choice and Alternative Explanations of Collective Political Action" (with Edward N. Muller; in *American Political Science Review,* 1988) and "A Spot Check: Casting Doubt on the Demobilizing Effects of Attack

Advertising" (with John G. Geer; in *American Journal of Political Science*, 1998). He is currently involved in a multi-country project investigating the effects of civic education on democratic attitudes, values, and behavior in emerging democracies. His most recent publication from this project is "Civic Education and the Mobilization of Political Participation in Developing Democracies" (*Journal of Politics*, 2002).

Paul Freedman is Assistant Professor in the Department of Politics at the University of Virginia. His work has appeared in *Public Opinion Quarterly*, the *American Journal of Political Science*, the *Journal of Politics*, *Political Communication*, and *Campaigns and Elections*. Freedman has worked as an election analyst for ABC News and is currently working on a book about campaign advertising and American democracy.

J. Tobin Grant is an assistant professor of political science at Southern Illinois University at Carbondale. His research lies in the areas of political behavior, campaign finance, legislative politics, and religion and politics. He has published articles in the *American Journal of Political Science*, *American Politics Research*, *Geographical Analysis*, *Legislative Studies Quarterly*, *Political Analysis*, *Political Behavior*, *Political Research Quarterly*, and *Public Opinion Quarterly*. He is working on a book-length manuscript, *Expression versus Equality: The Politics of Campaign Finance*, from his research for The Joyce Foundation's 2000 American Politics Study.

Timothy G. Hill is an assistant professor of political science at Doane College. His dissertation examines the electoral effects of interest-group endorsements and the psychological mechanisms that may induce such effects. He is currently studying the political consequences of entertainment-oriented media. He has presented papers at the meetings of the American Political Science Association and the Midwest Political Science Association.

William G. Jacoby is a professor in the Department of Political Science at Michigan State University. His major areas of interest include public opinion and political behavior, measurement and scaling methods, and statistical graphics. Professor Jacoby is the author of *Data Theory and Dimensional Analysis, Statistical Graphics for Univariate and Bivariate Data*, and *Statistical Graphics for Visualizing Multivariate Data*. He is currently editor of the *Journal of Politics*, and he has published articles in such professional journals as the *American Journal of Political Science*, the *Journal of Politics*, and the *British Journal of Political Science*.

Kristin Kanthak is an assistant professor of political science at the University of Arizona. Her dissertation, entitled "Kissing Different Rings: The Three Regimes of Power Selection Rules in the U.S. House of Representatives," focuses on how the rules governing who receives plum committee assignments in the House affect the voting behavior of legislators. Her current research interests include the use of evolutionary game theory to explain how legislative rules create better environments for some legislators over others, thus affecting the types of legislators who win reelection and the types who opt to leave the legislature.

John H. Kessel is Professor Emeritus at the Ohio State University. He taught at Amherst College and Mount Holyoke College, the University of Washington, and Allegheny College before moving to the Ohio State University in 1970. His books include *The Goldwater Coalition* (Bobbs-Merrill, 1968), *Presidential Campaign Politics* (Dorsey, 1980), *Presidential Parties* (Dorsey, 1984), and *Presidents, the Presidency, and the Political Environment* (CQ Press, 2001). He has been editor of the *American Journal of Political Science* and president of the Midwest Political Science Association.

David C. Kimball is an assistant professor of political science at the University of Missouri-St. Louis. He and Barry Burden recently completed *Why Americans Split Their Tickets*, published by University of Michigan Press. He is coauthor of "Organized Interests and the Decision of Whom to Lobby in Congress" (with Marie Hojnacki; *in American Political Science Review*, 1998) and "A New Approach to the Study of Ticket-Splitting" (with Barry Burden; in *American Political Science Review*, 1998) and author of articles in the *Journal of Politics* and other professional journals. His research interests include voting behavior, election reform, and interest groups.

Richard G. Niemi is Don Alonzo Watson Professor of Political Science at the University of Rochester, where he has taught for thirty-five years and has served as department chair, associate dean, and interim dean. He is coauthor or coeditor of *Comparing Democracies 2: New Challenges in the Study of Elections and Voting* (with Lawrence LeDuc and Pippa Norris; Sage, 2002); *Vital Statistics on American Politics 2001–2002* (with Harold Stanley; CQ Press, 2001); *Controversies in Voting Behavior*, fourth edition (with Herbert F. Weisberg; CQ Press, 2001); *Term Limits in the State Legislatures* (with John M. Carey and Lynda W. Powell; University of Michigan Press, 2000); *Civic Education: What Makes Students Learn* (with Jane Junn; Yale University Press, 1998); and other books. Dr. Niemi has written numerous articles on political socialization, voting, and legislative districting. His current research includes civic education, term limits, and voting technologies.

Helmut Norpoth is Professor of Political Science at the State University of New York, Stony Brook. He is author of *Confidence Regained: Economics, Mrs. Thatcher, and the British Voter* (University of Michigan Press), coauthor of *Politics and Government in Europe Today* (with Colin Campbell, Harvey Ferigenbaum, and Ronald Linden; Houghton Mifflin), and coeditor of *Economics and Politics: The Calculus of Support* (with Michael S. Lewis-Beck and Jean-Dominique Lafay; University of Michigan Press). He has also published numerous articles on voting and public opinion in the *American Political Science Review*, the *American Journal of Political Science*, and *Public Opinion Quarterly*.

Barbara Norrander is Professor of Political Science at the University of Arizona. She is the author of *Super Tuesday: Regional Politics and Presidential Primaries* (University Press of Kentucky, 1992); coeditor of *Understanding Public Opinion*, second edition (with Clyde Wilcox; CQ Press, 2002); and coauthor of *American Government: Using MicroCase ExplorIt*, eighth edition (with Michael Corbett; Wadsworth-Thomson, 2003). She has published a number of articles on presidential primaries and caucuses, state policymaking, and the gender gap. She will serve as president of the Western Political Science Association in 2004.

Thomas J. Rudolph is Assistant Professor of Political Science at the University of Illinois at Urbana-Champaign. His research interests include campaign finance, political behavior, and political psychology. He is the author of "Who's Responsible for the Economy? The Formation and Consequences of Responsibility Attributions" (*American Journal of Political Science*), "Institutional Context and the Assignment of Political Responsibility" (*Journal of Politics*), "Corporate and Labor PAC Contributions in House Elections: Measuring the Effects of Majority Party Status" (*Journal of Politics*), and the coauthor of "Value Conflict, Group Affect, and the Issue of Campaign Finance" (with Tobin Grant; *American Journal of Political Science*, 2003).

Harold W. Stanley is Professor of Political Science at the University of Rochester. He is the author of articles on voting, political parties, and elections as well as *Voter Mobilization and the Politics of Race: The South and Universal Suffrage, 1952–1984* (Praeger, 1987) and *Senate versus Governor, Alabama 1971: Referents for Opposition in a One-Party Legislature* (University of Alabama Press, 1975). He is currently doing research on voting rights, partisan change, and voting.

Herbert F. Weisberg is Professor of Political Science at the Ohio State University. He has research interests in voting behavior, Congress, survey research, and political methodology. He has edited books on the 1992 and 1996 elections and is coeditor of *Controversies in Voting Behavior*, fourth edition (with Richard Niemi; CQ Press, 2001) and *Classics in Congressional Politics* (with Eric S. Heberlig and Lisa M. Campoli; Longman, 1999). Dr. Weisberg has been president of the Midwest Political Science Association and coeditor of the *American Journal of Political Science*. He authored the chapter on political partisanship in the latest edition of *Measures of Political Attitudes* (with John P. Robinson, Phillip R. Shauer, and Lawrence S. Wrightsman, editors; Academic Press, 1999) and a chapter on the political psychology of party identification in *Electoral Democracy*. Dr. Weisberg's other current projects include the books on Survey Research and Survey Errors and on Reelection and Incumbency Effects in Presidential Elections.

Clyde Wilcox is Professor of Government at Georgetown University. He is the author of a number of books and articles on religion and politics, gender politics, and campaign finance. His most recent books include *The Financiers of Congressional Elections: Investors, Ideologues, and Intimates* (with Peter L. Francia, John C. Green, Lynda W. Powell, and Paul S. Herrnson; Columbia University Press, 2003) and *Religion and Politics in Comparative Perspective: The One, the Few, and the Many* (with Ted G. Jelen; Cambridge, 2002).

Models of Voting in Presidential Elections

1   The Puzzle of the Missing Landslide

CLYDE WILCOX AND HERBERT F. WEISBERG

If a writer had submitted a script to *West Wing* with the narrative of the 2000 presidential election, the producers would likely have rejected it as implausible and convoluted. The election did have all of the elements of prime-time entertainment. It had elements of dynastic revenge: the son of a former president defeated the son of a senator who had been part of the Democratic team that had defeated his father. It had elements of intrigue: Florida Republicans made plans to certify electors in Florida regardless of the results of the recount, while Democrats planned strategies to disqualify absentee ballots in Florida. It had elements of irony: as election officials in Florida debated the definition of a vote, Fidel Castro offered to send a team of observers to ensure a fair recount. Finally, it had elements of drama: the post-election maneuvering lasted thirty-six days, and the election was finally decided by a single vote—in the Supreme Court.

The election ended as almost a perfect tie (Ceaser and Busch 2001). The national popular vote margin was a scant five hundred thousand votes, or approximately one-half of 1 percent of the vote cast. Bush won in the electoral college by just five votes, a margin inflated by the protest abstention of one elector from Washington, D.C. The election produced a Senate that was an exact tie and narrowed the already razor-thin majority of the Republicans in the House to only six seats. In Florida, Bush was ahead by fewer than five hundred votes out of more than six million cast, a margin smaller than might have been produced had every voter simply flipped a fair coin to determine their vote (Erikson 2001). Other states were also close: the margin in New Mexico was less than five hundred votes, and in Iowa, Wisconsin, Oregon, and New Hampshire the final margins were quite small.

Although the United States has for years advised emerging democracies to count the votes carefully, slowly, and by hand in the event of a close election, in 2000 the nation carefully recounted the votes in none of these states. Recounts were started, then stopped, then started, and then stopped in two Florida counties, amid hot disputes about the precise definition of a vote. Instead of agreeing to recount all states in dispute, the two campaigns mobilized batteries of attorneys to offer a complex and shifting set of arguments in front of the Florida and U.S. Supreme Courts. In the end the U.S. Supreme Court halted the Florida recount, ironically basing their decision on the equal protection clause though the election was one in which thousands were disenfranchised by the technologies of voting.

Perhaps the most remarkable element of the election endgame was the scrambling by both parties to maximize their advantage. Anticipating the opposite outcome—Bush winning the popular vote but losing in the electoral college—Republicans set the stage for a planned advertising campaign to troll for unfaithful electors. On election night, Newt Gingrich planted the seed for this campaign by arguing on national television that "whoever wins the popular vote will find a way to win in the electoral college." Not surprisingly, this theme did not appear again in GOP discourse. The rhetorical exchanges were sometimes amusing: Gore's lawyers argued that it was important to count all votes though the Gore campaign planned to challenge absentee ballots, and Bush's advocates claimed with a straight face that the "dimpled chads" were evidence that many Florida voters had started to vote for Gore but recoiled at the last minute.

The 2000 elections will long have a place in history books. A photo of a tired Florida election official squinting at the punch-card ballot that he held up to the light quickly came to symbolize the drawn-out endgame of the election—the strategic maneuvers, legal battles, and complicated technical questions. The elections will have a long life in political trivia games as well. Distinctions between dimpled, hanging, and pregnant chads; "butterfly" ballot; and other colorful terms have entered the popular political vocabulary as a result of the 2000 presidential elections. But the election also raises deeper questions about models of electoral outcomes and vote choice.

The Puzzle of the Missing Landslide

For political scientists who study American elections, perhaps the most remarkable element of the 2000 election was the challenges it posed for well-established theories. At the American Political Science Association meeting in Washington in September 2000, several scholars presented the results of their estimates of the forthcoming vote based on statistical models of aggregate electoral outcomes that had been developed and fitted to past elections. Although these models vary in their predictors, they generally include one or more measures of the performance of the economy and some measure of the popularity of the incumbent president. Many of these models had done quite well in earlier elections and had correctly predicted George Bush's come-from-behind victory over Michael Dukakis in 1988. All of these models predicted a victory for Vice President Al Gore in November, with a two–party vote share of between 53 percent and 60 percent (see Table 3.1).

Individual-level models of vote choice also implied an easy victory for Gore. For many years, political scientists have believed that a large portion of the electorate engages in retrospective voting—rewarding the party of the president for good times, and punishing the party for bad times (Fiorina 1981). Ronald Reagan had articulated the logic of retrospective voting in the 1980 presidential debates, when he invited voters to "Ask yourself, are you better off than you were four years ago?" In most models of individual vote choice, evaluations of the performance of the economy or approval of the current president's handling of the economy are robust predictors of vote decisions. With a strong economy, a popular sitting president, and many other positive indicators, a Gore victory seemed a foregone conclusion. Although Gore did narrowly win the popular vote, it is clear that the 2000 elections pose a challenge to our models of electoral outcomes and of vote choice.

In 2000, the economy was slowing after the longest postwar economic recovery on record. Unemployment had been over 7 percent in early 1993 as Clinton and Gore took office; by the fall of 2000 it was less than 5 percent. Inflation had dropped from over 4 percent to approximately 1 percent. Interest rates had fallen, allowing many Americans to refinance their homes and save considerable sums. The budget deficit was $290 billion in 1993, but in 2000 there was a large surplus that was projected to endure for many years. Even after a sharp sell-off in the stock market, the Dow Jones industrials had increased over the Clinton years from an average of just over 3,000 to more than 9,000. In 1992, few Americans would have thought it possible that the budget deficit would disappear, and indeed a majority believed that their children would have a lower standard of living than they had enjoyed. By 2000, Americans were confident of the economic future. On Election Day, nearly nine in ten voters said that the national economy was good or excellent; in 1992, more than 80 percent had said that the economy was not so good or poor.

The good news was not limited to the economy. Welfare rolls had dropped sharply, and employment rolls had grown. Teenaged pregnancies and abortions had declined. School test scores were up after years of steady declines. Violent crime in the major cities fell to levels not seen since the 1970s. Small wonder that majorities of Americans told pollsters in the fall that they were satisfied with the way the country was going and that it was on the right track. National exit polls reported that fully 65 percent thought that the country was on the right track, compared to only 35 percent when Clinton and Gore had assumed office. Small wonder as well that political scientists expected Gore to win with little difficulty over the son of the president who had presided over the last recession.

Moreover, turnout increased only slightly in 2000, despite widespread agreement by media pollsters that the election would be extremely close; despite considerable spending by candidates, parties, and interest groups in carefully targeted states (Goldstein 2002); and despite campaigns by minor-party candidates. Thus, although the 2000 election will be remembered for its colorful images, desperate strategizing, and legal surprises, it also raises more enduring questions for those who study elections and voting behavior. After each election, political scientists ask questions about the campaigns, the issues, and the candidates, and about why voters responded as they did to the choices offered to them. After the 2000 elections, it is especially important to ask these questions, for although it is clear that the details of the 2000 election were extraordinary and that our fledgling forecasting models did not do well, it is not clear whether the election gives us reason to rethink our basic models of voting behavior.

The 2000 Presidential Election

Since the publication of *The American Voter* (Campbell, Converse, Miller, and Stokes 1960), most accounts of individual voting behavior have included some discussion of candidate evaluations, issues, and partisanship. Candidate evaluations are clearly short-term forces that change with the candidates and sometimes with events and advertisements. Issues are more enduring, with some, such as taxes, springing up in each election like perennials, but others like annuals blooming only in a single campaign. Partisanship is generally seen as the long-term force in the campaign. Although partisanship is clearly not immutable, it is resistant to change and helps to influence evaluations of issues and candidates. Aggregate models of presidential election outcomes often add one additional factor: evaluations of the sitting president. In the 2000 election, these evaluations appear to have been important and complex.

Ghosts of Presidents Past

In 1992 and 1996, incumbent presidents sought reelection. In 1992 Bill Clinton and Al Gore defeated George Bush and Dan Quayle, and in 1996 Clinton and Gore won reelection against Bob Dole and Jack Kemp. These reelection efforts are a regularity in American democracy (Weisberg and Box-Steffensmeier 1999), but American presidents are limited to two terms by Constitutional amendment. When presidents are barred from seeking reelection, someone from the president's administration—often the vice president—usually wins the party's nomination and seeks to win election at least in part on the record of the previous administration. These "succession" elections are also a regularity in American politics.

Thus, in 2000 the Democrats could not nominate Bill Clinton, who might have won reelection. Instead, they nominated Al Gore, Clinton's vice president and a former U.S. senator. Gore had been an active player in the Clinton administration, especially on environmental issues and governmental reorganization. Gore enjoyed the advantages of incumbency and could claim to have been an important member of the administration that restored American prosperity.

But successor candidates face a difficult tradeoff in devising their campaigns. They generally wish to claim credit for the successes of the previous administration, but they also want to establish their own political profile. When George Bush ran for president in 1988, he promised a "kinder and gentler" nation in advertisements that showed Bush playing with his grandchildren. Bush sought to claim the mantle of Reagan's conservatism and popularity but to distance himself from voter perceptions that the Reagan administration was not compassionate.

In 2000, Gore's problem was emphatically not an image that the Clinton administration was indifferent to average Americans. Instead, his problem was perhaps best captured by *The Onion*'s mock headline following the 1992 election, "New President Feels Nation's Pain, Breasts." Clinton was widely perceived as a very talented politician, and his administration's policies were quite popular, but he was also seen as a man who lacked self-control and perhaps a moral compass. Few Americans wanted Clinton to be removed from office for his affair with Monica Lewinsky or for his denial of that affair under oath (Andolina and Wilcox 2000), but most disapproved of Clinton's conduct. Many saw the Lewinsky story as part of a larger pattern of dishonesty by a man who claimed not to have avoided the draft or to have inhaled marijuana. Bill Clinton stands alone in recent American history in his power to inspire and to irritate, and it is likely that evaluations of Clinton played an even greater role in 2000 than evaluations of presidents in previous elections.

The 2000 election was an unusual succession election for one additional reason. The Republican candidate, George W. Bush, was the son of the president who Clinton and Gore had defeated in 1992—and he shared a remarkable likeness as well as a very similar name. Clearly, Bush did not want to run on his father's economic record, but he did seek to appeal to Republicans who had defected to Clinton in 1992 and 1996. In New Hampshire, an ebullient George Bush joined his son on the podium, and after media pundits focused on this paternal gesture at the expense of his son's message, the two men were seldom seen together at public events.

The Presidential Contest: Candidates, Issues, and Partisanship

The Candidates

Al Gore won the Democratic nomination easily, besting former senator Bill Bradley. At the start of the summer, however, Gore found himself running well behind George W. Bush. This was not unexpected: George Bush in 1988 had been far behind Michael Dukakis in the early summer. But the Gore campaign struggled to define the candidate, his character, and his issues.

More than previous successor candidates, Gore sought to distance himself from the incumbent administration. The carefully scripted, "spontaneous" long kiss he gave his wife at the Democratic convention was one effort to show that interns would be safe in a Gore Oval Office. But Gore's speech set the tone for his campaign: "This election is not an award for past performance. I'm not asking you to vote for me on the basis of the economy we have. Tonight I ask for your support on the basis of the better, fairer, more prosperous America we can build together." Throughout the campaign, Gore focused more on the future than the past. Moreover, he kept Bill Clinton—arguably the best campaigner of his generation—on the sidelines. Whether Clinton could have helped Gore with some carefully targeted appearances is a matter of intense debate among Democratic activists. Throughout the campaign, Gore struggled with how to deal with the good, the bad, and the ugly from the Clinton legacy.

Gore's campaign also struggled to define the character of the candidate. Gore was clearly perceived by prospective voters as knowledgeable and experienced, although his eagerness to demonstrate his knowledge made this less valuable than it might otherwise have been. The campaign sought to playfully overcome Gore's lack of spontaneity with humor, but many of its efforts seemed artificial (as when the campaign hired a consultant to help Gore project the image of an "alpha male"). But public perceptions that Gore was frequently ill at ease soon became the source of jokes by Jay Leno, skits on *Saturday Night Live*, and a hilarious claim on the Internet that Gore must be an extraterrestrial in human guise.

More troubling for Gore were perceptions that he might share some of Clinton's ethical lapses. Late in the campaign the media picked up the Bush campaign charge that Gore was a "serial exaggerator" who played loose with the truth in the search for votes. Before long, Gore's alleged claim that he had "invented the Internet" became shorthand for his exaggerations.[1]

Bush faced a different set of challenges—he needed to persuade the public to replace a vice president who had presided over good times with a one-term governor from a state dominated by its legislature. Bush's early courting of Christian Right leaders secured his base and allowed him to run as a moderate in the primaries, although he briefly detoured right to beat John McCain in South Carolina (Wilcox 2002). Bush initially faced a large field of opponents for the GOP nomination, but he managed to lock up an unprecedented number of elite endorsements and raise record sums early in the contest.

Bush's pitch to contributors and early backers was that he alone had the ability to raise the money to beat Al Gore. To a party deeply resentful of Clinton's success, this was sufficient to ensure unity. Ironically, Bush's claim of electability rested in part on his ideological agility and ability to neutralize Democratic issues—both important parts of Clinton's victories.

Bush was the son of a president who had presided over a recession, but he benefited from the public's economic myopia: most Republicans and many independents projected the current recovery backward. Thus, although most voters in 1992 thought the national economy was in bad shape, in 2000 many remembered the economy of 1992 as strong.

Most Americans believed that, unlike Gore, Bush said what he thought. But that was troubling in itself, for his speech often reflected great grammatical and syntactical irregularities. More troubling was Bush's lack of knowledge of major elements of public policy. He appeared to know little of world politics and to be confused about major American domestic policies as well. The Bush campaign sought to overcome this liability by attacking the vice president's credibility and by arguing that Bush was a manager who would hire smart people to give him advice. It also kept him away from spontaneous media events.

Issues

Issues are medium-term forces in politics. Some, like taxes and government services, are perennials in election campaigns. A few, like abortion, have been powerful factors in influencing vote choice and even partisanship for two decades (Abramowitz 1995; Cook, Jelen, and Wilcox 1992; Adams 1997). Other issues come and go as candidates raise them in campaigns.

During the primary elections, Bush's main opponent was Sen. John McCain, whose campaign centered on a promise to reform campaign finance and limit the size of contributions to parties. Al Gore picked up this issue during the general election and promised to make campaign finance reform the first issue of his administration.

In 1992 and 1996, Bill Clinton had sought to neutralize Republican advantages on issues such as crime and welfare by supporting the death penalty, proposing to hire more police officers, and promising to end "welfare as we know it." In 2000, the Bush campaign sought to duplicate Clinton's success by neutralizing Democratic advantages on education and Social Security. Bush centered his campaign on education, promising repeatedly to "leave no child behind." He promised to save Social Security by allowing citizens to manage a portion of their retirement in individual accounts. To rally regular Republicans, Bush promised a large cut in the income tax, an end to the estate tax, and a reduction in the size of government. Bush did not campaign on social issues such as abortion or gay rights, although he made his opposition to abortion clear.

Gore also campaigned for additional programs in education and the environment. He attacked Bush's tax cuts as welfare for the rich and his Social Security plan as risky. Although Gore was openly pro-choice in the campaign, he did not choose to emphasize his differences with Bush on gun control or the environment, despite a question in one debate that invited him to do so.

In the general election of 2000, the Bush campaign sought to craft an issue about trust and honesty in government. During the primary campaigns, Bush's biggest applause line was a promise to restore honor to the White House, and during the general election he attacked Gore for exaggerations.

Partisanship

Partisanship is usually conceived as the long-term source of voting behavior, providing stability against changing candidates and issues (Campbell et al. 1960). In 2000, the Democrats held a ten-percentage-point edge in partisanship, which should have advantaged Gore. This aggregate Democratic advantage had remained relatively constant since 1984, but beneath the surface there is evidence of change. During the late 1980s and throughout the 1990s, the policy positions of congressional Democrats and Republicans diverged (Adams 1997; Bond and Fleisher 2000). As the parties sent clearer ideological signals, the fit between the political views and partisanship of voters increased (Jacobson 2000). Between 1972 and 1980, the average correlation between ideology and partisanship in the NES was .35, but between 1992 and 2000 the figure was .50. There is evidence that at least some voters adjusted their partisanship during this period to match their views on some issues (Adams 1997), while others adjusted their policy views to fit their partisanship (Layman and Carsey 1998). As a consequence, partisans have become less likely to cross party lines in presidential voting: in 2000 fewer than 10 percent of partisans voted for the other major party's candidate.

Models of Presidential Voting

Several models of presidential voting have been proposed in the literature over the years (Niemi and Weisberg 2001, chapter 1) including social-psychological attitudinal models, economic forecasting models, political psychology models, group-based sociological models, and rational-choice models.

The social-psychological model (also known as the Michigan Model, see Beck 1986) emphasizes the distinction between long-term factors, such as social demographics, partisanship, and ideology, that are determined before the election year and short-term factors that are more election specific, such as issues, candidates, and the campaign. This approach has become the main model for empirical studies of voting.

Although the social-psychological model is applied to explain voting at the individual level, the economic forecasting model operates at the aggregate level to predict the vote percentages for the major-party candidates on the basis of economic conditions, presidential popularity levels, and other macro-level variables. The economic forecasting model received considerable publicity in the 2000 election, including national media coverage of predictions based on the model of an easy Gore victory (Kaiser 2000; Clymer 2000). The poor performance of both of these models led to considerable questioning of why these models had failed (Bartels and Zaller 2001; Lewis-Beck and Tien 2001; Wlezien 2001; Campbell 2001; Holbrook 2001). The answers often argued that the problem was with the Gore campaign rather than with the models. However, the seeming failure of these models was widely interpreted as discrediting political-science voting models, despite the fact that a wider range of voting models still produced valuable insights about the election. After all, models must be able to explain before they can be used to predict, and the explanatory social-psychology models are useful in understanding voting in the 2000 election.

The sociological model emphasizes the social-group basis of voting. In this model, social groups are seen as the building blocks of the parties, though voters have to resolve their membership in multiple groups when those groups affiliate with different parties. This model was the basis once for understanding American politics in terms of the New Deal coalition of southerners, Catholics, Jews, African Americans, urban dwellers, and the poor. However, its applicability is sometimes less clear now that the New Deal coalition has died away (Stanley and Niemi 1995). Although the sociological model is an older approach to understanding voting, it retains considerable interest since it corresponds closely to the targeting decisions that political parties must make during campaigns.

In contrast, the rational-choice approach emphasizes the strategic calculations candidates and voters make as they face elections. The basic Downs (1957) model, for example, views politics as a battle along a single liberal/conservative dimension, with citizens voting for the party that is closest to their own position on that dimension. Thus, the rational-choice model focuses our attention on ideology as a factor in elections, both in terms of how the candidates position themselves ideologically and the extent to which voters view the election in liberal/conservative terms. Additionally, this approach calls attention to the effects of strategies and rules on decisions, in the context of elections, how voters respond to multiple-candidate races, and how the electoral college functions as a decision rule. The third-party candidacies of Ralph Nader and Pat Buchanan make this model especially relevant to the 2000 election, as does the electoral college's awarding the election to a candidate who did not win a plurality of the popular vote.

These four models will be applied in the chapters that follow. The social-psychology model is central particularly to the attempts by Weisberg and Hill (chapter 2) and Kessel (chapter 4) to sort out the relative importance of different attitudes in affecting voter decisions in 2000. It is also central to Finkel and Freedman's (chapter 10) examination of voter turnout. Norpoth (chapter 3) directly deals with how economic forecasting models functioned in this election. The sociological model is the basis of Stanley and Niemi's (chapter 7) consideration of social-group voting generally as well as Kanthak and Norrander's (chapter 8) analysis of the gender gap. The rational-choice model is particularly relevant to Jacoby's (chapter 6) treatment of ideology and to Burden's (chapter 11) analysis of minor parties in the 2000 election.

To determine whether the standard models of electoral behavior apply to the 2000 elections, it is important to use the best available data and appropriate statistical models so other factors can be held constant or controlled for. This book examines how well our standard models apply to the 2000 elections, or whether the election requires us to revise our understanding. The chapters reflect the diversity of questions, approaches, and data that now typifies the study of electoral behavior.

Topics

The contributors to this book explore a variety of matters that were fundamental to the 2000 election. Recurring topics include the impact of Bill Clinton on the election, the apparent lack of an effect of a strong economy on the vote, the role of other issues, and the effect of ideology in an era of increased partisan polarization. Attention is also given to changing voting coalitions and the continuing role of the gender gap. Additionally, authors examine how divided government was temporarily ended, turnout effects in one of the closest elections in history, the effect of minor-party candidates in deciding the election, and, more generally, the relative importance of partisanship, candidates, and issues.

Data

This book also reflects the diversity of data sources and analytic approaches scholars now use in studying U.S. voting behavior. Many of the chapters rely on the 2000 National Election Studies (NES) survey—the latest in a series of academic surveys that have long been the cornerstone of voting behavior research. But contributors use other data as well: the Voter News Service (VNS) exit polls, Gallup and other tracking polls, historical election results, and state and local election results. One chapter relies on a unique source of data: the American Politics Study on attitudes toward campaign finance.

The following chapters all examine the 2000 election but within the context of other recent presidential elections. For example, both the Stanley and Niemi and the Kessel chapters (7 and 4, respectively) compare their results for 2000 with results they have obtained using the same models for the 1952–1996 period. Finkel and Freedman (chapter 10) examine change in turnout from 1996 to 2000, and Kimball (chapter 9) looks at split-ticket voting from the 1980s through 2000. Weisberg and Hill (chapter 2) analyze presidential succession by making comparisons to George H. W. Bush's succession to Ronald Reagan in 1988. The Burden chapter (11) compares third-party voting in 2000 with voting for H. Ross Perot and other recent independent candidates for president, while the Kanthak and Norrander chapter (8) shows how the gender gap has changed over the years. Norpoth (chapter 3) examines the effect of the economy on presidential voting over the 1872–2000 time frame.

Although the chapters in this book employ several different sources of data, the surveys are all either cross-sectional surveys or two-wave panels that interview the same people shortly before the election and again afterward (the NES design). Alternative possible longitudinal designs involve nightly polling, repeated interviewing of the same people in a multi-wave panel study, or a two-wave panel in which the first wave is before the election campaign begins. Each of these approaches has been used in innovative studies to investigate the 2000 election. For example, the Annenberg project (Johnston, Hagen, and Jamieson 2002; Romer et al., 2003) and the Vanishing Voter Project (Patterson 2002) did polling throughout the 2000 campaign year. That data can be used to examine campaign dynamics, although most of the interviews were completed before the election and thus do not include actual vote choice. Knowledge Networks conducted a multi-wave panel survey through its Internet polling (Hillygus and Jackman 2002), but there is coverage bias in such a sample. Jon Krosnick (Krosnick, Courser, Mulligan, and Chang 2002) commissioned several surveys in which respondents were asked about their vote intention in the summer of 2000. They were then resurveyed after the election to find out how they voted. Those surveys provide an excellent opportunity to examine vote change through the campaign, though they are no more helpful than other surveys in showing how vote intention developed before summer.

This is not to say that the standard National Election Studies design is ideal, only that its advantages and disadvantages are already well known. It would be very useful to be able to tie polling earlier in the election year to a person's final vote choice. Additionally, the NES surveys have been less flexible about changing the survey questions they ask than are many other surveys. This is because it is harder to change the written questionnaire used in the NES face-to-face interviews than the computer-assisted surveys used in most large-scale telephone and Internet polling. In previous years, that difference meant that NES could not keep up with the rapid pace of campaign developments. For example, it deleted detailed questions about Perot in 1992 after he dropped out of the race only to find that the questions could not be reinserted once he had reentered the race.

The 2000 NES survey was burdened by a series of interviewing and question-wording choices that make it more difficult than usual to analyze. The National Science Foundation has funded the NES since the 1970s, but it was expected to require that future election studies be telephone surveys because of the considerably lower cost of telephone interviews versus face-to-face surveys. As a result, NES conducted half of the 2000 interviews by phone, so there could be a one-time comparison between results for face-to-face and telephone interviews. However, that adds an element of noncomparability to the 2000 NES data. Further, the planned shift to telephone surveys led the NES to experiment with question wording. In particular, they tested branching formats in which people are asked one question and then asked a follow-up on the basis of their answer to the first question instead of the seven-point scale formats commonly used in face-to-face surveys.[2]

The combination of these two design features makes some of the NES data more than usually awkward to probe. In particular, the ideology question was asked in two different ways (the usual seven-point scale and a five-point branching format) to different random half-samples for both face-to-face and telephone interviews. As a result, the ideology question is very hard to analyze in the 2000 NES data, as evident in this book, where authors make very different decisions as to how to handle ideology as a predictor (see particularly Jacoby, chapter 6, note 1).

Note too that there was a slight Gore majority in the NES sample. Of course, Gore did win the popular vote, even though he eventually lost the electoral vote, but the NES sample overstates his vote margin. This difference, however, is in the usual range of sampling and measurement error. Moreover, it is not necessarily larger than in previous NES election surveys, as when NES substantially exaggerated Clinton's victory margin in 1992.

Analysis Techniques

Political scientists' efforts to develop one comprehensive model of voting have not been successful. It once appeared that improvements in research design and data analysis procedures would provide definitive answers as to how to understand voting. In particular, there was considerable anticipation that the 1972–74–76 NES panel survey would lead to a definitive test of the relative importance of different vote determinants, especially partisanship, issues, and candidate factors. Two major reports based on that study (Page and Jones 1979; Markus and Converse 1979) were published in the same issue of the *American Political Science Review*, both using state-of-the-art analysis procedures. Rather than provide definitive answers, they instead shattered the hope of finding a comprehensive voting model. Although there are similarities in the two reports' findings, their different assumptions produced opposite results in some crucial areas, especially on the relative importance of partisanship and issues in voting. It instantaneously became evident that even the most sophisticated models of voting would be vulnerable to their assumptions. As a result, even the best works that employ a single approach become suspect, since there is now recognition that they must be making assumptions that other researchers can challenge.

The longitudinal designs incorporated in the Annenberg, Knowledge Networks, Vanishing Voter, and Krosnick studies mentioned earlier seek to resolve some of these difficulties by looking at the sources of change over time. However, it remains difficult to parse the several simultaneous events that occur during an election campaign. For example, the increase in Gore's popularity after the Democratic convention can be seen as a result of his choice of Joe Lieberman as his running mate, the effectiveness of the convention on television, or Gore's kiss of his wife Tipper. Similarly, his later fall in popularity can be seen as a result of his ineffectiveness in the debates or the questions about his honesty that were raised after he was seen as exaggerating. It is tempting to ascribe a change in popularity to the event that occurred just before that change, but that does not take into account the inevitable lags in public awareness of those events. Causation is not easy to prove even in the best-designed longitudinal studies.

The ideal approach becomes instead to use multiple models to illuminate the voting process, in the hope that a triangulation strategy is more effective than the pursuit of the "correct" model. This appeal for tolerance of multiple models should not be read as a rejection of complex modeling approaches or of longitudinal surveys. Instead, it should be seen as a plea for further exploration of alternative approaches. Thus, the chapters in this volume employ a variety of approaches to understanding the vote. Table 1.1 summarizes the analysis methods, data, and dependent variables of the following chapters.

One common analysis procedure is to use logit (or probit) analysis to explain voting Republican or Democrat. However, two other techniques are also illustrated: a discrete-choice model that also includes voting for minor-party candidates (Burden) and a bivariate probit model to analyze

TABLE **1.1** Analysis methods, data, and dependent variables employed in analyzing the 2000 election

Chapter:	2	3	4	5	6	7	8	9	10	11
Author(s):	Weisberg & Hill	Norpoth	Kessel	Box-Steffensmeier, Grant, & Rudolph	Jacoby	Stanley & Niemi	Kanthak & Norrander	Kimball	Finkel & Freedman	Burden
Data:	1952–2000 NES	1992–2000 VNS exit polls & historical statistics	1952–2000 NES	2000 American Politics Study	2000 NES	1952–2000 NES	1952–2000 NES	1980–2000 NES & aggregate statistics	1992–2000 NES	VNS exit polls & aggregate statistics
Analysis Method:	Multi-stage logit	Logit & time series	Probit	Bivariate probit	Logit & interactions	Logit	Regression & interactions	Logit	Logit	Discrete choice
Dependent Variable:	Major-party vote	Major-party vote	Major-party vote	Voting turnout and major-party vote	Major-party vote	Party identification	Candidate thermometer difference	Split-ticket voting	Voting turnout	Vote, including minor parties

the turnout and vote direction decisions simultaneously (Box-Steffensmeier, Grant, and Rudolph). Weisberg and Hill employ what might be termed a multi-stage logit analysis, in which they analyze one stage of predictors at a time and then put together all the significant predictors in a single equation at the end. Kimball adds the further complication of analyzing presidential voting along with voting for the House of Representatives in a single split-ticket voting equation. Kanthak and Norrander show how interaction terms can be used to test whether men and women give different weights to different issues.[3] Jacoby's analysis tests whether voters with different levels of political sophistication rely on different factors in making their vote choice. Norpoth moves to time-series analysis in some of his exploration of the role of economic performance in voting. The Stanley and Niemi chapter differs from the other analyses in using party identification as its dependent variable rather than vote. This enables them to look for changes in party coalitions over time.

Several chapters also employ counterfactuals in election analysis, as in the chapters that estimate the outcome of the election if conditions from prior years had held in 2000. Finkel and Freedman do this in their analysis of turnout, for example, and Norpoth does it in analyzing the effect of the economy. It is important to remember, however, that changing one factor in the real world would inevitably also change other factors. For example, if the economy were very different in 2000 than it was, the candidates would have changed their emphasis on different issues as well. The Republican Party would have given more emphasis to the economy if it were in severe recession, and, as a result, other issues would have been more peripheral. Even asking people how they would have voted if Nader were not a candidate—the data that Burden relies on—is susceptible to the problem that the endgame of the campaign would have been different if Nader had never run: Gore would have been able to give more attention to states in which the Gore-Bush margin was small in the polls rather than the states in which Nader was riding high enough to threaten Gore. Also, Gore might not have run a populist campaign if Nader had not been in the race. The Gore-Bush contest might have been fundamentally different without Nader in the race. Counterfactuals are fascinating to spin out, but they should always be inspected with special care.[4]

Independent Variables

The chapters in this volume also demonstrate that different independent variables can be relevant for different purposes (see Table 1.2). The purest analysis is that by Kessel, which uses only the open comments that respondents make about the parties and candidates. Similarly, Finkel and Freedman

TABLE **1.2**   Types of predictor variables employed in analyzing the 2000 elections*

Chapter:	2	3	5	6	7	8	9	11
Author(s):	Weisberg & Hill	Norpoth	Box-Steffensmeier, Grant, & Rudolph	Jacoby	Stanley & Niemi	Kanthak & Norrander	Kimball	Burden
Partisanship:	yes	yes	yes	yes		yes	yes	yes
Economy:	yes	yes	yes	yes		yes		yes
Campaign finance:			yes					
Ideology:	yes			yes		yes	yes	yes
Issues:	yes			yes		yes		
Social issues:	yes	yes				yes		yes
Candidate personality:	yes			yes			yes	
Clinton:	yes			yes				
Perception of important party differences:							yes	
Demographics:	yes		yes		yes	yes		yes

*Chapter 4 (Kessel) uses only open-ended questions that ask what the respondent likes and dislikes about the parties and candidates. Chapter 10 (Finkel and Freedman) uses predictors that are better suited for the analysis of voting turnout.

use only a restricted set of predictors: only party identification in addition to the economic variables that are the focus of his chapter.

Table 1.2 shows the types of variables used in eight of the chapters. Partisanship, not surprisingly, is used in each of these chapters, and ideology is used in nearly all. Most use issue variables, though the exact set differs from one analysis to another. Candidate personality variables are included as predictors in some chapters, though others avoid those measures. Additionally, views about the retiring president are central to the Weisberg and Hill chapter and are also used in the Jacoby analysis. In addition to standard predictors, in his model of presidential voting, Kimball uses a main effect as well as interaction effects for perception of important party differences in order to test his party salience theory. The Stanley and Niemi chapter uses only demographic predictors since it is looking at the social-demographic characteristics of party coalitions.

Although there is near consensus across these chapters on some predictors, there is also a clear difference regarding including candidate variables (though they may be missing from some analyses only because they were not asked in the surveys being analyzed or were not asked for minor-party candidates). Some researchers might feel that the candidate variables are too close to the ultimate dependent variable, while others would argue that candidate variables are appropriate as predictors since they are prior to the vote decision.

Finally, Finkel and Freedman use a very different set of predictors because their focus is on voting turnout rather than vote choice. They include
election laws (in particular, registration closing dates), campaign contact,
political information, psychological attitudes (civic duty and political efficacy), reactions to the campaign (caring about the outcome and perceived
closeness of the race), and media use (newspaper reading), none of which
are usually used in studies of vote direction. They also use demographic
variables plus reactions to the candidates—which are often excluded in
studies of voter turnout—to test the extent to which turnout is motivated
by the candidates running in the election.

Demographic Predictors

There is further variation in these analyses in terms of the choice of demographic control variables (Table 1.3). This partly reflects the availability of
different demographic variables in different surveys. Stanley and Niemi use
a broad set of demographic predictors in their social-group analysis of partisanship. Further, they include particular combinations of these variables,
such as native southern white and white Protestant fundamentalist, and
they limit Hispanics to non-Cubans. Large numbers of demographic variables are also used in some other chapters (notably Finkel and Freedman,
Burden, and Weisberg and Hill). The Voter News Service exit polls analyzed

TABLE **1.3**   Social-demographic predictors employed in analyzing the 2000 elections*

Chapter:	2	5	7	8	9	10	11
Author(s):	Weisberg & Hill	Box-Steffensmeier, Grant, & Rudolph	Stanley & Niemi	Kanthak & Norrander	Kimball	Finkel & Freedman	Burden
Gender:	yes	yes	yes	yes		yes	yes
Race:	yes		yes			yes	yes
Hispanic:	yes		yes				yes
Region:	yes		yes		yes	yes	yes
Religion:	yes		yes			yes	
Religiosity:	yes		yes			yes	
Age:	yes	yes	yes			yes	yes
Marriage:	yes	yes				yes	yes
Education:	yes	yes				yes	yes
Income:			yes			yes	
Union:			yes			yes	
Length of Residence:						yes	yes
Home Owner:						yes	
Sexual Orientation:							yes

*Chapters 3 (Norpoth), 4 (Kessel), and 6 (Jacoby) do not include any social-demographic predictors.

by Burden even include sexual orientation. The turnout analysis by Finkel and Freedman makes use of some social-demographic variables that are not customarily included in the analysis of vote direction, including home ownership (though that variable has been used to analyze vote direction in some countries, notably Britain). By contrast, some analysts avoid demographic controls completely (Kessel and Norpoth) or nearly so (Kimball only uses a regional control for the South in his analysis of ticket splitting). Even Kanthak and Norrander's analysis of the gender gap does not include demographic variables beyond gender. Box-Steffensmeier, Grant, and Rudolph follow the intermediate strategy of using a limited set of demographic variables.

Another approach used in this book is to do separate analyses for different levels of theoretically significant demographic controls. This is comparable to Jacoby's use of separate analyses for different levels of political sophistication. Looking for interactive effects (as illustrated by Kanthak and Norrander's examination of gender effects) is particularly useful since it makes it possible to test whether other demographic variables have different effects for groups of interest.

The broader issue raised here is the meaning of these demographic variables. To Stanley and Niemi, they represent social groups that can be part of party coalitions, as typified by the New Deal coalition of days gone by. Others view sociodemographic variables as just proxy variables (Timpone 1998b) that pick up sources of variation for which we do not have more direct measures, such as viewing gender as encompassing a series of life experiences rather than a biological difference or a social group.

Unraveling the Puzzle of the 2000 Elections

What lessons do these models provide for understanding the 2000 election? The best way to answer this question is to summarize briefly the main results of each chapter and then draw some basic conclusions.

Chapters

The book begins with Herb Weisberg and Timothy Hill's consideration of the 2000 election in terms of a "succession election" in which the incumbent party's vice president was nominated to succeed the president. After portraying the 2000 candidates as "legacies," the authors develop a typology of presidential elections and discuss the nature of succession effects. They then analyze the 2000 National Election Studies survey. They begin with the effects of party identification on voting and then examine the effects of demographic differences, issue variables, and attitudes toward the major-party nominees. Weisberg and Hill demonstrate Bill Clinton's lasting effects on the vote, even though he was not running. Their final logit model of the vote includes all of the above factors, showing that attitudes toward Clinton had effects on the Bush-Gore race, above and beyond the effects of the other factors. Although feelings toward Clinton were critical to many vote decisions, the ambivalence of those feelings meant that the outcome was still very much in the hands of Gore and Bush. Weisberg and Hill's analysis shows that the virtually equal result of the 2000 presidential election came about because each candidate had an advantage on some dimensions but not a large enough upper hand on any variable to offset the other candidate's lead on other factors.

The next chapter focuses directly on one of the great puzzles of the 2000 election: why the strong economy during the Clinton-Gore administration did not result in an easy victory for Al Gore. In this chapter, Helmut Norpoth describes how the retrospective voting model has become the basis for election forecasting. The predictions it produced were far off the mark in 2000. He uses Voter News Service exit polls to examine systematically a series of explanations for this failure, including the possibility that voters do not reward good times as much as they punish bad times and that people base their vote on expectations about the economy in the future rather than past performance. He then uses time-series analysis to demonstrate that the lack of economic effect is due to the absence on the ballot of the sitting president who could be considered responsible for the strong economy. The vote for successors does not vary significantly with the state of the economy.

Chapter 4 considers the role of voter attitudes on the presidential election. John Kessel has employed an attitudinal model of voting to understand the elections since 1952, based on NES respondents' open-ended answers as to their likes and dislikes about the major parties and their presidential nominees. He extends this analysis to 2000, classifying these comments as relating to the candidates, the parties, or the issues. Kessel then subdivides these categories into more detailed candidate, party, and issue perceptions. The partisan advantage on each attitude is measured, after which he employs probit analysis to determine their importance to the vote decision. Finally, Kessel examines the combined effect of the partisan advantage and importance for each attitude object. His analysis finds that the close result of the election in 2000 was due to the very even balance between these attitude factors.

Chapter 5 concentrates on attitudes toward one specific issue: campaign finance reform. This has been an important issue for several decades, culminating in the passage of the Bipartisan Campaign Reform Act in the aftermath of the 2000 election. In this chapter, Janet Box-Steffensmeier, Tobin Grant, and Thomas Rudolph discuss the frames that have been used on each side of this debate as well as candidate positions on this issue. They use their 2000 American Politics Study, which contained detailed questions about the campaign finance issue. It showed that majorities of the public favor congressional spending limits and bans on soft money and political action committee contributions, while opposing both public financing and unlimited private contributions. Factor analysis shows that there are three separate dimensions underlying these attitudes: those on regulatory reforms, subsidy reforms, and deregulatory reforms. Box-Steffensmeier, Grant, and Rudolph apply a bivariate probit model to analyze together the determinants of turnout and vote direction. Campaign finance did not affect turnout, but attitudes on deregulatory reform were significantly related to presidential vote direction. On the other hand, attitudes on deregulatory and subsidized reforms affected the congressional vote direction.

William Jacoby focuses on the role of ideology in 2000 in chapter 6. Ideology has been an important factor in some presidential elections. Jacoby analyzes the NES respondents' placement of the candidates on a liberal/conservative scale to examine its importance. He uses multidimensional scaling to explore the dimensions underlying these placements and obtains two, including a liberal/conservative dimension. He estimates the direct effects of ideology on the vote in a logistic regression equation and also tests its indirect effects on issue attitudes, candidate personality assessments, and other variables. There is no sign of significant direct effects, even among the most politically sophisticated segment of the electorate, but ideology does have significant indirect effects. The 2000 presidential election can best be seen as nonideological, as the candidates blurred ideological distinctions so that ideology did not throw the election decidedly to either candidate.

The next two chapters examine the social demographics of voting. Harold Stanley and Richard Niemi employ a social-demographic model of partisanship in chapter 7. The social-group basis of partisanship is important because party identification is crucial to the vote decision. The demographics of party coalitions have been an interest since the earliest days of voting studies, but Stanley and Niemi are able to take advantage of the full 1952–2000 NES time frame to look for changes in support coalitions. They use logistic regression to determine the incremental probabilities of each demographic group identifying with the Democrats and the Republicans, controlling on the person's other demographic characteristics. Additionally, they derive the percentage of each party's coalition with a given group characteristic. For example, the Republican coalition in 2000 was a combination of southern whites and a strong religious base of Catholics, regular churchgoers, and Protestant fundamentalists. The Democratic coalition was marked by increased support from women and Hispanics, which was more than offset by losses of Catholics, union households, and regular churchgoers. The even finish in the 2000 election can thus be seen as the result of the Democrats losing their coalitional advantage without gaining sufficient support from new groups and the Republicans having assembled a coalition that is not yet a clear majority.

Chapter 8 turns to one particular social-demographic difference that has become important in American voting since 1980: gender. Kristin Kanthak and Barbara Norrander begin by discussing the sources of the contemporary gender gap in voting and tracing its growth over recent years. They use regression analysis on comparative ratings of the two nominees in the 2000 NES survey to determine the effects that several issues had on voting and whether men and women differed in their emphasis on those issues. Gender did not have a significant main effect. However, men and women differed in their views on some issues that affected the vote and in the emphasis they gave to some issues. Ideology had the largest impact on the gender gap in 2000, and views on the role of the government also had large impacts. By contrast, any gender gap in voting for Congress was simply the result of differences between men and women's partisanship and ideology. Through the lens of gender, the Bush-Gore near-draw was due to the liberal tendencies of women being balanced by the Republican and anti-government tendencies of men.

The last three chapters broaden the discussion beyond the restrictions imposed in the previous chapters. In chapter 9, David Kimball moves outside the focus on presidential voting by examining ticket splitting in voting for president and members of Congress. Kimball proposes a "party salience theory" of voting in which ticket splitting is a public response to elite polarization along partisan and ideological lines. There has been less ticket splitting in recent years as the policy and ideological divides between the Republican and Democratic parties have increased and become more salient to voters. Kimball uses logit analysis of NES surveys from the 1980s to 2000 to show that people who see important differences between the parties rely more heavily on party and ideology in their voting for both president and Congress. On the other hand, those who do not see important differences between the parties are most likely to engage in ticket splitting. Analysis of election returns for aggregate elections in the twentieth century shows that ticket splitting increases with greater ideological polarization between the parties. Thus, the (temporary) return to unified government with the 2000 elections was due to increased ideological polarization between the parties. The election saw the lowest level of president-House ticket splitting since 1968 and the fewest districts that voted for different parties for those two offices since 1952.

Chapter 10 directly focuses on voting turnout in the 2000 presidential election. Steven Finkel and Paul Freedman show that turnout increased slightly from 1996 to 2000, but remained low by world standards and varied considerably between states according to the states' laws on voting and their electoral conditions. Using the NES survey, Finkel and Freedman examine several factors that affected voting turnout in 2000. They employ logistic regression to analyze the determinants of voting in 2000 and then look at the effects of changes in the mean levels of those determinants from 1992 through 1996 and 2000. They find that the 2000 election was perceived as more competitive, had more voter mobilization, had less restrictive registration laws, and the electorate was more educated. However, turnout rose only marginally from 1996 because the electorate was fairly indifferent toward the major-party nominees. The candidates in 2000 not only were very balanced in terms of their support at the voting booths, but both lacked the appeal that would increase turnout as much as it should have given the other factors.

Finally, Barry Burden expands the book's purview to include the role of minor parties in chapter 11. After first determining whether there was a Condorcet winner in the 2000 election, he examines the trend in support for Ralph Nader over the course of the campaign. Analyzing a combination of Voter News Service exit polls and official vote totals, he uses multinomial logit analysis to examine the sources of third-party support. Both the Nader and Pat Buchanan candidacies affected turnout by bringing to the polls people who would otherwise not have voted, but they drew support from very different types of voters. The minor-party candidates may have affected the electoral college result in 2000, since in several states one or the other received more votes than the difference between the major-party candidates.

Lessons

Several important points emerge from the comparisons made in these chapters. One is the relevance of not only the candidates in the election, but also of the retiring incumbent president. This factor is important in all analyses of the elections in which an incumbent is not running, but it is especially important for unraveling the puzzle of the 2000 election—why Gore did not win as easily as economic forecasting models predicted. Clinton's moral failures complicated any notion of retrospective voting: in the exit polls 65 percent of the public thought that the country was on the right track, but only 35 percent thought that it was on the right moral track.

It is likely that the complexities of the evaluations of the incumbent president are unique to the 2000 elections. However, the analyses do suggest that voters responded both to the positive and negative elements of the Clinton legacy. In this regard, retrospective voting may in some circumstances go beyond economic evaluations and encompass other considerations.

Some analysts feel that Gore was so tied to Clinton that he might as well have tried to link himself more with the good economy of the Clinton years instead of running away from it. However, Norpoth argues (chapter 3) that the benefit of the good economy accrues less to a would-be successor than to an incumbent. Other voting specialists accept the results of the Gore campaign's focus groups, that Clinton would have hurt Gore nationally, so that he had to be used only in selected areas and among particular groups. Most analysts agree that Clinton has to be taken into account in understanding the 2000 election (see also Fiorina, Abrams, and Pope 2003), even if there is disagreement about the exact nature of his impact.

Another interesting comparison involves the role of ideology in the election. Jacoby (chapter 6) shows that it did not directly affect the vote (see also Weisberg and Hill, chapter 2, note 15), though he finds indirect effects of ideology. However, Kanthak and Norrander (chapter 8) demonstrate the interactive effects of ideology with gender: it has more of an effect for women than for men. Furthermore, Burden (chapter 11) shows that liberals were more likely to vote for Ralph Nader than for Bush or Gore. Thus, ideology should not be written off as a consideration in the 2000 election even if it was not significant in some equations for the major-party vote.

The discussion in this book also shows that determining the relative importance of different causal factors in election outcomes is more complicated that it once seemed to be. The relative importance of party identification, issues, and candidates can be compared, but other factors must be taken into account, such as evaluations of the retiring president when the incumbent is not running for reelection, turnout effects on the major-party vote, and the possibility of differential issue weights for different subgroups in the electorate. Thus, taken together, these chapters help us begin to unravel the puzzle of the 2000 election.

I   *Attitudinal Models*

The Succession Presidential Election of 2000:
The Battle of the Legacies

HERBERT F. WEISBERG AND TIMOTHY G. HILL

The 2000 presidential election was a notable contest even before its
close outcome afforded the state and national court systems opportunities
to help decide the final result. In particular, it was an unusual "succession
election"—an election in which the incumbent party's vice president was
nominated to succeed the president while the opposition party nominated
the son of its previous president in an attempt to regain the White House.
Succession elections are not unusual in the history of American presidential
elections. Indeed, they have been the norm for elections in which the sitting
president does not run, at least since the vice presidency assumed an important role in American politics in the mid twentieth century. Every presidential election after 1952 in which the sitting president was not running
featured an attempt by the vice president to succeed to the office: 1960,
1968, 1988, and 2000. But what made the 2000 election unusual is that it
was a "double succession election" that recalled 1968, when the incumbent
vice president faced off against the previous vice president.

Succession elections can involve an attempt by the incumbent president
to control his legacy, if the heir apparent is willing to be associated with that
legacy. In recent succession elections, Hubert Humphrey wanted to separate
himself from the foreign-policy legacy of the Johnson years, while George
Bush the First was more than willing to accept the legacy of the Reagan years.

A secondary question is what the legacy would be. Presidents would like
to control how they will be remembered in history, but they are not always
able to do so. Thus, Richard Nixon wanted to be remembered for his foreign-policy successes, not for the Watergate scandals. Similarly, Bill Clinton
would rather be remembered for the unprecedented economic growth wit-

nessed during his administration than for his involvement with Monica Lewinsky and his impeachment. Passing the presidency on to a designated successor is one way to try to control the legacy. Thus, Bill Clinton's presidency might be remembered more for its economic success if Al Gore had succeeded him rather than George W. Bush, who claimed he was inheriting an economic downturn.

The 2000 election involved the matter of legacy in one further sense of the term. Just as some private universities are more likely to admit the children of alumni because they are "legacies," so Governor Bush was a legacy in that he was the son of an ex-president. As a result, he was more easily recognized by the electorate than another governor might have been. At the same time, some Republican leaders viewed electing Bush as a way of restoring the earlier Bush presidency and vindicating a legacy that was tarnished when he lost to Clinton in 1992.[1]

Taking succession effects into account, our analysis of closed-ended questions in the 2000 National Election Studies survey shows that President Clinton both helped and hurt the Gore campaign. Other significant factors in the election also balanced each other out, leading to the razor-thin popular vote difference between the major party candidates.

Types of Elections

The American Voter (Campbell, Converse, Miller, and Stokes 1960) classified elections in terms of their being "maintaining," "deviating," or "realigning" elections, and a later article by the same team of authors (Converse, Campbell, Miller, and Stokes 1961) added a fourth category: "restoring" elections. This four-part classification has proved useful to scholars, but it is based on the election outcome and how that outcome differs from recent elections rather than on conditions that are evident before the votes are cast.

The classification of elections that is implicit in this chapter depends instead on the roster of major-party nominees: (1) an incumbency election in which the sitting president (either elected or a replacement when the elected incumbent passed away or resigned) runs, (2) a succession election in which the sitting president did not run but a designated successor (the vice president or, in earlier days, a member of the cabinet) runs, or (3) a nonsuccession election in which the candidate of the incumbent party is not associated with the administration. Incumbency and succession elections are both common, but the nonsuccession election has become the rarity in American presidential elections. The most recent occurred in 1952, and the only other such race in the twentieth century was in 1920.

Although this incumbency/succession classification has rarely been applied to presidential elections, it is commonly employed to analyze congressional elections, where there is a vast literature on incumbency effects, as well as in research on open-seat races. Succession effects in congressional elections have not been studied in the political science literature, but there is a considerable volume of anecdotal claims that spouses and children of deceased or retiring members of Congress have high rates of success when they run, instances that should be coded as succession elections.

Voting-behavior studies typically treat presidential elections as the equivalent of open-seat races, without recognizing sufficiently the carry-over effects associated with incumbency and succession. Open-seat races for president were the exception and not the rule in the twentieth century, and so it is urgent that our models better incorporate incumbency and succession effects (Weisberg 2002a).

This three-part classification of elections naturally leads to the question of what forces would lead to incumbency and succession effects. At the congressional level, incumbency effects are usually associated with the greater name recognition of the incumbent, and spouses and children of ex-legislators also expect to benefit from greater name recognition when they run. To be known is usually seen as an advantage, except in the case of members of Congress who have become embroiled in scandals (Peters and Welch 1980; Alford et al. 1994; Dimock and Jacobson 1995; Groseclose and Krehbiel 1994; Jacobson and Dimock 1994).

By contrast, the presidential election literature focuses on the concept of "retrospective voting"—that voters weigh how the last administration has performed in deciding whom to elect (Fiorina 1981). Conditions can be good or bad in the country, and so this retrospective evaluation can work for or against the incumbent party. However, retrospective voting is usually associated with issues and administration performance, whereas incumbency and succession effects suggest a more general assessment of the incumbent president, one that is weighted for successors by the extent to which the incumbent and successor are linked in the public's mind. Thus, incumbency and succession effects have to do with affective evaluations of the incumbent and not just cognitive retrospective judgments.[2]

Succession effects in presidential elections have been studied in Mattei and Weisberg (1994). They demonstrate succession effects in George Bush's 1988 victory as a result of his being linked positively to Ronald Reagan. They also examine the 1968 race and find that Lyndon Johnson's ratings had a significant effect on Hubert Humphrey's candidacy, even after controlling for issues and retrospective evaluations.

The extent of succession effects depends on the magnitude of the link between the incumbent and the heir apparent, which in turn depends on four factors. The first factor is the extent to which the incumbent treats his party's nominee as being his designated successor. Ronald Reagan treated George

Bush as the inheritor of his legacy in 1988, whereas Eisenhower nearly dis-
avowed Nixon in the 1960 campaign. A second factor is the extent to which
the nominee tries to associate himself with the incumbent administration.
The 1988 George Bush was willing to be seen as a continuation of the Reagan administration, whereas Al Gore tried to distance himself from the
moral scandals of Bill Clinton. The third factor is how much the opposition
party tries to tie the incumbent party's nominee with the sitting president. A
nominee may want to disassociate himself from the current administration,
but the opposition party may not permit that. Indeed, the Reagan campaign
in 1984 ran not only against Walter Mondale but also against the previous
Carter-Mondale administration, and the Republican campaign in 2000 did
not let the public forget about Gore's defense of Clinton during the impeachment period. Finally, the public may conjoin the heir with the incumbent because of the association built up over the previous four or eight
years. Thus, Al Gore was probably inevitably linked with Bill Clinton, just
as their sharing a name inevitably linked the George Bush of the 2000 election with former president Bush.

This linkage may be partially issue based, as when the nominee is held
responsible for the economic performance during the previous administration. However, the linkage need not be issue based, as when Governor
George W. Bush had instant name recognition because he was the son of ex-
President Bush. Al Gore clearly did not want to be linked to the Lewinsky
scandal, even if running as his "own man" meant he would not be able to
emphasize the issue-based linkage with the economic success of the Clinton
years.

Succession is inexorably tied to the notion of the incumbent president's
legacy. Presidents need not be concerned about their historical legacy, but
most are. Presidents, like Reagan, who want to change the direction of public policy will hope that the next president will keep their policies rather
than reverse them. Also, presidents expect, rightly or wrongly, that they will
play a larger part in the nation's life in the following four years if the next
president is someone from their party rather than someone who attacked
their administration throughout the campaign. Furthermore, presidents who
are brushed with scandal may feel partially vindicated if they can anoint
their chosen successor rather than be followed by a political adversary.

The question can be raised whether voting on the basis of non-issue-
specific succession effects is rational. However, such voting can be seen as
just a generalization of a citizen's voting on the basis of his or her comfort
with existing conditions. A person who liked the direction that the country
was moving under Ronald Reagan could rationally feel that Reagan's
anointed successor was most likely to keep the nation moving ahead. A person who was repelled by the Clinton presidency could rationally feel that
electing Clinton's heir apparent would not be a sufficient change. Thus, the

succession factor provides a possible shortcut for deciding how to vote: voting on the basis of satisfaction with the previous administration.

The argument made in this chapter is that in order to properly model the vote in a succession election we must take into account the association between the incumbent and the attempted successor. This association can work for or against the candidate, depending on how the public regards the incumbent, but failing to take this possible link into account would constitute a misspecification of the voting equation.

Our analysis will examine the 2000 National Election Studies survey data, with a focus on the closed-ended questions in which respondents must choose between a fixed set of alternative responses.[3] We shall begin by presenting separately the results for party identification, issue questions, candidate questions, and retrospective and succession questions. However, some of the effects on the vote that are ascribed to particular variables in that preliminary analysis may not be direct effects. Therefore, it is important to move to a model that has full controls. The variables that are significant in the separate models will be used to develop an overall model of the vote. Each of the steps along the way is important in its own right, but we shall proceed through them fairly quickly since our main interest is in the fully controlled model.

Party Identification and Demographics

We start with the distribution of party identification in 2000 since the partisan balance provides the baseline for understanding voting. The Democratic advantage in party identification remained intact in 2000. Indeed, Table 2.1 shows that the Democratic advantage was comparable to the level for 1992 and 1996.[4] The Democratic lead was higher than in the 1984–88

TABLE **2.1**   Party identification by year, 1952–2000 (in percentages)

	1952	1956	1960	1964	1968	1972	1976	1980	1984	1988	1992	1996	2000
Democratic	47.2	43.6	45.3	51.7	45.4	40.4	39.7	40.8	37.0	35.2	35.5	37.8	34.3
Independent	22.6	23.4	22.8	22.8	29.1	34.7	36.1	34.5	34.2	35.7	38.3	34.7	40.4
Republican	27.2	29.1	29.4	24.5	24.2	23.4	23.2	22.5	27.1	27.5	25.2	26.4	23.9
Dem Plurality	20.0	14.5	15.9	27.2	21.2	17.0	16.5	18.3	9.9	7.7	10.3	11.4	10.4
Dem + leaners	56.8	49.9	51.6	61.0	55.2	51.5	51.5	52.2	47.9	46.9	49.8	51.8	49.6
Pure Indep.	5.8	8.8	9.8	7.8	10.5	13.1	14.6	12.9	11.0	10.6	11.6	9.1	12.3
Rep + leaners	34.3	37.5	36.1	30.3	32.8	33.9	33.0	32.7	39.5	40.8	37.5	38.1	36.7
Dem Plurality	22.5	12.4	15.5	30.7	22.4	17.6	18.5	19.5	8.4	6.1	12.3	13.7	12.9

DATA SOURCE: *1952–2000 National Election Studies.*

period, but well below that of 1952–80. Identification with both parties actually fell a little since 1996, while political independence climbed and recovered from its slight drop in 1996. The proportion of pure independents was the highest since 1980, whereas the total proportion of independents (including partisans who admit being closer to one of the major parties) hit 40 percent of the respondents for the first time in NES surveys.

Ratings of the parties on the thermometer scale also show a continuing Democratic advantage (Table 2.2). There is no indication that either party suffered a loss of support due to the Lewinsky scandal or the impeachment episode. At the same time, there is no sign of the Republican Party gaining from that situation. The Democrats remain a bit less popular than they were in the 1980s, while the Republicans have fallen a few more points since then. The Democrats have been able to maintain a slight popularity advantage, but there is no resurgence in the popularity of parties.

As in previous years, there is a strong relationship between party identification and the vote (Table 2.3). People who strongly identify with their parties voted nearly unanimously for their party's candidate, with neither party suffering disproportionate losses. Weak partisans also overwhelmingly supported their party's candidate, but at the 85 percent level rather than at the 98 percent level of strong partisans. Pure independents broke in Bush's favor, but that advantage was minimized by their small number. Bush also was advantaged because 22 percent of independent Democrats voted Republican, while only 14 percent of independent Republicans voted Democrat, an 8 percent difference that applies to 25 percent of the sample who were independent partisans. These small advantages among pure independents and leaners helped Governor Bush neutralize the Democratic advantage in partisanship.

Most of the effects of demographic variables on the major-party presidential vote in 2000 were through party identification. We used logit analysis to test for direct effects of education, gender, race, Hispanic ethnicity, age, evangelical religion, religious commitment, region, and marriage, with partisanship controlled. (Full coding details are given in the methodological

TABLE **2.2** Party thermometer means, 1964–2000

Party	1964	1968	1972	1976	1980	1984	1988	1992	1996	2000
Democrats	72.3	65.8	66.4	62.9	63.9	62.1	61.5	59.0	58.8	59.0
Republicans	59.8	62.4	63.1	57.5	59.2	57.9	59.2	51.6	53.5	53.8
difference	12.5	3.4	3.3	5.4	4.7	4.2	2.3	7.4	5.3	5.2
correlation	−0.28	−0.18	0.02	0.01	−0.23	−0.40	−0.39	−0.27	−0.42	−0.34

DATA SOURCE: *1964–2000 National Election Studies.*
NOTE: *Respondents were asked to rate "Democrats" and "Republicans" in 1964–1980 and the "Democratic Party" and "Republican Party" in 1984–2000. The correlation shown is the correlation between the Republican and Democratic thermometers.*

TABLE **2.3** Vote by party identification, 2000

Party Identification	Gore % of Two-party Vote	% of Voters
Strong Democrat	97.0	22.1
Weak Democrat	85.3	15.5
Leaning Democrat	77.8	12.8
Pure Independent	44.7	7.2
Leaning Republican	14.1	12.8
Weak Republican	16.2	12.3
Strong Republican	1.7	17.2
Total		99.9

DATA SOURCE: *2000 National Election Study.*

appendix at the end of this chapter.) Studies show that African Americans, women, and non-Cuban Hispanics have been voting more Democratic in recent elections (Stanley and Niemi 1999), while married people (Weisberg 1987), evangelicals, and people with more religious commitment (Miller and Shanks 1996; Layman 1997; Weisberg and Mockabee 1999) have been voting more Republican. The analysis confirms some of these expectations (see equation 1 in Table 2.4): African Americans and women were more likely to vote for Al Gore, while people with greater religious commitment were more likely to vote for George W. Bush. Also, evangelicals, Southerners, and married people were more likely to vote for Bush. Any effects of the other demographic variables on the 2000 vote were expressed through their influences on party identification.[5]

Ideology and Issues

Liberal/conservative ideology can serve as another long-term predisposition that affects the vote. The Republican presidential campaign in 2000 was distinctive in that Governor Bush campaigned explicitly as a "compassionate conservative," which label could be expected to increase public awareness of ideology and to cement the association in the public's mind between being a Republican and a conservative. The Gore campaign was not explicitly ideological, so there is no reason to anticipate an increase in the relationship between being a Democrat and a liberal.

Starting in 1972 the NES surveys have asked people whether they are conservatives, moderates, or liberals. Table 2.5 shows the changes over time in the placement of respondents and the presidential candidates in recent elections. The values in this table have been adjusted so that positive values represent conservative positions and negative values represent liberal positions. None of the values for 2000 are particularly distinctive. The average respondent was as conservative as in 1996, Gore was seen as being as liberal

TABLE **2.4** Demographic, issue, and candidate effects on the Bush two-party vote in 2000

	Equation 1 (Standard Error)	Equation 2 (Standard Error)	Equation 3 (Standard Error)
Party Identification	1.155*** (.065)	1.076*** (.067)	.829*** (.075)
Education	−.060 (.046)		
Female	−.426* (.212)		
African American	−1.875*** (.503)		
Hispanic	−.060 (.513)		
Age	−.002 (.006)		
Evangelical	.962** (.310)		
South	.503* (.222)		
Married	.419* (.211)		
Religiosity	.289* (.139)		
Abortion		.376*** (.100)	
Retrospective Economy		.258** (.098)	
Health Insurance		.116 (.080)	
Tax Cut		.254*** (.063)	
Social Security		.103 (.082)	
Environment vs. Jobs		.036 (.103)	
Gun Control		.398*** (.105)	
School Vouchers		.030 (.059)	
Death Penalty		.133+ (.072)	
Candidate Competence			.114 (.113)
Candidate Integrity			.527*** (.129)
Candidate Empathy			.506*** (.108)
Candidate Leadership			.583*** (.090)
Constant	−3.038*** (.827)	−3.158*** (.680)	−2.531*** (.251)

(continued)

TABLE **2.4**   Continued

	Equation 1 (Standard Error)	Equation 2 (Standard Error)	Equation 3 (Standard Error)
N	1091	1081	1114
% Prediction	88.4%	88.4%	91.9%
Chi-square	859.071	875.439	1085.171
Degrees of freedom	10	10	5
−2 Log Likelihood	650.396	620.138	455.928

DATA SOURCE: *2000 National Election Study.*
NOTE: *The dependent variable is whether the respondent voted for Bush (1) or Gore (0). Values shown are logit coefficients. Issues have been coded so that conservative positions correspond to higher values.*
$^+p < .10; {}^*p < .05; {}^{**}p < .01; {}^{***}p < .001$ *(two-tailed).*

TABLE **2.5**   Average placement on a seven-point liberal-conservative scale, 1972–2000

	Average Respondent	Democratic Nominee	Republican Nominee	Distance Difference	Distance Between Candidates
2000	0.35	−0.76	0.93	−.53	1.69
1996	0.35	−0.78	1.05	−.43	1.83
1992	0.21	−0.81	1.04	−.19	1.85
1988	0.37	−0.76	1.11	−.39	1.87
1984	0.24	−0.55	0.96	−.07	1.51
1980	0.31	−0.26	1.21	.33	1.47
1976	0.23	−0.75	0.90	−.31	1.65
1972	0.14	−1.55	0.87	−.96	2.42

DATA SOURCE: *1972–2000 National Election Studies.*
NOTE: *Values are average scores on seven-point issue scales, where −3 is extremely liberal and +3 extremely conservative. Candidate means in 2000 are based on only a half-sample, since a five-point scale was used for the other half. Distance differences indicate how much closer the average respondent is to the Democratic candidate than to the Republican; positive values show that the average person is closer to the Democrat.*

as Clinton in 1992, and Bush was seen as slightly more moderate than Bush senior in 1992. The nominees were seen as being slightly less different from each other ideologically than in the previous three presidential contests. At the same time, the difference between the average respondent's ideological distance from the Democratic and the Republican nominees was greater than in most recent elections, a difference that worked to disadvantage Al Gore.

Several short-term issues were raised during the campaign. Among the issues that became relevant for which the NES included questions were abortion, retrospective evaluations of the economy, government-versus-private health insurance, whether taxes should be cut from the government surplus, protecting Social Security, a trade-off between protecting the environment and protecting jobs, gun control, school vouchers, and the death penalty.[6] Analyses of the 1996 election (Weisberg and Mockabee 1999; Lacy and Grant 1999) found that retrospective evaluations of the economy affected the vote that year even with controls on many other variables, whereas abortion did not. However, most accounts of the 2000 election insist that the economy did not play its usual role, Bush's tax cut proposal was not popular, and most of the other issues on this list did not matter.

We used logit analysis to examine the effects of issues, with partisanship controlled (see equation 2 in Table 2.4).[7] Some of the issues were significant. People who opposed abortion were more likely to vote Republican, as were opponents of gun control. People who felt that the economy had become better were less likely to vote Republican, a conventional result but one that challenges the media's view that Gore did not benefit from the strong U.S. economy. The tax-cut item was found to be significant, with people who favored tax cuts being more likely to vote for Bush. The other issues did not have significant direct effects in the multivariate analysis, though position on the death penalty was marginally significant.[8]

Candidate Images

The major-party presidential nominees in 2000 were new to voters but familiar at the same time. Al Gore had been vice president for eight years, but since that is usually a relatively invisible position Gore virtually had to introduce himself to the public as part of the presidential campaign. He was best known for being Bill Clinton's vice president (and for defending him publicly at some stages of the impeachment episode) and for his questionable fund-raising techniques in the 1996 campaign. Neither association helped Gore. Indeed, he faced a challenge that many vice presidents who run for the presidency have to face: how to show voters that they are their own man rather than just the continuation of a presidency of which the country had grown tired.

The George Bush name was very familiar to the public, or at least to people who were old enough to have been politically aware during the senior George Bush's administration from 1989 through 1992. As a large-state governor, George W. Bush was only somewhat known to the public, so he also had to define himself to the voting public. Some of his initial support was probably due to people associating him with his father, but that association was also a potential problem in that voters had rejected George H. W. Bush's attempt for a second term. Governor Bush campaigned as someone who had already demonstrated executive leadership skills, but the impression developed that his knowledge level was limited, and he had to fight that perception.

Gore was expected to have the advantage in the presidential debates, but, as is often the case, that expectation itself is a handicap to a candidate. Gore's performance did not live up to those expectations, varying from

TABLE **2.6**   Nominee thermometer means, 1968–2000

Nominee	1968	1972	1976	1980	1984	1988	1992	1996	2000
Democratic	61.7	49.1	63.1	56.6	57.4	56.8	56.1	59.7	57.3
Republican	66.5	66.0	60.6	56.1	61.2	60.6	52.3	52.0	56.6
Independent	31.4			52			45.4	40	
Winner's lead	4.8	16.9	2.5	−0.5	3.8	3.8	3.8	7.7	0.7
D-R correlation	−.18	−.40	−.30	−.29	−.50	−.38	−.39	−.45	−.39

DATA SOURCE: *1968–2000 National Election Studies.*
NOTE: *The mean score given to Nader in 2000 was 52.0, and the mean score given to Buchanan was 41.0.*

overly pushy in the first debate to overly restrained in the second and about right only in the third debate. Bush did better than expected, at least in the sense of not making any serious gaffes, and he bettered Gore overall in that his performance was more steady across the debates. Thus, the effect of the debates was probably to weaken any advantage Gore might have had in terms of incumbency while making Bush seem more capable and experienced.

The candidate thermometers (Table 2.6) show that neither candidate was wildly popular or unpopular, and their average ratings were virtually identical. The difference between their ratings was smaller than in any year other than 1980, and their ratings were in the range of Carter and Reagan that year as well as Clinton's range in 1992—which is also the same range of Mondale and Dukakis when they lost. George Bush was somewhat more popular than was his father in 1992 or than Bob Dole in 1996, and he was liked enough to be a stronger candidate than they were. Attitudes toward Gore were about as polarized as attitudes toward Bush, as indicated by a standard deviation of 25.6 for ratings of Gore versus 24.5 for Bush.[9]

Since 1980, the NES surveys have asked respondents whether they feel the presidential nominees have each of a series of traits. Kinder's (1986; see also Funk 1996 and 1999; and Weisberg 2000) research shows that these trait questions measure four dimensions: leadership, competence, integrity, and empathy. Table 2.7 shows the results for 2000 in comparison to those for earlier years. George Bush stands out on being seen as a strong leader, with the highest ratings on that question of any candidate since Ronald Reagan as an incumbent in 1984. At the same time, his ratings on being knowledgeable and intelligent are below that of any other candidate since Reagan in 1980, though the vast majority of the public rated him favorably on those traits. The two candidates were seen as equally moral, but a slightly greater percentage of people saw Gore as dishonest. More people saw Gore rather than Bush as caring about people, but Gore's rating was below that of Mondale in 1984, Dukakis in 1988, and Clinton in 1992. Bush's rating in this category was above that of his father in 1992 and Dole in 1996 and on par with that of Reagan in 1984. Altogether, Gore has the advantage on the

TABLE **2.7** Candidate trait perceptions, 1980–2000

Trait	2000			1996			1992		1988		1984		1980	
	Bush	Gore	Clinton	Dole	Clinton	Perot	Bush	Clinton	Bush	Dukakis	Reagan	Mondale	Reagan	Carter
Leadership														
Strong leader	67	59	66	60	59	38	56	62	54	57	71	49	60	39
Inspiring				38	52	35	39	59	39	49	59	44	49	37
Gets things done				65	57	53	41	68						
Competence														
Knowledgeable	71	84	88	84	83		83	83	83	82	77	81	70	
Intelligent	77	85	86		88		82	87	78	88	83	86		75
Integrity														
Moral	73	74	17	79	39	67	80	48	78	80	82	85	71	
Honest		28		69	41	59	59	51	67	78				81
Dishonest	23		66											
Empathy														
Cares about people	47	58	51	42	56	39	35	66	50	65	47	64		
Compassionate					69		59	79	62	73	60	79		
Out of touch	41	37	39											

DATA SOURCE: *1980–2000 National Election Studies.*

competence and empathy dimensions, while Bush has the advantage on leadership and a small edge on integrity. However, the differences are generally not large and are certainly much smaller than the advantage that Clinton had over Bush senior eight years earlier.

All in all, the candidate factor looks like it broke fairly even. Gore may have had a slight advantage, which is about what could be expected given the Democratic lead in party identification. The media depicted the campaign as being between competence and integrity, but the data suggest that the difference between the candidates was somewhat larger on leadership and that the governor was able to trump the vice president on that dimension.

To test the relative importance of competence, integrity, empathy, and leadership, we created four composite candidate trait variables. Each measures the extent to which the respondent favored Bush over Gore with respect to the relevant traits. Logit analysis, with a control for party identification, shows that all except competence were significant, all, of course, in the expected direction (see equation 3 in Table 2.4).[10] That the competence dimension was not related to the vote worked to Gore's disadvantage, as it could have been his strong card. With that dimension irrelevant, what was left was Bush's advantage on leadership and integrity, countered only by Gore's advantage on empathy.

Succession Effects

The succession theme for this chapter suggests that it is necessary to look at reactions to one more individual: President Clinton. Al Gore was closely linked to Bill Clinton as part of the Clinton-Gore administration, a linkage that had both positive and negative implications. Being associated with the economic growth of the 1990s could have been a positive for the vice president, but being seen as a defender of Clinton during the impeachment period would be seen as a negative for him. The press depicted the relationship between Clinton and Gore as very close during the early years of their administration, but apparently it soured after the Lewinsky scandal and was no longer personally close by election time. The Clinton people were said to be upset that the Gore campaign did not make more use of Clinton in the 2000 campaign.

The NES survey included a thermometer and the standard job-approval rating on President Clinton. Clinton's average popularity was 56, a reading that was on par with those of the presidential nominees but down a few degrees from his popularity when he was reelected in 1996. As was the case during the impeachment period, Clinton scored even better on the standard job-approval measure, with 67 percent approving his job as president, but 24 percent strongly disapproving.

TABLE **2.8** Succession effects on the Bush vote in 2000

	Equation 4 (Standard Error)	Equation 5 (Standard Error)
Party identification	.654** (.077)	.676*** (.078)
Clinton thermometer	−.022*** (.007)	
Clinton job approval	−.078 (.116)	
Candidate differential (Bush–Gore)	.060*** (.006)	.062*** (.006)
Clinton economy		−.553*** (.169)
Clinton security		−.222 (.155)
Clinton crime		−.231 (.205)
Clinton moral climate		−.585** (.153)
Constant	−.854 (.669)	−6.554*** (.792)
N	1098	1100
% Prediction	92.1%	92.6%
Chi-square	1086.838	1116.006
Degrees of freedom	4	6
−2 Log Likelihood	432.850	406.644

DATA SOURCE: *2000 National Election Study.*
NOTE: *Succession variables have been coded so that pro-Clinton answers correspond to higher values.*
$^+p < .10$; $^*p < .05$; $^{**}p < .01$; $^{***}p < .001$ *(two-tailed).*

Table 2.8 examines the effects of retrospective and succession predictors, again keeping party identification as a control variable in each equation. First (equation 4), we use the Clinton thermometer to measure general affect toward him along with the standard presidential job-approval measure. These variables have usually been employed separately in vote-prediction equations because they were thought to have considerable overlap. However, the Lewinsky scandal brought home the public's ability to distinguish between approval of the president and of his job performance. Estimating succession effects with just Clinton variables and party identification would be a serious misspecification in that no predictor relates directly to the current election. We follow the solution employed by Mattei and Weisberg (1994) of using the difference in the thermometer ratings of the current presidential candidates as a control variable. This candidate differential is not of direct interest, but we use it because it should control for most of the candidate-specific aspects of the election. These four variables alone can predict the vote well. Equation 4 shows that reactions to Clinton are significantly related to the vote even when the candidate differential is in-cluded—but his job performance is not. Clinton's job performance may have helped save his presidency when he was threatened with removal from office, but there is no sign here that Gore benefited from that. However, Gore was still affected by general affect toward Clinton.[11]

The NES survey also included several questions that measured partici-pants' evaluations of the contributions of Bill Clinton. We use the questions on how his administration handled the economy, national security, crime, and the moral climate of the country. A typical question was "Would you say that the Clinton administration made the nation's crime rate better, worse, or hasn't it made much difference either way?"[12] These predictors are interesting because they do not include anything directly related to the Gore-Bush race. In assessing the importance of these variables, we include two ad-ditional controls—party identification, once again, and the candidate dif-ferential—so that there is a variable relating to the 2000 race.

There is evidence that reactions to President Clinton affected voting in 2000 (equation 5 in Table 2.8). Evaluations of his handling the economy af-fected the vote, as did his effect on the moral climate of the nation, while his handling of national security and crime had insignificant effects.

This analysis implies that President Clinton had a direct effect on the 2000 election, even after controlling for partisanship and the candidate dif-ferential. His handling of the economy helped Vice President Gore, while the moral implications of his presidency hurt the vice president's electoral chances. Thus, the election could be seen as a battle between two Clinton legacies: an economic legacy and a moral one. The economic performance variable might be seen as a retrospective evaluation (a mediated retrospec-tive evaluation, in Fiorina's terms), but the moral and Clinton thermometer variables are non-issue succession variables.

The Attitudinal Basis of the Election

To summarize the separate effects presented in this chapter and to insti-tute appropriate controls, we have developed an overall model of major-party presidential voting in 2000. The model includes the sets of variables we discussed in earlier sections of this chapter: party identification, several standard demographic variables, issues, net evaluations of the candidates on the trait dimensions, and variables measuring reactions to President Clin-ton. All of the smaller logit equations we reported earlier had high levels of predictive success, so it is important to admit that a simple model with only party identification (not shown) predicts 87.7 percent of the cases correctly. Thus, the more complex equations improve on that predictive power only marginally, though it is, of course, impossible to obtain much improvement when a baseline model performs that well.[13] In any case, the next step is to

TABLE **2.9**   Final model, with estimated effects, for the Bush vote in 2000

	Logit Value (Standard Error)	Mean	Range	Partisan Valence	First Difference
Party Identification	.672*** (.085)	2.814	0 to 6	−.06	.31
Demographics					
Female	−.492+ (.292)	.554	0 to 1		−.12
African American	−1.405* (.587)	.104	0 to 1		−.29
Evangelical	.276 (.419)	.200			
South	.158 (.310)	.348			
Married	.317 (.277)	.600			
Religiosity	.057 (.200)	1.336			
Issues					
Abortion	.103 (.148)	−2.901			
Retrospective Economy	−.072 (.133)	2.708			
Tax Cut	.151+ (.083)	−2.585	−5 to −1	.21	.06
Gun Control	.187 (.148)	2.013			
Death Penalty	.085 (.094)	−2.210			
Candidate Traits					
Integrity	.401** (.144)	.116	−4 to +4	.03	.15
Empathy	.506*** (.121)	−.240	−4 to +4	−.06	.21
Leadership	.550*** (.097)	.251	−4 to +4	.06	.26
Succession Variables					
Clinton Thermometer	−.015* (.007)	53.166	0 to 100	−.06	−.11
Clinton Economy	−.453* (.178)	2.186	1 to 5	−.41	−.10
Clinton Moral Climate	−.583*** (.171)	3.654	1 to 5	.33	−.13
Constant	−3.552 (1.323)				
N	1075				
% Prediction	92.5%				
Chi-square	1110.027				
Degrees of freedom	18				
−2 Log Likelihood	377.425				

(*continued*)

TABLE **2.9** Continued

DATA SOURCE: *2000 National Election Study.*
NOTES: *The Partisan Valence column shows the departure of the variable's mean value from its middle value, divided by its possible departure from that middle value, with positive values showing a Republican advantage. For example, the Clinton thermometer for voters was 3.17 points above its neutral value of 50, compared to a potential 50 points, yielding −.063 advantage against the Republicans.*

The first difference values show the effect of moving from −.5 standard deviation to +.5 standard deviation on the variable, with the others at their means, except that the values shown for the dummy variables (gender and race) show the effects of moving men to women and from non-African Americans to African Americans.
$^+p < .10; ^*p < .05; ^{**}p < .01; ^{***}p < .001$ *(two-tailed).*

combine these sets of predictors to see whether together they have more explanatory power.

To keep the number of predictors reasonable, we calculated a logit equation for major-party voting using as predictors only those variables that were significant in the previous equations at the .10 level.[14] Many of these variables did not prove to have significant direct effects in a full model (Table 2.9). The only demographic variable that retains significance is race plus a marginal effect of gender. Thus, even the full barrage of controls does not suffice to explain the greater Democratic vote among African Americans. The only issue variable with even a marginal effect is the tax-cut issue, which may monitor a long-term difference between the parties.[15] Affect toward President Clinton helped Gore. Evaluations of Clinton on the economy were significant, as were evaluations of the moral climate under Clinton.[16] Candidate integrity, empathy, and leadership were also significant, as would be expected given how close comparative candidate reactions are to the vote decision itself.

Note that several of the variables that were significant in the earlier analysis, including all of the issues, are not significant in the full model. Issues such as gun ownership received considerable attention in the media, especially after bivariate analysis of exit polls showed they were strongly related to the vote. However, the issues that are significant in an issue-only analysis (equation 2 in Table 2.4) do not have significant direct effects on the vote when full controls are instituted. Their effects are presumably instead mediated through other variables in the model, including the candidate terms and the retrospective and succession terms.[17] That does not mean that these issues were not important, but that these issues helped shape other attitudes, which in turn affected the vote more directly.

It is important to emphasize that three separate succession variables had significant direct effects on the vote: Clinton's general thermometer rating and the assessments of his contributions to the economy and to the nation's moral climate. One might expect that the Clinton thermometer rating would encapsulate the moral dimension, but affective reactions to him had a separate effect. After eight years in office, Clinton had become a dominant political figure who would influence the election result directly, beyond the issue and moral aspects of his tenure.

The means for the variables are shown in the third column of Table 2.9, along with the ranges of the significant variables. The Partisan Valence column provides an indication of how much the mean of the variable lay in the Republican direction. That is crucial information that must be considered in order to determine whether a candidate is helped or hurt by a variable. The last column of the table gives estimates of the impact of each significant variable (based on the difference between the estimated values of the equation for a one-half-standard-deviation range of the variable, with all other variables at their means). The two final columns of the table together show the net importance of each significant variable.

The important question becomes, Which variables had the greatest impact on the vote? Four of the significant attitudinal variables worked in favor of Gore, but those with the greatest advantage for the Democrats generally did not have a large impact on the vote. As would be expected, party identification clearly had a large impact on the vote decision, but its mean was not Democratic enough to give Gore a large boost. Race clearly had a very strong impact, with the African-American vote helping Gore. The African-American vote has long been crucial to the Democratic Party, but Bush would have walked away with an easy victory in 2000 if the African-American vote had not been so completely one-sided. Empathy had a large impact and helped Gore, as it helped Clinton four years earlier, but the advantage on empathy for Gore was slight. The first differences for three other variables that helped Gore were smaller. Gender worked toward Gore's favor, though it was only marginally significant. General attitudes toward Clinton narrowly helped Gore. Finally, Clinton's performance on the economy helped Gore, and this variable was most strongly in the Democratic direction.

Although the empathy dimension helped Gore, it was compensated for exactly by the degree to which the leadership dimension swung in the Republican direction. The latter's impact on the vote was slightly higher. The first differences for the other variables that helped Bush were smaller. The candidate-integrity dimension also was in the Republican direction, but it had less impact. The tax-cut issue worked to Bush's favor, but the first difference is very small. However, one succession factor did have a more substantial effect: evaluations of Clinton's contribution to the moral climate of the nation, which were decidedly negative and therefore helped the Republicans.

This analysis suggests that Gore started out with an advantage due to partisanship, his lock on the African-American vote, and an advantage among women. Empathy could have worked in his favor, but it was compensated for by Bush's advantage on leadership, and the integrity dimension pushed the candidate factor into the Bush column. That leaves the retrospective and succession variables. Gore benefited slightly from overall affect toward Clinton and from attitudes on Clinton's handling of the economy. However, this benefit was compensated for by negative evaluations of morality involving Clinton, so the retrospective and succession variables helped Bush. From this perspective, it is not surprising that the election was so close: most of the factors that helped either candidate did not help him much, whereas the only two variables with a large impact worked in opposite directions.

Conclusion

By definition, it is impossible to explain the outcome of an election that was so close that no one will ever know who really won. And it is equally impossible to explain an election in which the popular-vote difference was a trivial 539,947 out of 101,452,285 votes cast and counted for the major-party candidates—a difference of just 0.53 percent. However, the analysis presented here does explain how the election became so close. Some variables that are usually important did not have significant effects in 2000. In particular, retrospective economic evaluations usually stand out in importance but did not in 2000. We will leave others to continue their debate as to whether this is because Gore did not make effective use of the nation's economic well-being, because a country that experiences a long period of economic well-being will no longer vote on the basis of the economy, or because the country recognized that the economy was beginning to weaken and therefore was not willing to give much credit for its strength (see Bartels and Zaller 2001; Lewis-Beck and Tien 2001; Wlezien 2001; Campbell 2001; Holbrook 2001).

Additionally, the election became so close because neither candidate had much of an advantage on any important matter, and the advantages that the two candidates had pretty much balanced out. Partisanship benefited the Democrats, but not enough to expect it to ensure a Democratic victory. Neither candidate particularly excited the electorate, and neither candidate completely turned the electorate off. When comparing the traits that people ascribed to the candidates, neither candidate had enough of an advantage to matter. Each had an advantage on some dimensions, but neither had a large advantage across the board.

When the incumbent is not running, it is conventional to view the race as an open-seat race. That characterization, however, would miss the substantial carryover effects of the previous administration when one of the major-party nominees is associated with that administration. Affect toward the sitting president affected voting, as did evaluations of his handling of the nation's moral climate and the economy. However, the lack of a direct effect from Clinton's job approval indicates that Gore did not gain the full electoral advantage that an heir apparent can gain from being linked to the incumbent—the advantage that Bush's father had in 1988 (Mattei and Weisberg 1994, Table 2).

Given that the literature usually restricts the term *retrospective voting* to issue-based voting, it is important to emphasize that broader succession effects were obtained in this study. Clinton's effect on the moral climate of the nation, which we interpret as the impact of his involvement with Monica Lewinsky, had a significant effect on the vote, though it is neither directly related to the 2000 candidates nor to issues. Also, the respondent's thermometer rating of Bill Clinton was significantly related to the vote in the final model, even with the full set of controls for handling specific issues during his presidency. This again emphasizes that succession effects do not just involve issue-based matters. There was issue-based retrospective voting in the 2000 election, but there were also more general succession-related effects.

The presidential elections of the past hundred years have rarely been open-seat races in which neither candidate is associated with the administration. Even when the sitting president is not running, the vice president or another designated heir (cabinet secretaries in 1908 and 1928) has usually attempted to provide for continuity in succession to the presidency. Treating presidential elections as open-seat races overlooks the importance of the incumbent president.

The 2000 election was not conducted as a blank-slate election in which only the current party nominees mattered. Two succession variables had decided partisan directions: evaluations of Clinton on the economy and on moral climate. Unfortunately for Vice President Gore, the moral legacy of the administration was more related to the vote than was its economic legacy. If Gore could not disassociate himself from the administration's moral legacy, he had to associate himself more with its economic legacy in order to win decidedly. He did not succeed in doing so.

In the end, the electorate balanced the administration's record in the moral and economic realms. Economic success was not enough to outweigh moral bankruptcy. Succession effects can be devastating when the sins of the incumbent are visited on the designated successor.

METHODOLOGICAL APPENDIX
Variables Used from 2000 NES Survey

Party Identification: V000523, third party and apoliticals deleted

Demographics

Education: V000910
Female: V001029
African American: V001006a, coded 1 for African American, 0 otherwise

Hispanic: V1006a, coded 1 for Hispanic, 0 otherwise

Age: V000908

Evangelical: 1 if BOTH Born Again AND Interpret Bible Literally, 0 otherwise
  Born Again—V000903, coded 1 if R has had a born-again experience, 0 otherwise
  Interpret Bible Literally—V000876, coded 1 if R interprets Bible literally, 0 otherwise

South: V000092, coded 1 for South, 0 otherwise

Married: V000909, coded 1 for married or partnered, 0 otherwise

Religiosity: Prayer + Attend Services
  Prayer—V000874, coded 1 if R prays "a few times a week" or more, 0 otherwise
  Attend Services—V000879, coded 1 if R attends "once or twice a month" or more, 0 otherwise

Ideology: V000439, missing data coded at center

Issues
(missing data has been coded to the middle position on all but abortion and economy)

Abortion: V000694 * −1 [This issue and some other issue variables have been multiplied by −1 in order to give them consistent directions, with conservative positions having higher values.]

Retrospective Economy: V000491

Health Insurance: V000614

Tax Cuts: V000690 * −1

Social Security: V000693

Environment vs. Jobs: V000713

Gun Control: V000731

School Vouchers: V000744 * −1

Death Penalty: V000752 * −1

Candidate Traits

Notes: Candidate traits were recoded to 1 to 5 scales, with missing data recoded to 3. All candidate differences are in the format of Gore minus Bush. V000528, V000530, V000535, and V000537 were reverse-coded before performing the transformation listed below. Higher scores represent rating Bush as better than Gore on the dimension.

Candidate Competence: ((V000526 + V000529)—(V000533 + V000536))/2

Candidate Integrity: ((V000524 + V000528)—(V000531 + V000535))/2

Candidate Empathy: ((V000525 + V000530)—(V000532 + V000537))/2

Candidate Leadership: (V000527—V000534)

Candidate Differential: V000361—V000360

Clinton Job Approval: V000341 * −1 [This variable and the succession variables below are multiplied by −1 in order to give them consistent directions, with pro-Clinton answers having higher values.]

Clinton Thermometer: V000359

Succession Variables
(missing data recoded to center)

Clinton Economy: V001603a * −1

Clinton Security: V001612a * −1

Clinton Crime: V001620a * −1

Clinton Moral Climate: V001628a * −1

3 Bush v. Gore: The Recount of Economic Voting

HELMUT NORPOTH

In the contest between Al Gore and George W. Bush, a sure winner ended up a loser. The 2000 presidential election was supposed to be a slam-dunk victory for economic voting. The growth of the U.S. economy was brisk, inflation tame, unemployment invisible, the stock market booming, the federal budget in the black, and the American public in a cheerful mood. How on earth could the party in the White House fail to retain that office under those circumstances? Forecast models were unanimous in their prediction of victory for the candidate of the party that had steered the economy on its glorious course. The only disagreement was over the size of the victory margin. Although Gore beat Bush in the popular-vote count, and may very well have edged him in Florida as well, the economy was unable to deliver a comfortable victory for the Democratic candidate in the 2000 presidential election. What went wrong?

Perhaps the answer is simply, "It's *not* the economy, stupid!"—not in 2000, or in any election. Maybe it is time to abandon the idea that economics is a major factor in elections, let alone the deciding one. But that reaction would be like throwing out the baby with the bathwater. Granted, other factors besides the economy certainly matter for voting, in the 2000 election no less than in others, but the economy provides an issue too plausible and compelling to discard altogether. To do so, one would have to ignore too many bodies of evidence documenting the influence of economic conditions on the vote. While leaving to others the task of probing the influence of noneconomic factors, this chapter intends to pursue promising clues provided by the economic-voting theory itself. Consider, in particular, the following propositions about economic voting that may help resolve the 2000 election puzzle:

– Economic voting is asymmetric: good times pay less of an electoral benefit compared to the cost exacted by bad times. That may be especially so after a prolonged spell of good times, as voters get used to them. Hence voters with a favorable view of the economy in 2000 may not have been especially inclined to reward the incumbent party with their votes.

– Voters behave as "bankers," not as "peasants." Economic voting is prospective, not retrospective. It did not matter that the economy *was* booming; what mattered was what was lying *ahead*. Pessimism about the economy after the 2000 election nullified the effect of good times enjoyed before the election.

– Economic voting requires an institutional configuration that was missing in the 2000 election: Bill Clinton, the sitting president responsible for the booming economy, was not on the ballot in 2000 — a casualty of the two-term limit. Economic voting will not work as strongly for the incumbent party with another candidate such as Al Gore. In other words, this is personal, not partisan. Credit and blame for economic performance are not fully transferable.

The research in this chapter combines survey and aggregate data. It relies on the exit poll conducted by the Voter News Service on Election Day on a sample of the national electorate (ca. 13,000 cases), and time series of economic performance and presidential elections (1872–2000). To provide sufficient background for an examination of the three possible explanations just outlined, let us begin with a review of the economic-voting model that made a Democratic victory in 2000 look like a sure thing.

Retrospective Voting

The standard model implicit in most studies of economic voting presumes a retrospective calculus of reward and punishment (for recent reviews, see Lewis-Beck and Stegmaier 2000; Norpoth 1996a). Election Day is judgment day in which good performance earns incumbents reelection and bad performance defeat. During the 1980 presidential campaign, Ronald Reagan popularized that model when he posed the question, "Ask yourself, are you better off now than you were four years ago?" As Kramer (1971, 134) put it more formally: "If the performance of the incumbent party is 'satisfactory' according to some simple standard, the voter votes to retain the incumbent governing party in office, while if the government's performance is not 'satisfactory', the voter votes against the incumbent."

A voter's decision, accordingly, focuses on the incumbent, while ignoring the opposition; takes account of the past, while ignoring the future; and judges performance, while ignoring policies. The retrospective model is

TABLE **3.1**   Forecasts of the Democratic vote in the 2000 presidential election

Forecaster	Forecast	Issued	Predictors
Abramowitz	53.2%	August 1	Presidential approval closest to July 1 (59%) First-half real GDP growth (2.5%) More than second term (1)
Campbell	52.8%	August 29	Trial heat around Labor Day (49%) 2nd quarter real GDP growth (1.3%)
Holbrook	60.3%	Early July	Presidential approval 2nd quarter average (58.3%) Consumer satisfaction index (138) More than second term (1)
Lewis-Beck & Tien	55.4%	August 25	Presidential approval in early July (59%) First-half real GNP growth (2.5%) Peace and prosperity index (100)
Lockerbie	52.9%	July 7	Change in real disposable income in year before election (3.0%) Prospective consumer attitudes (43) Years the in-party has been in White House logged (.903)
Norpoth	55.0%	July 26	Primary performance (New Hampshire since 1952) Democratic vote in last election (54.7%) Democratic vote in election before that (53.5%)
Wlezien & Erikson	55.2%	August 25	Presidential approval for 3rd quarter (58%) Cumulative growth in leading economic indicators (.13)

DATA SOURCE: *APSA Roundtable on Election Forecasting, Washington, D.C., August 31, 2000.*
NOTE: *The forecast is Al Gore's percentage of the two-party vote.*

simple and undemanding. A voter does not have to be familiar with the economic policies pursued by government, or with the proposals introduced by the opposition. All that matters is whether at the end of the day economic times are good or bad, according to some simple standard. It does not matter whether the incumbent government really deserves the credit or the blame for the state of the economy. Nor does it matter whether or not the opposition would have done equally well or poorly, or whether its proposals are likely to improve a bad situation.

The retrospective model has proved quite congenial for election forecasting. In 1996, those forecasts all predicted, before the event, a Democratic victory in the presidential election, and the forecast turned out to be right (Campbell and Garand 2000). In 2000, as can be seen in Table 3.1, they all forecast a Democratic victory again, but with less success this time (Kaiser 2000; Clymer 2000). A favorite predictor of these forecast models is a measure of past economic performance such as GDP growth or change in disposable income prior to the election (Abramowitz 2001; Campbell 2001; Lewis-Beck and Tien 2001; and Lockerbie 2001). Another widely used predictor, the approval rating of the incumbent president, also pertains to retrospective performance, though not necessarily solely economic (Holbrook 2001; Wlezien and Erikson 2001). Moreover, the use of performance in presidential primaries as a vote predictor (Norpoth 2001) also was inspired by the logic of retrospective behavior. Although some of the forecast equations go beyond the retrospective calculus, that calculus without much doubt constitutes the core of all those efforts.

Aside from the schadenfreude among skeptics of election forecasting, the poor record of the 2000 predictions prompted questions especially about the wisdom of the retrospective model and the emphasis on the economy as a vote predictor. Two defenders of the basic model (Bartels and Zaller 2001), who themselves had not ventured into forecasting before the election, offered a stunningly simple absolution: the U.S. economy prior to the election was by no means as strong as had been assumed by the forecast models. By their measure of real disposable income, the economy actually was in weak enough shape to lead to a 50–50 electoral outcome. Hence, there is no reason to question the retrospective model or the influence of the economy; it is just a matter of relying on the proper measure. Of course, this is advice proffered with the benefit of hindsight after the electoral outcome was known. How good or bad was the U.S. economy in 2000? As far as the electoral impact is concerned, the most compelling answer comes from the way voters saw and judged the state of the economy when they cast their vote.

Table 3.2 presents evaluations of economic conditions rendered by voters on Election Day. In 2000, a near-unanimous verdict pronounced the nation's economy to be in good health, with barely one in ten rating it not so good or poor. To see how "satisfactory" that was, consider the results for 1992 and 1996. In 1996, a bare majority gave the national economy an excellent or good rating (56%), and Bill Clinton had no difficulty winning reelection. If the economy was good enough in 1996 for an incumbent victory, the economy in 2000, everything else being equal, should have produced an even better outcome. Indeed, nothing short of a landslide triumph would have done justice to that kind of economy. Consider the following exercise. Had the economic views held in 2000 guided the presidential vote in the same manner as they did four years earlier, Al Gore would have swept George W. Bush with 59.4 percent of the major-party vote, assuming party identification held constant. In light of economic performance, the real mystery of 2000 is not that the Democratic candidate lost the White House, but that he failed to surpass the electoral mark of 1996.

To see what kind of economy it takes to bring on election defeat, look no further than 1992. That year, according to Table 3.2, eight in ten voters rated the economy as either poor or not so good. They also were more inclined to say no rather than yes to the "Reagan Question": 34 percent considered themselves to be "worse off" in 1992 compared to four years ago, while 24 percent picked "better off." In 2000, by contrast, the ratio in favor of "better off" was five to one, surpassing even the good year of 1996.[1] Note that while views of economic conditions fluctuated widely between 1992 and 2000, the balance of party identification hardly budged at all, with

TABLE **3.2**   Economic views and partisanship in presidential elections, 1992–2000

	1992	1996	2000
Nation's Economy Now			
Excellent	1%	4%	20%
Good	18%	52%	67%
Not so good/poor	81%	44%	14%
Family Financial Situation, compared to four years ago			
Better today	24%	34%	51%
About the same	42%	46%	39%
Worse today	34%	21%	11%
Issue That Mattered Most			
Economy/Jobs	27%	26%	21%
Party Identification			
Democrat	38%	39%	39%
Independent	27%	26%	27%
Republican	35%	35%	35%
(Range of N)	(6,652–13,229)	(6,785–15,400)	(5,795–12,427)

DATA SOURCE: *Election Day national exit polls conducted by Voter Research & Surveys 1992 and Voter News Service 1996 and 2000.*

Republicans at near parity with Democrats. That competitiveness for the Republican Party in national politics is the legacy of the partisan realignment that took place in the 1980s (Meffert, Norpoth, and Ruhil 2001). Still, partisanship gave the Democratic candidate a slight edge, making it all the more daunting to explain why a good economy failed to keep that party safely in the White House.[2]

The Asymmetry Effect

One possibility, grounded in social psychology, is that economic voting is asymmetric (Katona 1975; Lau 1985). Although bad performance hurts incumbents at the polls, good performance does not help as much, if at all. To paraphrase V. O. Key's famous saying, the electorate is more inclined to act as a "god of vengeance" than as a "god of reward" (Key 1964, 568). The reasons for such asymmetric behavior are not hard to come by. Like Gresham's law, bad news drives good news out of circulation. People are more sensitive to losses than to gains. The economy is more likely to make the headlines when it is in trouble than when it is doing all right. A good economic record is what the public expects. When this expectation is disappointed the economy becomes a public concern and voters begin to look for culprits.

Such a "negativity effect" has attracted considerable attention in the study of electoral behavior. The classic text *The American Voter* noted that a "party already in power is rewarded much less for good times than it is punished for bad times" (Campbell et al. 1960, 555). In American elections from 1896 to 1970, economic downturns appeared to hurt the vote of the incumbent party, whereas prosperity paid no electoral dividend (Bloom and Price 1975). If that were true in general, the 2000 election puzzle would not be hard to solve. As the candidate of the governing party, Al Gore would have had no reason to expect an electoral benefit from good economic times. He was simply the victim of a negativity bias leading to an asymmetric form of economic voting. But how credible is this effect? Both Bill Clinton's reelection victory in 1996 and Ronald Reagan's reelection in 1984 seem inexplicable without the benefit of a good economy. There is evidence that shows voters to be "evenhanded in their economic judgments, voting *for* governments that are liked, *against* governments that are disliked" (Lewis-Beck 1988, 79; also Kiewiet 1983). Some have suggested that negative voting may be an artifact, with such behavior being concentrated among previous supporters of the incumbent party (Fiorina and Shepsle 1989).

Though hard to accept in general form, asymmetric voting may prove a useful guide in certain elections. Good times may indeed pay a handsome electoral dividend when prosperity is a relative novelty. When the economy is recovering from a recession at a brisk pace (i.e., 1984 and 1996), the electorate may be quite sensitive to good news. But when the boom has run its course for a while and is becoming all too familiar, voter attention may drift elsewhere. In such an election, like the one in 2000, voters may be less inclined to reward the governing party for good economic performance.

The test presented in Table 3.3, with a control for party identification, offers no support for negative asymmetric voting in the 2000 election. The parameter estimate for the positive category (excellent) of the national economy is strong and far more significant than is the parameter estimate for the negative category (not so good/poor). The case is even stronger for family finances. Here the negative side (worse today) falls short of significance while the positive side (better today) comes through with both strength and significance. If there is any asymmetry in this pattern it is one that favors the positive side, contrary to the original hypothesis, which presumes asymmetric behavior with a negativity bias. Judging by voters' own sense of issue importance, the economy was nearly as salient an issue in the 2000 election as in the previous two (Table 3.2). That times were good did not render the economy an irrelevant issue. All that, of course, only deepens the mystery of that election. Not only were times exceptionally good, but favorable impressions had a stronger electoral pull than did negative ones. How could that combination fail to deliver a winning margin to the incumbent party in 2000? Short of discarding the economic factor altogether, we must consider the possibility that voters saw something ominous on the economic horizon

TABLE **3.3** Positive versus negative views of economic conditions and the presidential vote, 2000

	Presidential Vote	
Nation's Economy Now		
Excellent	.92***	—
	(.10)	
Not so good/poor	−.64***	—
	(.11)	
Family Financial Situation		
Better today	—	.97***
		(.08)
Worse today	—	−.06
		(.13)
Party Identification	2.26***	2.24***
	(.05)	(.05)
Constant	−4.70***	−5.08***
	(.12)	(.13)
Correct Prediction	82%	83%
N	(5,852)	(5,862)

DATA SOURCE: *Voter News Service, National Exit Poll 2000.*
NOTE: *Entries are logit estimates; standard errors in parentheses. Only votes for Bush (coded 0) and Gore (coded 1) were included in the analysis.*
***$p < .001$.

and set aside their good feelings about recent economic performance. The economic downturn in the year following the election would certainly prove such pessimism right.

The Banker Model

In theory, the decision made on Election Day is a choice about the future: who should govern the country in the next few years? A rational voter ought to reach that decision based on a comparison of future benefits. With respect to the economy, voters should ask themselves which candidate (party) is most likely to deliver good times after the election, not what the parties have done lately (Chappell and Keech 1991; Fiorina 1981; Lewis-Beck 1988). Some have gone as far as to depict voters as "bankers" (instead of "peasants"), who rely on "an informed view of the nation's economic prospects," not on a narrow view of their pocketbooks (MacKuen, Erikson, and Stimson 1992). Granted, voters are not required to do their own economic forecasting. All they have to do is simply pick up cues about "economic prospects" from what transpires in the media. So long as expert forecasts are covered in the economic news, the average viewer may end up as farsighted and sophisticated as a "banker."

TABLE **3.4**   Retrospective versus prospective views of economic
conditions and the presidential vote, 2000

	Presidential Vote	
Nation's Economy Now	.76***	—
	(.07)	
Family Financial Situation,	—	.65***
compared to four years ago		(.06)
Nation's Economy Next Year	.12	.05
	(.06)	(.06)
Party Identification	2.25***	2.23***
	(.05)	(.05)
Constant	−6.44***	−6.29***
	(.21)	(.11)
Correct Prediction	82%	83%
N	(5,687)	(5,684)

DATA SOURCE: *Voter News Service, National Exit Poll 2000.*
NOTE: *Entries are logit estimates; standard errors in parentheses. Only votes for
Bush (coded 0) and Gore (coded 1) were included in the analysis.*
***$p < .001.$

It may be questionable, however, whether ordinary citizens pay enough
attention to economic news to be so informed about the future. Surveys of
consumer attitudes show that a large portion of the American public admits
not following economic news. What is more, the economic views of those
who do not get such news are remarkably similar, in the aggregate, to the
views of those who tune in (Haller and Norpoth 1997). Even a rational-
choice proponent like Downs (1957) is not very sanguine about voters' capacity to judge future performance, so much so, in fact, that he allows current performance to be used as the best bet regarding the future. In other
words, if you want to make a prospective judgment, rely on retrospection.
Indeed, consumer expectations about the economy strongly follow in the
path of how recent economic performance is being evaluated, especially
when times are good. It is only during economic downturns that the two diverge, with expectations turning optimistic ahead of the actual recovery
(Haller and Norpoth 1994). Although some studies have shown that economic expectations, though significant, do not overwhelm retrospective
evaluations (Clarke and Stewart 1994), others have found no support for
the banker model (Norpoth 1996b). Still, most of this debate has been
fought in the domain of presidential popularity, not actual voting decisions.
Although the question about a president's current job performance may
mostly elicit a retrospectively flavored response, the choice on Election Day
may put voters in a more prospective mind.

Even so, the results of Table 3.4 are not encouraging for the prospective
case. In fact, they are devastating. Views about the nation's economy next

year, that is, the year following the election, fail to register a significant effect on the vote in the 2000 election. Meanwhile, views about the economy now record a strong and highly significant effect. The same is true for personal financial assessments instead of views of the national economy. In terms of the metaphors introduced by MacKuen, Erikson, and Stimson (1992), it is just the opposite of what they postulate. In the straight fight between bankers (national economic prospects) and peasants (family finances now compared to the past), it is the peasants who win a knockout victory.

Returning to the vote in the 2000 election, one must conclude that rosy retrospective assessments of economic conditions were not overturned by whatever forecasts voters may have made about the future of the U.S. economy. A very simple reason why that could not have happened in the 2000 election is that so few voters voiced any pessimism about the economic prospects. Only one in ten expected the economy to get worse in the year ahead, whereas three in ten saw it getting even better, with the remainder seeing the same (good times) ahead. The voter who predicted a downturn while agreeing that the economy was in good shape was a rarity. Any clouds that might have been darkening the economic sky lurked far beyond the horizon in 2000. As it was, times were good in 2000, and more of the same and perhaps even better times lay ahead. That puts us back at square one. If voters were so pleased with the economy, why did the incumbent party fail to win comfortably? Now that we have dismissed both the possibilities of asymmetric and prospective voting, what, if anything, is left to consider within the realm of economic voting?

The Missing Incumbent

To recapitulate the basic model of economic voting, elections are judgments about government performance, and the operational meaning of government is "incumbent party." That definition, of course, is not as straightforward as it may sound, even for a two-party system. Does the absence of a sitting president from the ballot matter for the value of incumbency? Should we expect government performance to matter as much for the presidential vote when the incumbent president is not running for reelection as when he is running? In other words, could Al Gore expect to reap the same electoral benefit from the good economy as Bill Clinton would have done had he been allowed to run for a third term?

Whether or not the incumbent party is running with the same or a new candidate may make little difference in elections where candidates are little known to most voters. But that is hard to accept for electoral contests that feature highly visible contenders. The vote for president in American politics bears a heavy imprint of candidate evaluations, as demonstrated by the voting classic, *The American Voter* (Campbell et al. 1960, chapters 3 and 4) and many studies since (e.g., Miller and Shanks 1996). Although past performance in office leaves a mark on those evaluations, the effect varies sharply according to whether an incumbent president is in the race or not. Incumbency affects how many key determinants affect electoral choice in presidential elections (Weisberg 2002a). Sitting presidents seeking reelection are overwhelmingly evaluated by retrospective performance, but fresh candidates of the incumbent party much less so (Miller and Wattenberg 1985). Granted, an incumbent vice president running for the presidency may be subject to a "succession" effect (Mattei and Weisberg 1994; also Weisberg and Hill, Chapter 2 in this book), but that does not preclude the possibility that the successor is judged less strongly in terms of incumbent performance than the incumbent would have been (Nadeau and Lewis-Beck 2001). How can we estimate this gap in the incumbency effect in presidential elections? How can we come to grips with someone not in the race, whether it is Bill Clinton in 2000, Ronald Reagan in 1988, and so on?

The Presidential Term Limit

The only way to do so is by comparing presidential elections across time. Fortunately, for this purpose, the United States not only has an extended history of popular voting, but there are also numerous instances where sitting presidents did not run for reelection. For that, one must thank the two-term limit. In deciding against seeking a third term, George Washington set a precedent not violated for nearly a century and a half. Franklin Roosevelt's departure from that tradition in 1940 sparked an effort to make a two-term limit a constitutional requirement. The Twenty-Second Amendment adopted in 1951 set term limits in stone for American presidents. But whether by law or tradition, the two-term limit has been the rule (with one exception) in presidential elections. The rule guarantees that the incumbent president is missing from the ballot with some predictable regularity. It is a regularity that should register in the time flow of the presidential vote.

Figure 3.1 charts the Democratic percentage of the major-party vote for president from 1828 to 2000, a period covering forty-four elections altogether.[3] It is a perfect picture of equilibrium (Norpoth 1995; Stokes and Iversen 1966). The movement of the two-party division of the vote is constrained within boundaries of roughly 35 and 65, and within those boundaries the vote crosses the 50–percent mark quite frequently.[4] In other words, neither party can expect to hold on to the presidency for very long. How long, on the average? If the two-term limit affects voting in presidential elections, one would predict a tenure of the presidential party in the White House of close to 2 terms. As it happens, the actual average is 2.6 terms. So turnover in the White House does not quite occur with the regu-

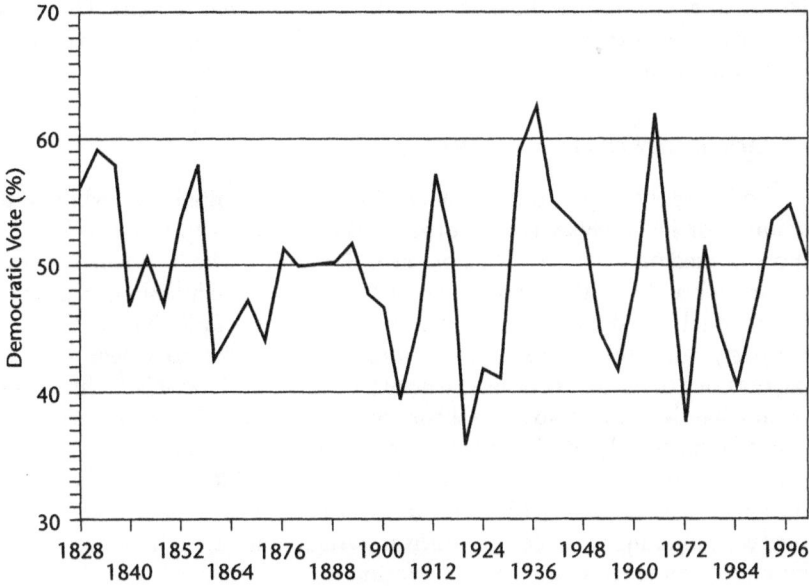

FIGURE 3.1   The Democratic Percentage of the Major-Party Vote for President

larity of the tide calendar. But cyclical movement, albeit with irregular period and amplitude, is evident in the vote in presidential elections.

This type of cycle can be modeled with the help of a second-order autoregressive model (see Box and Jenkins 1976; Clarke, Norpoth, and Whiteley 1998). For the Democratic vote series (VOTE), centered around its overall mean, the estimates are as follows, with standard errors in parentheses:

$$\text{VOTE}_t = .41 \text{ VOTE}_{t-1} - .35 \text{ VOTE}_{t-2}$$
$$\quad\quad (.14) \quad\quad\quad (.14)$$

Adj. R^2 = .21   SER = 5.6   N = 44

Most telling, the parameter for VOTE_{t-2} is negative, whereas the parameter for VOTE_{t-1} is positive; and both are roughly equal in absolute size.[5]
These results confirm estimates derived for shorter vote series (Norpoth
1995, also Midlarsky 1984). The party winning a presidential election in a
contest that drives the other party from the White House can expect to hold
on to the office in the election immediately following, with the sitting president seeking reelection. At the same time, the presidential party must reckon
with a reversal at the next election, as the incumbent party seeks reelection
without the sitting president in the race. When a president leaves the White

House after two terms, the party's hold on that office is in peril. That was Al Gore's predicament in the 2000 election. What vote could he expect to reap even in good economic times under those circumstances?

Incumbency and Economic Voting

To probe the impact of the economy on the presidential vote, while controlling for incumbency (also Norpoth 2002), one has to make do with a more limited time horizon. Data on the U.S. economy can be tracked at best as far back as 1872, the measures being GNP growth and inflation.[6] Since the presidential vote continues to be defined as the Democratic share of the major-party vote, the economic indicators must be adjusted whenever that party is out of office. Obviously, whenever the White House is not in Democratic hands, the retrospective theory does not predict that good times will help that party's electoral fortune, or that bad times will hurt it. It is just the other way around. So for elections in which Republicans held the presidency, the economic variables must be inverted.[7] For the sake of parsimony, the two economic variables, real GNP growth and inflation, have been combined into an index of economic performance (ECON).[8]

The impact of the presidential term limit will be estimated through the second-order autoregressive dynamic as identified for the vote series all the way back to 1828 in the previous section. The vote equation for the Democratic percentage of the major-party vote in presidential elections (VOTE) yields the following estimates for the economic performance index (ECON) and the term-limit–induced dynamic (standard errors in parentheses):

$$\text{VOTE}_t = 48.9 + .51 \text{ ECON}_t + .41 \text{ VOTE}_t - .40 \text{ VOTE}_{t-2}$$
$$\phantom{\text{VOTE}_t =} (7.6) \quad (.12) \qquad\qquad (.13) \qquad\qquad (.13)$$

Adj. R^2 = .60   SER = 4.5 $\chi^2(8)$ = 6.5   N = 33 (1872–2000)

Although significant, the electoral influence of economic performance must contend with the fallout from the two-term limit, as registered by the autoregressive dynamic, and especially the negative weight attached to the vote two elections before. What does this model say about the Democratic vote in the 2000 election? With the 2000 election included in the analysis, the expected vote for Al Gore comes to 51.5 percent. Compare that to the expected vote based solely on economic performance: 54.1 percent. The control for the term-limit effect on the presidential vote sharply curtails the electoral benefit that a superior economy would be expected to award the incumbent party.[9]

In retrospect, the 2000 election turned out to be very much as an economic-voting model with term limits would have suggested. Seen in the per-

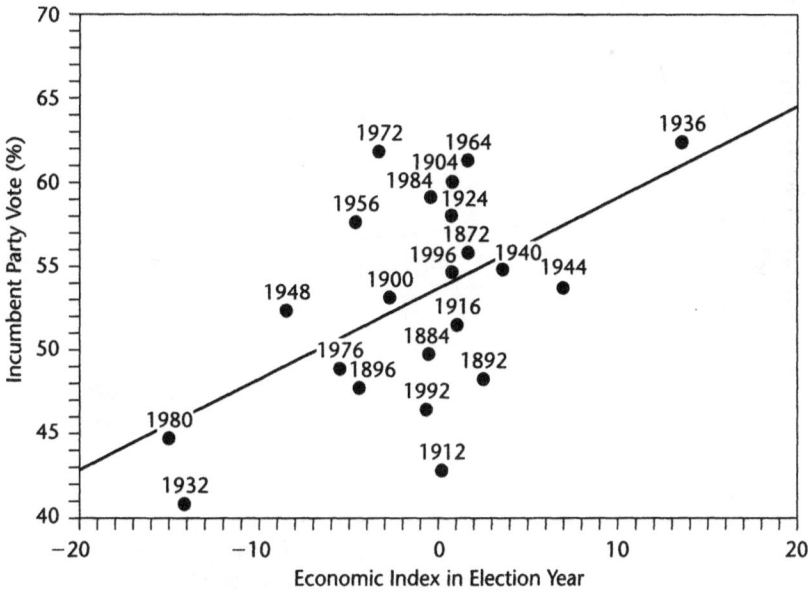

FIGURE 3.2   Economy and Voting in Presidential Elections with Incumbents

spective of elections since 1872, the 2000 performance of this model actually ranks as one of its better moments. There are only five other elections, out of a total of thirty-three, that fit the model better. So there is nothing puzzling about the 2000 election. What happened to the influence of the economy in the contest between Gore and Bush? Though economic times were fabulous, the absence of the sitting president sharply diminished the electoral value of that asset for the incumbent-party candidate.

To buttress that conclusion, let us take one further stab at the confluence of economics and incumbency in presidential elections. This additional line of inquiry makes an explicit distinction between contests that feature sitting presidents and those that do not. Is economic voting, in fact, sharply reduced in open-seat contests compared with those where a president is running for reelection? Since this tack aims squarely at the incumbent party, its vote share will now be used as the dependent variable. Figures 3.2 and 3.3 plot the incumbent-party vote against economic performance for the two types of presidential contests. It seems quite clear that whenever an incumbent president is running for reelection (Figure 3.2), the relationship between economic performance and the incumbent-party vote is as expected. In contrast, in open-seat races (Figure 3.3), the relationship appears to be

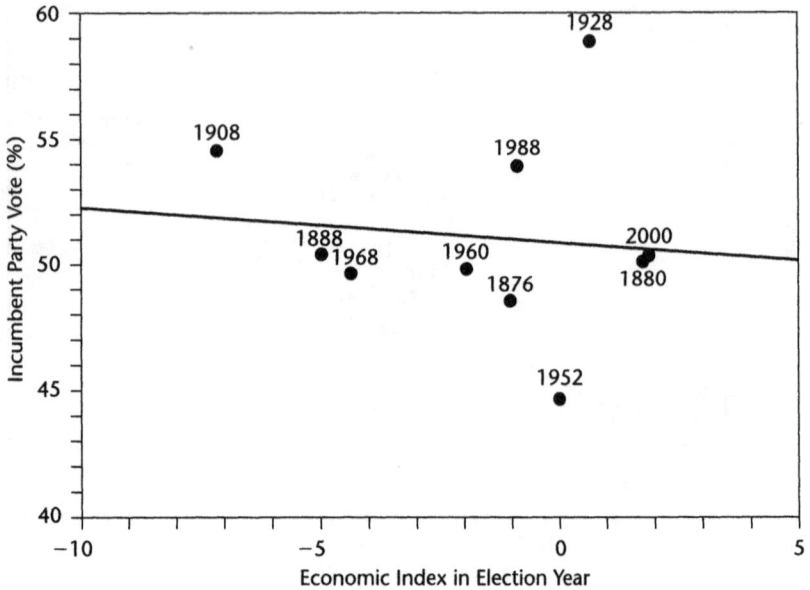

FIGURE 3.3   Economy and Voting in Presidential Elections without Incumbents

much weaker. The statistical estimates of the vote function for the two types of contests, with standard errors in parentheses, are as follows:[10]

Elections *with* Presidential Incumbents:

$$INC.VOTE_t = 53.8 + .49 \ ECON_t$$
$$\quad\quad\quad\quad (.93) \ (.17)$$

Adj. $R^2 = .19$ SER $= 5.1$ $N = 22$

Elections *without* Presidential Incumbents:

$$INC.VOTE_t = 50.8 - .14 \ ECON_t$$
$$\quad\quad\quad\quad (1.5) \ \ (.45)$$

Adj. $R^2 = -.11$ SER $= 4.1$ $N = 10$

The contrast is quite sharp. When a sitting president is running for re-election, the economy influences the vote in American presidential elections to a much greater extent than is true for elections in which the sitting president is not on the ballot. Depending on the state of the economy, the incumbent president either gets a far bigger reward for good times or far more punishment for bad ones than would a nonincumbent candidate of the presidential party. Whatever electoral bounce Al Gore was able to derive from the good economy in the 2000 election, as the evidence in Table 3.3 suggested he did, it was only a fraction of what the incumbent himself would have realized. It is probably not wise to make too much of the sign of the economic effect for the open-seat elections, given the small number of cases and the lack of statistical significance. In any event, the retrospective model offers much less guidance in contests that lack a sitting president in the race than it does in those with an incumbent in the race—the preponderant type of presidential election.

In a presidential election without an incumbent, such as the one in 2000, the candidate of the incumbent party, according to the estimate just given, should expect to get roughly an even split (50.8 percent of the major-party vote), regardless of the performance of the economy.[11] That comes close to the prediction made by the economic-voting model with term limits for the 2000 election (51.5 percent). Without the incumbent in the race, the economy was of little help in 2000 to the incumbent party. Yes, Al Gore was the sitting vice president and arguably had a hand in economic policy-making. But whatever "succession effect" (Mattei and Weisberg 1994; and Weisberg and Hill, chapter 2 in this text) he may have benefited from fell way short of what a good economy would have done for the incumbent himself.

Conclusion

An election that was poised to offer a resounding confirmation of the theory of economic voting instead came perilously close to discrediting it. How can that theory resolve the failure of the incumbent party to ride the wave of prosperity to a comfortable victory in the 2000 presidential contest? Of the three probes sunk into the economic-voting terrain of that election, only one paid off. To begin with the failures, the exploration of asymmetric voting came up empty, as did the one about prospective behavior. In other words, it was not the case that good news about the economy failed to count because voters are more attuned to bad news. Even after a run of eight years, good economic times paid electoral dividends for the incumbent party. It was also not the case that economic prospects undermined assessments of recent performance. Not only were voters far too optimistic about the future economy, but those expectations utterly failed to matter for the vote in 2000. The banker model of economic voting is of no use for solving the 2000 election puzzle.

The successful probe keyed on a critical requirement of economic voting in presidential elections: the incumbency factor. The basic model, which assumes a retrospective calculus, works quite well in elections in which the sitting president was on the ballot. That is what an analysis of the presidential

Bush v. Gore: The Recount of Economic Voting

HELMUT NORPOTH

In the contest between Al Gore and George W. Bush, a sure winner ended up a loser. The 2000 presidential election was supposed to be a slam-dunk victory for economic voting. The growth of the U.S. economy was brisk, inflation tame, unemployment invisible, the stock market booming, the federal budget in the black, and the American public in a cheerful mood. How on earth could the party in the White House fail to retain that office under those circumstances? Forecast models were unanimous in their prediction of victory for the candidate of the party that had steered the economy on its glorious course. The only disagreement was over the size of the victory margin. Although Gore beat Bush in the popular-vote count, and may very well have edged him in Florida as well, the economy was unable to deliver a comfortable victory for the Democratic candidate in the 2000 presidential election. What went wrong?

Perhaps the answer is simply, "It's *not* the economy, stupid!"—not in 2000, or in any election. Maybe it is time to abandon the idea that economics is a major factor in elections, let alone the deciding one. But that reaction would be like throwing out the baby with the bathwater. Granted, other factors besides the economy certainly matter for voting, in the 2000 election no less than in others, but the economy provides an issue too plausible and compelling to discard altogether. To do so, one would have to ignore too many bodies of evidence documenting the influence of economic conditions on the vote. While leaving to others the task of probing the influence of noneconomic factors, this chapter intends to pursue promising clues provided by the economic-voting theory itself. Consider, in particular, the following propositions about economic voting that may help resolve the 2000 election puzzle:

Four of the thirteen presidential elections since 1952 have been extraordinarily close. The popular vote totals for the major-party candidates were very tight in 1960, 1968, and 2000, and victory in the electoral college depended on just a handful of states in 1960, 1976, and 2000. The 2000 election was unique among these close elections: Vice President Al Gore won the popular vote, but Gov. George W. Bush won a narrow victory in the Supreme Court and subsequently in the electoral college. But the sources of the 2000 popular vote can be explored using the same models and techniques that are useful in studying other close presidential elections.

Most aggregate models of presidential voting predicted that Gore would easily win the election. His tiny margin in the popular vote is therefore a puzzle that needs explanation. In this chapter I will explore the reasons why the election was so close, using responses to the National Election Studies' (NES) open-ended questions to measure attitudes toward the candidates, parties, and issues as well as the impact of these attitudes on the vote.

I shall investigate the virtual tie of 2000 using a model I created nearly thirty years ago, building on Donald Stokes's six-component model (Stokes, Campbell, and Miller 1958; Campbell, Converse, Miller, and Stokes 1960, chapter 19). Stokes created measures of partisan advantage on these open-ended questions in six areas: attitudes toward each of the candidates separately, domestic and foreign issues separately, group-related attitudes, and parties as managers of government. He then calculated a measure of the strength of the relationship between each component and vote choice.[1] He reported the product of the two as an attitude force that was moving the electorate in a Democratic or Republican direction.

From my perspective, however, the Stokes categories were both too narrow and too broad. They are too narrow in that they do not easily reveal the relative importance of candidates, parties, and issues to the vote decision. Yet they are too broad in that they combine very different attitudes in the same components, such as voters who admire economic policies of one party and the social policies of the other, or voters who regard a candidate as a good administrator but also untrustworthy. Thus, two models are needed, one that is more broadly gauged and one that is gauged more narrowly.

In place of Stokes's six areas, I have created measures of three summary components and also a sixteen-component model that reveals more distinctive candidate and issue attitudes.[2] When applied to the 1952–1976 presidential elections, these models correctly predicted between 85 and 90 percent of the individual vote choices between major party candidates (Kessel 1980). For the 1980–1996 elections, between 87 and 93 percent of the individual vote choices were correctly predicted (see appendix, Table 4A.1).

These models are very good for making historic comparisons across elections (Smith and Kessel 1995; Smith, Radcliffe, and Kessel 1999). The NES has asked the underlying open-ended questions about parties and candidates in every election since 1952. This makes these items especially useful for comparing the sources of vote decisions across elections—even more so since they are the only questions that have been asked in the entire series of NES presidential election-year surveys.

Now, what can these models tell us about the all-but-absolute tie between Al Gore and George W. Bush in 2000? In brief, they show how a series of themes favored one side or the other, as well as how strongly each theme affected vote choice. Appropriately, the themes that were significantly related to the vote choice ended up tied: a half-dozen favoring Bush, an equal number leaning toward Gore, and a last one virtually tied.

Valences: Measuring Partisan Advantages

As they approach an election, American voters have many different opinions. "George Bush has the management skills needed to handle the presidency," says one. "You can trust the Democratic Party," says another. "I like what Al Gore is saying about Social Security," says a third. These commonplace observations can be heard in many preelection conversations. But although they are simple, they contain two basic elements of attitude analysis. First, each statement focuses on a particular *object*: a candidate, a party, or an issue. In these examples, George Bush was the candidate, the Democrats were the party, and Social Security was the issue. Second, each statement has a *valence*—a positive or negative judgment about the object.

The NES open-ended questions provide an ideal means of measuring the valence toward the candidate, party, and issues objects in the election. In 1952 the University of Michigan researchers began by asking such questions as, "Is there anything in particular you like about the Democratic Party?"

TABLE **4.1**   Frequencies of open-ended comments and their valences

Object	Pro-Rep.	Anti-Rep.	Pro-Dem.	Anti-Dem.	Total	Partisan Valence
Three-Predictor Model						
Candidates	887	877	830	873	3467	−0.8
Parties	259	323	331	386	1299	0.3
Issues	1647	1641	1979	1315	6582	5.0
Sixteen-Predictor Model						
Candidates						
General	283	216	264	208	971	−0.6
Record-Incumbency	67	93	146	36	342	19.9
Experience	20	57	29	52	158	4.4
Management	171	126	125	126	548	−4.2
Intelligence	71	127	100	45	343	16.2
Trust	176	129	91	234	630	−15.1
Personality	99	129	75	172	475	−7.1
Parties						
People in the Party	89	87	96	215	487	−12.4
Party Affect	170	236	235	171	812	8.0
Issues						
General	436	178	228	388	1230	−17.0
International Involvement	134	42	33	84	293	−24.4
Economic Management	459	675	575	322	2031	11.5
Social Benefits	275	291	682	154	1402	19.4
Civil Liberties	327	396	315	310	1348	2.7
Natural Resources	15	57	142	54	268	24.3
Agriculture	1	2	4	3	10	10.0

NOTE: *Positive valence scores favor the Democrats; negative favor the Republicans.*
DATA SOURCE: *2000 National Election Study.*

and "Is there anything in particular about Eisenhower that might make you want to vote for him?"[3] They have been asking similar questions before every presidential election since. These questions provide an equal opportunity for respondents to say what they like and don't like about the Democratic and Republican Parties and candidates.[4]

We code responses to these open-ended questions into partisan valence scores. The valence of each statement in a particular domain is coded and then summed, weighting each comment equally. Consider a respondent who thinks George Bush is too cocky, approves of Bush's profession of religious beliefs, and believes Al Gore is not a strong person. Whereas the pair of evaluations of Bush balance each other out, the single evaluation of Gore is negative, so these statements therefore can be interpreted as leaning in a Republican direction.

We can determine a partisan valence score for the electorate by performing analogous calculations on the mass level. Table 4.1 contains the number of positive and negative comments for both parties, broken down by attitude objects. Look first at the three-predictor model at the top of the page. The comments about the candidates are quite similar, with a few more positive than negative comments about Governor Bush and a few more negative than positive comments about Vice President Gore. There are slightly more negative than positive comments about both parties. Moreover, there are more positive than negative reactions on the issues for both parties, although the Democratic policies have a perceptible edge in the positive column over the Republicans' suggestions.

We can reduce the four columns of positive and negative comments to a single summary measure. We shall express these measures in terms of Democratic partisan valences as a matter of convention. Since positive attitudes about the Democrats and negative attitudes about the Republicans would both tend to produce Democratic votes, we take the sum of these two figures as a percentage of all comments: 100 * ((pro-Democratic) + (anti-Republican))/N. For example, with the candidate comments, this gives 100 * (830 + 877)/3467 = 49.2. Finally, we adjust these values into partisan valences by subtracting 50 so that the neutral point is set at zero. Thus, the Democratic candidate valence of 49.2 becomes −0.8.[5]

Returning now to the substantive information contained in the three-predictor model in Table 4.1, we see partisan valences of −.8, .3, and 5.0 for candidates, parties, and issues, respectively. The pattern for 2000 is consistent with that of past elections. Attitudes about the candidates have been favorable to the Republicans in every election save 1964. Attitudes about issues have been pro-Democratic in every election but 1968, 1972, and 1980. Attitudes about parties have swung back and forth; the Republicans have benefited in five elections, and the Democrats have benefited in seven elections. However, in 2000, with tiny advantages on candidates and parties and a reasonable Democratic advantage on issues we see a hint of a virtual tie in the making.

Finally, note the distribution of the total number of comments. A clear majority, 6,582, concerns issues, even though respondents are not asked directly about issues. Next comes candidates with 3,467. Parties, with 1,299, are the least visible. This pattern of salience—issues first, then candidates, and parties last—has also been standard in the second half of the twentieth century. Only in 1956, and somewhat more so in 1976, were there more candidate comments than issue comments. Moreover, parties have never been nearly as visible as either candidates or issues.

The three-predictor model is quite robust and can be used to make judgments about any election. It provides quick overviews, allowing one to say that candidates (or parties or issues) were either more important or less important in a given election. But it doesn't indicate what aspect of that attitude object is most important. If candidate attributes are found to play a vital role in an election victory, for example, is that due to the candidates' experience, intelligence, management skills, personality, or what? Similar questions arise with respect to what aspects of parties or which specific issues are important.

To see more subtle patterns, the three broad components must be decomposed into more specific dimensions. The candidate component will be divided into seven subcategories, the party cluster will be separated into two more specific categories, and the issue references will be decomposed into seven more classes.[6] These sixteen categories have remained constant across many elections, but the specific nature of the comments in them varies with the candidates and campaigns.

Views of the Voters: A Closer Look

In each of these sixteen categories, voters expressed views on a variety of topics. As an example, Table 4.2 presents a detailed look at one category—general attitudes about candidates. This category is purposefully vague since the nature of attitudes toward candidates varies widely across elections. There are six general themes that significant numbers of respondents mentioned. The frequencies listed in Table 4.2 have been summed from individual categories in the NES Master Code.[7]

Among the general candidate comments, there are two family motifs: references to family and feelings that the candidate was a good family man. The former has a pro-Republican valence and consists primarily of references to Governor Bush's father, the former president. The latter has a pro-Democratic valence and is principally composed of references to the candidate's relationships with his wife and children.[8] Respondents' objections to fund-raising were completely negative and concerned Al Gore. There were more negative than positive comments about the campaigning of both Bush and Gore, but this category had a pro-Democratic valence because the negative-to-positive ratio was greater for Bush. Respondents' views about the candidates' appearances yielded a small edge for Bush, and claims that their candidate was the better man were a little more favorable to Bush. Republicans thought that Bush was the better candidate; Democrats thought that

TABLE **4.2** Frequencies of general candidate comments and their valences

Object	Pro-Rep.	Anti-Rep.	Pro-Dem.	Anti-Dem.	Total	Partisan Valence
Reference to Family	54	26	9	6	95	−13.2
A Good Family Man	12	0	50	1	63	29.4
Financial Scandals	0	0	0	59	59	−50.0
Campaigning or Tactics	7	29	19	21	76	13.2
Appearance	11	15	8	14	48	−2.1
The Better Candidate	41	0	32	0	73	−6.2

DATA SOURCE: *2000 National Election Study.*

Gore was the better candidate. When all was said and done, it was the balance between positive and negative comments about both candidates that led to the near-zero overall valence.

This detailed look at the elements that comprise general candidate characteristics shows the impact of the campaigns. The Bush campaign succeeded in turning Al Gore's previous fund-raising irregularities into a character issue, despite the fact that Bush raised more money in large contributions than any presidential candidate in history—by a large margin. The Gore campaign succeeded in turning the relationship between the vice president and his wife (symbolized by the long kiss at the convention) into a positive—principally to insulate Gore from any spillover effect from Clinton's extramarital affair.

The entries in this table do not fully capture all of the general comments about the candidates. Only 42.6 percent of all general candidate comments were included, with the rest scattered across myriad topics. This was true for other dimensions as well: the comments concerning personality, management, and international involvement were also too scattered for efficient summary. In other dimensions, most comments are captured in a few themes.

Each of the other fifteen dimensions is also composed of several themes. Having provided in Table 4.2 a detailed example of the subtopics that undergird my discussion of one specific dimension, I will present only verbal summaries of the contents of the remaining dimensions in election year 2000.

Candidate Evaluations

General candidate attitudes, detailed in Table 4.2, result in a virtual tie between the two candidates. The next two candidate attributes are closely related, and both benefit Vice President Gore. Record-incumbency deals with what the candidate has done in office. Experience embraces other specific kinds of experience that are seen to be germane: military experience, foreign-policy experience, political experience, and specific activities (e.g., military combat) where this type of experience would be acquired. That Gore would receive an advantage in experience is not surprising, given his long service in the Senate and as vice president versus Bush's single completed term as governor. There were more pro-Bush comments regarding his record as governor than his experience, but Gore had an even stronger advantage in the record-incumbency category because of the much larger number of pro-Democratic comments.

Management, the next candidate predictor, had a pro-Bush valence. Bush benefited primarily from a cluster of positive statements about his ability to provide good, efficient, businesslike administration and a smaller set of statements that Gore was inefficient. Republicans have traditionally had an advantage on this dimension.

Intelligence produced a strong pro-Democratic valence of 16.2. This category includes intelligence and education, being well informed, being realistic, using common sense, being accepting of new ideas, and having a well-defined set of beliefs. Governor Bush's highly publicized misstatements and misunderstandings coupled with Gore's greater familiarity with national issues helped produce a large pro-Democratic valence. But on trust, Bush had an equally large advantage. Gore suffered from a large number of negative comments about his honesty, a sign that Gore's "misstatements" and the Bush campaign's amplification of those misstatements caught hold in the public mind. Bush fared better than Gore on comments that he was principled, while most comments about nonsexual scandals were anti-Bush. However, most comments in this category were about honesty, which determined the overall valence.

Bush also benefited somewhat from comparisons of personality. What is striking about the comments in this domain is that *both* candidates were more likely to be seen as weak rather than strong, overconfident rather than humble, and inarticulate rather than eloquent. When voters said that their candidate was better, they did not mean they were entirely satisfied but that their favored candidate's deficiencies were preferable to his opponent's flaws. As between the two, Gore was criticized as weak. However, complaints that a candidate was too cocky, or that he had difficulty explaining things, more often had Bush as their target. Bush did benefit from comments about his religious posture, but that was the only salient personality attribute of either candidate that was positive.

Taken together, these various dimensions of candidate evaluation produce a slight advantage for Bush. Gore benefited from his experience in office and his record, but the Bush campaign succeeded in neutralizing this somewhat by promoting Bush's record as governor in Texas and by the normal GOP advantage in the public's perception of the candidate as a potential manager. Gore had a large advantage on intelligence, but this was balanced by a large Bush lead in trust.

Party Perceptions

There were far fewer comments about political parties than about candidates, and these lead to only one distinct category: comments about other party members besides the candidate. Everything else is collected into a predictor called "party affect."

In their open-ended comments, many respondents mentioned other people in the party and the ties between the candidates and those party figures. Governor Bush had a significant advantage in perceptions of people in the party. Gore suffered from his links to Clinton. However, there were mentions of his ties to other national party leaders, and these were four times more likely to be negative than positive. Bush also benefited from positive statements about Republican Party leaders.[9]

Bush's advantage on people in the party was offset by a pro-Democratic valence on party affect. As a catchall category, this includes a variety of comments, but most comments repeated certain themes. "Gore is a typical Democrat," and "Bush is a typical Republican" were the most frequent comments. In Gore's case, this was a reason to vote for him, whereas being a Republican was a reason to vote against Bush as often as to vote for him. The most common remarks in this category refer explicitly to the parties. The leading comment is that "He's a Democrat" approvingly, or "He's a Democrat" as in "what do you expect?"

Republicans had a lead in comments about trust in the party: the Republican Party was almost as likely to be trusted as distrusted, but four times as many voters distrusted the Democratic Party as trusted it. Three less-frequent remarks were all pro-Democratic: the Democratic Party was thought to be more representative, Democrats were more likely to listen to the people, and habitual party voting was more likely to be Democratic. There were also negative comments about both parties concerning campaign tactics: that one party spent too much money on its campaign or did too much mudslinging.

General party affect produced a sufficient Democratic advantage to produce a slight pro-Democrat valence in attitudes toward parties. However, this broad set of attitudes, like those toward candidates, essentially produced a tie.

Issue Perceptions

Although much of the literature in political science argues that the issues have a limited impact on vote decisions, the largest number of open-ended statements dealt with issues. Most of them fall into one of the following seven categories: general issue comments, international involvement, economic management, social benefits, civil liberties, natural resources, and agriculture.

The general issue comments include responses favoring more or less government activity. In neither case do the respondents say what activity they have in mind. The category also embraces responses favoring greater social change and others rejecting change that the respondents regard as socialistic. There are references to liberalism or conservatism. Either the respondent approves of a liberal or conservative proposal, or disapproves because a proposal is too liberal or too conservative. Finally, there are general assessments too broad to be assigned to any specific categories.

General issue comments strongly favored the Republicans. The most frequently expressed remarks criticized the Democrats for favoring too much government activity and commended the Republicans for opposing that activity. Republicans also benefited from positive statements about conservatism and negative statements about liberalism. Republicans even benefited from unspecified comments such as "I like their ideas." Only the topic of social change produced a partisan valence favorable to Democrats.

Throughout the decades of the Cold War, voters frequently expressed foreign-policy concerns—Vietnam, the U.S. position vis-à-vis the Soviet Union, and so on. Some interest in international involvement was expressed in 2000, but the number of references was much smaller than comments about the major domestic issues. The specific comments on defense spending, missile defense, and general preparedness created a decidedly pro-Republican valence.

The policy area that drew the most number of comments was economic management. For the third election in a row, the largest number of remarks on economic management concerned ties between the parties and the major economic strata. Once again, voters saw the Republican Party as being much too close to big business. There were fewer responses concerning the middle class, but here too the Democratic Party was credited as supporting middle-class concerns. A great many statements praised the Democrats for standing up for the common person. As long as the Republicans continue to be seen as supporting the rich, and can't at least split perceived credit with the Democrats as being good for the middle class, their electoral fortunes are going to be handicapped.

The other economic attitudes were split in their electoral effects. Taxes was the second-largest economic category, with Bush getting credit for lower taxes but being blamed by those who mentioned specific tax-reform proposals. On general questions of economic posture Democrats were criticized for government spending, and Republicans garnered credit for their work ethic. Democrats were given credit for the good times, but, unfortunately for Gore, this was the least salient economic topic.

The overall pro-Democratic valence on economic management was boosted by the voters' judgments about relations between the parties and the various economic strata, prosperity, and Republican opposition to tax reform. That valence was reduced, however, by pro-Republican attitudes about government spending, the work ethic, and Bush's advocacy of lower taxes.

Social benefits produced an even more pro-Democratic valence: all but one of the specific attitudes in this category favored the Democrats. Despite Bush's frequent appearances in the classroom and emphasis on education, this set of comments had a large pro-Democratic edge, and was the most common topic in this domain. Gore also benefited from comments on health programs (mental health, aid for disabled, and AIDS), on programs for seniors (Medicare, prescription drugs, etc.), Social Security, and aid for poor people. The only social program that lacked a pro-Democratic valence was welfare. There were more welfare comments concerning the Democrats than the Republicans, but the ratio of positive to negative remarks helped the Republicans a little more. The contrast between the Democratic advantage on "aid for poor people" and the GOP edge in "welfare" suggests that issue framing remains important in this policy domain.

During the 1960s, civil liberties meant civil rights, equal admission to public facilities, and perhaps the rights of defendants to fair trials. Now, however, public attention has shifted to the continuing debates over abortion, gun control, and the death penalty as well as the more general issues of morality and "pro-family" policies. These were areas in which there was great partisan contention in 2000. Overall, this category produced a very slight pro-Democratic valence, with each party enjoying advantages in some issues. Abortion was by far the most frequently mentioned topic, but as was the case in 1996, there were more negative than positive abortion comments about *both* parties. Republicans had some advantage in the statements about gun control, and Bush had a more decided edge as a champion of traditional morality. On the other hand, Republicans were criticized because of their position on the death penalty, and in spite of George Bush's repeated claim to be a compassionate conservative, the Democrats were seen to be the more compassionate and generous party and the Republicans less so.

When we turn to natural resources, public attention is centered on air and water pollution. The debate is between those who favor cracking down on polluters in order to protect the environment and those who believe that business owners have a right to develop resources. This issue category produced a very large pro-Democratic valence, with voters expressing many favorable statements about Democratic positions and many negative ones about Republicans. Finally, although agriculture has provided a number of comments in past elections, there were far too few references to the topic in 2000 to sustain any analysis.

If one looks at the partisan valence scores in Table 4.1, it seems that the Republicans gain from general issue comments and international involvement, and the Democrats benefit from the other issue areas. Having delved into these categories, we see a somewhat more complex picture. International involvement is purely Republican, natural resources purely Democratic, and in 2000 the valences happened to be almost the same. With single exceptions, the general issues help the Republicans, and social benefits aid the Democrats. And although the overall valences favor the Democrats in economic management and civil liberties, there are some specific issues within these categories that favor the Republicans.

Maximum Likelihood Estimates: Links to the Vote Decision

Of course, each of these attitudes is not equally important in voters' choices. Some attitudes are more important in vote choice, and some are less important. Presidential campaigns try to increase or decrease the importance

TABLE **4.3**   Probit analysis of the 2000 presidential vote,
three-predictor model

Object	Standardized Maximum Likelihood Estimate
Candidates	1.68***
Parties	1.07***
Issues	3.16***
N	1120
Chi-square	934.5 (df = 2) p < .001
Pseudo-R^2	.60
−2 Log Likelihood	307.47
% correctly predicted	89.3%
% baseline prediction	52.6%

DATA SOURCE: *2000 National Election Study.*
*p < .05, **p < .01, ***p < .001, NS = not significant at .05 level.

of these attitudes to voters. Sometimes attitudes with large partisan valences will be relatively unimportant in vote decisions, whereas a small partisan advantage on another issue may assume great importance in vote decisions. Accordingly, we need a separate measure of the linkage between an attitude and the choice that a voter makes. If we can predict vote choice by knowing the value of a given component, we can assume that the component in question is important in making that decision. Conversely, if we cannot make such a prediction, we say that the component does not affect vote choice. Statistically, this means the variables are independent of one another; substantively, this means that the component is unimportant to the vote decision.

As this linkage measure, we shall use the maximum likelihood estimates (hereafter MLEs) derived from probit analysis. The model's capacity for handling dichotomous dependent variables makes it particularly appropriate for analyzing choice between two candidates.[10] In making this determination, we want to use *standardized* maximum likelihood estimates. These estimates are computed by multiplying the MLEs by the ratio of the standard deviation of the independent variable to that of the dependent variable— here the standard deviation of the particular component divided by the standard deviation of the vote.[11] The standardized components are particularly useful for comparing the importance of components across elections (see Kessel 1992, appendix 9.1).

Two general conclusions are evident in the three-predictor model shown in Table 4.3. First, knowing an attitude's partisan valence does not tell you anything about its importance in vote choice. The partisan valence scores for the three-predictor model in Table 4.1 do not depart very far from the neutral zero. The Democrats have a modest advantage in issue attitudes, but the Republicans have only a minuscule advantage in candidate attitudes while the Democrats have an even tinier edge in party attitudes. Yet the maximum likelihood estimates reveal a clear ordering. Issue attitudes are the most important, candidate attitudes are second, and party attitudes are the least important. So partisan valence scores and maximum likelihood estimates are clearly measuring different things.

Second, the 2000 ordering of MLEs is customary. In eleven of the thirteen elections since the middle of the twentieth century, issue attitudes have been most important, then candidate attitudes, and finally party attitudes. The only exceptions have come in 1952, when party attitudes were more important than candidate attitudes, and in 1976, when candidate attitudes were the most important consideration.

The Full Model

When we include all sixteen factors, the results provide an interesting insight into the 2000 presidential election (see Table 4.4). With the nation just emerging from a period when serious questions were raised about the incumbent president, trust was the most important candidate trait in predicting vote choice. Trust was also the most important candidate attitude in 1972 and 1976 (after Nixon) as well as in 1996 (after one term of Clinton). When presidential behavior raises alarms about integrity, trustworthiness tends to gravitate to the center of voters' cognitive structures.

General candidate attitudes were the next most important. As we have seen, this category is a mélange. Yet as the candidate grouping that attracts the most comments, it is bound to be consequential in voting choice. In fact, it is one of only three predictors that have been significantly related to vote in all thirteen elections.

Personality was the third most important. Personality does not always rank this highly; the MLE is a bit higher than average. But voters had reservations about the personal characteristics of both candidates in 2000. These apprehensions invested personality with a little more importance in determining vote choice.

The voters' judgments about the candidates' management skills made a moderate contribution to their voting decisions. Management has been edging up a bit in recent elections, and it appeared to be a characteristic that was helpful to voters in distinguishing between Governor Bush and Vice President Gore.

Record-incumbency had the lowest MLE of all the significant candidate attitudes in 2000. Its values were higher in 1968, 1976, 1980, 1988, and 1992 when there were sitting presidents (or their designated successors) running for election, and the voters may have been taking their records into consideration.[12] The low impact of record-incumbency combined with the large impact of trust show the failures of the Gore campaign.

TABLE **4.4**   Probit analysis of the 2000 presidential
vote, sixteen-predictor model

Object	Standardized Maximum Likelihood Estimate
Candidates	
General	.70***
Record-Incumbency	.29*
Experience	NS
Management	.40**
Intelligence	NS
Trust	.81***
Personality	.51***
Parties	
People in the Party	.46***
Party Affect	.91***
Issues	
General	.97***
International Involvement	.44**
Economic Management	1.55***
Social Benefits	.82***
Civil Liberties	1.20***
Natural Resources	.39**
Agriculture	NS
N	1120
Chi-square	949.8 (df = 15)
	p < .001
Pseudo R^2	.61
−2 Log Likelihood	299.47
% correctly predicted	89.2%
% baseline prediction	52.6%

DATA SOURCE: *2000 National Election Study.*
*$p < .05$, **$p < .01$, ***$p < .001$, NS = *not significant at*
.05 level.

Two of the candidate items in the sixteen-predictor model had insignificant effects and therefore cannot be said to have made any significant contribution to voters' decisions in 2000.[13] These were experience and intelligence. The weak standing of intelligence as a predictor of presidential choice
is depressingly familiar. In eight of the last thirteen elections, intelligence
has either been insignificant or the weakest candidate item in influencing the
selection of a person to hold the most demanding job in the world. This is
my personal choice for the most discouraging datum in political science.

We shall consider the combined effect of valence and importance pres-
ently, but for the moment note the association between partisan valence and
the candidate MLES. Trust, general candidate attitudes, personality, and
management all had pro-Bush valences. Record-incumbency, experience,
and intelligence all had pro-Gore valences, but, though the electorate had

some favorable opinions of Vice President Gore, these attitudes had little impact on voting choices. Among candidate characteristics, those that favored Bush were the most important.

Party affect is more important in influencing votes than the public's perceptions of people in the party. In the Eisenhower-Stevenson elections of the 1950s, party attitudes were of some moment. Party affect, the more important party predictor, was the most important of all sixteen predictors in 1952 and 1956, and the second-most important in 1964 and 1968.[14] Thereafter (except for 1984), it declined in importance in voting choice. But in both 1996 and 2000, it showed some real strength again. As Table 4.4 shows, party affect had a higher MLE than *any* of the candidate predictors.

In 2000, economic management was the most influential attitude among issues, as well as the most influential attitude across the whole set of sixteen predictors (see also Norpoth, Chapter 3 in this book). The former has often been the case. Remember James Carville's 1992 assertion, "It's the economy, stupid." Moreover, economic management was the most influential of all attitudes from 1976 through 1992. Topics such as spending, taxes, relations with various economic strata, and related items guarantee that economics will be consequential. If the economy is in trouble (as in 1976, 1980, and 1992), this just augments already important attitudes. But economic management does not always dominate the issue debate. In 1960, 1964, and 1996, it ranked only third or fourth among issues.

Civil liberties was the second-most important issue in its influence on vote, and the second-most important overall. A glance at Table 4.4 reveals that civil liberties has a very substantial MLE. This policy area has an interesting history. It was not significantly related to the vote in 1952, 1956, 1960, or 1968; it emerged first in 1964; and it exercised a growing influence from 1972 onward. Then through the 1990s, it was the second-most influential issue. The source of its present influence seems reasonably clear. Civil liberties embraces abortion, gun control, morality, and family topics, all issues on which many people feel passionately and that are likely to influence one's vote.

General issue comments was the third most important issue category in 2000. It, too, has exercised considerable influence over a series of elections, being the most important category of all from 1960 through 1972. Of course, there is some tendency for issue attitudes to vary in influence depending on what is happening in other issue areas. The general issues area reflects this. For example, in 1960 when only two specific policy areas were significantly related to vote, general issue attitudes were more important than any other predictor. But in 1988 when five specific policy areas were significantly related to vote, general issue attitudes fell to fifth place.

The general issue component seems to be better than specific issue components at picking up the mood and the tone of a campaign. Perhaps for this reason, candidates with favorable partisan valence in this component have won twelve of the thirteen recent elections.

Foreign events naturally affect the importance of international involvement. With but a single exception, international involvement was one of the strongest predictors throughout the Cold War.[15] It was never at the top of the list, but almost always had respectable MLEs, and in 1980, 1984, and 1988 it was the second most influential issue.[16] As attention to international affairs waned in the 1990s, so did the influence of this predictor. It narrowly missed being significant in 1996, and exercised only a moderate influence in 2000.

Social benefits embraces a wide array of federal programs: Social Security, aid to education, assistance for seniors, health, welfare, and so on. Although these have an appeal across the whole electorate, they are of more intense concern to the constituencies that are directly affected by these policies. As such, social benefits is always part of the public agenda. Republicans and Democrats differ on what should be done, usually on the scale and governing structure of the programs that should be undertaken. This third major domestic predictor is consequential, but tends to have less impact on voting than economic management or civil liberties.

Agriculture and natural resources, the two minor predictors, are an interesting pair. In both 1952 and 1956, agriculture was a visible but minor force in shaping the vote. But since that time, it has been seen only in 1976 and 1988. In the other nine elections, it was not significantly related to vote choice. Natural resources, on the other hand, did not play an important role for forty years. Since 1992, the MLE for natural resources has been quite stable at about .4. In 1992, natural resources was about as important as social benefits, and in 2000, it was of nearly the same consequence as international involvement.[17] What may lay behind these changes are the disappearance of the farm bloc as a consequential group in presidential politics and the seeming emergence of an environmental bloc casting green votes.[18]

To recapitulate, general candidate attitudes, general issue attitudes, and economic management have been significantly related to vote choice in all thirteen elections from 1952 to 2000. Party affect has been significant in twelve; international involvement in eleven; record-incumbency, trust, personality, and social benefits in ten; and civil liberties in nine. From there on, component impact falls off until it reaches agriculture, significant in only four elections, and natural resources, significant in only two.

In 2000, four of the most important attitudes in voter's decisions were those that have exercised continuing influence: economic management and the three broadest categories of general issue attitudes, party affect, and general candidate attitudes. The other strongest influences were civil liberties, social benefits, and trust, all three attitudes that have been important in several elections and tapped meaningful facets in 2000.

Potency: The Combined Effect of Partisanship and Importance

To this point, we have established two different effects, partisanship and importance. But in actuality, these forces work together. If a voter has an attitude, it tends to favor one party rather than the other, and it is more or less important in the voting decision. To visualize these combined effects in action, we need a single measure that will reflect both. For this purpose, I suggest *potency*—the product of the partisan valence and the maximum likelihood estimate—since a category can swing the vote to a candidate only if the valence is toward that candidate and the MLE is large. I regard potency as a heuristic, suggesting implications, rather than as a precise statistical measure. However, potency is an extremely convenient heuristic to have at hand.

Table 4.5 shows some varieties of potency from the 2000 election. We can see in this table that some attitudes, such as toward the experience of the candidates, yield a low valence and a low MLE, suggesting that experience had little impact on the vote. In contrast, civil liberties was a set of issues where neither candidate had a clear advantage but that moved many voters in offsetting directions. Natural resources, and especially economic management and general issues, helped one side or the other because the issues favored one side, and voters used these issues to decide their votes.

TABLE **4.5**   Varieties of potency with examples from 2000

Pattern:	Valence very low; MLE very low. Equilibrium close to neutral; forces moving voters quite weak.
Example:	Experience (not significant)
Meaning:	Voters slightly impressed with Gore's experience, but he didn't get any benefit.
Pattern:	Valence very low; MLE moderate. Equilibrium close to neutral; forces moving voters a little stronger.
Example:	Personality ($-.04$)
Meaning:	Bush favored on personality; got a little help from that attitude.
Pattern:	Valence very low; MLE very high. Voters driven one way and another by strong forces, but equilibrium still close to neutral.
Example:	Civil Liberties (.03)
Meaning:	Many passions aroused by civil liberties issues, but Democrats didn't get much help because the net result of much movement was still close to neutral.
Pattern:	Valence high; MLE moderate. Voters moved by moderate forces, which allowed equilibrium to remain some distance from the neutral point.
Examples:	Natural Resources (.095); International Involvement ($-.11$)
Meaning:	Democrats derived benefit from natural resources; Republicans derived benefit from international involvement.
Pattern:	Valence relatively high; MLE high. Voters moved by strong forces that amplify the distance from the neutral point.
Examples:	Economic Management (.18); General Issues ($-.17$)
Meaning:	These were the Democrats' and Republicans' strongest issues. Democrats gained substantially from economic management; Republicans gained substantially from the conservative tone of the general issue debate.

TABLE **4.6**   Potency of significant predictors,
sixteen-predictor model

Object	Potency
Pro-Gore	
Economic Management	.18
Social Benefits	.16
Natural Resources	.095
Party Affect	.07
Record-Incumbency	.06
Civil Liberties	.03
Pro-Bush	
General Issues	−.17
Trust	−.12
International Involvement	−.11
People in Party	−.06
Personality	−.04
Management	−.02
Effectively Tied	
General Candidate	−.004

DATA SOURCE: *2000 National Election Study.*
NOTE: *Positive potency scores favor the Democrats; negative favor the Republicans.*

Now, what can potency suggest about the virtual tie in the 2000 election? The potency values of the significant predictors are presented in Table 4.6. The predictors that have pro-Democratic valence all have pro-Gore potency values. Conversely, the predictors that have pro-Republican valences all have pro-Bush potency values. Both have higher values if their equilibria are further away from neutral and their MLEs are stronger. Accordingly, Vice President Gore benefited from attitudes on economic management, social benefits, natural resources, party affect, record-incumbency, and civil liberties. Economic management contributed the most to his vote total, and civil liberties contributed the least. In the same way, Governor Bush profited from general issues, trust, international involvement, people in the party, personality, and management. For him, general issues contributed the most to his vote total, and his reputation as a manager contributed the least.

The data in Table 4.6 are very interesting as an explanation of the tied result. There are six pro-Gore potency values matched by six pro-Bush potency values. Moreover, the potency values from most pro-Gore to least pro-Gore are approximately the same as the pro-Bush comments about general issues through the comments about the candidates' management abilities. And if the general candidate attitudes are regarded as a tie, then there are six pro-Gore attitudes balanced by six pro-Bush attitudes, followed by a tie. The data in Table 4.6 are beautiful if one is trying to explain a tied outcome.

Conclusion

In any election as close as 2000, many explanations can be offered about the outcome: the decisions made about where the candidates ought to campaign, the split in the electoral college, the legal debate that eventually led to the Supreme Court decision, and so forth. Any one of these is correct; almost any small change in electoral strategy or in methods of counting the vote would have altered the outcome enough to change the result. But the attitude analysis in this chapter ought to be added to the array of explanations. Whether one prefers the more detailed sixteen-predictor model, or the more approximate three-predictor model, these models offer some understanding about why there was such an even division of votes in the first place.

An election as close the 2000 contest does not, of course, confer a mandate on the person it puts in office. However, the pattern of results shows which dimensions President Bush capitalized on in 2000 and might be expected to pursue while in office. The catchall general issue category does not provide specific clues in this regard, other than a general preference for less government and for conservative over liberal solutions. However, the importance of trust to the Bush victory is clear, as is the role of international involvement. Trust requires being the un-Clinton when it comes to personal matters. Subsequent events have thrown Bush headlong into foreign affairs, in terms of the war on terrorism, the fight against al-Qaida and the Taliban in Afghanistan, taking on Saddam Hussein in Iraq, dealing with nuclear threats in North Korea, and handling Iran, the third leg of his Axis of Evil. If George Bush has any mandate, the results of this chapter suggest that these foreign affairs issues are its main components.

Meanwhile, the analysis suggests three components that Bush should try to neutralize before his 2004 election campaign. Economic management is of vital importance, though the prolonged recession threatens his ability to defuse that issue. Social benefits are of similar importance, which means that education reform must be followed by other successes in this realm. Natural resources provide a continuing challenge to Republican hopes for the future, particularly to the extent that GOP energy policy is portrayed as anti-environment.

The NES began surveying the American public in the decade of the 1950s, when a popular Republican incumbent was reelected. That was followed by two decades in which no person served a full eight years in the Oval Office. By contrast, the 1980s and 1990s saw the reelection of two popular presidents (along with the defeat of one incumbent). Whether the 2004 election will continue the reelection pattern of the past two decades or will revert to the pattern of the 1960s and 1970s will depend, at least in part, on the extent to which George Bush can build on those pro-Republican dimensions while neutralizing the pro-Democratic ones.

APPENDIX

TABLE **4A.1** Probit analysis of major party presidential vote, sixteen-predictor model from 1952 through 1996

Object	1952 Valence	1952 MLE	1956 Valence	1956 MLE	1960 Valence	1960 MLE	1964 Valence	1964 MLE	1968 Valence	1968 MLE	1972 Valence	1972 MLE
Candidates												
General	-14.7	.26	-16.8	.44	-8.4	.82	16.5	.86	-6.7	.64	-17.6	.75
Record-Incumbency	36.3	NS	-36.9	.38	-14.7	.22	43.1	NS	11.6	.49	-44.5	.58
Experience	11.1	.29	-13.4	.40	-19.1	1.02	26.4	NS	-10.2	.33	-28.0	NS
Management	-28.7	.29	-8.5	.44	-15.4	.24	14.7	NS	-16.0	NS	-27.9	.28
Intelligence	8.5	NS	15.9	NS	13.0	.26	25.5	NS	.0	NS	-38.9	.37
Trust	-28.2	.63	-31.2	NS	-3.5	NS	-31.8	.38	2.1	.39	10.6	.85
Personality	-23.3	.26	-21.7	.51	8.2	NS	2.9	.53	-1.8	.44	-29.8	.62
Parties												
People in the Party	-16.7	NS	5.6	.29	-10.6	NS	-1.0	NS	9.1	.44	-11.0	NS
Party Affect	-5.0	1.36	4.8	1.10	3.9	.76	16.7	1.12	2.8	.76	-2.8	NS
Issues												
General	-4.2	.77	-4.3	.71	14.3	1.38	4.5	1.59	-5.6	1.23	-13.8	.94
International Involvement	-29.9	.76	-33.1	.58	-17.7	.80	4.4	.65	-22.8	NS	-17.2	.61
Economic Management	12.5	1.25	24.1	.71	6.1	.32	9.5	.55	5.0	.61	25.0	.80
Social Benefits	30.9	NS	33.5	.51	3.4	NS	38.7	.38	17.6	NS	-2.3	.35
Civil Liberties	-9.3	NS	-3.8	NS	14.6	NS	17.3	.64	.1	NS	-11.2	.44
Natural Resources	32.1	NS	17.4	NS	26.2	NS	27.3	NS	-	NS	21.4	NS
Agriculture	30.1	.34	29.7	.47	20.8	NS	14.9	NS	-14.3	NS	16.7	NS
% Correctly Predicted	87%		86%		88%		90%		88%		86%	

(*continued*)

TABLE **4A.1** Continued

Object	1976 Valence	1976 MLE	1980 Valence	1980 MLE	1984 Valence	1984 MLE	1988 Valence	1988 MLE	1992 Valence	1992 MLE	1996 Valence	1996 MLE
Candidates												
General	-.2	.68	10.2	.65	-4.6	1.20	4.3	.42	13.6	.86	7.8	1.26
Record-Incumbency	-1.9	.73	-.5	.71	-30.2	.47	-29.8	.76	-8.3	.79	-9.4	NS
Experience	-21.1	.44	13.3	NS	-9.3	.34	-44.6	NS	-42.2	.46	-33.6	NS
Management	-20.4	.64	-24.3	.57	-1.2	.48	-6.9	.29	5.7	.46	-7.4	.57
Intelligence	-1.6	.27	12.0	NS	14.0	.32	3.7	.41	17.9	.51	18.8	NS
Trust	-9.2	.80	7.8	.31	-2.9	.55	5.6	NS	-12.7	.78	-37.9	1.85
Personality	-2.0	.47	-9.8	.57	-23.3	.28	7.2	NS	-13.1	.30	5.1	NS
Parties												
People in the Party	19.6	.25	6.8	NS	-17.7	.46	9.8	.32	8.4	NS	-.5	.67
Party Affect	6.0	.39	4.6	.39	8.7	.79	2.4	.50	8.4	.65	5.0	1.03
Issues												
General	.3	.48	-14.1	.75	-16.2	.78	-12.7	.83	1.9	1.04	-10.3	1.41
International Involvement	-11.6	.31	-15.8	1.30	2.7	.95	-4.8	1.22	-1.3	.71	-6.7	NS
Economic Management	24.9	1.10	-1.3	1.33	-.4	1.93	4.8	1.46	20.9	1.85	17.1	1.12
Social Benefits	19.1	.23	13.0	.63	26.8	.61	24.2	.95	32.5	.37	18.2	.85
Civil Liberties	-4.7	.28	7.4	.81	10.5	.57	-12.7	.92	8.0	1.70	2.7	1.27
Natural Resources	33.5	NS	-2.4	NS	44.5	NS	16.4	NS	34.0	.42	38.0	NS
Agriculture	31.4	.25	-9.1	NS	17.9	NS	9.7	.64	10.0	NS	-50.0	NS
% Correctly Predicted	85%		87%		90%		87%		91%		93%	

DATA SOURCE: *1952–1996 National Election Studies.*
NOTE: *Cell entries show partisan valences and standardized MLE coefficients. Positive valences favor the Democrats. NS = not significant at the .05 level.*

5   The Effects of Campaign Finance Attitudes on Turnout and Vote Choice in the 2000 Elections

JANET M. BOX-STEFFENSMEIER, J. TOBIN GRANT,
AND THOMAS J. RUDOLPH

The 107th Congress is unlikely to be remembered for its legislative achievements. With divided government, a slim majority in both houses, and all but one appropriations bill unfinished before the 2002 election, there was little of significance signed into law. One notable exception was the Bipartisan Campaign Reform Act (BCRA), which was signed into law on March 27, 2002. This bill, which was supported by 56 percent of House members and 60 percent of Senators, included a ban on "soft money" contributions. As long as it was used for "party-building activities" and not "coordinated" with candidates' campaigns, soft money had previously been unregulated and could be contributed in unlimited amounts. Such contributions were widely viewed by critics as thinly veiled campaign activities that violated the spirit, if not the intent, of existing campaign finance laws. In the 2000 election cycle alone, roughly $500 million was funneled into federal campaigns through soft-money contributions (Federal Election Commission 2001). The BCRA also restricted issue ads during the sixty days before an election. Although most of the public's attention and congressional debate focused on these new regulations, the law also deregulated some hard-money provisions. Specifically, individuals can now give $2,000 to a candidate per election instead of $1,000. This limit is raised for candidates facing a wealthy opponent who is personally funding his or her campaign. If they survive the constitutional challenges that are already pending, the provisions of the BCRA are expected to change the way campaigns are financed for years to come.

Several factors contributed to the passage of the BCRA. First, Sen. John McCain (R-AZ), sponsor of the bill and presidential candidate in the 2000 Republican primaries, demanded that the Senate consider the legislation early in the session. This gave the bill enough time to pass both houses. Second, members of the House were able to force the bill to the floor despite opposition by the Republican leadership. Although these procedural tactics provide a partial explanation of why BCRA was passed, one question remains outstanding. Why did Congress suddenly decide to enact major campaign finance reform legislation after years of consideration? Was there something about the 2000 election that motivated members to pass campaign finance reform? Did this issue contribute to voters' decisional calculus in the 2000 elections, and, if so, what message did voters send to their elected officials?

In this chapter we investigate public attitudes toward campaign finance reform by using a uniquely suited data set, the 2000 American Politics Study. This data set contains information about citizens' attitudes toward a series of specific reform proposals, such as banning soft money, increasing contribution limits, and establishing a system of public financing. Using this data set we discern three general factors for categorizing one's preferences about campaign finance reform, which we identify as regulatory, deregulatory, and subsidy reforms.

We answer a series of important questions about the effects of the campaign finance issue in the 2000 elections. How deep and widespread was public support for campaign finance reform? Did candidates' arguments regarding campaign finance reform resonate with voters? Was campaign finance reform a decisive issue in the 2000 presidential election, or were traditional issues such as taxes and the economy more consequential? Incumbents in both the House and the Senate have been forced to take public votes on campaign finance reform legislation. What impact did the campaign finance issue have on the congressional races? Finally, did support for campaign finance reform increase voter turnout? In short, we find that campaign finance attitudes failed to rally voters who otherwise would not vote. However, once in the polling booth, voters' attitudes toward campaign finance influenced their choice of candidate.

The Issue of Campaign Finance Reform

Campaign finance reform remains a controversial issue in large part because it forces individuals to consider and to balance the competing democratic values of political equality and free speech (Grant and Rudolph 2003). It is an issue that involves what Sniderman et al. (1996) refers to as a "clash of rights." These two competing democratic values frame the elite discourse on campaign finance. Proponents of reform argue that attitudes toward campaign finance reform should be guided by concerns about political equality and equal representation. They argue that economic inequalities pose a serious threat to political equality, allowing affluent individuals and organized groups to exert undue influence in the political process (e.g., Adamany and Agree 1975; Fiss 1996; Foley 1994; Hasen 1996, 1999; Neuborne 1999a, 1999b; Raskin and Bonifaz 1993; Sunstein 1993, 1994; Wertheimer and Manes 1994). Because such individuals and groups are not representative of the mass electorate, reformers argue that their influence is problematic (Brown, Powell, and Wilcox 1995; Sorauf 1992; Verba, Schlozman, and Brady 1995). To impede the conversion of economic power into political power, reformers strongly advocate the adoption of more stringent campaign finance laws.

In framing their arguments, opponents of reform tend not to emphasize the principles of political equality and equal representation. Rather, invoking the First Amendment, they propose that campaign finance reform be viewed in terms of free speech (e.g., McConnell 2001; Smith 1996, 1997, 1998, 1999, 2001). Those arguing that the use of money in campaigns is essentially a form of political speech, and thus should be protected under the First Amendment, favor deregulation. They submit that limitations on campaign contributions and expenditures are unconstitutional abridgments of free speech and vigorously oppose reformers' efforts to strengthen existing campaign finance regulations.

Political equality–versus–free speech arguments are difficult to balance. Despite repeated attempts, the Supreme Court has failed to satisfy either side of the campaign finance reform debate. In evaluating the constitutionality of the regulatory regime established by the Federal Election Campaign Act (1971) and its 1974 amendments, the Court rendered a somewhat mixed verdict. Although striking down the FECA's expenditure limits, the Court upheld the FECA's contribution limits as an acceptable protection against the reality or appearance of corruption. As evidenced by the growing body of case law, the *Buckley* decision clearly has failed to put the constitutional questions surrounding campaign finance regulations to rest (*Federal Election Commission v. National Conservative Political Action Committee*, 1985; *Colorado Republican Federal Campaign Committee v. Federal Election Commission*, 1996; *Nixon v. Shrink Missouri Government PAC*, 2000; *Federal Election Commission v. Colorado Republican Federal Campaign Committee*, 2001). Reformers argue that the Court needs to go further, and they seek more stringent regulations on campaign contributions and expenditures. Opponents, in contrast, submit that the current campaign finance system requires only deregulation.

Candidate Positions on the Issue of Reform

The issue of campaign finance reform played a prominent role during the 2000 campaign season and was particularly visible at the presidential level. Senator McCain's presidential bid pushed campaign finance onto the issue agenda simply because of his track record as a strong proponent of reform. But McCain's proposals are but one set of many that could be advocated. Reformers, scholars, and partisan elites have proposed a number of reforms over the years. Sorauf (1994) observes that the consensus agenda for mainstream reform is comprised of three broad proposals. He explains that reformers wish (1) to reduce the amount of "interested" money, such as contributions from PACs and other interest groups, (2) to reduce the amount of money raised and spent in campaigns, and (3) to eliminate loopholes in the current system like soft money and bundling. Each of these mainstream reforms may be classified as *regulatory* reforms.

One suggestion for reducing "interested" money is to enact *subsidy* reforms, an expanded public financing system to be used in both presidential and congressional elections (e.g., Ackerman 1993; Foley 1994; Hasen 1996; Magleby and Nelson 1990; Raskin and Bonifaz 1993; Wertheimer and Manes 1994). Supporters of public financing argue that such a move would decrease candidates' financial dependence on special interests. Others suggest that reducing communication costs associated with modern campaigns would minimize candidates' dependence on special-interest money (e.g., Magleby and Nelson 1990; Raskin and Bonifaz 1993). Magleby and Nelson (1990) propose subsidizing candidates' mailings and television advertising.

Not all reform proposals, however, have been designed to limit the amount of private money in political campaigns. In fact, many have argued that *deregulatory* reforms, rather than increased regulation, are the proper road to reform (e.g., Gais 1998; McConnell 2001). Sen. Mitch McConnell (R-KY) best articulates this position. Defending the rights of so-called special interests, McConnell argued that "[t]heir speech, political activity, and right to 'petition the government for a redress of grievances' (that is, to lobby) are protected by the First Amendment" (McConnell 2001).

Of these three types of reforms (regulatory, subsidy, and deregulatory), which ones were advocated by the presidential candidates? In the 2000 presidential election, Gore clearly supported regulatory reforms. Whether motivated by principled policy convictions, a desire to distance himself from questionable fund-raising practices during the 1996 campaign, or an interest in attracting former McCain presidential supporters, Al Gore made campaign finance reform a central pillar of his policy platform in his acceptance speech at the Democratic National Convention: "If you entrust me with the presidency, I will put our democracy back in your hands, and get all the special-interest money—all of it—out of our democracy, by enacting campaign finance reform. I feel so strongly about this, I promise you that campaign finance reform will be the very first bill that Joe Lieberman [the Democratic vice-presidential candidate] and I send to Congress" (Gore 2000). Gore, along with the Democratic leadership in Congress, supported many provisions of the McCain-Feingold reform package, particularly its ban on soft money. In addition, the Democratic party platform also called for a "crackdown on special interest issue ads" and a ubiquitous insistence on "tough new lobbying reform."

Gore also supported some subsidy reforms. While staying clear from an outright call for public funding of campaigns, he proposed a "public-private, non-partisan Democracy Endowment." This endowment would raise money from the private sector that would then finance congressional campaigns. If candidates accepted the funds, then they would not be allowed to accept campaign contributions from other sources. In addition, Gore, in the Democratic party platform, advocated "publicly-guaranteed TV time for debates and advocacy by candidates." As with his Democracy Endowment, this would not be publicly funded but would be a de facto subsidy for candidates.

George W. Bush did not make campaign finance reform a centerpiece of his campaign, but he did stake out clear positions on this issue, some of which were distinct from Gore's. Like Gore, Bush advocated regulatory reforms, including a ban on soft money. However, unlike Gore, Bush would have placed two exceptions on this regulation. First, he advocated this ban only if such a ban included "paycheck protection," a provision that would keep unions from using members' dues for political purposes without their consent. Second, Bush opposed banning soft-money contributions from individuals. Bush also advocated some regulatory reforms not explicitly supported by Gore. In particular, the platform includes a pledge to "level the playing field by forbidding incumbents to roll over their leftover campaign funds into a campaign for a different office." Thus, although Gore was more outspoken on his position for campaign finance reform, both Bush and Gore could both claim to advocate similar regulatory reforms.

The difference between Bush and Gore on this issue is distinct in the areas of subsidy and deregulatory reforms. Whereas Gore advocated some subsidy reforms, Bush favored deregulatory reforms. Although Bush supported full disclosure via the Internet, he fought regulations on the amount of money that interest groups could spend on issue-advocacy ads. Bush also favored an increase to the $1,000 ceiling for individuals' contribution limits. In addition, the Republican platform included a provision to "Preserve the right of every individual and all groups—whether for us or against us—to express their opinions and advocate their issues. We will not allow any arm of government to restrict this constitutionally guaranteed right." This support for more deregulation is one point of difference between the parties on this issue.

Why should we expect public opinion on the issue of campaign finance to affect vote choice in the 2000 elections? Public-opinion scholars have observed that citizens' attitudes toward policy issues are powerfully influenced by elite discourse (Zaller 1992). Elite cues are important factors in opinion formation for several reasons. First, they reduce information costs for citizens by reducing complex issues into simpler and more manageable parts. Most citizens are ill informed about the issue of campaign finance (Center for Responsive Politics 1997). By framing the issue in terms of more widespread and more accessible constructs such as free speech or political equality, elite cues make it relatively easy for citizens to form opinions on an otherwise complicated issue. Second, elite cues are often directional in that they encourage citizens to think about an issue in a positive or negative light.

In the debate over campaign finance reform, elite cues were usually, but not always, divided quite sharply along partisan lines. Consider first the issue of regulatory reform. Partisan cues on this issue were somewhat mixed, as both major parties advocated at least some forms of regulatory reform. As a result, rank-and-file partisans may not always have received clear signals from their leaders on this issue. If they are formed in the absence of distinct partisan cues, citizens' attitudes toward regulatory reform may later have little bearing on their choices between partisan candidates. On the issues of deregulatory and subsidy-based reform, however, cues from partisan elites were unmistakably clear. The Republican establishment repeatedly called for deregulatory reforms, either by raising contribution limits or by removing them entirely. The Democratic Party was unified in its opposition to such reforms. In contrast, many Democrats championed subsidy-based reform by calling for public financing or free television time. Virtually no Republicans supported such measures. Since they benefited from very clear and distinct cues from partisan elites, citizens' attitudes toward deregulatory and subsidy-based reforms can be expected to have a much stronger relationship to voting behavior than attitudes toward regulatory reform.

Public Attitudes toward Campaign Finance Reform

To gauge public support for campaign finance reform, we use data from the 2000 American Politics Study, a nationally representative survey specifically focused on campaign finance.[1] The survey was administered in the weeks following the 2000 election to measure public attitudes toward proposed campaign finance reforms.[2] We presented respondents with a list of ten reform proposals (submitted by reform debate players either formally or informally) and asked whether they strongly agreed, agreed, disagreed, or strongly disagreed with each of them. Respondents' attitudes toward these reform proposals are reported in Table 5.1.

The public is extremely supportive of reform proposals that would strengthen campaign finance regulations. A substantial majority (85.1%) agrees or strongly agrees that congressional candidates should be subject to spending limits. More than eight in ten Americans (84.1%) agree that congressional candidates ought to raise a certain percentage of their money in their home state. Nearly three-quarters of citizens (73.0%) favor a ban on

TABLE **5.1**   Public support for campaign finance reform proposals

	Strong Disagree	Disagree	Agree	Strong Agree	Total	N
Limit spending by candidates	0.7	14.2	67.4	17.7	100%	1201
Limit TV advertising by candidates	2.3	29.9	49.2	18.6	100%	1210
Ban soft-money contributions	2.1	24.8	57.6	15.4	100%	1103
Ban PACs from giving money	2.0	39.8	49.6	8.7	100%	1118
Require candidates to raise % of money in their home state	0.9	15.0	73.8	10.3	100%	1193
Let individuals give more	4.1	52.2	41.2	2.5	100%	1194
Let parties give more	7.3	58.8	32.6	1.2	100%	1170
Remove limits, but disclosure	4.7	39.1	47.1	9.1	100%	1153
Provide public funding	10.6	50.8	35.7	2.9	100%	1175
Provide free media, postage	10.4	51.1	33.9	4.7	100%	1201

DATA SOURCE: *American Politics Study 2000.*

soft money, and two-thirds (67.8%) favor limits on candidates' television advertising. A majority of Americans (58.3%) also supports a ban on contributions made by political action committees.

The American electorate expresses less support for the public financing of congressional elections. Slightly more than one-third of respondents (38.6%) favors the use of public funds to finance congressional elections. An equally small percentage supports the extension of free media time and postage to congressional candidates. The public, it seems, does not advocate proposals that achieve reform through public subsidies. The public expresses only modest support for deregulatory reforms. Less than one-half of respondents (43.7%) agree that individuals should be permitted to give more money to candidates. In addition, only one in three respondents (33.8%) feels that political parties should be allowed to contribute more money. Only one of the three deregulatory reforms enjoys majority support among the mass public. A slight majority (56.2%) favors the removal of contribution limits provided that full disclosure is ensured.[3]

Considerable variation remains in the public's attitudes toward alternative campaign finance reform proposals. In the next section we examine whether individuals' campaign finance attitudes impacted voter turnout and vote choice in the 2000 presidential and congressional elections.

Modeling the Effects of Campaign Finance Attitudes

We begin the modeling exercise by conducting an exploratory factor analysis of the ten reform proposals we discussed earlier. The goal of the factor analysis is to reduce the number of variables and to detect structure in the relationships between the variables. As we discussed previously, there are three types of reforms advocated in public debate—regulatory, subsidy,

TABLE **5.2**   Factor analysis of campaign finance reform proposals

	Regulatory Reforms	Subsidy Reforms	Deregulatory Reforms
Limit spending by candidates	0.720	0.080	−0.031
Limit TV advertising by candidates	0.608	−0.186	−0.066
Ban soft-money contributions	0.632	0.246	−0.140
Ban PACs from giving money	0.676	0.088	−0.014
Require candidates to raise certain % of money in their home state	0.446	0.077	0.289
Allow individuals to give more	−0.122	0.067	0.788
Allow parties to give more	−0.372	0.218	0.615
Remove limits, require full disclosure	0.242	−0.154	0.545
Provide public funding	0.123	0.762	0.046
Provide free media time, postage	0.059	0.795	0.014
Eigenvalue	2.236	1.498	1.229

DATA SOURCE: *American Politics Study 2000.*
NOTE: *The above results were obtained by factor analysis using direct oblimin rotation with Kaiser normalization.*

and deregulatory reforms. The factor analysis results will then be used to model the effects of these attitudinal indices on voter turnout and presidential and congressional vote choice in the 2000 elections.

Table 5.2 shows that the rotated structure matrix produced three distinct factors, each of which corresponds to one of the forms of reforms. The first factor, "regulatory reform," accounts for about 22 percent of the total variance. Five proposals strengthening campaign finance regulations comprise the regulatory reform factor: limiting candidate spending, limiting television advertising, eliminating soft money, banning PAC contributions, and requiring money to be raised at home. A second factor, "subsidy reform," explains an additional 15 percent of the variance and is composed of the two proposals involving public subsidies: public funding for congressional candidates and free media time for candidates. A third factor, termed "deregulatory reform," accounts for an additional 12 percent of the variance. Three proposals that would loosen campaign finance regulations, allowing individuals to contribute more, allowing parties to contribute more, and eliminating contribution limits, constitute the third factor. Informed by these factor-analytic results, we created three factor-based indices of reform support: support for regulatory reform, support for deregulatory reform, and support for subsidy reform.[4]

In modeling the vote in the 2000 elections, our primary concern is to estimate the effect of support for these three forms of reform on the vote. For this issue voting to occur, it is important that the parties and candidates clearly delineate their differences on the issue (Key 1966; Page and Brody 1972; Abramson, Aldrich, and Rohde 1983). At the elite level, attitudes toward subsidy and deregulatory campaign finance reform(s) are, for the most part, divided quite cleanly along partisan lines. Democratic leaders tend to support subsidy reforms and to oppose deregulatory reforms. Conversely, the Republican establishment favors deregulatory reforms and opposes subsidy reforms. On mainstream regulatory reforms, the parties differ, but less substantially. As discussed previously, both Bush and Gore support some type of ban on soft-money contributions, some restrictions on advertising, and changes to the way lobbying is done. The differences are subtle, such as the paycheck protection, and thus may not be noticed by the average voter. Do such attitudinal differences at the elite level resonate at the mass level? Do citizens recognize parties' positions on particular campaign finance reforms, and do individuals' attitudes toward these reforms affect their voting decisions? If so, we expect that, given partisan differences at the elite level, supporters of subsidy reforms will be more likely to vote for Al Gore and Democratic candidates for Congress. Those who favor deregulatory reforms are expected to favor George W. Bush and Republican candidates for Congress. As for regulatory reforms, we expect that voters who support regulatory reforms will be more likely to vote for Democratic candidates, but this hypothesis depends on whether the average voter can distinguish between the parties on this issue.

We test whether voters based their decision to vote and for whom to vote for, at least in part, on these positions. Specifically, we estimate a model of turnout and presidential vote choice that includes three indices measuring support for three separate types of reforms: regulatory, deregulatory, and subsidy. We expect that the more one supports increased regulation, opposes deregulation, or supports subsidy reforms the more likely one is to vote for the Democratic candidate, Gore, rather than the Republican candidate, Bush. In addition, we test whether campaign finance reform, by turning out nonvoters and thus rallying supporters, served as a mobilizing issue. That is, those in favor of reform would be more likely both to support candidates who agree with them and to go to the polls for those candidates. Our model allows us to estimate the effect of the campaign finance issues at both stages of the vote decision. First, we include the measures of campaign finance reform attitudes as part of the decision to turn out. Second, we include them as part of the choice between candidates. Our model has two dependent variables:

$y_1 = 1$ if a respondent voted in the election

$y_2 = 1$ if the respondent voted for the Democratic candidate

Theoretically, two independent binomial models should not be used to estimate these decisions because the observation of the vote is censored; it cannot be observed unless a person votes. To account for this, we employ an extension of the bivariate probit model (cf. Greene 1997). Researchers have used this estimator to model both voter turnout, where one cannot observe a citizen voting unless he or she is registered (Timpone 1998a), and the vote choice, where one first decides whether to vote (Dubin and Rivers 1989). Our work mimics the latter application. This model is

$$y_1 = 0, y_2 = 0: \qquad P(y_1 = 0) = 1 - \Phi(\beta'_1 x_1),$$

$$y_1 = 1, y_2 = 0: \qquad P(y_1 = 1, y_2 = 0) = \Phi_2[-\beta'_2 x_2, \beta'_1 x_1, -\rho],$$

$$y_1 = 1, y_2 = 1: \qquad P(y_1 = 1, y_2 = 1) = \Phi_2[\beta'_2 x_2, \beta'_1 x_1, \rho],$$

where y_1 is a dichotomous dependent decision (1 = turnout; 0 = abstain), and y_2 is a successive dichotomous dependent decision (1 = vote for Democrat; 0 = vote for Republican). Unlike two independent binomial probit models, this model is a system where Φ is the normal cumulative distribution function, and Φ_2 is the bivariate normal cumulative distribution function. The model depends not only on the effects of the independent variables but also on the correlation of the errors (ρ).[5]

For the turnout portion of the model, we include measures of political engagement, partisanship, policy attitudes (with special attention given to campaign finance reform), and demographics. We include three measures of political engagement as determinants of turnout in our model. First, those who are more efficacious—those who think that their voice will be heard by government—should be more likely to vote. Second, those who have a higher level of interest in politics and elections should also be more likely to vote. Finally, increased political knowledge should raise the probability of turning out to vote. We include partisanship and expect that the surge and decline arguments of Campbell (1960) and Campbell (1987, 1992) will result in independents being less likely to vote than partisans. We include several measures of policy attitudes. These account for other sources of issue-based mobilization but also serve as controls for the ideology of the respondent. Specifically, we include the following: retrospective evaluations of the national economy, government spending, and the federal government's role in protecting family values. In addition, we include measures of a person's attitudes toward campaign finance reform. These measures are indices based on the factor analysis presented earlier. We include three measures of support for reform: regulatory, deregulatory, and subsidy campaign finance reforms. Lastly, we include several demographic measures. Those who are married, older, or have higher levels of education should be more likely to vote than those who are not. We include each of these measures as part of the turnout equation.

The variables we included as part of the candidate-choice portion of the model are very similar to the turnout model. Candidate choice is modeled by partisanship, policy attitudes, attitudes toward campaign finance reform, and demographic characteristics. Our interest in this model centers upon whether, after controlling for partisanship, policy attitudes, and demographics, voters chose candidates based on their positions on campaign finance reform.

To identify the model, at least one of the coefficients must be constrained to zero in one of the models. That is, if there were a set of variables that should affect only one decision and not the other, then those should be constrained to zero. We constrain the political-engagement variables (efficacy, political interest, and knowledge) to zero for the candidate-choice equation. By constraining these variables we are able to estimate our statistical model.

Table 5.3 presents the results of the model. Of the three reform attitudes, deregulatory reform was the only one that was statistically significant from zero.[6] We interpret this as confirmation of our hypothesis that this is evidence of voters responding to the candidates who show clear differences on this issue. However, we do so hesitantly. The model does not include a general measure of ideology because the survey lacks data on this. As a result, we must be somewhat cautious in our interpretation because the deregulatory attitude may be a reflection of a more general stance against government regulation.[7] Finally, there is no evidence of issue mobilization, as none of the attitudes toward reform had an effect on voter turnout.

Consistent with the literature on presidential vote choice, voters base their choices on party identification, the economy, and policy attitudes. Of great interest to this analysis is the direction and statistical significance of the three campaign finance reform measures. Voter turnout, in contrast, is not based on issue mobilization but is determined by individual characteristics: efficacy, interest in politics, knowledge, and demographics, and, again, partisanship.

To compare the magnitude of the issues for candidate choice, we calculate the change in the predicted probabilities that a person would abstain from voting, would vote for Bush, or would vote for Gore. For each variable, we calculated the change in probabilities given a shift from a low value for the explanatory variable (greatest of either the mean minus two standard deviations or lowest value) to a high value (lowest of either mean plus two standard deviations or highest value), holding all other values at their respective means.[8] Table 5.4 presents the changes in the predicted probabilities.

As Table 5.4 clearly shows, attitudes toward deregulation of the campaign finance issue had a relatively large impact on presidential vote choice in 2000. Not surprisingly, partisanship has the largest impact on vote choice (Democrats have a 0.26 greater probability of voting for their candidate than Republicans; independents have a 0.25 greater probability). Of the issues in the model, deregulating the campaign finance system had the same impact on voting for Bush as attitudes toward government spending and the

TABLE **5.3** Model of presidential vote

	Voter Turnout	Vote for Gore
Political Engagement		
Efficacy	.535***	—
	(.190)	
Interest in Politics	1.205***	—
	(.200)	
Political Knowledge	.650*	—
	(.266)	
Partisanship		
Democratic Identifier	−.102	2.863***
	(.133)	(.180)
Independent	−.843***	1.505***
	(.212)	(.315)
Policy Attitudes		
Economic Evaluation	.183	.611*
	(.213)	(.305)
Government Spending	−.082	.958*
	(.266)	(.392)
Middle-Class-Only Tax Cut	.059	.239
	(.238)	(.362)
Family Values	−.148	.759*
	(.236)	(.339)
Campaign Finance Reform		
Regulatory Reforms	.405	−.369
	(.456)	(.641)
Deregulatory Reforms	.270	−1.029[+]
	(.396)	(.599)
Subsidized Reforms	−.122	.322
	(.323)	(.464)
Demographics		
Married	.226[+]	−.314[+]
	(.119)	(.180)
Female	.174	.124
	(.119)	(.169)
Age	.832***	.125
	(.286)	(.420)
Education	1.047[+]	.226
	(.606)	(.794)
Constant	−2.101***	−1.960***
	(.597)	(.954)
ρ	−.010	
	(.349)	

DATA SOURCE: *American Politics Study 2000.*
NOTE: *Sample selection probit model. N = 752. Standard errors in parentheses.*
[+]$p < .10$; *$p < .05$; ***$p < .001$.

TABLE **5.4**   Change in probability for presidential vote model

	No Vote	Vote Republican	Vote Democratic
Democratic Identifier	0.04	−0.26	0.23
Independent	0.23	−0.25	0.02
Economic Evaluation	−0.06	−0.05	0.11
Government Spending	0.03	−0.10	0.07
Middle-Class-Only Tax Cut	−0.02	−0.02	0.04
Family Values	0.05	−0.08	0.03
Regulatory Reforms	−0.08	0.04	0.04
Deregulatory Reforms	−0.06	0.08	−0.02
Subsidized Reforms	0.03	−0.04	0.00

DATA SOURCE: *American Politics Study 2000.*
NOTE: *Change in probability given a change from a low value (highest of either mean minus two standard deviations or lowest possible value) to a high value (lowest of either mean plus two standard deviations or highest possible value). Estimates are based on the model presented in Table 5.3.*

federal role in protecting family values. Other issues—family values, tax cuts, and the economy—all had lower impacts on vote choice than campaign finance reform.[9] Voting for Gore was affected by attitudes toward government spending, family values, the economy, and, finally, deregulation of the campaign finance reform system. These estimates show that attitudes toward deregulation—the most conservative of the reform proposals— were clearly an important determinant of the voting decision in the 2000 presidential election.

We now turn to the congressional model. We again use the sample selection model and the same variables with three sets of exceptions.[10] First, we include measures to control for incumbency and challenger quality. Because our candidate choice is partisan (i.e., 1 = Democrat, 0 = Republican), we use three dummy variables to account for the quality of the candidates: Democratic incumbent and high-quality Republican challenger, Democratic incumbent and low-quality Republican challenger, and Republican incumbent and high-quality Democratic challenger. Races with Republican incumbents and low-quality Democratic challengers are the baseline. We expect citizens who have Democrat incumbents to be more likely to vote for the Democrat and those who have a Republican incumbent and high-quality Democratic challenger to show a greater probability of voting for the Democrat in comparison to the baseline category. Second, we include a measure of the difference between Democratic and Republican campaign expenditures. Finally, we include the incumbent's grade by Common Cause to control for the candidates' stance on electoral and government policies. We include these three sets of measures as part of the candidate-choice equations because we expect them to affect the vote choice but not turnout.

Table 5.5 presents the congressional model.[11] Voter turnout in the congressional model was similar to that in the presidential model. Voter turnout

TABLE **5.5** Model of congressional vote

	Voter Turnout	Vote for Democratic Candidate
Political Engagement		
Efficacy	.413***	—
	(.158)	
Interest in Politics	1.039***	—
	(.202)	
Political Knowledge	1.014***	—
	(.228)	
Partisanship		
Democratic Identifier	−.137	1.630***
	(.118)	(.237)
Independent	−.450*	.725***
	(.199)	(.279)
Policy Attitudes		
Economic Evaluation	−.052	.389
	(.190)	(.259)
Government Spending	.076	.642*
	(.234)	(.312)
Middle-Class-Only Tax Cut	.254	−.122
	(.211)	(.291)
Family Values	−.214	.477+
	(.202)	(.266)
Campaign Finance Reform		
Regulatory Reforms	.257	−.846
	(.395)	(.531)
Deregulatory Reforms	−.043	−1.264***
	(.353)	(.495)
Subsidized Reforms	−.332	.886*
	(.284)	(.379)
Campaign Characteristics		
Democratic Spending Ratio	—	−.306
		(.447)
Democrat Incumbent & High-Quality Challenger	—	1.136***
		(.422)
Democrat Incumbent & Low-Quality Challenger	—	.973*
		(.413)
Republican Incumbent & High-Quality Challenger	—	.566*
		(.238)
Incumbent Common Cause Grade	—	−.259
		(.217)
Demographics		
Married	.119	.003
	(.106)	(.038)
Female	−.021	.212
	(.105)	(.145)
Age	1.051***	−.380
	(.251)	(.374)
Education	1.498***	−1.127
	(.524)	(.708)
Constant	−2.736***	.264
	(.529)	(.939)
ρ	−.710***	
	(.236)	

DATA SOURCE: *American Politics Study 2000.*
NOTE: *Sample selection probit model. N = 726. Includes incumbent races only. Robust standard errors in parentheses; observations clustered by congressional district.*
$^{+}p < .10;$ *$^{*}p < .05;$ $^{***}p < .001.$*

TABLE **5.6**   Change in probability for congressional vote model

	No Vote	Vote Republican	Vote Democratic
Democratic Identifier	0.05	−0.35	0.30
Independent	0.12	−0.14	0.02
Economic Evaluation	0.02	−0.12	0.10
Government Spending	−0.03	−0.16	0.19
Middle-Class-Only Tax Cut	−0.10	0.06	0.04
Family Values	0.07	−0.14	0.06
Regulatory Reforms	−0.06	0.15	−0.09
Deregulatory Reforms	0.01	0.20	−0.21
Subsidized Reforms	0.10	−0.22	0.12
Democrat Incumbent & High-Quality Challenger	0.00	−0.26	0.25
Democrat Incumbent & Low-Quality Challenger	0.00	−0.20	0.20
Republican Incumbent & High-Quality Challenger	0.00	−0.10	0.10

DATA SOURCE: *American Politics Study 2000.*
NOTE: *Change in probability given a change from a low value (highest of either mean minus two standard deviations or lowest possible value) to a high value (lowest of either mean plus two standard deviations or highest possible value). Estimates are based on the model presented in table 5.5.*

was influenced by individual characteristics—efficacy, interest in politics, knowledge, and demographics. The vote-choice model is similar to the presidential vote model in that partisanship and issues both determine vote choice. The model also shows the importance of the quality of the two candidates. Those voters with Democratic incumbents are more likely to vote for the Democrat. Those with Republican incumbents are more likely to vote for the Republican. In addition, voters are more likely to choose incumbents if the opposition candidate has no prior experience.

Attitudes toward campaign finance reform also affect the vote choice between Democratic and Republican candidates. Those who believe that the current system should be deregulated are more likely to vote Republican; those who disagree are more likely to vote Democratic. Similarly, those who believe that the government should subsidize our campaigns and elections are more likely to vote Democratic; those who disagree are more likely to vote Republican.

We present the change in probabilities in Table 5.6 to show the relative impact of these determinants on the voting decision. Compared to Republicans, Democrats have a 0.30 greater probability of voting the Democratic candidate; independents have a 0.02 greater probability. The greatest determinant after partisanship is incumbency and the quality of the challenger. Incumbents are more likely to receive votes than opposition candidates; stronger opponents do better than less-experienced opponents. Of the issues, campaign finance reform has the greatest effect on the vote because attitudes toward both deregulation and subsidies determine the choice between candidates. Those who favor deregulation have a 0.20 greater probability of voting for a Republican and a 0.21 lesser probability of voting for a Democrat. Those who favor subsidies for campaigns have a 0.12 greater probability of voting for a Democrat and a 0.22 lesser probability of voting for a Republican. As in the presidential model, attitudes toward reform are strong determinants of congressional vote choice.

Discussion and Conclusion

Americans clearly wish to see the campaign financing system overhauled. Given the twenty-eight-year gap between the FECA (1974) and the BCRA (2002), it is not surprising that loopholes need to be closed and adjustments made. As Potter (2001, 1) points out, "no law is a permanent fix."

Our work moves beyond recognizing the widespread call for reform to investigating the specific reforms that Americans support as well as the impact of public attitudes about campaign finance on turnout and vote choice in the 2000 presidential and congressional elections. We conclude that although most Americans want the campaign finance system reformed, and although the call for reformation reached a high level of prominence during the 2000 campaign season, the issue did not impact turnout. Among the myriad of factors that could affect voters' decisions in the 2000 elections, voter attitudes on campaign finance reform did matter, though this was limited to attitudes toward reforms on which the parties took opposing positions. Vote choice was affected by "extreme" proposals—deregulation and subsidies—and not "mainstream" regulatory attitudes. Voter cynicism is reaching a high point in American politics and is partially driven by dissatisfaction with the current campaign finance system.

Beyond showing the effect of campaign finance reform at the polls, the modeling results have normative implications for any discussion of campaign finance reform. Specifically, one is immediately struck by the important role of incumbency and challenger quality in the congressional model of turnout and vote choice. That reform is needed is suggested by the following facts: that incumbent war chests deter competition (Goldenberg, Traugott, and Baumgartner 1986; Fritz and Morris 1992; Box-Steffensmeier 1996), the buildup of which is facilitated by the current financing system, and that incumbency plays a large role in congressional voting decisions. Specifically, the lack of competitive congressional races shows that the scale that balances the democratic ideals of free speech and equality should be tipped toward equality while respectfully recognizing the value of free speech. A shift in the balance should increase competition, and ultimately the quality of congressional races and the responsiveness of elected officials. Moreover, such a shift would satisfy the expressed preferences of the American electorate (Gallup 2001).

MEASUREMENT APPENDIX

Campaign Finance Reform Proposals: I'm going to read you some different proposals to change the way federal election campaigns are run. As I read each proposal, tell me if you would strongly agree, agree, disagree, or strongly disagree with the change. How about this proposal . . . (question order was determined by randomized start)

1. Place a limit on spending by congressional candidates?
2. Limit TV advertising of congressional candidates?
3. Provide public funding for congressional candidates?
4. Eliminate large soft-money contributions?
5. Ban political action committees from giving money to congressional candidates?
6. Allow individuals to make larger gifts to candidates?
7. Eliminate all limitations and require full disclosure?
8. Allow parties to make larger gifts to candidates?
9. Give free media time and free postage to candidates?
10. Require candidates for the U.S. House and Senate to raise a certain percentage of their campaign funds within their own states?

Political Efficacy: Our measure of political efficacy is an additive index of three questions. Higher values on this index indicate greater political efficacy.

1. "How much do elections make government pay attention to what people think?" (always, most of the time, some of the time)
2. "Public officials don't care much what people like me think." (strongly agree, agree, disagree, strongly disagree)
3. "People like me don't have any say about what the government does." (strongly agree, agree, disagree, strongly disagree)

Political Knowledge: Our measure of political knowledge was formed by summing correct responses to five questions. Three of the questions dealt with respondents' knowledge of campaign finance while two inquired about politics more generally.

1. "As far as you know, how much money does current law allow private citizens to give directly to the campaigns of candidates for president and Congress? As much as they want, only a limited amount, or are they not allowed to contribute any money?"
2. "As far as you know, how much money does current law allow private citizens to give to political parties for party-building activities such as get-out-the-vote efforts? As much as they want, only a limited amount, or are they not allowed to contribute any money?"

3. "Do you happen to know which party received the most money in campaign contributions this year?"

4. "Who has the final responsibility to decide if a law is constitutional or not . . . is it the president, the Congress, the Supreme Court, or don't you know?"

5. "Do you happen to know which party had the most members in the House of Representatives in Washington before the November election?"

Political Interest: To measure political interest, respondents were asked the following question. "In general, how interested are you in politics and elections? Would you say . . . very interested, somewhat interested, not too interested, or not at all interested?"

Economic Evaluations: How about the economy as a whole? Would you say that over the past year the nation's economy has gotten better, stayed about the same, or gotten worse? [If respondent replies better or worse] Would you say it has gotten much [better/worse] or somewhat [better/worse]?

Attitude on Government Spending: The government should spend more money to help people, even if it means increasing taxes (strongly agree, agree, disagree, strongly disagree).

Attitudes on Tax Cuts: The government should cut taxes for the middle class but not for the very wealthy (strongly agree, agree, disagree, strongly disagree).

Attitudes on Government Protection of Family Values: The federal government needs to protect traditional family values and morality (strongly agree, agree, disagree, strongly disagree).

Partisanship: Party identification was measured by the following instrument: "Generally speaking, do you usually think of yourself as a Republican, Democrat, independent, or what?"

Age: Respondents' age in years.

Sex: A dummy variable was used to denote respondents' sex (female = 1).

Education: What is the highest grade or year of school you have completed?

Married: A dummy variable was used to denote married respondents (married = 1).

Voter Turnout: In talking to people about elections, we often find that a lot of people were not able to vote because they weren't registered, they were sick, or they just didn't have time. How about you? Did you vote in the elections this November?

Vote Choice: How about the election for president? Who did you vote for?

6 Ideology in the 2000 Election: A Study in Ambivalence

WILLIAM G. JACOBY

Many treatments of the 2000 election have emphasized themes that are specific to the various presidential candidates. Questions about George W. Bush's intelligence, concerns about Al Gore's sincerity, and speculation about Ralph Nader's motivations provide three prominent examples. Interestingly, however, most popular treatments of the election have downplayed a phenomenon that has been shown to exert a pervasive impact on many aspects of American politics: liberal and conservative ideology. This lack of attention is particularly surprising, given the ideological tone of some Republican campaign rhetoric along with the aggressively conservative policy agenda that President Bush has pursued since taking office.

This chapter will try to bridge the "ideological gap" in our understanding of the 2000 presidential election by examining the prevalence and impact of liberal and conservative thinking within the 2000 American electorate. In other words, to what extent did liberal and conservative ideas serve to structure the electoral environment, citizens' issue orientations, political perceptions, and voting choices during the contest between George W. Bush and Al Gore? I will employ data from the 2000 National Election Study (NES) to address this question.

The answer appears to be somewhat mixed: on the one hand, the campaign environment was infused with an unusually high level of explicitly ideological rhetoric, stimulated for the most part by Bush's "compassionate conservatism." Voters clearly recognized this and responded accordingly in their assessments of the candidates.

On the other hand, individual liberal-conservative identifications had little, if any, direct impact on citizens' choices between Al Gore and George Bush. Accordingly, 2000 could be characterized as a clear example of a nonideological election. Thus, the fact that attention has been focused elsewhere might not be unreasonable after all.

Ideology in the 2000 Political Environment

Several decades ago, political scientists would have divided the topic of elections into two distinct and separate components, corresponding to mass behavior (i.e., how do citizens make up their minds when confronted with the voting decision?) and elite behavior (i.e., how do candidates and parties try to maximize popular support for themselves?). At least since the 1970s, however, the discipline has recognized that the classification is just not that neat and simple. Instead, elections clearly involve an *interaction* between the mass public and political elites: the components of voter decision-making are affected by the content and structure of the political environment that confronts the mass public.

Given the preceding fact, it is important to determine just how prominent liberal-conservative themes were during the 2000 electoral campaign. If we were to confine our attention to the candidates alone, it would appear that ideology played an important role. On the Republican side, George W. Bush explicitly called himself a "conservative," albeit a "compassionate" one. And his public image was repeatedly pushed in a rightward direction, due to the intraparty challenge he faced from John McCain. Among the Democrats, Al Gore seldom (if ever) used the term *liberal* to describe himself. However, his campaign made no effort to disguise its appeals to traditional Democratic constituencies. In fact, it harked back to the New Deal era of the 1930s (e.g., organized labor) and the civil rights struggles of the 1960s (e.g., minorities)—in other words, liberal sociopolitical groups in American society. At the same time, third-party challenges on both the left (Nader's Green Party) and right (Buchanan's Reform Party) injected additional ideological fervor into the campaign by charging that the respective major-party candidates had abandoned the principles that they should have been espousing. Thus, the "true content" of the 2000 campaign environment clearly reflected ideological rhetoric. But did the public actually pick up on this? Several types of evidence drawn from the 2000 NES suggest that they did.

Ideological Placements of Parties and Candidates

First, let us consider ideological placements of major political actors. Obviously, it would be impossible to have ideologically motivated political action unless citizens recognize the ideological positions of the parties and candidates. So, it is reasonable to begin by checking the number of people who are willing to place the major parties and their candidates along the

TABLE **6.1**   Citizen placements of the 2000 parties and candidates along the liberal-conservative continuum

	Percentage Placing Along the Liberal-Conservative Scale	Percentage Placing at "Correct" Location Along Liberal-Conservative Scale	Percentage Placing at "Incorrect" Location Along Liberal-Conservative Scale	Mean Placement Along the Liberal-Conservative Scale
Parties				
Democratic Party	88.1	63.7	11.8	2.30
Republican Party	87.1	66.5	10.8	3.78
Candidates				
Clinton	88.3	45.0	7.8	2.34
Gore	86.8	38.2	12.2	2.56
Bush	86.6	46.8	10.1	3.60
Buchanan	62.1	40.3	6.3	3.99

DATA SOURCE: *2000 National Election Study.*
NOTE: *Placements are made along a five- or seven-point liberal-conservative scale. Regardless of item format, the scale consists of equally spaced values from one to five. A value of one means "Strong [or 'extremely'] liberal" and a five means "Strong [or 'extremely'] conservative."*

liberal-conservative continuum.[1] The leftmost column of Table 6.1 provides the appropriate figures. It is immediately apparent that almost the entire public is willing to specify ideological positions for the major parties and candidates. The percentages are all very high, and the differences are negligible across the various stimuli, ranging from 86.6 percent for George W. Bush to 88.3 percent for Bill Clinton. The 2000 NES included liberal-conservative placements for only one of the minor-party candidates, Pat Buchanan. Even this lesser-known political figure had a fairly clear ideological public image; 62.1 percent of the NES respondents placed him along the liberal-conservative continuum.

For our present purposes, the public's general *willingness* to provide dimensional placements of the candidates and parties is not, in itself, enough. Given the abstract nature of ideological terminology and the well-known tendency for acquiescence among survey respondents, it is necessary to go further and assess the *accuracy* of these placements. For present purposes, it is reasonable to specify that Clinton, Gore, and the Democratic Party are all liberal stimuli, while Bush, Buchanan, and the Republican Party are conservative. The second column of Table 6.1 shows the percentages of the NES respondents that gave "correct" placements for each of these political actors.[2] As one would expect, these values are all lower than those in the previous column, suggesting that there is quite a bit of confusion, mistaken understanding, and/or outright guessing involved when citizens place the candidates and parties along the ideological dimension.

When we limit our attention to those whose placements seem to be an accurate reflection of political reality, a much smaller number of people "pass the test." Consistent with prior research, the major parties seem to be the "carriers of ideology" within the electorate (Campbell, Converse, Miller, Stokes 1960; Nie, Verba, Petrocik 1979). But even here, only about two-thirds of the respondents placed the Democrats on the proper, liberal side of the continuum (64%) and the Republicans on the appropriate, conservative side (66%). The percentages of correct placements for all of the candidates are significantly lower than this. Of those, Bush's figure is the highest, at 47 percent. And it seems reasonable to attribute this to his own overt self-identification as a conservative. In contrast, barely more than one-third of the NES respondents correctly placed Gore on the liberal side (38%). Although this may reflect his own avoidance of the "liberal" label it is still somewhat surprising, given that Gore was definitely *not* a new figure on the political scene.

Any pessimistic conclusions that one might draw from the small sizes of the preceding figures must be tempered somewhat by the information provided in the third column of the table. The values presented there show the percentages of *incorrect* placements for each party or candidate—that is, placements with the Democratic Party, Clinton, or Gore on the conservative side of the scale and the Republican Party, Bush, or Buchanan on the liberal side. These figures are all quite small, never going above 12 percent. Even though the electorate appears somewhat hesitant to assign the proper ideological labels to electoral stimuli, there are still very few people who are blatantly wrong in their assignments. This does leave about one-fourth of the respondents who locate each of the parties at the moderate position, and about one-half who assign a similar stance to each of the candidates. Given the kinds of rhetoric employed by the major-party candidates in 2000 —again, Bush's "compassionate" conservatism and Gore's emphasis on new directions for the twenty-first century—it is not entirely unreasonable that citizens were somewhat reluctant to associate the parties and, particularly, the candidates with traditional liberal or conservative orientations.

Finally, the fourth column of Table 6.1 shows the mean scores assigned to the various stimuli, calculated on a scale ranging from one for "strong liberal" to five for "strong conservative." Although there may have been substantial variability among individual perceptions, the central tendencies all make a great deal of sense. Once again, the ideological positions of the parties are more clear-cut than are those of their respective candidates. On the Democratic side, Clinton is perceived to be more liberal than Gore (although the difference is not statistically significant). In contrast, the NES respondents placed Buchanan at a significantly more conservative position than either Bush or the Republican Party. Thus, the overall "shape" of the public's ideological perceptions seems to reflect accurately the realities of the 2000 political environment.

At the same time, however, the variability in the ideological placements cannot be ignored. It remains to be determined why some people specify locations for the parties and candidates that do not conform to the "true" ideological content of these stimuli. The most obvious factor is political sophistication. A long line of previous research has repeatedly demonstrated that highly sophisticated individuals are much more likely to think about politics in liberal-conservative terms than are less sophisticated people (Converse 1964; Luskin 1987; Jacoby 1988b, 1995). And this would clearly have direct implications for political perception. So, we will consider beliefs about the ideological positions of the parties and candidates across sophistication strata within the general public.

For our present purposes, political sophistication is defined in terms of the NES respondents' abilities to answer correctly ten factual questions about partisan control of the U.S. Congress, the positions held by various public figures, and the home states of the presidential and vice-presidential candidates.[3] The resultant political knowledge scores (i.e., the number of correct answers given by each person) range from 0 to 10. The distribution is skewed positive, with a mean of 3.61 and a median of 3. A four-category version of this variable is created by dividing the original distribution at its approximate quartiles.

Figure 6.1 traces the mean liberal-conservative placements for the parties and candidates across the four levels of political sophistication. The effects are clear-cut: there is a strong tendency toward greater ideological polarization among the perceptions of more sophisticated NES respondents.

Note that the *relative* ordering of the stimuli seldom changes, from the least- to the most-sophisticated subset. The Democratic Party is usually viewed as the most liberal stimulus, followed by Bill Clinton, and so on, down to Pat Buchanan, the most conservative figure by far. So, it would be inappropriate to say that these strata view the political world in fundamentally different ways. But it definitely seems that the *clarity* of the ideological content of the political world is enhanced among those individuals who are most capable of seeing it—that is, the people who are most familiar with politics in the first place.

The Ideological Content of General Candidate Perceptions

The analysis in the previous section demonstrated that people can identify liberal-conservative positions for parties and candidates when they are prompted to do so. But, to what extent do ideological themes permeate the public's general evaluations of the candidates? Stated simply, do citizens distinguish parties and candidates along liberal-conservative lines *on their own*? And, as a related issue, does the ideological content of these perceptions vary with levels of political sophistication?

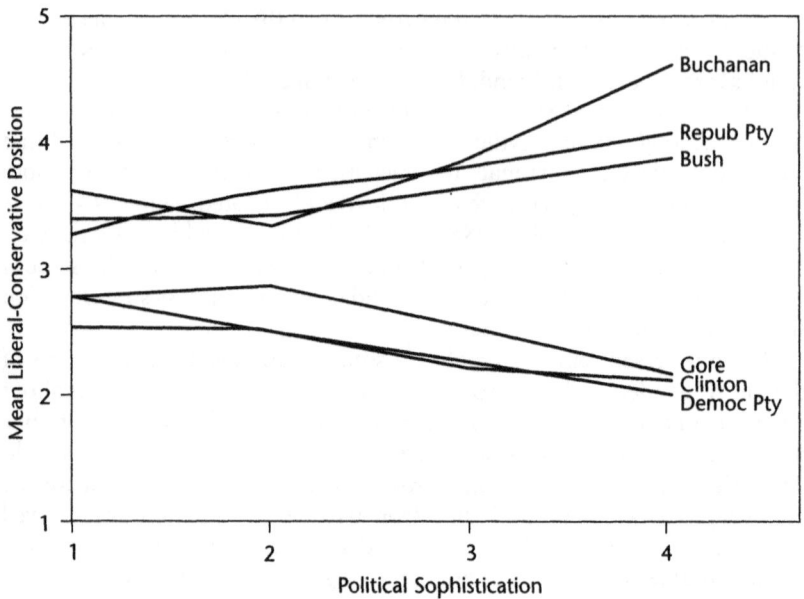

FIGURE 6.1   Mean Liberal-Conservative Placement of Parties and Candidates, by Level of Political Sophistication

To answer these questions, I perform a weighted multidimensional scaling (MDS) analysis. Generally speaking, MDS models dissimilarities between stimuli (candidates and parties, in this case) as distances between points in a dimensional space: greater dissimilarity between two objects corresponds to larger distance between the points representing those objects. Multidimensional scaling is a useful approach in this context because it enables us to recover the "cognitive map" that people bring to bear on the candidates and parties, without any prior specification of the exact criteria that they employ to evaluate these stimuli. Indeed, determining the latter is usually the objective of the MDS itself.

The input data for the MDS are a series of perceptual dissimilarity matrices that are created from the feeling thermometer battery in the preelection wave of the 2000 NES using the line-of-sight (LOS) methodology developed by Rabinowitz (1976).[4] In order to test for sophistication effects, a separate dissimilarities matrix is created for each of the four knowledge strata. All four resultant matrices are input to the MDS routine, which allows for differential dimension salience (or "weights") within each of the four subsets.

Major goals of an MDS analysis include ascertaining the number and nature of the judgmental standards that people use to evaluate the stimuli in

question. Of course, we would hypothesize that one of the dimensions underlying public perceptions corresponds to the standard liberal-conservative
continuum, like that discussed in the previous section. And, if sophistication
effects are present, then the weights attached to the liberal-conservative dimension should increase as we move upward through the respective political knowledge subgroups. The nature of any other dimensions is determined
empirically, by inspecting the point coordinates along the relevant coordi-
nate axis in the MDS space.

The MDS of the LOS dissimilarities from the 2000 National Election Study
data reveals that two dimensions are sufficient to provide an accurate model
of the public's perceptions.[5] Figure 6.2 shows the resultant "map" of perceived candidate and party points. Let us begin by considering the nature of
the dimensions. The horizontal direction within the graph does seem to represent an ideological continuum. Points representing more liberal stimuli
(Gore, Bill and Hillary Clinton, Bradley, Nader, and the Democratic Party)
are located toward the left and those for more conservative stimuli (Bush,
Cheney, McCain, and the Republican Party) toward the right.

To verify this interpretation, the best strategy is to correlate the point coordinates along the horizontal axis with some external measure of each object's liberal-conservative position. However, finding such a separate gauge

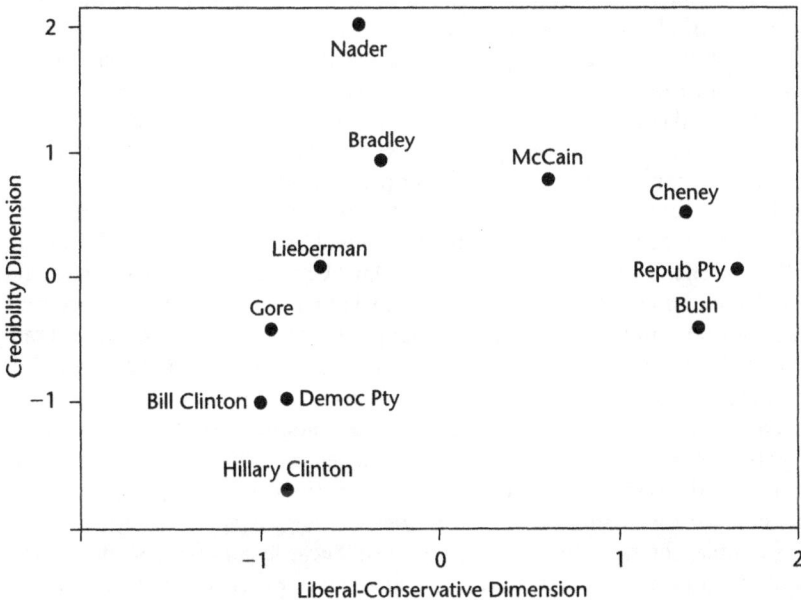

FIGURE 6.2   Perceptual Space for 2000 Candidates and Parties

of ideological position for each of the parties and candidates is problematic since the NES obtained liberal-conservative placements for only a few of them. Therefore, I will use an indirect strategy: for each of the eleven stimulus objects in the MDS analysis, I will take the difference between the mean feeling thermometer rating provided by conservatives and the mean feeling thermometer rating provided by liberals. The resultant values should summarize ideologically based variability in citizens' reactions toward the candidates and parties.

The correlation between this candidate-party ideology measure and the set of horizontal axis point coordinates is extremely large, at 0.98. Indeed, the two are virtually identical to each other. So, the more systematic analysis confirms the visual evidence: citizens' perceptions of the political parties and presidential candidates in 2000 are based, at least in part, on liberal-conservative distinctions. This result is particularly telling because the NES respondents were *not* explicitly instructed to use ideological criteria in their evaluations. Instead, they apparently do so without any outside prompting.

The vertical axis in Figure 6.2 is perhaps a bit more difficult to characterize. The major feature in this direction seems to be the wide separation between Nader and (to a lesser extent) Bradley and McCain, and the remaining candidates and the two parties. Accordingly, I would argue that this dimension represents some kind of "credibility" standard or "insider-versus-outsider" distinction.[6] Similar kinds of dimensions have emerged in analyses of electorate perceptions during other presidential election years since 1980, although the precise substantive interpretations have varied quite a bit from one researcher to the next.

External confirmation of this interpretation is somewhat problematic. A credibility criterion of the type I propose represents the extent to which each figure is a viable candidate for his/her party. Therefore, I compare two variables. The first variable is the vertical distance (in Figure 6.2) from each candidate point to his/her party point (assuming Bush, Cheney, and McCain are all Republicans, while Bill Clinton, Hillary Clinton, Gore, Lieberman, and Nader are all Democrats). The second variable is the mean thermometer rating for each candidate provided by identifiers with his/her own party (again, using the preceding allocation of candidates to parties). If the vertical dimension does, indeed, represent credibility then candidates who are perceived to be closer to their respective parties should be held in higher esteem by the citizens who identify with those parties. And this is exactly what does occur in the data. The correlation between the candidate-party point distances and the within-party thermometer ratings is very strong, at -0.87. Of course, the negative sign makes sense because *smaller* distances correspond to more positive evaluations. Thus, the empirical evidence clearly suggests that a major component of the electorate's overall judgments about the candidates involved their status as reasonable representatives of their respective parties.

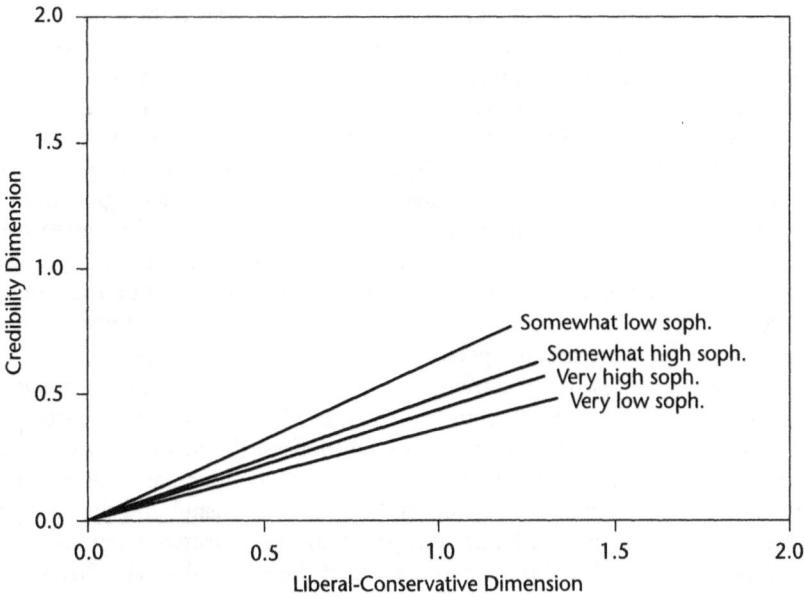

FIGURE 6.3   Dimension Weights for Citizens' Perceptions of 2000 Candidates and Parties

The discussion of the MDS results so far has focused on the substantive criteria that underlie mass perceptions. It is also important to see whether the "mix" of perceptual criteria varies across levels of political sophistication. Here, the answer is a simple and immediate "no." Figure 6.3 plots the dimension weights for the four political knowledge subgroups. The two axes in the figure are identical to the axes in Figure 6.2. Each subgroup is represented by a vector. The smaller the angle between a vector and an axis, the greater the weight on that evaluative criterion, within that subgroup.

There are two major features of Figure 6.3 that stand out immediately. First, the weights for all four knowledge strata are larger on the horizontal axis than on the vertical axis. This shows that the perceptions of the NES respondents were more heavily influenced by liberal-conservative differences among the stimuli than by questions of candidate credibility. Moreover, this result provides further confirmation that citizens really did use ideological considerations to shape the ways they thought about the candidates and parties in the 2000 election.

Second, it is also apparent that the four vectors in Figure 6.3 point generally in the same direction. The differences that do exist appear to be random "noise" rather than systematic, sophistication-based variations in the underlying evaluative criteria that people use to evaluate parties and candidates. This lack of variability among the vector orientations shows that, contrary to prior expectations, the salience of the liberal-conservative continuum does *not* increase among the political perceptions of more knowledgeable segments within the mass public.

The preceding result is extremely surprising. It certainly contradicts a pattern that has emerged repeatedly over the past twenty years. A massive amount of research on mass-belief systems has shown that ideological thinking is much more common among sophisticates than within less attentive, educated, and/or politically involved portions of the mass public (Jacoby 2002). And that is just not the case here. Perceptions of parties and candidates are imbued with a fairly consistent degree of liberal-conservative content, regardless how much a person knows about American politics.

So, what causes this apparently anomalous finding? Although it is impossible to provide an answer with any degree of certainty, there is certainly a factor that looms large in speculative responses: the ideological rhetoric employed by the Bush campaign as well as the two minor-party candidates. Perhaps Bush's language of "compassionate conservatism" and the charges leveled by Buchanan and Nader did penetrate the collective consciousness to a degree that colored mass perceptions of the political world. Given the dominant scholarly reservations about the reasoning capacities of the American electorate, such an interpretation should probably be treated with at least some skepticism. On the other hand, it is hard to think of another explanation for the uniformity of the ideological component to mass political perceptions during the 2000 presidential campaign.

Ideology and Voting Choice

The analysis so far has shown that ideology helped to shape the electorate's perceptions of candidates, parties, and issues in the 2000 presidential election. But the most important question is whether personal liberal-conservative feelings had any impact on individual voting choices. To test this, I estimate a two-part model using the NES data.

The first part of the model contains those factors that are hypothesized to have a direct effect on electoral decision-making. The dependent variable is each citizen's binary choice between George W. Bush (scored 1) and Al Gore (scored 0). There are six independent variables. First, there is the seven-point liberal-conservative identification scale.[7] Second, there is the familiar seven-point index of party identification. These variables are both coded so that larger values indicate more conservative and Republican identifications, respectively. Third, there is a summated rating scale of issue attitudes that summarizes the respondents' positions on eight different issues included in the NES interview schedule.[8] Once again, larger values correspond to more conservative issue stands. Fourth, there is a variable that measures relative assessments of Gore's and Bush's personality traits. Larger values indicate more positive assessments of Bush and negative assessments of Gore.[9] Fifth, there is a measure that summarizes individual beliefs about national economic performance over the preceding year (larger values indicate more dissatisfaction with the economy).[10] And finally, there is a variable that summarizes each person's beliefs about Bill Clinton's personal characteristics (larger values indicate higher levels of approval for Clinton's personality traits).[11]

All of the preceding independent variables are derived from longstanding theory and analytical practice in the field of mass political behavior. Two of them constitute reference groups—ideology and party identification (e.g., Conover and Feldman 1981; Jacoby 1988a). Two represent partisan political attitudes that are highly proximal to the voting act itself—issue attitudes and candidate personality assessments (e.g., Campbell et al. 1960; Miller and Shanks 1996). Finally, two are retrospective judgments—sociotropic economic judgments and evaluations of Clinton (Downs 1957; Fiorina 1981; Popkin 1991). Taken together, these six variables cover the major empirical theories of voting choice that have been proposed in the scholarly literature over the past four decades.

The second part of the voting model allows for indirect effects on citizens' electoral decisions. Party identification and ideological self-placement are widely regarded as longstanding symbolic predispositions (e.g., Sears, Lau, Tyler, Allen 1980). As such, most models of voting behavior assign these factors a position that is prior to, and relatively distant from, the final candidate choice (e.g., Schulman and Pomper 1975; Markus and Converse 1979; Rahn, Aldrich, Borgida, Sullivan 1990). In this capacity, ideology as well as partisanship could easily exert influences *through* other, more proximal factors like issues (Jacoby 1991), assessments of the candidates' personalities (Kinder 1986), and retrospective economic judgments (Duch, Palmer, Anderson 2000). Such indirect effects will be tested by using liberal-conservative self-placement and party identification as independent variables in a set of equations that predict each of the other four direct influences on voter choice (again, issue attitudes, Bush-Gore personality assessments, sociotropic economic judgments, and Clinton personality evaluations).

Direct Effects

The direct effects on voting choice are estimated using logistic regression. The empirical results are shown in Table 6.2. The leftmost column of the table gives the MLE's for the coefficients, along with the standard errors. The right-hand column contains the odds ratios. For each independent variable, the latter show the proportionate change in the odds of an observation falling within the dependent-variable category coded "1" that occurs with

TABLE **6.2** Influences on voter choices between Al Gore and George W. Bush

	MLE's of Logistic Regression Coefficients (and Standard Errors)	Odds Ratios
Liberal-conservative self-placement	0.109 (0.104)	1.115
Party identification	0.728* (0.086)	2.072
Bush-Gore personality assessments	2.496* (0.266)	12.132
Issue attitudes	0.591* (0.264)	1.805
Sociotropic economic judgments	0.060 (0.153)	1.062
Clinton personality assessments	−1.096* (0.312)	0.334
Likelihood ratio chi-square	1027.258	
Degrees of freedom	6	
Prob (chi-square)	0.0001	
Pseudo R^2	0.725	
Number of observations	1022	

DATA SOURCE: *2000 National Election Study.*
Coefficient is statistically different from zero, 0.05 level, one-tailed test.

a unit increase in that independent variable. The odds ratios are useful for interpretation because the independent variables' effects are expressed in a linear and additive manner (unlike the logistic regression coefficients or derived probabilities).

The equation fits the data very well, with a pseudo-R^2 value of 0.725. An inspection of the independent variables' effects reveals some expected patterns, along with some surprises. Assessments of the candidates' personality characteristics and individual partisan identifications have the strongest impacts, with highly significant coefficients of 2.496 and 0.728, respectively. The odds ratios express these effects somewhat differently. A unit increase in the personality-assessment variable corresponds to more than a twelve-fold increase in the odds of a vote for Bush. One unit of movement along the party-identification continuum doubles the odds of a Bush vote. An assessment of citizens' issue attitudes and Clinton's personality had smaller, but still significant, effects on voting choices, with coefficients of 0.591 and −1.096, respectively. Thus, electoral decisions were determined by "the iron triangle" of personalities, party, and issues (in that order of importance). In other words, the analytic results for the 2000 electorate conform almost perfectly to standard scholarly understandings of voting behavior. The additional influence of Clinton evaluations is also very reasonable. It could be either a decision-making heuristic based upon "low-information rationality" (Popkin 1991; Sniderman, Brody, and Tetlock 1991) or a reflection of the close public association (for better or worse) between Clinton and Gore.

The surprising aspects of Table 6.2 center around the variables that did *not* affect voters' decisions. The coefficients for liberal-conservative self-placement and sociotropic economic judgments have the correct signs (both positive). However, they are both quite small (0.109 and 0.060, respectively), and neither one achieves statistical significance. The minuscule sizes of the effects can be seen very easily in the odds ratios. One unit of movement along the liberal-conservative continuum results in only a 12 percent increase in the odds of a Bush vote, while a unit increase in the economic judgment variable (which actually means a more pessimistic assessment) produces an even smaller 6 percent increase in the odds. Whatever the substantive implications of the 2000 presidential election, the empirical results suggest an unambiguous *negative* conclusion regarding these two variables: the election provided neither an ideological mandate to the victorious Republican candidate nor a referendum on recent economic performance in the nation.

The apparent lack of direct ideology effects revealed in Table 6.2 may be due to extreme individual differences within the electorate. In other words, liberal-conservative influence on voting choice could be limited to the most sophisticated stratum of citizens, as is the case with many other forms of ideological thinking. Political sophisticates comprise a fairly small segment of the general public. Therefore, ideology effects may get "lost" when they are subsumed within the overall electorate. In fact, precisely such individual differences in voting behavior have appeared in a number of other elections.

The empirical test for sophistication-based variability in the impact of ideology is presented in Table 6.3. The table shows the same six-variable model of voting choice, with the coefficients estimated separately across the four levels of the discrete political-sophistication variable. In the interest of brevity, the table presents only the odds ratios (which are, again, more convenient for making comparisons of effects across subgroups) and the pseudo-R^2 values for each equation. Significant effects (0.05 level, one-sided tests) are marked with asterisks.

The first row of Table 6.3 shows the odds ratios for liberal-conservative identification, and if we inspect the values across the columns we see that the hypothesized pattern does occur: the proportionate change in the odds of voting for Bush due to a positive unit change in the ideology scale increases across the levels of political sophistication. At the lowest sophistication level, the odds ratio is less than one (0.842), revealing that the probability of a Bush vote actually *decreases* as people become more conservative —the opposite of substantive expectations. The odds ratio changes sign and increases in size through the remaining levels, up to a maximum of 1.276 among the most sophisticated subset of NES respondents. However, al-

TABLE **6.3**   Influences on voter choices between Al Gore and George W. Bush, broken down by levels of political sophistication

	Level of Political Sophistication			
	Very Low	Somewhat Low	Somewhat High	Very High
Liberal-conservative self-placement	0.842	1.023	1.198	1.276
Party identification	2.058*	1.917*	1.965*	2.511*
Bush-Gore personality assessments	7.074*	5.293*	15.729*	41.949*
Issue attitudes	1.165	1.581	2.797*	1.492
Sociotropic economic judgments	0.795	1.042	1.362	1.090
Clinton personality assessments	0.391	0.256*	0.184*	1.040
Pseudo R^2	0.567	0.586	0.750	0.841
Number of observations	101	209	291	421

DATA SOURCE: *2000 National Election Study.*
NOTE: *Table entries are odds ratios from logistic regression equations. Entries marked with an asterisk represent an effect that is statistically significant at the 0.05 level, in a one-tailed test.*

though the form of this pattern is reasonable in substantive terms, it is important to point out the exceedingly weak magnitude of the effect. The overall amount of change in the odds ratio across the sophistication levels is very small, and the ratios are never significantly different from one (i.e., the odds of a Bush vote do not change at all, or a null result) in any case.

A more general examination of the entries in the table shows that the pseudo-R^2 values increase steadily, from 0.567 among the least-sophisticated respondents up to 0.841 within the most-sophisticated subset. Thus, political sophistication affects the efficiency of the process through which citizens "translate" their preferences into a vote choice. But across the four sophistication strata, the relative magnitudes of the independent variables' effects remain fairly constant: personality assessments of Bush and Gore have, by far, the strongest impact, followed by party identification and assessments of Clinton. After these three factors, by a sizable margin, come the effects of issues, ideology, and sociotropic economic judgments. For our present purposes, the important result is that political sophistication does *not* affect the strength of the individual-level relationship between ideological self-placements and electoral decisions.

Indirect Effects

The empirical results necessary for testing indirect effects are shown in Table 6.4. Specifically, the table shows the OLS estimates from four regression equations, which measure the impact of party identification and liberal-conservative self-placement on each of the other four predictor variables from the voting model tested back in Table 6.2. These four predictor

TABLE **6.4**   The impact of party identification and liberal-conservative ideology on issue attitudes, Bush-Gore personality assessments, sociotropic economic judgments, and Clinton personality assessments

	Party Identification	Liberal-Conservative Self-placement	Intercept	R^2
Issue Attitudes	0.326 (0.042)	0.098 (0.008)	2.075	0.241
Bush-Gore personality assessments	0.270 (0.010)	0.099 (0.013)	−1.286	0.459
Sociotropic economic judgments	0.070 (0.013)	0.028 (0.017)	2.257	0.034
Clinton personality assessments	−0.146 (0.007)	−0.032 (0.008)	3.173	0.332

DATA SOURCE: *2000 National Election Study.*
NOTE: *Table entries are* OLS *regression coefficients, with standard errors in parentheses. All coefficients are statistically different from zero (one-tailed test). The number of observations in each equation varies from 1,497 through 1,604.*

variables are the summary scales of issue attitudes, relative assessments of the presidential candidates' personality traits, judgments about the national economy, and assessment of Clinton's personal characteristics. Each of these equations is estimated using the entire sample of NES respondents.

The results are very consistent across all four regression equations: partisanship and ideology always show a statistically significant impact, in the expected direction. Their influences are relatively weak in the equation for economic judgments—the R^2 value for this equation is very small, at 0.034. Recall, however, that the latter variable did not have a significant effect on voting choice in any case. Party identification and ideology do have greater explanatory power for the other three variables, with R^2 values ranging from 0.241 (in the equation for issue attitudes) to 0.459 (in the equation for Bush-Gore personality assessments). And, of course, all of these variables showed strong effects on voters' decisions. Thus, party identification and ideology both definitely exert an indirect influence, by operating through their effects on citizens' policy orientations and personality assessments.

The relative magnitudes of the impacts attributable to liberal-conservative self-placement and party identification are quite different. The latter is always stronger than the former. However, this is probably to be expected given scholarly understandings about the difference between the two factors as evaluative criteria. The major political parties serve as reference groups providing clear and easily discernible cues for guiding citizens' orientations. Ideological labels are more abstract, so the connections between terms like *liberal* and *conservative*, on the one hand, and issue stands, candidate traits, and economic performance on the other, are a bit more attenuated. Nevertheless, they do still exist. Clearly, liberal-conservative ideology joins party identification as one of the critical "background" variables that shape the more immediate factors impinging on citizens' electoral decisions.

The results presented in Table 6.4 are important for two reasons. First, they show that the 2000 election was *not* completely devoid of ideological content. However, to the extent that liberal-conservative considerations had any influence on voter' choices, they reached that point by an entirely indirect route. Second, the indirect impact of liberal-conservative identifications demonstrates that the apparently nonideological character was *not* entirely due to citizens' inability to deal with ideological abstractions. If that were the case, then liberal-conservative identifications should not be related to anything else. But, as we have just seen, they are indeed related to other factors. Instead, the ideological labels were simply not directly relevant to the voting decision between candidates Bush and Gore.

The general conclusions to be drawn from this part of the analysis seem relatively straightforward: the 2000 presidential election was not an overtly ideological contest in the eyes of the American electorate. Moreover, in contrast to many other election years, this was true *throughout* the public. Liberal-conservative considerations did not even come close to dominating the thoughts of even the most sophisticated subsets of the electorate.

Conclusion

The results of this analysis suggest that ideology had a very ambivalent role in the 2000 presidential election. The political environment was clearly imbued with ideological content. Citizens were able to place candidates and parties quite accurately along the liberal-conservative continuum. In fact, ideologically consistent perceptions occurred *throughout* the electorate—they were not confined to the most sophisticated strata, as has been the case in most prior election years.

At same time, however, the 2000 electorate did not translate ideological loyalties directly into electoral choices. The analysis presented in this chapter shows that individual voting decisions are quite predictable if we use a set of independent variables that might be characterized as some of "the usual suspects" within the field of mass political behavior. However, ideology is notable for its absence from the latter group. Liberal-conservative orientations showed no direct impact whatsoever on candidate choice. And this is even true among the most sophisticated subset of the electorate—precisely the stratum of citizens that, traditionally, has been most strongly attuned to ideological abstractions.

Still, it is important to emphasize that the apparently nonideological character of the 2000 election was *not* due (at least, entirely) to the "ideological innocence" of the American mass public. For one thing, liberal-conservative self-placements did influence a number of other orientations that were relevant to voters' decisions. In this sense, ideology did exert a pronounced, albeit indirect, effect by shaping the considerations that weigh more directly into electoral choices. This would not be the case if the public really suffered from the ideological incoherence that is often attributed to it.

Furthermore, the lack of a direct ideological effect may be due to the candidates rather than the voters—particularly, to George W. Bush. By calling himself a "compassionate conservative," Bush tried to appeal to two distinct ideological positions (i.e., moderate as well as conservative). In so doing, he raised ideology to a relatively prominent position within the electoral environment, but also muted its effects by equivocating.

The net result is that other judgmental standards—most prominently, candidate personalities and individual party identification—were simply more salient and easier to apply than liberal-conservative distinctions. If this is the case, then the nonideological character of the 2000 election occurred precisely because citizens reacted to the overt content of the campaign environment. Thus, it would be incorrect to equate "nonideological" with "nonrational," "incapable," or "disattached" when speaking about the qualities of the American electorate.

II *Group Voting Models*

7 Partisanship, Party Coalitions, and Group Support, 1952–2000

HAROLD W. STANLEY AND RICHARD G. NIEMI

Over the past few decades there has been a weakening of longtime patterns of party support and the beginnings of new support coalitions. The so-
called New Deal coalition, which took shape in the 1930s, referred to broad
support of the Democrats by native white Southerners, labor union and
working-class households, African Americans, Jews, and to a lesser extent,
Catholics. During the 1950s, breaks in this coalition began to appear, as native southern whites supported Republican candidates for the presidency.
Yet the coalition remained largely intact for a considerable time. Some further weakening occurred in the ensuing years, but it was not until after the
1992 election that we felt "it is time to declare the New Deal [Democratic]
coalition dead" (Stanley and Niemi 1995, 237). Republican control over the
House since 1994 and over the Senate after the 2000 and 2002 elections have
reinforced that conclusion.

Yet no sooner is one coalition gone than we want to know the shape of
that to follow. Is there a consistent pattern of group support since 1994 that
defines a new party support structure and suggests what lies ahead? Did the
2000 elections provide further definition to the coalitional structure that
gave Republicans the White House and the upper hand in Congress? Or, despite Democratic setbacks in 2000, did Bill Clinton's presidential victories in
1992 and 1996 reinvigorate elements of the old New Deal coalition, or even
spark the dawn of a new Democratic coalition? More specifically, do changing patterns of party support suggest the beginning of a new, long-lasting
form of coalitional behavior that will favor either Republicans or Democrats? Or rather do they indicate competitive elections, with the party in the
majority shifting from election to election?

The fortunes of the political parties have surged and declined over the
1990s as success, failure, and recovery have characterized both the Repub-

licans' and Democrats' fates. In 1991 Republican President George H. W. Bush set historic records in presidential approval; the following year he could not even secure reelection against Bill Clinton, who campaigned as a "New Democrat" and secured the first Democratic presidential victory since 1976. Clinton's presidential win in 1992 was in turn followed by a resounding victory for Republicans in 1994 when they gained majority control of the House of Representatives for the first time in over forty years. Clinton bounced back to trounce Republican Bob Dole in 1996, but Democrats were unable to retake control of either the House or Senate. Despite presidential impeachment proceedings, the president's party gained House seats in the 1998 midterm elections, the first time this had happened in over a half-century. But two years later, in a climate of economic prosperity and peace that ordinarily helps the incumbent party retain power, partisan contests ended in a virtual tie in the presidential vote and in the composition of the House and Senate, with Republicans (barely) controlling all three.

In this chapter, we look beneath these volatile partisan trends to examine the support base for each party. Gaining an appreciation of the shifting bases of the parties will help us model voting for the 2000 election. We approach the question of partisan trends not by directly analyzing the vote, but by considering expressed loyalties underlying support of the political parties —that is, self-reported partisanship. Of course, partisanship serves as a potent voting cue that encapsulates enduring evaluations of parties, candidates, issues, and events. Overwhelming majorities of partisans almost always back their party's nominees. Yet partisanship is no unmoved mover. Over the years partisanship can itself be changed by the political currents unleashed by these same candidates, issues, and events.

The potential for such changes in partisanship, reflected in the shifting group composition of the party coalitions, motivates this chapter. Here, we will update our over-time analysis of group support, now extending to almost half a century. We are concerned with continuity from past to present, but we are especially interested in the potential for a new group basis for the party coalitions. This new group basis may signal the start of yet another fundamental change in voters' relations with the parties—that is, the rise of a new party system. Thus, while presenting group partisanship figures for all presidential and almost all midterm elections since the 1950s, we will concentrate our analysis on the changing patterns found since 1994.

Analyzing Group Support

Group support can mean a number of different, though related things. In the past, we have looked primarily at what is called party identification— that is, which party people say they "generally support" (Stanley and Niemi 1995, 1999). Political scientists and pollsters use self-reports of this sort to assess "enduring" or long-term support for the parties, in contrast to the more short-term support gathered by specific candidates.[1] It is now generally conceded that self-reports of party support are not entirely immune from the direction political winds happen to be blowing in response to particular campaigns, partisan scandals, and so on (see, for example, Niemi and Weisberg 2001, part 5). Nevertheless, party identification, or partisanship, is less transient than individuals' voting behavior. This is especially true when one thinks of presidential voting. The presidential election is so visible that all but the most isolated individuals (who are not likely to vote in any event) have heard or read about and probably exchanged thoughts about both candidates. Hence, presidential preferences fluctuate to a degree that partisanship does not. Therefore, it is useful to consider party support in this "generic," more fundamental sense.

Having decided to rely on self-reports of party leanings, there remains the question of how, statistically, we should assess the support of the various groups for each party. We could simply show the raw partisanship of each group—that is, how many native southern whites, females, African Americans, white Protestant fundamentalists, and so on, say they generally support Democrats or Republicans. For some purposes, this approach is exactly what one wants. A problem is that such simple accounts are misleading because the groups are overlapping. For example, many native southern whites are also white Protestant fundamentalists, and vice versa. Thus, if we find that both of these groups tend to support Republicans, there is substantial overlap across the groups. Do both characteristics tend to make people Republican? And if so, by how much? Trying to answer such questions raises several problems, but one is certainly aided by the use of multivariate statistical procedures (i.e., procedures that incorporate multiple variables "all at once" rather than one at a time). In this chapter we use multivariate logit analysis.[2] Although this technique is complicated, a careful reading of our tables and of the explanations we provide for them should make the results understandable.

The Models

We begin by describing the multivariate models that form the basis of our analysis. In this presentation, we draw on National Election Studies data from twenty-three presidential and congressional elections since 1952. We define four models of party support that collectively cover the 1952–2000 period.[3] For comparisons over the entire period, it is important to consider all the models, and we have previously done so. For the present analysis, we emphasize the latest model, which can be estimated virtually without change since 1990. That model incorporates the New Deal elements, gender, church attendance, income, white Protestant fundamentalists, Hispanic origin, and three birth cohorts: 1943–1958 (baby boomers), 1959–1970 (so-called Generation X), and 1971–1982.[4] The primary dependent variables to be explained are Democratic identification and Republican identification.[5]

For several reasons, we use separate models for Democratic and Republican identification. First, to the extent that the New Deal coalition has broken up—a position we advanced in the mid-1990s (Stanley and Niemi 1995) —we want to be certain of the continued validity of that judgment, and a model of Democratic identification is most appropriate for that test. More significantly, we want to see the extent to which formerly Democratic groups have moved over into support for the Republican Party (as opposed to becoming independent), so we need to create a model for each party. Finally, for newer groups, we want to see whether hypothesized connections to the Republicans have taken hold. Our focus here is on the continuing nature of the changes as reflected in the 1990s, especially from 1994 on.

Results

The groups of interest are of three kinds. First, some groups have largely retained their traditional levels of allegiance to the Democratic Party despite the decline of the New Deal coalition. Three groups have done this: African Americans, Jews, and members of labor-union households. Second, other groups were part of the New Deal coalition, but their support declined sharply from what it was in the 1950s. Native white southerners, whose political support changed steadily and dramatically, and Catholics, for whom the decline occurred later and less sharply, are two groups of this type.[6] Finally, some groups have become larger or more politically visible in the past ten to fifteen years. Such groups include women, those who are well off financially, Hispanics, churchgoers in general and Christian fundamentalists in particular, and groups defined by age or "generation." They represent the greatest possibility of volatile movement or of a slow but systematic shift toward one of the parties.

In examining the support coming from these groups, we consider support for each party separately. Although support that does not go to one party most often goes to the other, voters are more independent than they were prior to the 1960s, so one sometimes finds that neither party receives a boost from a particular group. The top half of Table 7.1 presents the mean predicted probability (based on the results from the logit analysis) that a group member claims Democratic identification in each election year since 1952. Essentially, these numbers are the proportions of Democrats in each group before imposing any controls for other group memberships. Note that Democratic partisanship declined for every group in 1994 except for those born between 1959 and 1970, 1971 and later, and Hispanics. The changes are often small; but recall that partisanship is generally quite stable in the face of temporary partisan tides. Thus, the force of the Republican tide in 1994 is demonstrated by the fact that virtually all groups were affected. In the case of many of the New Deal groups, this represented the continuation of a change that had been taking place for many years. Note, for example, the continued slide of white Southerners, Catholics, and members of union households. The same was true of support from Christian fundamentalists and of baby boomers (born between 1943 and 1958), where support dropped precipitously in 1994.

The movement away from the Democrats could not be maintained, however. Not only did virtually every group swing back toward the Democratic Party in 1996 (all except union households), but the pattern over the next two elections was mixed. Even if one compares only the presidential years— and whether one concentrates on 1996 and 2000 or all of the presidential years since 1988—there is no uniform movement toward one party or the other. Thus, the initial figures about self-reported loyalties in the 1990s conform to the partisan volatility observed in the vote.

Although the proportion of Democratic supporters within groups changed erratically after 1994, the incremental impact of membership in a particular group, shown in the bottom half of Table 7.1, gives us a different view of group effects. These numbers show how much more likely an individual is to be a Democratic identifier because of membership in a specific group. That is, they consider all of the other group ties of each individual and how likely those other ties are to make the person Democratic. These incremental probabilities show very clearly the continuation of long-term trends. African Americans reported levels of Democratic partisanship—net of other influences—that were as high as or higher than in most previous years. Support for the Democrats among Jews appears to have slipped compared to other recent years, though it was still very high.[7] Moreover, members of union households reversed a short-term fall and in 2000 expressed Democratic leanings that matched or exceeded most years since 1970.

Long-term trends are also evident in the decline—now in its fifth decade —of the Democratic Party among white southerners. In 2000, for the first time since these measurements started, such individuals were *less* likely to be Democratic than others with similar characteristics. The appointment of so many Southerners to leadership positions in the George W. Bush White House reflects that change but also is likely to encourage still further departures from the Democratic ranks among southern whites.

Current politics are also reflected in the sharp decline in Democrat partisanship among Catholics. President George W. Bush's appearances with the Catholic hierarchy, his vocal support of faith-based charities, and his careful decision on stem cell research reflect strong efforts to align the Republican Party with this large bloc of voters. In this shift among political elites combined with the observed movements in the electorate, we could be

TABLE **7.1**   Mean and incremental probabilities of Democratic identification for members of social groups

Group	'52	'56	'58	'60	'64	'66	'68	'70	'72	'74
Mean Probabilities[a]										
African American	.53	.51	.51	.45	.73	.62	.85	.78	.67	.69
Catholic	.56	.52	.57	.64	.59	.54	.53	.53	.50	.51
Jewish	.73	.62	.71	.52	.57	.68	.50	.54	.52	.53
Female	.48	.42	.51	.49	.53	.46	.48	.46	.43	.43
Native southern white[b]	.77	.71	.74	.72	.71	.60	.52	.46	.52	.52
Union household	.54	.51	.59	.57	.64	.56	.50	.55	.46	.47
Regular churchgoer	.50	.46	.47	.49	.53	.48	.47	.46	.44	.40
Income: top third	.43	.40	.46	.44	.42	.42	.39	.39	.34	.31
White Protestant fundamentalist									.46	.43
Hispanic, non-Cuban										
Born 1943–1958										
Born 1959–1970										
Born 1971–										
Incremental Probabilities[c]										
African American	.17	.20	.14	.11	.30	.24	.49	.42	.37	.40
Catholic	.21	.20	.20	.30	.19	.16	.18	.16	.20	.22
Jewish	.39	.32	.31	.18	.20	.35	.18	.21	.27	.28
Female	−.01	−.05	.03	.04	.02	.02	.03	.02	.05	.04
Native southern white[b]	.45	.42	.39	.41	.33	.26	.19	.12	.18	.23
Union household	.14	.12	.14	.15	.18	.16	.08	.15	.09	.08
Regular churchgoer	.00	−.02	−.09	−.03	−.01	.01	−.01	.03	.03	−.03
Income: top third	−.07	−.04	−.04	−.06	−.14	−.05	−.06	−.06	−.07	−.11
White Protestant fundamentalist									.08	.03
Hispanic, non-Cuban										
Born 1943–1958										
Born 1959–1970										
Born 1971–										

DATA SOURCE: *1952–2000 National Election Studies.*
NOTE: *The four models containing the different variables were evaluated through 2000. However, presentation is greatly simplified by showing only the following: 1952–1970 values are based on the model with eight variables; 1972–1978 values are based on the model with nine variables; 1980–1988 entries are based on the model with twelve variables; 1990–2000 entries are based on the model with thirteen variables. Values that can be estimated with more than one model seldom differ by more than .01 from one model to another.*

seeing the most important change in the group basis of party support in many years. Note that until the late 1970s, Catholics had an incremental probability of about .20 of supporting the Democratic Party. Support dropped in the 1980s and 1990s, but the increment remained at about .15. As such, it was higher than the push that came from membership in a union household. In the last two election years, however, support of Catholics dropped off

'76	'78	'80	'82	'84	'86	'88	'90	'92	'94	'96	'98	'00
.72	.64	.73	.81	.62	.72	.63	.64	.64	.61	.66	.72	.64
.50	.49	.43	.54	.43	.45	.37	.45	.41	.39	.43	.41	.35
.58	.55	.81	.59	.60	.36	.36	.62	.63	.55	.63	.58	.63
.42	.42	.44	.49	.40	.43	.40	.43	.39	.37	.43	.41	.38
.52	.44	.49	.55	.41	.43	.39	.37	.33	.30	.36	.33	.25
.48	.49	.48	.52	.47	.46	.42	.51	.47	.44	.44	.46	.46
.43	.43	.40	.47	.37	.43	.39	.43	.36	.33	.36	.36	.34
.31	.34	.35	.37	.32	.33	.28	.35	.29	.21	.26	.34	.31
.43	.43	.56	.48	.41	.39	.37	.34	.31	.27	.34	.23	.31
		.56	.57	.45	.53	.45	.46	.43	.44	.51	.58	.40
		.39	.43	.34	.36	.34	.43	.37	.30	.37	.39	.38
		.32	.35	.32	.35	.27	.30	.30	.31	.36	.33	.30
							.29	.25	.29	.38	.35	.29
.43	.34	.46	.47	.34	.43	.39	.31	.38	.37	.35	.42	.36
.22	.20	.14	.20	.14	.15	.09	.12	.15	.16	.13	.06	.05
.36	.31	.55	.31	.34	.07	.17	.32	.39	.33	.32	.26	.29
.03	.03	.08	.06	.05	.05	.09	.03	.06	.06	.08	.05	.08
.23	.12	.13	.20	.08	.12	.11	.02	.06	.04	.03	.01	-.05
.12	.15	.12	.11	.13	.10	.11	.15	.15	.13	.08	.11	.14
.03	.02	-.04	.01	-.04	.00	.02	.02	-.03	-.02	-.07	-.06	-.05
-.11	-.10	-.06	-.11	-.06	-.08	-.06	-.09	-.10	-.16	-.14	-.02	-.04
.05	.11	.25	.07	.10	.05	.07	.01	.04	.03	.04	-.07	.03
		.17	.10	.05	.10	.09	.08	.07	.09	.08	.27	.11
		-.09	-.06	-.11	-.11	-.09	-.04	-.05	-.08	-.04	-.08	-.06
		-.16	-.18	-.16	-.16	-.19	-.18	-.14	-.11	-.10	-.15	-.15
							-.21	-.22	-.15	-.11	-.15	-.18

[a] Cells are the mean of the predicted probabilities of Democratic identification for all group members in each year.
[b] Native southern whites, 1952–1988; all southern whites, 1990–2000.
[c] Cells are the average of the difference, for each group member, between the individual's predicted probability of Democratic identification (based on all of the other characteristics in the multivariate model) and what the individual's probability would have been without the effect of the group membership.

again, this time to below that of many other groups. If President Bush is successful, Catholics could become the second group in the old Democratic coalition—native southern whites being the first—to lose completely their tendency to be Democratic once other group characteristics are taken into account.

Adding significance to the drop in the marginal Democratic tendencies of Catholics is the continued movement of regular churchgoers away from the Democrats. The magnitude is not yet great, but it is clearly above the very weak, oscillating tendencies of much of the previous fifty years. Interestingly, white Protestant fundamentalists—seen in previous years as a strong bastion of Republican support (e.g., Wilcox 1996)—have not, except for 1998, been pulled away from the Democrats.

The gender gap, which arose in the early 1980s, continued undiminished into the new century. As we noted previously, neither party can afford to limit its appeal to males or females. Nonetheless, this division is likely to be sustained by Republican support for pro-life policies, their positions on other gender issues (e.g., toward gays and lesbians), and Democratic policies that are seen as more supportive of women (e.g., with respect to equal pay). In contrast, what appeared to be a continuing, perhaps growing partisan gap between rich and poor in the first half of the 1990s shriveled to the low levels of the 1950s.

Republicans have also made concerted, recent efforts to court Hispanic voters. And, indeed, judging by mean probability figures, these efforts at least dented Democratic support among Hispanics, except in 1998. But judging by the incremental probability of supporting Democrats, these efforts have yet to pay off. Indeed, Hispanic support for Democrats spiked in 1998, perhaps energized by Republican sponsorship of restrictionist immigration policies along with Democratic support for more liberal policies (Glastris 1997).

What about the Republican Party? As groups increase or decrease their support for the Democrats, is there compensating movement to the other side? Among southern whites, the answer is clearly yes. Indeed, for three of the past four election years, mean probabilities of partisan identification have been greater for Republicans than Democrats, and incremental probabilities have favored Republicans in the last two (table 7.2). Declining Democratic partisanship among Catholics and regular churchgoers was also matched by increasing identification with Republicans. Incremental probabilities for Catholics are still negative (meaning that, net of other characteristics, Catholics are less likely than non-Catholics to consider themselves Republican), but they are at their lowest levels ever. Correspondingly, the gap between the parties in mean probabilities has narrowed. Among regular churchgoers, small positive incremental probabilities favoring the Republicans have become larger. Mean probabilities, which once favored the Democrats by margins of two to one, are now virtually even.

At the same time, the difficulty the Republicans face of putting together a new coalition is apparent in the receding identification they received from those in the top third of the income distribution. Incremental probabilities, which had inched upward in the early 1990s, dropped in the two most recent elections. Attracting women and even white Protestant fundamentalists also remained a problem. The prospects of a generational appeal—either to boomers or to subsequent generations—do not find much support here either. The incremental push from particular generations can be described as an anti-Democratic force but as only a weak and inconsistent pro-Republican force. Both of the age groups in tables 7.1 and 7.2 have consistently high increments in favor of independence (not shown). This reflects the dealigning forces that have characterized American politics since the mid-1960s. It is worth pointing out that even as levels of party identification change among groups defined by ethnicity, religion, and so on, there has been no systematic change in party leanings in the generational groups. Consistent with arguments about the importance of the years in which one enters adulthood, aging by itself has not led to changing party allegiances, in either an absolute (mean probability) or relative (incremental probability) sense.

Republicans' difficulties in attracting Hispanic support, noted earlier, are also evident in the Republican mean and incremental probabilities. The public attention focused on Elian Gonzales, the Cuban boy rescued in the Caribbean and later returned to Cuba, and protests over bombing on the Puerto Rican island of Vieques are reminders of the high-risk stakes for parties as they court ethnic groups and seek to retain other supporters. In any case, Hispanics have not found increasing favor with Republicans during the 1990s. The mean probability has, if anything, declined marginally during the decade. Incremental probabilities have also become less favorably Republican.

The change in group support has been dramatic over the entire period for which we have data. But it has taken the form of a wearing away of an old coalition—the New Deal coalition—rather than the formation of new, distinct group alliances. The change is best described "negatively"—that a given group is no longer part of, or no longer so heavily a part of, the Democratic or Republican coalition. There has been no genuine group realignment, if one means by that changes in which a group that was at one time highly supportive of one party is now highly supportive of the other (or even that a group that was neutral is now highly supportive of one party). Now, decades after the beginning of the breakup of the old, we may finally be seeing the start of a new, "positive" pattern. For the first time in twenty-three surveys stretching over a half century, southern whites in 2000 showed a greater (if still small) affinity with Republicans than with Democrats. Regular churchgoers have shown a growing, decade-long tilt in favor of the Republicans. Catholics show signs of shifting their support as well. African Americans have strongly supported Democrats since the 1960s, but that should not obscure the increased support compared to the 1950s. Women have perhaps supported Democrats in sufficient proportions and for a sufficient length of time to be called a part of their base coalition. And Hispanics, who when we first observed them were not so much an unaligned group as one too small to be of much importance, have remained Democratic sup-

TABLE **7.2**   Mean and incremental probabilities of Republican identification for members of social groups

Group	'52	'56	'58	'60	'64	'66	'68	'70	'72	'74
Mean Probabilities[a]										
African American	.13	.19	.15	.18	.07	.10	.02	.04	.08	.04
Catholic	.18	.21	.17	.15	.17	.16	.15	.16	.14	.14
Jewish	.00	.11	.12	.08	.06	.05	.05	.05	.09	.12
Female	.29	.32	.28	.30	.25	.25	.23	.25	.24	.23
Native southern white[b]	.09	.12	.12	.11	.08	.11	.09	.14	.15	.12
Union household	.22	.21	.17	.17	.14	.18	.19	.14	.16	.14
Regular churchgoer	.28	.29	.31	.30	.26	.25	.24	.26	.26	.25
Income: top third	.31	.34	.33	.30	.32	.25	.28	.29	.30	.29
White Protestant fundamentalist									.21	.17
Hispanic, non-Cuban										
Born 1943–1958										
Born 1959–1970										
Born 1971–										
Incremental Probabilities[c]										
African American	−.27	−.21	−.25	−.26	−.27	−.25	−.34	−.29	−.25	−.29
Catholic	−.24	−.20	−.25	−.28	−.21	−.18	−.22	−.17	−.19	−.18
Jewish	−.41	−.30	−.25	−.31	−.31	−.31	−.32	−.30	−.29	−.23
Female	.03	.07	−.01	.02	.01	−.01	−.02	.01	.01	.01
Native southern white[b]	−.35	−.32	−.32	−.35	−.30	−.27	−.29	−.22	−.17	−.20
Union household	−.09	−.12	−.14	−.17	−.16	−.10	−.09	−.14	−.12	−.12
Regular churchgoer	.05	.05	.10	.07	.06	.03	.04	.03	.05	.05
Income: top third	.05	.06	.04	.02	.10	−.01	.03	.06	.08	.07
White Protestant fundamentalist									−.05	−.05
Hispanic, non-Cuban										
Born 1943–1958										
Born 1959–1970										
Born 1971–										

DATA SOURCE: *1952–2000 National Election Studies.*
NOTE: *The four models containing the different variables were evaluated through 2000. However, presentation is greatly simplified by showing only the following: 1952–1970 values are based on the model with eight variables; 1972–1978 values are based on the model with nine variables; 1980–1988 entries are based on the model with twelve variables; 1990–2000 entries are based on the model with thirteen variables. Values that can be estimated with more than one model seldom differ by more than .01 from one model to another.*

porters. Thus, after a long period of breakdown and uncertainty, we may, at last, be seeing the development of a new group profile in party support.

Group Support and the Party Coalitions

So far we have focused on the probability that individuals with a given characteristic identify with one party or the other. Now our attention turns

'76	'78	'80	'82	'84	'86	'88	'90	'92	'94	'96	'98	'00
.05	.07	.05	.02	.04	.05	.06	.05	.04	.05	.03	.04	.05
.16	.13	.19	.17	.20	.22	.27	.23	.19	.25	.24	.25	.23
.08	.05	.00	.18	.10	.21	.12	.10	.05	.10	.07	.14	.06
.27	.23	.23	.23	.27	.26	.28	.23	.24	.31	.24	.25	.21
.16	.16	.19	.18	.22	.22	.21	.21	.27	.39	.31	.35	.32
.14	.14	.13	.17	.20	.21	.21	.20	.15	.22	.17	.18	.18
.28	.24	.28	.26	.32	.27	.32	.28	.31	.36	.36	.33	.33
.30	.25	.30	.32	.35	.30	.34	.33	.34	.43	.40	.34	.30
.21	.18	.16	.20	.22	.26	.26	.28	.32	.40	.34	.41	.30
		.13	.10	.11	.18	.15	.14	.14	.18	.13	.13	.12
		.21	.20	.28	.24	.26	.24	.27	.35	.30	.26	.24
		.14	.27	.25	.26	.28	.28	.24	.33	.27	.29	.28
							.19	.19	.26	.22	.32	.15
−.28	−.24	−.26	−.30	−.35	−.31	−.34	−.29	−.30	−.36	−.32	−.27	−.22
−.18	−.18	−.12	−.17	−.16	−.13	−.08	−.10	−.17	−.17	−.13	−.02	−.04
−.28	−.27	−.33	−.20	−.33	−.13	−.31	−.26	−.34	−.32	−.27	−.14	−.18
.05	.02	−.02	−.02	.00	.00	.00	−.04	−.05	−.03	−.08	−.04	−.06
−.16	−.11	−.09	−.14	−.08	−.11	−.15	−.12	−.10	−.01	−.05	.03	.05
−.14	−.11	−.15	−.11	−.11	−.07	−.13	−.11	−.16	−.11	−.17	−.11	−.08
.06	.05	.08	.04	.08	.04	.06	.06	.09	.07	.13	.09	.15
.08	.05	.09	.11	.10	.05	.06	.09	.11	.12	.13	.09	.07
−.06	−.10	−.13	−.08	−.13	−.05	−.06	−.01	−.02	−.03	−.03	.08	−.01
		−.06	−.10	−.11	−.04	−.12	−.09	−.07	−.12	−.12	−.19	−.12
		−.01	−.06	.03	−.02	−.02	−.02	.00	.04	.00	.01	.00
		−.06	.05	.02	.03	.02	.05	.00	.07	.02	.05	.05
							−.02	−.03	.01	−.01	.11	−.04

[a] Cells are the mean of the predicted probabilities of Republican identification for all group members in each year.
[b] Native southern whites, 1952–1988; all southern whites, 1990–2000.
[c] Cells are the average of the difference, for each group member, between the individual's predicted probability of Republican identification (based on all of the other characteristics in the multivariate model) and what the individual's probability would have been without the effect of the group membership.

to the party coalitions. In the first two sections of tables 7.3 and 7.4 we show the mean predicted probability of Democratic or Republican identification in the United States and, below that, the percentage of each coalition with a given group characteristic. This breakdown of the coalitions is in terms of overlapping groups. The percentages describing the party coalitions thus add to more than one hundred because, for example, an African-American female churchgoer is counted in each of three categories.

TABLE **7.3** Size and composition of the Democratic coalition

Group	'52	'56	'58	'60	'64	'66	'68	'70	'72	'74
Predicted Probability of Democratic Identification in the U.S.[a]										
	48	44	49	47	52	46	45	44	41	41
Percentage of Democratic Coalition with a Given Group Characteristic[b]										
African American	10	10	9	8	14	14	17	17	17	17
Catholic	27	25	26	29	26	26	26	24	30	30
Jewish	5	5	4	4	3	5	3	4	3	3
Female	55	53	56	59	56	56	58	59	60	63
Native southern white[c]	26	27	26	28	20	19	19	20	21	25
Union household	32	32	30	33	30	34	28	29	30	30
Regular churchgoer	42	45	43	50	44	42	40	40	42	43
Income: top third	37	28	32	39	29	35	27	34	27	23
White Prot. fundament.									17	18
Hispanic, non-Cuban										
Born 1943–1958										
Born 1959–1970										
Born 1971–										
Percentage of Democratic Identifiers in Group Continuing to Claim Democratic Identification										
African American	68	61	73	75	59	61	42	46	44	43
Catholic	62	61	64	52	68	70	67	70	61	57
Jewish	46	48	57	66	65	48	64	60	47	48
Female	102	111	94	91	97	95	93	95	89	90
Native southern white[c]	42	41	47	43	53	56	64	74	64	56
Union household	75	77	76	74	71	71	85	73	81	82
Regular churchgoer	100	104	119	107	102	97	102	94	93	107
Income: top third	117	110	108	115	133	112	116	116	122	137
White Prot. fundament.									82	92
Hispanic, non-Cuban										
Born 1943–1958										
Born 1959–1970										
Born 1971–										
Relative Size (%) of Democratic Coalition After Removing Group Characteristic										
African American	97	96	98	98	94	95	90	91	91	90
Catholic	90	90	91	86	92	92	91	93	88	87
Jewish	97	98	98	99	99	97	99	99	98	98
Female	101	106	97	95	98	97	96	97	93	94
	85	84	86	84	91	92	93	95	92	89
Union household	92	93	93	91	91	90	96	92	94	95
Regular churchgoer	100	102	108	103	101	99	101	98	97	103
Income: top third	106	103	103	106	110	104	104	105	106	109
White Protestant fundamentalist									97	99
Hispanic, non-Cuban										
Born 1943–1958										
Born 1959–1970										
Born 1971–										

DATA SOURCE: *1952–2000 National Election Studies.*
[a] *These estimates, derived from the model, are virtually identical to the actual percentage of Democratic identifiers.*
[b] *Figures derived from taking the mean predicted probability of Democratic identification for a group in a particular year (table 7.1) multiplied by that group's number of respondents, and dividing this product by the number of Democratic identifiers.*

'76	'78	'80	'82	'84	'86	'88	'90	'92	'94	'96	'98	'00
40	40	42	46	38	41	36	41	37	34	39	38	35
19	16	21	21	19	27	25	23	25	23	22	26	22
32	32	27	29	32	28	26	32	30	33	31	36	25
4	4	6	3	4	1	1	3	4	4	3	4	4
60	58	61	60	60	59	65	58	58	60	62	61	60
20	16	22	22	20	20	23	21	21	24	26	24	18
28	32	29	25	27	24	24	23	23	23	20	19	19
44	41	38	44	38	43	42	44	42	44	39	40	37
29	29	26	29	27	25	26	30	29	20	21	30	28
15	16	20	18	16	16	19	16	15	15	16	8	12
		5	3	8	7	10	10	9	11	11	16	9
		35	35	34	34	36	34	34	29	29	33	35
		4	7	13	16	16	18	21	26	24	21	24
							2	3	5	8	13	13

After Removing Democratic Tendency of Defining Group Characteristic[d]

'76	'78	'80	'82	'84	'86	'88	'90	'92	'94	'96	'98	'00
40	47	37	42	45	40	38	52	40	39	47	41	43
56	59	68	63	68	67	75	73	64	59	69	85	86
38	44	32	47	43	80	54	48	37	41	49	54	53
93	93	82	88	87	89	78	93	86	83	82	88	80
57	73	74	63	81	73	71	94	82	87	92	97	119
75	70	76	79	72	79	73	71	68	71	81	77	69
93	95	109	98	111	99	95	96	109	105	119	116	115
134	130	118	131	119	123	123	127	136	174	154	105	112
88	75	55	84	75	87	81	97	88	89	87	132	89
		69	83	89	82	80	82	83	81	83	54	74
		122	114	132	132	126	110	114	125	111	121	115
		150	150	151	147	169	158	147	135	128	147	149
							173	185	153	128	145	164
89	91	87	88	89	84	84	89	85	86	88	85	87
86	87	91	89	90	91	93	91	89	87	91	95	96
98	98	96	99	98	100	99	99	98	98	98	98	98
96	96	89	93	92	93	86	96	92	90	89	93	88
91	96	94	92	96	94	93	99	96	97	98	99	103
93	90	93	95	93	95	94	93	93	93	96	96	94
97	98	104	99	104	100	98	98	104	102	107	106	106
110	109	105	109	105	106	106	108	110	115	111	101	103
98	96	91	97	96	98	96	99	98	98	98	103	99
		98	99	99	99	98	98	98	98	98	93	98
		108	105	111	111	109	103	105	107	103	107	105
		102	103	107	107	111	110	110	109	107	110	112
							102	102	103	102	106	108

[c] Native southern whites, 1952–1988; all southern whites, 1990–2000.

[d] Figures derived by recalculating the probabilities of Democratic identification without the effect of, say, white Protestant fundamentalist identification, then taking the mean of these probabilities for all respondents who were white Protestant fundamentalists. The ratio of this revised mean probability to the mean probability that includes the effect of white Protestant fundamentalism gives the ratio of the hypothetical size to the actual one.

TABLE 7.4 Size and composition of the Republican coalition

Group	'52	'56	'58	'60	'64	'66	'68	'70	'72	'74	'76	'78	'80	'82	'84	'86	'88	'90	'92	'94	'96	'98	'00
Predicted Probability of Republican Identification in the U.S. [a]																							
	27	29	28	29	25	25	24	24	24	23	24	21	23	24	27	25	29	25	26	32	29	27	23
Percentage of Republican Coalition with a Given Group Characteristic [b]																							
African American	5	6	5	5	3	4	1	1	3	2	2	3	2	1	2	3	3	3	2	2	2	2	2
Catholic	15	15	14	10	15	15	14	13	15	15	18	17	21	17	21	22	24	26	20	22	24	31	25
Jewish	0	1	1	1	1	1	1	1	1	1	1	1	0	1	1	1	1	1	0	1	1	1	1
Female	57	61	55	55	56	56	53	58	57	61	65	60	57	53	57	58	57	51	49	53	48	52	49
Native southern white [c]	5	7	7	7	5	7	6	11	10	10	10	12	15	14	15	17	15	19	24	33	30	35	34
Union household	22	20	16	15	14	21	20	14	17	16	14	17	14	15	16	17	14	14	10	12	11	10	11
Regular churchgoer	40	43	52	47	46	40	38	40	42	49	47	43	49	46	44	43	43	47	51	50	54	51	53
Income: top third	47	36	41	41	47	39	36	46	41	39	46	40	40	49	40	37	39	44	48	43	43	42	39
White Protestant fundamentalist									13	13	12	12	10	14	12	17	17	21	21	22	21	21	17
Hispanic, non-Cuban													2	1	3	4	4	5	4	5	4	5	4
Born 1943–1958													33	31	38	37	34	30	35	35	33	30	33
Born 1959–1970													3	10	14	19	21	26	24	28	24	26	33
Born 1971–																		2	3	5	6	17	11

DATA SOURCE: 1952–2000 National Election Studies.

[a] These estimates, derived from the model, are virtually identical to the actual percentage of Republican identifiers.

[b] Figures derived from taking the mean predicted probability of Republican identification for a group in a particular year (Table 7.2) multiplied by that group's number of respondents, and dividing this product by the number of Republican identifiers.

[c] Native southern whites, 1952–1988; all southern whites, 1990–2000.

The changing group profiles of the parties can be seen in these figures, though with nuances that distinguish coalition composition from the marginal propensities shown earlier. Beginning with the Republicans, it is apparent in table 7.4 that Catholics, southern whites, and regular churchgoers are now a significant, perhaps dominant part of the party. White Southerners and Catholics, each one-quarter to one-third of the Republican Party's supporters, are now as large a proportion of Republican identifiers as they were of Democratic identifiers in the 1950s. In addition, white Protestant fundamentalists have managed to hold their own at about one-fifth of the party adherents, altogether making a formidable religious force. In contrast, members of union households, who at one time made up one-fifth of the Republican coalition despite their tilt toward the Democrats, make up no more than one-tenth of the Republican Party's supporters.

Given the current party makeup, the emphasis that President George W. Bush has placed on religious issues and organizations is understandable. Still, religious heterogeneity is apparent as well. Relatively speaking, fundamentalists have lost ground to Catholics, and fundamentalists have not always been happy with their influence on Republican Party doctrine. However, in the case of stem cell research, it appears to have been Catholic conservatives who were most unforgiving (Goodstein 2001). Bush's efforts in support of school vouchers are generally applauded by the right, but they could end up providing a substantial boost to Catholic schools, something the Protestant right is not happy about. Maintaining a coalition in which both Protestant fundamentalists and Catholics are major parts will not be easy.

In the Democratic Party, the biggest observable shifts are in the increasing proportions of women and Hispanics. Women, always a majority of the party, are now edging up to over three-fifths of Democratic identifiers. Further growth, if any, is likely to be slow because the group itself is not growing. Hispanics, on the other hand, are an expanding part of the overall population, and Republicans have had difficulty attracting them. This portion of the Democratic coalition is likely to become larger rather quickly unless President Bush is successful in his attempts to draw some of that support to the Republican side.

Democrats continue to be a diverse lot, however. Catholics, for example, continue to make up a substantial fraction of Democratic identifiers, despite the greatly diminished incremental probabilities noted earlier (table 7.3). Indeed, because of other changes in the Democratic coalition—the declining number of white Southerners (who are generally Protestant) and the growing number of Hispanics (who are generally Catholic)—there is a higher proportion of Catholics in the party now than in the 1950s and 1960s (ignoring the anomalous decline in 2000). African Americans, not surprisingly, also are a substantial proportion of Democratic identifiers, though their proportion has remained about the same over the past fifteen years. And members of union households, although declining among identifiers as union membership falls nationwide, are still about one-fifth of the Democratic following.

What would happen if a party lost its distinctive appeal for various members of its coalition? Because these groups have overlapping membership, at least some members would remain loyal to the party because of another of their group memberships. Here, we show results only for the Democratic coalition (table 7.3, second panel).[8] These results reinforce the importance of certain group memberships. African-American and Jewish supporters appear the most vulnerable, with members of union households not far behind. If the Democratic Party were to lose its appeal among these groups as such, support from those group members would fall sharply. Among Hispanics, in contrast, other characteristics would keep more of them under the Democratic banner, though the results for the most recent elections suggest that they are becoming a more vulnerable group as well.

Still, because of the diversity of the Democratic coalition, it is relatively resilient, as shown dramatically in the final panel in table 7.3. These figures show the effect that removing each group characteristic has on the size of the Democratic coalition. In recent years, the numbers dip below 90 percent only for African Americans and for women in 1996 and 2000. This suggests that the party would remain close to its current size even if it lost its specific appeal to any one group. Democratic efforts to appeal to a broad range of groups and to avoid being "captured" by any one of them have lessened their vulnerability to any given group. On the other hand, any systematic loss of support would loom large at a time when the party balance is as close as it was in the 2000 election.

Conclusion

From a long-term perspective, changes in the 1990s and the beginning of the twenty-first century could be viewed simply as a continuation of processes that began decades ago. The movement away from the Democratic Party by southern whites, for example, began in the 1960s. Catholics' lesser identification (lower incremental probabilities) with the Democrats began around 1980. The proportion of Democratic identifiers who are members of union households began to fall in the 1970s. And the Hispanic population and its contribution to the Democratic coalition have been on the rise for at least fifteen years.

Yet the changes that we see in the most recent data might well signal the beginning of a distinct new group basis for the party coalitions. Note, first of all, that several watershed changes have occurred very recently. Southern whites, perhaps for the first time ever, had an incremental push favorable to the Republicans in 2000, and in the past two elections they were estimated to be a greater fraction of Republican than of Democratic identifiers.

In 1996, members of union households sank to just one-fifth of all Democratic supporters and dropped a point further in the two subsequent elections. Hispanics, although not increasing their marginal support for the Democrats, are now a much more substantial fraction of the coalition, while the contribution of African Americans to the Democratic coalition has stabilized or is possibly declining.

Significantly, recent changes appear to be defining group support for the Republican Party more sharply than has been the case for many years. Regionally, the party now finds a strong base in the South, which is no longer just "less Democratic." Southern whites lean more toward the Republicans, and they make up a substantial part of the Republican coalition. This is, of course, apparent at the elite as well as the mass level. Even more noteworthy is the strong religious base of Republican identifiers, as Catholics, regular churchgoers, and Protestant fundamentalists have found greater favor with the Republican Party. This is also reflected at the elite level, as President Bush seeks religious support by his behavior and by his policies regarding abortion, faith-based initiatives on social policy, and, most recently, stem cell research.

The Democrats' coalition, in contrast, appears to have lost important group support that has not been replaced by the support of significant new groups. For decades, the party weathered the steady erosion of southern support without losing its majority in the House, though that erosion explains the Democrats' inability to elect more than an occasional president (all of whom since Lyndon Johnson in 1964 were from the South). By 1994, however, the loss of support from other groups, along with still-declining support from the South, left the Democrats unable to maintain their congressional majority. Not even the increased support of women, which had begun in the early 1980s, and the growing Hispanic population were sufficient to offset the loss of Catholic, union households, and regular churchgoing voters. Nor has the party been able to establish a firm partisan base among younger cohorts.

Overall, the problem for the Republicans is to maintain and enhance the coalition they have put together, including a fragile religious combination. A larger, more heterogeneous Republican coalition brings its own strains. Both parties vie for greater support among Hispanics. This group's population growth, and its geographic concentration in states rich with electoral college votes, such as California, Florida, and Texas, highlights the desirability of wooing and winning Hispanics. The problem for the Democrats is that they cannot remain content with their current partisan base. To be competitive and position themselves for electoral victory, Democrats must find new coalition partners or regain support that the party has lost. But how? Which group? An attractive prospect would be the youngest generation among the electorate, as neither party has a hold on this group's loyalties. But capturing the attention and the commitment of the young, though tempting, has proven to be a challenging test for partisans. The likelihood of bringing Catholics or southern whites back into the Democratic fold does not appear promising—and the prospects for recapturing union households or regular churchgoers appear only a tad more favorable.

If neither party gains a more dominant support coalition, the volatility in outcomes typical of the 1990s may continue for some time. Greater voter independence and a close partisan balance may characterize American party politics into the future.

8   The Enduring Gender Gap

KRISTIN KANTHAK AND BARBARA NORRANDER

The 2000 presidential election has been called the perfect tie, but if the election had been held only among men, or only among women, it would have been a landslide. Al Gore carried the women's vote in the Voter News Service (VNS) exit polls by 54 to 42 percent, and George W. Bush won among men by 53 to 43 percent. This gender gap in presidential voting is not new, but in 2000 for the first time polls showed that a majority of women voted for one candidate, and a majority of men supported the other.[1]

The gender gap in 2000 was notable because of the substantial efforts that both campaigns took to broaden their appeals (Brownstein 2000). George W. Bush's "compassionate conservative" campaign was carefully constructed to appeal to white women, and often during the campaign he surrounded himself at campaign stops with prominent GOP women. Al Gore's campaign sought to downplay his support for gun control, and consultants worked to create an image for him that would appeal to white men. These efforts cannot be labeled as failures, for in the absence of such appeals the gender gap might have been much larger than nine points. Nevertheless, it is striking that exit polls found a larger gender gap in 2000 than in 1996, despite clear efforts by both campaigns to narrow it.

The media discovered the gender gap in 1980, and though it has offered various explanations for it, social science research generally fails to confirm these explanations. During the 1980s, journalists frequently linked women's cooler attitudes toward Ronald Reagan to his opposition to the Equal Rights Amendment and the Republican platform's pro-life position. Yet scholars found that men and women held similar positions on those two issues and that the gender differences in support for Reagan were linked to social welfare and military issues (Gilens 1988; Mansbridge 1985).

Journalistic coverage of subsequent elections also frequently focused on gender themes. When a large number of new women were elected to Congress in 1992, journalists dubbed that election "The Year of the Woman." Media accounts linked the victory of these women candidates to the politicization of gender issues during George H. W. Bush's presidency, when the Supreme Court's 1989 *Webster* decision allowed states more leeway in regulating abortion, Bush vetoed the family leave bill, and Anita Hill charged that Supreme Court nominee Clarence Thomas sexually harassed her. Yet scholars argued that the success of these woman candidates was mostly attributable to their careful building of political careers in lower offices, their strategic move to take advantage of a large number of open-seat contests, ample campaign contributions, and a willingness by voters to support female candidates (Cook and Wilcox 1995).

With the Republican takeover of Congress in 1994, journalists looked for an explanation for the votes of the angry white males, who were supposedly upset over advantages given to African Americans and women by affirmative action programs. Yet support for such programs only slightly decreased in the early 1990s, and this decrease was uniform across all types of Americans. In other words, differences between men and women or African Americans and whites had not grown before the 1994 election (Citrin 1996; DiIulio 1997). Two years later, journalists were looking toward the vote of "soccer moms" as being key to the election outcome. *Newsweek* accredited Clinton's victory to the vote of these soccer moms, though African Americans, Latinos, Catholics, Jews, union members, and the poor all gave stronger percentages of votes to Clinton (DiIulio 1997; Nelson 1997). Journalists are quick to stamp a gender theme on recent elections. Social-science analysis confirms these gender patterns but for different reasons.

The Gender Gap in Context

In politics, men and women are more alike than they are different (Sapiro 2002). Both sexes rally behind a president during an international crisis, most men and women believe that women should have an equal role in politics, and both sexes often consider the state of the national economy when deciding which presidential candidate to support. On most issues, the majority of men and women fall on the same side, although often the percentage of men and women who take each position differs. These "gender gaps" on issues, partisanship, and candidate choices mostly range from between five to ten percentage points, but on some issues the differences are greater.

Gender differences are historically greatest on questions regarding the use of force, such as military intervention, gun control, and the death penalty. For example, in the 2000 National Election Study (NES), 69 percent of women versus 46 percent of men wanted tougher gun control laws, one of the largest gender gaps in the survey. Gender differences in policy preferences are also large on compassion issues. Women are more likely than men to support government aid to individuals experiencing economic difficulties, whereas men are more likely to believe in individual self-reliance. For example, in every NES survey from 1972 to 2000, men have on average been ten percentage points more likely than women to respond that "the government should just let each person get ahead on his/their own" rather than advocating that the government guarantee a job for everyone.[2] The gender gap on many compassion issues grew somewhat in 1980s but stabilized in size by the 1990s.

On moral issues women tend to be more conservative than men. For example, women are more likely than men to favor stronger government regulation of pornography, to oppose euthanasia, and to favor school prayer. In part, these differences stem from the fact that women are more religious than men. Gender differences are sporadic and inconsistent for women's issues, such as abortion or women's role in society (Shapiro and Mahajan 1986; Norrander 1999a; "Women and Men" 1982). Meanwhile, a gender gap in ideological identification first emerged in the 1980s and increased in the 1990s. Men, to a greater extent than women, began to label themselves as conservatives (Norrander 1999a).

The gender gap in partisanship predates the 1980 election and emerged from a slow secular realignment of partisan preferences that began in the 1960s (Abramowitz and Saunders 1998; Kaufmann and Petrocik 1999; Norrander 1999a, 1999b). Men, especially white southern men, increasingly became more Republican. White women in the South also became more Republican but at half the rate of southern men. Outside the South, white men moved into the Republican Party as well, at a pace slightly slower than southern women. White women's partisan preferences outside the South show no change over time (Norrander 1999b). Figure 8.1 traces male and female support nationwide, and for all races, for the Republican and Democratic parties. The partisan percentages include those independents who are leaning toward each party to compensate for men being slightly more likely to profess a leaning-independent identity and for women being slightly more likely to adopt a weak partisan label (Norrander 1997).

The top two lines of Figure 8.1 represent men's and women's preferences for the Democratic Party beginning in the earliest era. In the 1950s, women were less Democratic than men.[3] Between 1964 and the late 1980s, men's support for the Democratic Party declined sharply, while women's support declined at a slower rate. By the late 1980s, women's support for the Democratic Party was increasing, while men's remained constant. Men's

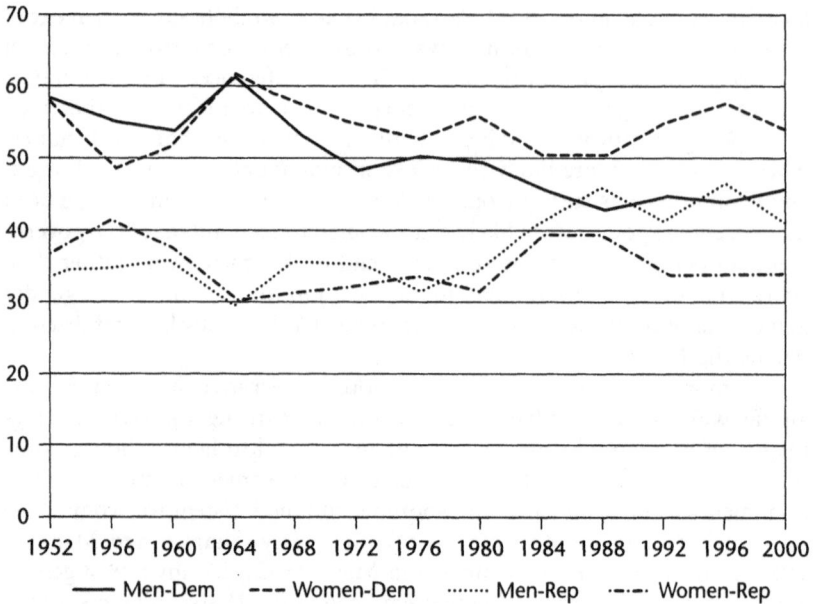

Men-Dem   --- Women-Dem   ········ Men-Rep   ·—·— Women-Rep

FIGURE 8.1   Male and Female Support for the Democratic and Republican Parties (Including Leaners), 1952–2000

and women's preferences for the Republican Party were fairly similar from 1960 to 1984. After that point, men's support for the Republican Party grew faster, while women's support of the party declined.

The widening of the partisan gender gap after 1990 may be due to two factors: the increased polarization of the political parties at the elite level in the 1980s and 1990s and the subsequent ideological realignment in citizens' partisan preferences (Abramowitz and Saunders 2002). The Reagan administration more clearly crystallized the conservative nature of the Republican Party. The two parties became more ideologically distinct in Congress as well, and these divisions became more apparent to the general public with the Republican takeover of Congress after the 1994 elections. Men's and women's differences on a host of issues as well as on ideological identifications may have led to divergent evaluations of the two more ideological parties. This resulted in the rise in support for the Republican Party among men and the increase in support for the Democratic Party among women.

Figure 8.2 illustrates how these changes in partisanship created a gender gap in partisan preferences and presidential election voting. The gender gap is measured as the difference in Democratic identification or voting for men versus women. The reverse gender gap held true in the 1950s, when women were less Democratic and voted less often for the Democratic candidate. These gender differences were statistically significant in the 1956 NES survey. The current gender gap in partisanship and presidential-vote choice first reached statistical significance in 1972, disappeared during the Carter election, and reemerged in the 1980s. Except for 1976, the gender gap in partisanship and voting tended to hover around five percentage points through the 1970s and 1980s. The gender gap grew in the 1990s, with both the partisan and electoral gender gaps peaking around fifteen percentage points in 1996. In 2000, the partisan gender gap stood at seven percentage points, and the gender gap for Al Gore and George W. Bush on Election Day stood at nine percentage points, according to the NES survey.

The Gender Gap in the 2000 Presidential Election Cycle

Both candidates aggressively courted women's votes in the 2000 election. George W. Bush relied on his mother, former First Lady Barbara Bush, and his wife, Laura Bush, to help him appeal to women voters, with tactics such as their "W Stands for Women" campaign tour. At the same time, Gore placed his daughter Karenna Gore Schiff in charge of Gorenet, a group created to increase political participation among younger voters. Gore also relied on Karenna to shore up votes and motivate volunteers during the New Hampshire primary (Cobb 2000; Roberts and Roberts 2000) and enlisted actresses Sharon Stone and Christine Lahti as well as feminist activist Gloria Steinem to campaign on his behalf (Marinucci 2000).

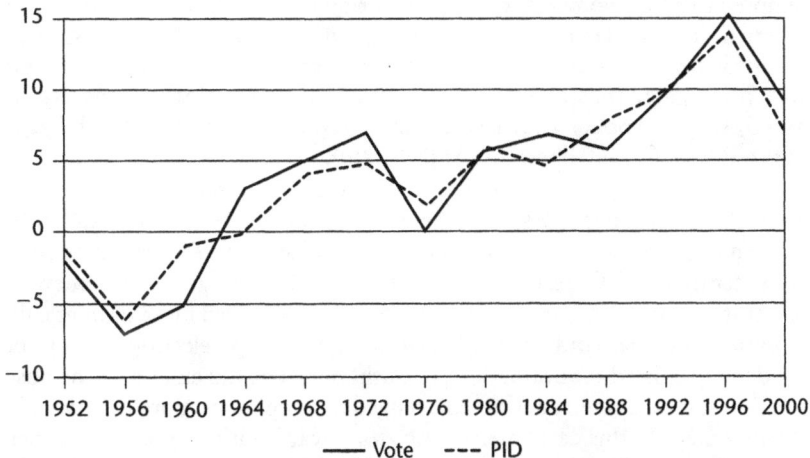

FIGURE 8.2   Gender Gap in Presidential Vote and Party Identification, 1952–2000

TABLE **8.1**   Gender gap in candidate preferences in 2000 election

	Gore	Bush	Gore–Bush	Nader	Buchanan	Clinton
Preelection Survey						
Men	54.6	57.3	−2.7	51.3	39.2	55.4
Women	59.4	56.1	3.1	52.6	42.7	56.5
t-ratio	−3.97	.97	−2.90	−.98	−3.04	−.73
Sig.	.00	.33	.00	.33	.00	.46
N	1773	1761	1745	1253	1456	1795
Postelection Survey						
Men	50.1	58.6	−8.5	47.2		52.4
Women	57.5	55.2	2.5	48.1		55.4
t-ratio	−5.09	2.48	−4.43	−.76		−1.99
Sig.	.00	.01	.00	.45		.05
N	1526	1530	1519	1262		1530

DATA SOURCE: *2000 National Election Study.*
NOTE: *Entries are mean thermometer ratings. Evaluations of Buchanan were not asked in the postelection survey.*

At the same time, candidates on both sides of the aisle worked hard to bridge the gender gap, with Democrats courting male voters and Republicans wooing female voters. Democratic pollster Stan Greenberg wrote a memo to Democratic candidates entitled "Winning Back Men," in which he outlined how Democrats could increase their appeal among male voters. Gore adopted a more populist stance and downplayed his support for gun control to appeal to working-class white male voters. Bush, meanwhile, attempted to court women voters by appearing on *The Oprah Winfrey Show*, where he discussed issues such as marriage and his wife's difficult pregnancy. Bush further attempted to bring more women into the Republican camp with a campaign theme that described him as a compassionate conservative and by stressing policies such as education reform (Brownstein 2000; Eagan 2000; Edsall 2000; Gilbert and Skiba 2000).

To gauge how these candidates' strategies affected the gender gap, Table 8.1 lists the average thermometer ratings of the presidential candidates by men and women in the preelection and postelection NES surveys. Women consistently rated Gore higher than did men, but the gap was somewhat larger in the postelection survey as men's attitudes cooled more dramatically toward Gore than did women's attitudes. In the preelection survey, no gender gap existed for evaluations of Bush, but a gap did emerge in the postelection survey, as men once again changed their opinions more dramatically than women. In this case, men's attitudes toward Bush increased by 6 percentage points. The third column in Table 8.1 combines attitudes toward both of the major candidates by subtracting Bush's thermometer rating from

Gore's thermometer rating. In the preelection survey, the average male re-spondent rated Bush nearly 3 percentage points higher than Gore while the average female respondent rated Gore 3 percentage points higher than Bush. The size of the preference gap grew considerably larger for men in the postelection period, with their ratings of Bush increasing to 8.5 percent-age points over Gore. Women's postelection preferences more closely mir-rored their preelection preferences, with a 2.5-percentage-point lead for Gore over Bush.

The thermometer ratings also enable us to test for a gender gap for the two minor-party candidates in the 2000 election as well as for President Bill Clinton. Ralph Nader experienced no gender gap in preferences in either time period, and his ratings cooled among both sexes in the postelection survey. Evaluations of Buchanan were gauged only in the preelection survey, but showed a statistically significant gender gap. Women rated Buchanan somewhat more highly than did men. In some aspects, this is an odd pattern since in the past men were more likely than women to support third-party candidates. Perhaps Buchanan's strong antiabortion stand attracted support from some conservative women. Also unusual is the disappearance of the gender gap for Bill Clinton in the preelection survey. After all, it was during Clinton's presidency that the gender gap grew to its largest margins. Maybe both sexes participate equally in the phenomenon in which presidential evaluations tend to rise at the close of their administration. Nevertheless, the gender gap in evaluations of Bill Clinton reemerged in the postelection wave as men's attitudes toward Clinton cooled.

Sources of the Gender Gap in the 2000 Presidential Election

Gender differences in election choices can be manifested in two ways. First, men and women can hold different opinions on the issues that influ-ence presidential vote choices. For example, the social-psychological model posits a central role for party identification in voting decisions, and we know that men and women hold different partisan preferences. If the entire gender gap in candidate preferences could be explained by distributional differences on partisanship and issues, then gender would not have a direct effect on vote choice. The coefficient for gender would be statistically insig-nificant when used in a multivariate equation along with partisanship and issues. Gender would affect voters' choices indirectly through differences in issue positions. However, some gender differences in issue opinions may not affect the electoral gender gap because these issues do not influence voters' choices in the specific election. For example, men and women hold quite dis-tinctive opinions on whether gays should be allowed to serve in the military, but opinions on this issue did not influence voters' preferences for presiden-tial candidates in the 2000 election.

TABLE **8.2**   Distributional differences in partisanship, ideology, and issue positions

	Men	Women	Difference	t-ratio	Sig.	N
Party Identification	.48	.43	.06	3.42	.00	1723
Ideology	.58	.54	.04	2.74	.01	1558
Personal Economy	.41	.44	−.03	−2.66	.01	1620
National Economy	.44	.45	−.01	−.82	.41	1735
Isolationism	.71	.68	.03	1.24	.21	1688
Defense Budget	.63	.59	.04	2.69	.01	1333
Death Penalty	.74	.69	.05	2.54	.01	1653
Gun Control	.33	.19	.14	11.28	.00	1735
Government Services	.46	.39	.07	4.53	.00	1426
Guaranteed Job	.65	.58	.08	4.36	.00	1522
Health Insurance	.48	.45	.03	1.74	.08	1554
Environment versus Jobs	.39	.40	−.01	−.98	.33	1508
Environmental Regulations	.39	.33	.05	3.24	.00	1263
Government Aid to Blacks	.62	.61	.00	.09	.93	1478
Affirmative Action – Blacks	.81	.77	.04	2.08	.04	1583
Gays in the Military	.39	.21	.18	9.10	.00	1641
Abortion	.38	.39	−.01	−.34	.73	1703
Women's Role	.17	.13	.05	3.57	.00	1688

DATA SOURCE: *2000 National Election Study.*
NOTE: *Entries are mean opinions of men and women. All issues have been recoded to a 0 to 1 scale. Higher values indicate conservative opinions, internationalist opinion, and worsening views of the economy. Only respondents who rated both Gore and Bush in the preelection survey are included.*

The second way in which gender differences can emerge in electoral choices is if men and women place different weights on specific issues when choosing among the candidates. In other words, the coefficient of influence for a specific issue would be different for men and women. A number of analyses attempt to show that men and women place different emphases on issues by displaying separate multivariate equations for men and women. That procedure, however, does not test whether differences in coefficients meet criteria for statistical significance. One method for testing the statistical difference between the emphases that men and women place on specific issues is to use a multivariate equation that combines both sexes but uses interaction terms between gender and each of the other independent variables. Statistically significant interaction effects indicate that men and women place different emphases on an issue.

Table 8.2 presents information on the distributional differences in men's and women's opinions on a number of issues during the 2000 presidential election.[4] Each of the variables has been recoded to a zero-to-one scale. Most have been coded so that a higher score indicates a more conservative opinion. High scores on partisanship indicate Republican identification. High scores on personal and national economic evaluations indicate a sense of a worsening economic situation. High scores on the internationalism variable indicate an acceptance of an internationalist role. Twelve of the issues have statistically significant gender gaps, with men being more likely than women to be Republican and to hold more conservative positions on all the issue questions. Women were more pessimistic about their own economic fortunes, but unlike other election years did not differ from men in evaluations of the national economy (Chaney, Alvarez and Nagler 1998). The largest gender differences were for gays in the military and gun control. Also showing somewhat large gender gaps were opinions on the level of government services, the government's role in guaranteeing jobs, and environmental regulation. The lack of a statistically significant difference between the two sexes on the other environmental issues (environmental regulations versus jobs) fits well with past evidence that women are more "green" on only some environmental questions (Tolleson-Rinehart and Somma 1997).

To test for emphasis differences in the 2000 election, we performed a regression analysis in which the dependent variable was the differences in thermometer ratings between Gore and Bush (Gore thermometer rating minus Bush thermometer rating) in the preelection survey.[5] Table 8.3 presents results of this regression analysis. Gender had no direct effect on voters' candidate preferences since the regression coefficient for sex is statistically insignificant. Thus, the gender gap in 2000 can be explained by distributional and emphasis differences on the other issues in the analysis. Six variables had significant direct effects on voters' preferences: partisanship, evaluations of the national economy, preferences for defense-spending levels, the government's role in guaranteeing jobs, environmental regulation, and abortion. Opinions on gun control are marginally significant ($p \leq .10$ level), and in a regression equation that lacks interaction effects these opinions do have a statistically significant effect ($p \leq .01$ level). Only three emphasis differences were uncovered. Women weighed ideology more heavily than did men in evaluating Bush and Gore, while men weighed opinions on government services and government guarantee of jobs more heavily than did women. Ideology may have a different meaning for men than for women. A study of European public opinion found that men's ideological identification was shaped mostly by economic issues, while women's ideological identification included traditional values as well as economic positions (Jelen, Thomas, and Wilcox 1994). Thus, the lack of influence that ideology had on men's vote choice in the 2000 election may be due to a greater overlap of ideology with their opinions on government services and government size, which are also included in the regression model. Finally, some past analysis has argued that women are more likely to emphasize sociotropic evaluations and men are more likely to be pocketbook voters (Welch and Hibbing 1992). However, these patterns tend not to be statistically significant (Norrander 1998), and such was the case in the 2000 election as well.

We found a number of distributional and three emphasis differences for candidate preferences in the 2000 election. Table 8.4 combines these two

TABLE **8.3**   Emphasis differences across sexes in determinants of comparative candidate
preferences during the 2000 presidential election

	Simple Effects		Interactive Effects			
	b (Std. Err.)	Sig.	b (Std. Err.)	Sig.	b Male	b Female
Gender (1 = women)	−2.48 (5.76)	.67				
Party Identification	−63.36 (3.95)	.00	−.93 (5.12)	.86		
Ideology	−7.00 (4.40)	.11	−16.93 (5.32)	.00	−7.00	−23.93
Personal Economy	−1.72 (4.84)	.72	5.17 (6.00)	.39		
National Economy	−11.70 (3.77)	.00	−3.79 (5.09)	.46		
Internationalism	.16 (2.35)	.94	−3.21 (3.08)	.30		
Defense Budget	−12.43 (3.86)	.00	.10 (4.39)	.98		
Death Penalty	−4.54 (2.91)	.12	4.16 (3.67)	.26		
Gun Control	−7.30 (4.36)	.09	−9.33 (5.99)	.12		
Government Services	−8.26 (4.33)	.06	10.63 (5.49)	.05	−8.26	2.37
Guaranteed Job	−8.49 (3.57)	.02	9.94 (4.30)	.02	−8.49	1.45
Health Insurance	2.76 (3.46)	.42	−4.54 (4.34)	.30		
Environment versus Jobs	−2.55 (3.91)	.51	5.89 (4.93)	.23		
Environment Regulation	−13.48 (4.28)	.00	2.23 (5.41)	.68		
Gov't Aid to Blacks	−1.38 (3.64)	.70	−1.17 (4.37)	.79		
Affirmative Action for Blacks	−3.74 (3.34)	.26	1.69 (4.03)	.68		
Gays in Military	−1.73 (2.77)	.53	−2.04 (4.10)	.62		
Abortion	−14.79 (3.27)	.00	3.38 (4.21)	.42		
Women's Role	.50 (4.23)	.91	.07 (5.90)	.99		
Constant	74.93 (4.69)	.00				
R^2	.53					
N	1745					

DATA SOURCE: *2000 National Election Study.*

TABLE 8.4 Sources of gender differences in 2000 presidential election

	Distributional Differences		Emphasis Differences			Level-Importance Statistic		
	Men Mean	Women Mean	b – both	b – men	b – women	Men	Women	Diff.
Party Identification	.48	.43	-63.36			-30.41	-27.24	-3.17
Ideology	.58	.54		-7.00	-23.93	-4.06	-12.92	8.86
Personal Economy	.41	.44	-11.70					
National Economy								
Internationalism								
Defense Budget	.63	.59	-12.43			-7.83	-7.33	-.50
Death Penalty	.74	.69						
Gun Control	.33	.19	(-7.30)			(-2.41)	(-1.39)	(-1.02)
Government Services	.46	.39		-8.26	2.37	-3.80	.92	-4.72
Guaranteed Job	.65	.58		-8.49	1.45	-5.52	.84	-6.36
Health Insurance								
Environment versus Jobs								
Environmental Regulations	.39	.33	-13.48			-5.26	-4.45	-.81
Government Aid to Blacks	.81	.77						
Affirmative Action – Blacks	.39	.21						
Gays in the Military								
Abortion	.17	.13	-14.79					
Women's Role								

DATA SOURCE: 2000 National Election Study.
NOTE: All coefficients and differences between means are statistically significant at the .05 level, except for those listed in parentheses.

effects with a level-importance statistic that multiplies the regression coefficient by the mean value of the independent variables (Achen 1982, 72–73). (If level-importance values were devised for all of the independent variables and were added to the constant from the regression equation [here 74.93] they would reproduce the mean value on the dependent variable.) To illustrate gender differences, separate level-importance statistics are reported for each sex, but only when these differences are significant. Gender differences become significant in three ways: (1) statistically significant distributional differences on issues that influenced voters' choices in the election, (2) men and women placing different emphases on an issue when making their choices, and (3) both distributional and emphasis differences.

Table 8.4 shows that three issues with distributional differences influenced the electoral gender gap because these issues also were linked to voters' choices. Distributional differences on partisanship, levels of defense spending, and environmental regulations translated into differential support for the two candidates. Distributional differences on gun control also may matter, though the significance level of the regression coefficient may be more marginal. Three of the issues that shaped voters' preferences in the 2000 election did not translate into the gender gap in candidate preferences because there were no distributional differences in opinions on these issues. Men and women held similar opinions on the national economy, internationalism, and abortion. Five issues (personal economy, death penalty, affirmative action, gays in the military, and women's role) on which there were distributional differences did not shape the electoral gender gap because these issues did not influence voters' choices in the 2000 election. No issue translated into gender differences in voters' choices based solely on emphasis differences. Rather, the remaining three issues (ideology, government services, government jobs) had both distributional and emphasis differences.

Seven attitudes account for the gender gap in candidate preferences in the 2000 presidential election. Because all of the independent variables were recoded to the same zero-to-one scale, gender differences in the sizes of the level-importance statistics can tell which of the issues had the strongest influences on the gender gap. The final column in Table 8.4 lists these differences. Having the most sizable impact on the gender gap in the 2000 presidential election were distributional and emphasis differences on ideology. Women were less conservative than men and placed more weight on ideology than men in choosing between the two candidates. Meanwhile, significant differences arose for men's support of the two candidates in that men were more conservative and placed more weight on the issues of government services and government guarantee of jobs. Men and women emphasized partisanship at the same level, but because men are more Republican and women more Democratic, partisanship was the fourth component to the electoral gender gap. The remaining three issues (defense budget, gun control, environmental regulations) had lesser effects on the gender gap in the 2000 election.

The Gender Gap in the 2000 Congressional Elections

Congressional elections provide a very different means for exploring the gender gap in the 2000 election because, unlike presidential elections, both female and male candidates competed for congressional seats. Female candidates were common in the 2000 election. Indeed, there were fifty-three women incumbents, fifty-six women challengers, and thirteen female candidates in open-seat races. In eleven congressional districts, both the challenger and the incumbent candidates were women. In total, one-quarter of the 2000 congressional elections had a female candidate. Further, the 2000 election resulted in a record thirteen female senators and fifty-nine members of the House. The increasing number of female candidates allows us to discern how a potential gender gap may develop.

Two types of gender gaps could occur in congressional elections. First, female voters may show greater preferences for Democratic congressional candidates than do male voters. This form of the gender gap would be similar to that found at the presidential level. The question, however, might be whether or not this gender gap would primarily reflect a core gender gap in partisanship, as voters may not have sufficient information about congressional candidates to differentiate them from general party traits (e.g., Democratic candidates are more liberal than Republican candidates). A second form of gender gap possible at the congressional level is for the presence of female candidates to influence gender patterns in voting. Are female voters more likely than male voters to support female candidates?

Most of the research on a gender gap in voting analyzes presidential or statewide elections. A few studies of congressional elections find a gender gap influencing voters' choices, though this may occur for only certain types of congressional elections or may disappear when the partisanship of voters is controlled (Cook 1998; Mattei and Mattei 1998). Similarly, most studies searching for the effects of female candidates on voters' choices analyze other electoral settings or use experiments involving hypothetical candidates. Among the studies of congressional elections, Dolan (1998) found that women were more willing than men to vote for female congressional candidates, but McDermott (1997) found no gender difference in support of female candidates.

We investigate a gender gap in congressional elections by using the same methodology we employed to investigate the gender gap in the presidential election. The dependent variable is the level by which the Democratic candidate's thermometer score exceeds or falls below that of the Republican candidate. Because voters are less familiar with congressional candidates, instead of investigating the effects of a list of issue attitudes, the congressional model uses only measures of respondents' partisanship and ideology. Incumbent candidates possess a number of advantages (Wright 1993) that lead them to be reelected at high rates. Thus, we add two dummy variables to measure whether the incumbent candidate is a Democrat or a Republican. Finally, we add three variables that measure the presence of a female candidate as either an incumbent, challenger, or candidate in an open-seat race. These three variables are coded (1) for a Democratic female candidate, (0) for no female candidate, and (−1) for a Republican female candidate.[6] We test whether men and women evaluate female candidates differently by using an interaction term between gender and each of the types of female candidates.

First, we find little evidence of a gender gap in voters' evaluations of congressional candidates. On average, male respondents evaluated Republican candidates one point higher than Democratic candidates (score on dependent variable = −.88), while female respondents rated Democratic candidates slightly higher (2.30). A simple difference-of-means test shows no statistically significant difference between the ratings given by men and women ($t = -1.20$, sign. = .231). These evaluations, however, may be confounded by variations in the partisanship of incumbent candidates and the presence of female candidates. Thus, we turn to the regression analysis presented in Table 8.5.

The regression analysis continues to show no gender gap in evaluations of congressional candidates beyond what might be explained by distributional differences in partisanship or ideology. The gender variable is statistically insignificant. Further, respondents as a whole did not rate male candidates higher than female candidates, as evidenced by the lack of statistical significance on the variables for female incumbents, challengers, or open-seat contestants. The dummy variables measuring the incumbency advantages are in the appropriate direction, but only the Republican variable approaches significance.

Is it possible that women rate female candidates more highly than men, thus creating a congressional gender gap that is disguised in the simple effects regression? The results of the interaction effects in Table 8.5 show that this is not the case.[7] Women and men rated female candidates the same. The source of any gender gap in congressional elections appears to be due solely to distributional differences in partisanship and ideology. Men and women do not emphasize these two factors differently (i.e., the interaction terms are statistically insignificant), but distributional differences on partisanship and ideology lead men to rate Democratic candidates more negatively than do women.

TABLE **8.5**   Gender gap in comparative evaluations of candidates in 2000 House elections

	Simple Effects		Interactive Effects		Level-Importance Statistics		
	b (Std. Err.)	Sig.	b (Std. Err.)	Sig.	Men	Women	Diff.
Female	−4.76 (4.70)	.31					
Party Identification	−37.30 (5.37)	.00	.29 (7.05)	.97	−18.34	−15.30	−3.04
Ideology	−25.78 (6.78)	.00	7.51 (8.39)	.37	−15.62	−13.53	−2.09
Democratic Incumbent	5.00 (3.54)	.16					
Republican Incumbent	−5.98 (3.55)	.09					
Female Incumbent	4.68 (5.82)	.42	−1.96 (8.13)	.81			
Female Challenger	−.52 (4.67)	.91	−2.47 (5.96)	.68			
Female Open Seat	3.03 (10.33)	.77	−13.56 (12.93)	.29			
Constant	33.22 (4.66)	.00					
R^2	.32	.00					
N	573						

DATA SOURCE: *2000 National Election Study.*
NOTE: *Dependent variable is Democratic candidate thermometer score minus Republican candidate thermometer scores. Female candidates are scored: (−1) female Republican candidate, (0) no female candidate, and (1) female Democratic candidate.*

Conclusion

The gender gap in presidential voting grew slightly in 2000 despite carefully planned appeals by both campaigns aimed at reducing it. Men gave Bush a clear majority of their votes, and women did the same for Gore. The perfect tie of the 2000 election was the result of two offsetting votes, with majorities of men and women voting differently. If the Republicans could increase their appeal among women, or the Democrats increase theirs among men, it would have a significant impact on electoral politics. Yet the gender gap persists despite the efforts of the parties' elites to close it.

The gender gap persists because it is anchored in core identities, such as partisanship and ideology, and in basic beliefs about the role of government. In congressional elections as well, gender differences in evaluations of candidates are shaped primarily by gender differences in partisanship and ideology. There is little evidence that male and female voters react differently to women candidates. But why do men and women differ so much in their core identities and beliefs about government?

Men and women hold different positions on some issues and base their vote decisions on a different mix of issues. In 2000, there were several issues, such as affirmative action and gays in the military, where men and women held different positions but on which neither sex based their vote decisions. On some other issues, such as defense spending and environmental regulations, the gender gap had an impact because men and women both based their vote decision on them.

The largest source of the gender gap in the 2000 election, however, was on three issues—ideology, government services, and governmental jobs. On these, men and women held different views and differed in the impact those views had on their vote. Men and women have different expectations about what government can and should do to help disadvantaged groups, and these differences were a major source of the gap in the 2000 elections. At the start of the twenty-first century, the gender gap in presidential elections had existed for more than thirty years, and it appears to be poised to influence future elections. But the lesson of the 2000 election is that the gender gap is an ideological and role-of-government gap. Candidates concerned about mitigating the effects of a gender gap would do well to emphasize issues rather than daytime talk-show appearances and passionate postconvention-speech kisses.

APPENDIX

TABLE **8A.1** Emphasis differences across sexes in determinants of comparative candidate preferences during the 2000 presidential election (using listwise deletion of cases)

	Simple Effects		Interactive Effects			
	b (Std. Err.)	Sig.	b (Std. Err.)	Sig.	b Male	b Female
Gender (1 = women)	−6.68 (12.32)	.59				
Party Identification	−61.18 (6.10)	.00	−4.11 (8.63)	.63		
Ideology	−13.23 (7.20)	.07	−21.49 (10.22)	.04	−13.23	−34.72
Personal Economy	4.35 (7.46)	.56	8.37 (10.65)	.43		
National Economy	−12.16 (5.84)	.04	−10.45 (8.52)	.22		
Internationalism	2.20 (3.89)	.57	−6.27 (5.63)	.27		
Defense Budget	−18.53 (7.00)	.01	7.84 (10.00)	.43		
Death Penalty	.43 (4.63)	.93	7.69 (6.38)	.23		
Gun Control	−10.52 (6.57)	.11	−4.09 (9.74)	.67		
Government Services	−17.54 (6.85)	.01	20.82 (9.87)	.04	−17.54	3.28
Guaranteed Job	−13.05 (6.59)	.05	−3.09 (9.13)	.74		
Health Insurance	8.31 (5.62)	.14	3.19 (7.66)	.68		
Environment versus Jobs	−.10 (6.81)	.99	.44 (10.17)	.97		
Environment Regulation	−11.18 (7.46)	.13	−4.81 (10.50)	.65		
Gov't Aid to Blacks	1.50 (6.95)	.83	−5.51 (9.81)	.57		
Affirmative Action for Blacks	6.80 (5.90)	.25	7.20 (8.71)	.41		
Gays in Military	−3.35 (4.10)	.41	−3.42 (7.19)	.63		
Abortion	−16.60 (5.23)	.00	9.68 (7.30)	.19		
Women's Role	5.23 (6.71)	.44	11.15 (10.76)	.30		
Constant	66.28 (7.74)	.00				
R^2	.64					
N	592					

DATA SOURCE: *2000 National Election Study.*

TABLE **8A.2** Gender gap in comparative evaluations of candidates in 2000 House elections (using listwise deletion of cases)

	Simple Effects		Interactive Effects	
	b (Std. Err.)	Sig.	b (Std. Err.)	Sig.
Female	−5.19 (5.39)	.34		
Party Identification	−36.84 (5.59)	.00	.68 (7.35)	.93
Ideology	−26.45 (7.36)	.00	7.69 (9.54)	.42
Democratic Incumbent	2.91 (3.66)	.43		
Republican Incumbent	−7.12 (3.65)	.05		
Female Incumbent	5.79 (6.46)	.37	−2.70 (8.85)	.76
Female Challenger	−1.92 (4.85)	.69	−1.10 (6.12)	.86
Female Open Seat	3.91 (11.02)	.72	−15.39 (13.62)	.26
Constant	34.70 (5.06)	.00		
R^2	.32			
N	534			

DATA SOURCE: *2000 National Election Study.*
NOTE: *Dependent variable is Democratic candidate thermometer score minus Republican candidate thermometer score. Female candidates are scored: (−1) female Republican candidate, (0) no female candidate; and (1) female Democratic candidate.*

III *Beyond the Two-Party Presidential Vote*

9 A Decline in Ticket Splitting and the Increasing Salience of Party Labels

DAVID C. KIMBALL

> The voice of the people is but an echo chamber. The output of an echo chamber bears an inevitable and invariable relation to the input. As candidates and parties clamor for attention and vie for popular support, the people's verdict can be no more than a selective reflection from among the alternatives and outlooks presented to them.
>
> —V. O. Key, *The Responsible Electorate*

Split party control of the executive and legislative branches has been a defining feature of American national politics for more than thirty years, the longest period of frequent divided government in American history. Even when voters failed to produce a divided national government in the 2000 elections, the party defection of a lone U.S. senator (former Republican James Jeffords of Vermont) created yet another divided national government. In addition, the extremely close competitive balance between the two major parties means that ticket splitters often determine which party controls each branch of government. These features of American politics have stimulated a lot of theorizing about the causes of split-ticket voting.

In recent years, the presence of divided government and relatively high levels of split-ticket voting are commonly cited as evidence of an electorate that has moved beyond party labels (Wattenberg 1998). Another theory holds that some voters split their ballots in a strategic fashion to produce divided government and moderate policies (Fiorina 1996; Alesina and Rosenthal 1995). However, the 2000 and 2002 elections narrowly produced a unified national government as ticket splitting declined to the lowest levels in over thirty years. What explains the decline in ticket splitting? How strong is the public preference for divided government, and what happened to divided government and ticket splitters in the 2000 election?

Under what might be called a "party-salience theory of voting," the decline in ticket splitting is best understood as a public response to elite polarization along party and ideological lines. The ideological distance between the major parties determines the salience of party labels and ideological considerations when voters cast their ballots. Voters who see important differences between the parties are more likely to rely on party and ideology when casting their ballots. In contrast, voters who see no ideological differ-

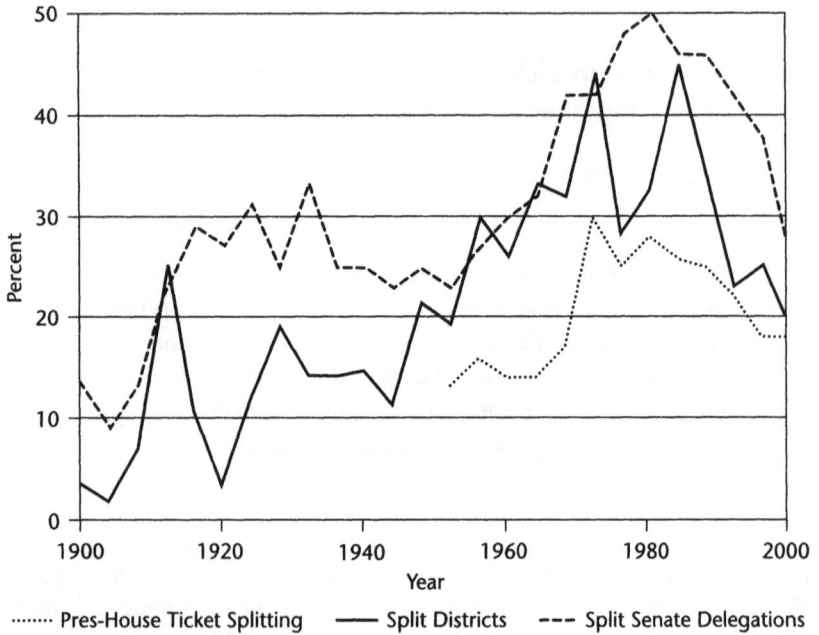

50 ┤

40 ┤

Percent

30 ┤

20 ┤

10 ┤

0 ┤

1900   1920   1940   1960   1980   2000

Year

········ Pres-House Ticket Splitting   ——— Split Districts   – – – Split Senate Delegations

figure 9.1   Indicators of Ticket Splitting, 1900–2000

ences between the parties are more likely to rely on nonpolicy considerations when voting and are more likely to be ticket splitters. As the political parties have engaged in sharp policy disputes and become more unified around ideological messages, voters have come to see politics in more partisan terms. Thus, ticket splitting has declined as the ideological gulf between the major political parties has grown wider. These developments reinforce the idea that the collective choices of American voters are, in part, a response to the ideological reputations of the parties in government.

The Recent Decline in Ticket Splitting

By a number of measures, major-party ticket splitting in national elections declined substantially over the past twenty years. Figure 9.1 displays the percentage of split congressional districts (i.e., districts carried by a presidential candidate of one party and House candidate of another party), the percentage of split Senate delegations (since 1900), and the percentage of major-party president-House ticket splitters (since 1952).[1] The same pattern is evident from all three measures: increasing levels of ticket splitting from the 1950s to the 1980s and a significant decline thereafter. In addition, the 2000 elections produced the lowest levels of ticket splitting observed in several decades. The frequency of president-House ticket splitting in 2000 (18%) is the lowest observed since 1968. The number of split districts in 2000 (86) is the fewest since 1952, and the number of split Senate delegations in 2000 (14) is the lowest observed since 1956.

Given the closely competitive partisan environment in recent elections, there remains a nontrivial amount of ticket splitting in the United States. However, the frequency of ticket splitting in national elections has dropped to levels last seen in the 1950s and 1960s. This substantial drop in ticket splitting is consistent with evidence of increased partisanship in the mass public during the past twenty years (Miller 1991; Bartels 2000; Hetherington 2001; Jacobson 2001; Weisberg 2002b). These developments require an explanation, and they provide us with an opportunity to test theories of split-ticket voting.

Theories of Ticket Splitting

Theories of split-ticket voting abound. One explanation attributes the bulk of ticket-splitting behavior to "candidate-centered politics" (Wattenberg 1991). According to this point of view, weakening party loyalties among voters, an increasing reliance on mass-media communications in campaigns (often bypassing party organizations), a growing incumbency advantage, and (until recently) a Democratic advantage in fielding quality candidates for Congress all produced increasing levels of ticket splitting (Wattenberg 1991, 1998; Jacobson 1990). From this perspective, ticket splitting is a by-product of independent voting decisions that rely heavily on candidate characteristics as opposed to partisan or ideological considerations (Burden and Kimball 2002, 1998).

From the candidate-centered perspective, a potential explanation for the recent drop in ticket splitting might focus on congressional incumbency. Abundant evidence indicates that the incumbency advantage in congressional elections is an important source of ticket splitting (McAllister and Darcy 1992; Alvarez and Schousen 1993; Born 1994; Burden and Kimball 1998; Born 2000a; Mattei and Howes 2000; Garand and Lichtl 2000). Perhaps the incumbency advantage has declined during the 1990s, prompting a concomitant decline in ticket splitting? As it turns out, however, one common measure (Gelman and King 1990) indicates that the incumbency advantage remained large throughout the 1990s. In fact, the 2000 election produced the largest incumbency advantage observed during an on-year election over the past one hundred years.

The candidate-centered approach also emphasizes the strength of partisanship among voters. It is well documented that strength of partisanship is inversely related to ticket splitting: strong partisans are less likely to split their tickets than independents (Campbell et al. 1960; Campbell and Miller 1957). The recent drop in ticket splitting can be partly explained by a slight drop in the proportion of pure independents and a slight increase in the proportion of strong partisans in the electorate (Weisberg 2002b; Bartels 2000). In addition, there is evidence that party loyalty in voting has increased since the 1980s (Bartels 2000). The candidate-centered approach provides a sound explanation for rising ticket splitting in the 1960s and 1970s, but it requires some elaboration to account for the recent drop in ticket splitting. In particular, this chapter argues that growing party polarization among elites has helped the parties overcome, to some extent, the candidate-centered nature of campaigns by strengthening mass partisanship.

Another theory of ticket splitting emphasizes certain structural features of the American electoral system. The Australian ballot (Rusk 1970) increases the likelihood of ticket splitting. At the same time, straight-party ("one-punch") ballot devices and the party-column ballot format (Campbell and Miller 1957; McAllister and Darcy 1992; Kimball 1997; Burden and Kimball 1998) reduce ticket splitting by modest amounts. However, ballot format cannot account for the drop in ticket splitting, since states have gradually been eliminating the party-column ballot as well as one-punch devices designed to promote straight-party voting (Kimball, Owens, and McLaughlin 2002).

A third explanation of ticket splitting is "policy balancing" (Fiorina 1988, 1996). This theory posits that moderate voters behave strategically and split their ballots in order to strike a balance between two ideologically extreme parties, which produces divided government and middle-of-the-road policies (also see Alesina and Rosenthal 1995; Ingberman and Villani 1993; Lacy and Niou 1998; Lacy and Paolino 1998; Smith, Brown, Bruce, and Overby 1999; Mebane 2000; Mebane and Sekhon 2002). With national elections in the 1990s perpetuating divided government, it has become common for political pundits and leaders of both parties to speculate that American voters prefer divided government and strategically split their tickets as a result (Kimball 1997; Lang, Lang, and Crespi 1998).[2]

One way in which policy-balancing theories might explain the recent decline in ticket splitting is if fewer voters now see divided government as desirable. However, slightly more than half of the respondents to the 2000 survey conducted by the National Election Studies expressed a preference for divided government, and earlier surveys show similar levels of support for divided government (Petrocik and Doherty 1996). Although this survey question is not a good predictor of voting behavior, it suggests that voters have not grown weary of divided government (Beck et al. 1992; Sigelman, Wahlbeck, and Buell 1997; Lacy and Paolino 1998). Alternatively, perhaps moderate voters (those with the strongest ideological motivation for ticket splitting) comprise a smaller share of the voting public today than in the 1970s. However, the share of moderates in the electorate has remained stable for the past twenty years, including 2000 (National Election Studies 1995–

2000). Thus, it does not appear that a substantial change in voter preferences led to the decline in ticket splitting.

However, if moderate voters are inclined to balance control of government between two ideologically polarized parties, and if the share of moderates in the electorate remains stable, then ticket splitting should increase in frequency when the parties move further apart on the ideological spectrum. As Fiorina hypothesizes: "When the parties are relatively close, near the center of gravity of the electorate, ticket splitting declines. When the parties move away from each other, following their own internal dynamics toward the extremes of the voter distribution, they open up a large policy range in which ticket splitting is the voter response" (Fiorina 1996, 81). Thus, the policy-balancing perspective suggests that the recent decline in ticket splitting could be explained if the two major parties had moved toward the center of the ideological spectrum. Instead, the parties have polarized during the past twenty years, especially in Congress as more extreme factions in each party have gained control of the leadership positions (Rohde 1991; Poole and Rosenthal 1997; Carmines and Layman 1997).[3]

A final perspective argues that ticket splitting is the result of sincere policy-based proximity voting (Frymer 1994; Frymer, Kim, and Bines 1997; Grofman et al. 2000; Brunell, Grofman, and Merrill 2001). Since American parties are diverse coalitions, congressional candidates may hold ideological positions that are quite different from the presidential candidates of their own party. In addition, median voter and party preferences vary from one district to another, even within the same state. As a result, some voters may find themselves closer to the policy positions of a presidential candidate of one party and a congressional candidate of the opposite party. This argument may be best understood when considering white southerners who regularly voted for Republican presidential candidates and conservative Democratic House candidates in the 1960s, 1970s, and 1980s. This theory may also explain the recent drop in ticket splitting. As the parties (and their candidates for Congress) have polarized, fewer candidates are trying to run away from their party's positions. As a result, fewer voters find themselves proximate to presidential and congressional candidates of opposite parties. However, there is more to the decline in ticket splitting than the growing ideological homogeneity of each party's candidates for Congress. Increased party polarization has the added effect of making voters view politics in more partisan and ideological terms.

A Party-Salience Theory of Ticket Splitting

It is possible to make sense of the recent decline in ticket splitting by noting the growing ideological gulf between the two major political parties. When parties offer clear choices to voters, then party labels are more salient decision aids when voters cast their ballots, which reduces the chances that voters will cast split ballots. A fuller explanation and empirical test of these ideas follows.

This argument rests on two primary claims. The first is that voters rely on party labels to make inferences about the ideological positions of candidates and the policies candidates will pursue if elected. This inferential process is especially important in low-information races (like many congressional contests), where voters often do not learn much about the candidates during a campaign. For example, Franklin (1991) finds that voters' perceptions about the ideological position of an incumbent legislator depend, in part, on the ideological location of the incumbent's party.

The second tenet is that the degree to which voters make ideological inferences based on party labels depends on the ideological distance between the two major parties. The salience of party labels depends on the degree to which the two parties offer clear and contrasting policy positions. Party labels are less useful to voters when both parties have similar policy positions. This is certainly not a new idea. As this chapter's epigraph suggests, V. O. Key (1966) argues that voters rely on policy preferences when parties and candidates provide clear choices during the campaign. However, when voters confront indistinguishable or vague policy alternatives, they rely on other considerations, such as candidate traits and experiences (see also Downs 1957, 137; Campbell et al. 1960, 170).

There is empirical evidence based on candidate statements and positions to support this conditional view of issue voting. When competing candidates offer similar or ambiguous policy proposals, voters often rely on character assessments and personal traits in making voting decisions (Page 1978; Asher 1988). In contrast, ideological considerations have a stronger influence on vote choice when opposing candidates take clear and contrasting policy positions (Page 1978; Wright 1978; Abramowitz 1981; Wright and Berkman 1986).

I argue that the ideological positions of the major parties have a similar effect on voters. As the ideological distance between the two major parties increases, party labels become more informative, and it becomes easier for voters to identify and vote for the candidate or party closest to their policy preferences. In contrast, as the parties converge toward the ideological median, it becomes harder for voters to recognize ideological differences between the parties, issues become less relevant, and voters rely on nonpolicy criteria. Assuming that nonpolicy characteristics (such as appealing candidate traits) are distributed to candidates independently of party affiliation, then voters will be more likely to split their ballots when the parties converge toward the center.

In sum, the party-salience explanation offers predictions at the individual and aggregate level. At the individual level, the party-salience theory predicts that voters who see no policy differences between the parties are less likely to rely on party labels and ideological positions and are thus most likely to cast split ballots. At the aggregate level, the party-salience theory predicts that ticket splitting should be more common when party positions move toward the center. Thus, Key's (1966) echo chamber metaphor illustrates why ticket splitting should decrease when the parties polarize. When parties offer a meaningful choice, voters respond by clearly selecting one of the parties in several different races. In contrast, when parties and their candidates move toward the ideological center and blur their differences, the response from the electorate should be equally vague: ticket splitting and divided government. Clarity from the parties begets clarity from the voters; confusion begets confusion.[4]

Have Voters Recognized Growing Party Polarization?

There is ample evidence of growing ideological distance between the two parties nationally during the past thirty years, especially when examining Congress and convention delegates (Rohde 1991; Cox and McCubbins 1993; Poole and Rosenthal 1997; Green, Jackson, and Clayton 1999). In order to link this development to the recent decline in ticket splitting, it is first necessary to determine whether voters have recognized this growing party polarization. If voters are generally unaware of the relative ideological positions of the two major parties, the motivation for making policy inferences and voting decisions based on party labels largely disappears.

The simplest test is to compare an objective measure of party polarization to a measure that is based on public perceptions of the parties. Figure 9.2 plots the percentage of NES respondents who see "important differences" between the parties against the ideological distance between the Republican and Democratic parties in the House of Representatives. The ideological distance measure is the difference between the mean DW-NOMINATE scores (Poole and Rosenthal 1997) for Republicans and Democrats in the House during the session that preceded each presidential election from 1952 to 2000.[5] As Figure 9.2 indicates, there is a strong positive correlation ($r = .84$, $p < .01$) between the two variables. As the ideological distance between the parties in the House increases, more voters perceive "important differences" in what the parties stand for. This relationship encompasses significant party polarization during the past thirty years. In 1972, the mean policy distance between Republicans and Democrats in the House was .4 on the DW-NOMINATE scale, and only 46 percent of NES respondents saw important differences between the parties. By 2000, the mean distance between the parties in the House was over .8, and 66 percent of NES respondents saw important differences between the parties. Other public opinion measures of perceived party polarization show similar movement over the past several decades (Hetherington 2001; Weisberg 2002b; Mockabee 2001).

Interestingly, the party-differences measure is not correlated with the

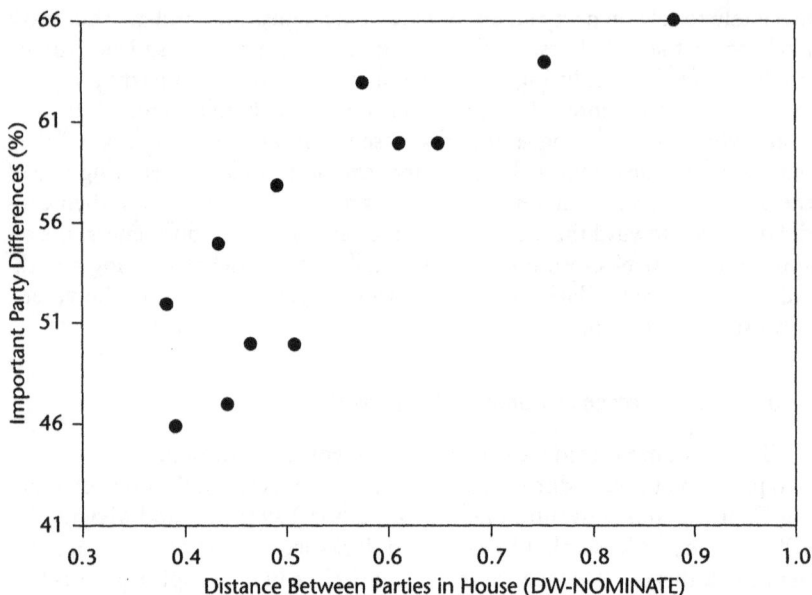

FIGURE 9.2   Comparing Measures of Party Distance, 1952–2000

ideological distance between presidential candidates ($r = -.19, p = .59$) or the relative extremism of the two candidates for the White House ($r = .08$, $p = .82$).[6] Thus, public perceptions about party positions seem to depend more on the aggregate positions of party members in Congress than on the relative positions of the two presidential candidates.

Do Perceptions of Party Differences Influence Voting Decisions?

Now that we have established that public perceptions of party polarization are closely related to an objective indicator of party positioning, the next question is whether these perceptions make any difference in voting decisions. The party-salience theory hypothesizes that voters who see a wide ideological gap between the parties should be more likely to cast their ballots on the basis of party labels and ideological considerations than voters who see no differences between the parties.

It is possible to test this hypothesis using data from the NES Cumulative Data File and the 2000 Election Study. I estimate a model of vote choice in presidential elections (first column) and House elections (second column) using three main factors: party, ideology, and candidate attributes.[7] In the presidential model, the candidate factor is measured by the candidate-affect differential: the sum of the number of likes for the Republican and dislikes for the Democrat minus the number of likes for the Democrat and dislikes for the Republican (up to five mentions). Incumbency (coded −1 for a Democratic incumbent, 0 for an open seat, and +1 for a Republican incumbent) measures the candidate factor in the House model. Only contested House races, where voters have a choice between at least two candidates, are included in this analysis.

To test the hypothesis, I interact each of the three main factors with the "important party differences" NES variable (coded 1 if the voter sees important differences between the parties, 0 if not). The interaction terms should be positive and significant for the party and ideology factors, indicating that party and ideology weigh more heavily in the voting decisions of people who see major policy differences between the parties. The interaction term should be negative and significant for the candidate factor, indicating that candidate attributes weigh more heavily in the voting decisions of people who see no policy differences between the parties.

The results are presented in Table 9.1. The dependent variable in each case is dichotomous (coded 1 for Republicans, 0 for Democrats), so logistic regression is used to estimate the voting models. For voting in presidential and House elections, the results support the first two parts of the proposition but fail to support the third. All three factors are significant predictors of vote choice for voters who see no differences between the parties, as indicated by the logit coefficients for the main factors. The positive and significant interaction terms for party identification and ideology in both models indicate that people who see important differences between the parties indeed rely more heavily on party and ideology when making voting decisions. In contrast, the interaction between party differences and the candidate factor falls well short of statistical significance. Apparently, incumbency and candidate affect equally shape the voting decisions of all voters, regardless of their perceptions of party positions. Nevertheless, voters' perceptions about party differences shape the degree to which party and ideology influence voting decisions.

Is Ticket Splitting Less Common Among Voters Who See Important Differences Between the Parties?

If voters who see no important differences between the parties place less emphasis on party and ideology, their votes are more likely shaped by nonpartisan and nonpolicy considerations, such as other candidate traits. Assuming that other candidate traits (experience, speaking ability, appearance, etc.) are evenly or randomly distributed between the parties, voters who see no differences between the parties should be more likely to vote for candidates of different parties in different contests.

TABLE **9.1**   A multivariate analysis of voting in national elections, 1984–2000

	Dependent Variable: Vote Choice	
	President	House
Constant	.14	−.04
	(.09)	(.07)
Party Identification	.53***	.54***
	(.05)	(.03)
Ideology	.43***	.19*
	(0.10)	(0.08)
Incumbency	—	1.23***
		(0.07)
Presidential Candidate Affect	.59***	—
	(.04)	
Important Party Differences	−.11	−.03
	(.13)	(.08)
Party Identification * Important Party Differences	.19**	.14**
	(.07)	(.04)
Ideology * Important Party Differences	.29*	.31**
	(.14)	(.10)
Incumbency * Important Party Differences	—	−.04
		(.09)
Presidential Candidate Affect * Important Party Differences	.05	—
	(.06)	
Number of cases	4584	5290
Model Chi-square	4403.8***	2911.1***
Pseudo-R^2	.69	.40

DATA SOURCE: NES *Cumulative Data File 1948–96, 2000 Pre- and Postelection Study.*
NOTE: *The House vote model only includes races that were contested by both major parties. The dependent variables are coded 1 for Republican votes and 0 for Democratic votes. Cell entries are logit coefficients (standard errors in parentheses).*
[+]*p < .1,* *p < .05,* **p < .01,* ***p < .001 (two-tailed).*

To see whether perceptions of party differences are an important determinant of ticket splitting when controlling for other factors, I estimate a multivariate model of president-House ticket splitting using data from the National Election Studies. Several independent variables are included in the model to test different theories of ticket splitting. In an era of candidate-centered politics, it is commonly stated that ticket splitting reflects a weak psychological attachment to either major party (Campbell et al. 1960; Wattenberg 1998). Thus, strong partisans (as opposed to independents) and those who care a great deal about the outcome of the presidential contest (as opposed to those who don't care) are less prone to ticket splitting (Campbell and Miller 1957; Beck et al. 1992; Mattei and Howes 2000). Both measures are included in the analysis here.[8] Since both measures are strongly correlated with perceptions of party differences (Hetherington 2001), including them in a multivariate model makes it more difficult for perceptions of party differences to account for any variation in ticket splitting.

Second, the multivariate model includes a measure for testing policy-balancing theories of ticket splitting. Other things being equal, ideological centrists should be more motivated to split their ballots than other voters. Thus, the model includes a dichotomous variable that indicates whether a voter places herself in between the two major parties on the liberal-conservative spectrum. Similar measures have been used in other studies (Born 2000b; Mattei and Howes 2000; Garand and Lichtl 2000).

Third, it is important to control for the quality of the competing House candidates. One obvious determinant of ticket splitting is incumbency. Voters are more likely to split their ballots when confronting an incumbent of the opposite party on the ballot (McAllister and Darcy 1992; Alvarez and Schousen 1993; Born 1994; Brody, Brady, and Heitshusen 1994; Sigelman, Wahlbeck, and Buell 1997; Born 2000a, 2000b). Thus, the model includes two measures that indicate whether the House contest features an incumbent of the same or opposite party of the voter's chosen presidential candidate.

Given that incumbency is a crude measure of candidate quality, it is important also to control for candidate familiarity. Some incumbents face strong, highly visible challengers while many others face relatively unknown, token opposition. Ticket splitting should be more common in the latter contests. To account for these variations in candidate quality (especially for challengers), the model includes measures that indicate whether voters can recall the names of the House candidates from their own party and the opposite party.

Fourth, one must allow for the fact that the quality of the presidential candidates influences ticket splitting. Some voters may split their ballots simply because they find the presidential candidate from their party to be inferior to the opposition candidate (Mattei and Howes 2000). Thus, the model includes two dichotomous variables that indicate whether partisans are cross-pressured by finding the opposition presidential candidate more appealing.[9]

Finally, I include controls for region and ballot format. A dummy variable for residents of southern states accounts for higher rates of ticket splitting among those voters (Alvarez and Schousen 1993). There is a historical pattern unique to the South of selecting Republican presidential candidates while electing Democrats to Congress, although this regional distinction has gradually disappeared (Burden and Kimball 2002). An additional dummy variable indicates states that have a straight-party device on the ballot, which reduces ticket splitting (Campbell and Miller 1957; McAllister and Darcy 1992; Burden and Kimball 1998).

The results of a multivariate analysis of president-House ticket splitting can be seen in Table 9.2. The sample used for this analysis includes NES respondents from 1980 to 2000 and excludes third-party votes and House races that were not contested by both major parties.[10] Thus, the analysis

TABLE **9.2**   A multivariate analysis of president-House ticket splitting, 1980–2000

	Coefficient (Std. Error)	Change in Probability
Important Party Differences	−.49*** (.10)	−.11
Strength of Party Identification	−.34*** (.05)	−.20
Care About Outcome	−.27* (0.11)	−.06
South	.19+ (.10)	.05
Straight-Party Ballot Device	−.20* (.09)	−.05
Place Self Between the Major Parties	.18+ (.10)	.04
House Incumbent of Own Party	−1.12*** (.16)	−.22
House Incumbent of Opposite Party	1.09*** (.14)	.27
Recall Name of Own Party House Candidate	−.96*** (.12)	−.19
Recall Name of Opposite Party House Candidate	.95*** (.11)	.23
Presidential Pull on Republicans	1.32*** (.18)	.31
Presidential Pull on Democrats	.91*** (.17)	.22
Constant	−.10 (.20)	—
Number of Cases	4200	
Model Chi-square	1152.6***	
Pseudo-R^2	.26	

DATA SOURCE: NES *Cumulative Data File 1948–96, 2000 Pre- and Postelection Study.*
NOTE: *Analysis only includes House races that were contested by both major parties. The dependent variable is coded 1 for a split ticket and 0 for a straight ticket. Cell entries are logit coefficients (std. errors in parentheses). Change in probability values are calculated by moving the variable of interest from its minimum to maximum value while holding all other variables constant at modal values.*
+$p < .1$, *$p < .05$, **$p < .01$, ***$p < .001$ *(two-tailed).*

covers a period in which president-House ticket splitting declined substantially (from 27% in 1980 to 17% in 2000 among voters in this sample). The first column of Table 9.2 provides the estimated logit coefficients and standard errors for each explanatory variable. Since logit coefficients are not easily interpreted, I also calculate the change in the predicted probability of casting a split ballot when varying each independent variable from its minimum to maximum value while holding the other explanatory variables constant (see the second column of Table 9.2).[11] The change-in-probability values provide a more substantive comparison of the relative impact of each explanatory variable.

As expected, perceptions of important party differences are a significant predictor of ticket splitting even after controlling for several other important factors. Candidate-centered factors (incumbency and name recall in House contests, candidate affect in presidential contests) have the strongest impact on ticket splitting. However, a fair amount of ticket splitting can be attributed to voters who blur any distinctions between the parties (i.e., political independents, those who don't care about the outcome of the presidential election, and those don't see important party differences).

Furthermore, the decline in ticket splitting from the 1970s to 2000 can be explained almost entirely by changes in the composition of the electorate for these three variables. In 2000, 79 percent of the voters in the sample saw important differences between the parties, as compared to 55 percent in 1976. In 2000, 89 percent of the voters cared a great deal about the presidential outcome, as compared to 67 percent in 1976. In 2000, 41 percent of the voters were strong partisans, as compared to 32 percent in 1976. This represents a significant increase in the salience of party labels among voters, and provides a compelling explanation for the recent decline in ticket splitting. None of the other variables in the model, with one exception (discussed later in this chapter), move in a direction that would lead to less ticket splitting over the past twenty years.

Another factor contributing to the decline in ticket splitting is greater unity among Democrats in affection for the party's presidential candidate. Only 5 percent of Democrats in 2000 were conflicted in their evaluations of the presidential candidates, down from 11 percent in 1976. In addition, increased electoral competition in the South, the result of a gradual shift of voters to the Republican Party, also accounts for the recent drop in ticket splitting (Aistrup 1996; Brunell and Grofman 1998; Burden and Kimball 2002). In the three most recent presidential elections, president-House ticket splitting was no more common in the South than in any other region of the country.

It is worth noting that Table 9.2 lends some support for policy-balancing theories. Ticket splitting is positively associated with being located between the parties on an ideological spectrum (note the positive logit coefficient and change-in-probability score for the "place self between the major parties" variable). On the other hand, the model coefficient barely reaches conventional levels of statistical significance. Moreover, the substantive impact of being a moderate is weaker than the other explanatory variables, including whether one lives in a state that has a straight-party ballot mechanism. In addition, the number of voters who place themselves in between the two major parties has remained constant over the past twenty years (at around 23%), so ideological moderation does not help to account for the recent decline in ticket splitting. On the whole, the evidence in Table 9.2 provides support for a party-salience theory of ticket splitting. When party labels are less salient and less informative about candidates' policy positions, there is less to prevent a voter from crossing party lines.

Does Ticket Splitting Increase When the Parties Offer Similar Policies?

A final hypothesis from the party-salience theory is that aggregate ticket splitting should be more common when the parties converge ideologically and less common when the parties diverge. One way to test this hypothesis is to examine the number of congressional districts that have split outcomes each year (i.e., districts that are carried by a presidential candidate of one party and a House candidate of a different party). I estimate a regression equation in which split-district outcomes from 1900 to 2000 are modeled as a function of party polarization, presidential victory margin, and incumbency.

As in Figure 9.2, I used Poole and Rosenthal's (1997) DW-NOMINATE scores to measure party polarization. I simply calculate the difference between the mean Republican and Democratic DW-NOMINATE scores in the House for the Congress preceding each presidential election as my measure of party polarization. According to the party-salience theory, party polarization should be inversely related to ticket splitting. In contrast, policy-balancing theory predicts a positive relationship between party polarization and ticket splitting.

In an era of "candidate-centered" politics, many argue that ticket splitting occurs when an appealing candidate manages to attract voters from the opposite party (Wattenberg 1991; Beck et al. 1992). The multivariate analysis includes the president's margin of victory (in percentage points) to account for the expectation that popular presidential candidates may generate more ticket splitting by attracting an unusually large number of votes from the opposition. The final explanatory variable is a measure of the incumbency advantage in House elections, which was developed by Gelman and King (1990). Given that incumbency is a strong predictor of ticket splitting, when the incumbency advantage increases, we should observe more ticket splitting.

It is possible that presidential landslides only influence ticket splitting in the modern candidate-centered campaign era with smaller presidential coattails. Thus, I estimate a second regression model that includes as an explanatory variable an interaction between the margin of victory in the presidential race and a dummy variable that marks elections in the "candidate-centered" period of modern American politics. I choose 1952 as the beginning of the candidate-centered era, since Dwight Eisenhower and Adlai Stevenson were the first presidential candidates to use television ads in a presidential campaign (Ansolabehere, Behr, and Iyengar 1993). The main effect for victory margin should be insignificant, while the interaction term

TABLE **9.3**   A multivariate analysis of split-district outcomes, 1900–2000

	Model 1	Model 2
Constant	27.73**	27.52**
	(7.13)	(7.01)
Mean Distance Between Parties (D-NOMINATE)	−31.65**	−25.42**
	(8.34)	(8.47)
President Victory Margin (Percent)	0.28+	0.01
	(0.15)	(0.19)
Incumbency Advantage (Gelman-King)	2.26***	1.75*
	(0.45)	(0.67)
Modern Era (since 1952)	—	−1.99
		(5.67)
President Victory Margin * Modern Era	—	0.60*
		(0.28)
Number of cases	26	26
Adjusted R²	.75	.79
Std. Error of Estimate	5.97	5.50
Durbin-Watson d	1.95	2.18

DATA SOURCE: *Stanley and Niemi (2000); Keith Poole.*
NOTE: *The dependent variable is the percentage of House districts that were won by a presidential candidate of one party and a House candidate of another party. Cell entries are OLS coefficients (standard errors in parentheses).*
$^{+}p < .1$, $^{*}p < .05$, $^{**}p < .01$, $^{***}p < .001$ *(two-tailed).*

should produce a positive and significant coefficient. This would be consistent with the idea that candidate-driven ticket splitting is a characteristic of the modern era of American politics.

As the regression estimates in Table 9.3 indicate, party convergence, incumbency, and lopsided presidential elections are associated with higher levels of president-House ticket splitting. These results hold in both models presented in Table 9.3, with one caveat to be discussed later in this chapter.[12] Thus, we find more support for a party-salience theory of ticket splitting. When the parties converge toward the ideological center, ticket splitting increases. When the parties polarize, ticket splitting decreases.[13] Again, a substantial increase in party polarization since the 1970s goes a long way toward explaining the decline in split districts during the past twenty years. In the 1970s and 1980s, over 30 percent of congressional districts produced split results in presidential and House elections. In 2000, only 20 percent of districts generated split outcomes. The difference between mean party DW-NOMINATE scores in the House has increased from .39 in 1972 to .87 in 2000 (on a scale that runs from −1 to +1). According to the regression equations in Table 9.3, this increase in party polarization should have reduced split districts by about twelve to fifteen percentage points, not far from the decline that actually occurred.

The results in Table 9.3 also suggest that the association between the president's winning margin and split districts is stronger for the latter half of this century. As expected, the interaction term is positive and significant in the second model, while the main effect for the victory margin variable is not statistically significant.[14] Landslide presidential elections generally failed to produce divided government before the 1950s because the fate of congressional candidates was closely linked to the performance of the party's presidential candidate. In contrast, lopsided presidential contests are more likely to produce divided outcomes today because congressional campaigns are more independent of the race at the top of the ticket.

Conclusion

It is still commonly argued that party attachments among voters are weakening and that ticket splitting is on the rise (Lawrence 1999, 173; Wattenberg 1998, 27; Patterson 2001, 221). However, it is apparent that the conventional wisdom regarding partisan decline and ticket splitting needs to be revised. There is abundant evidence of increasing partisanship among the mass public and a substantial decrease in ticket splitting in recent elections. The increased ticket splitting of the 1960s and 1970s is certainly related to weakened party attachments and the rise of candidate-centered campaigns during that period. More recently, however, we have witnessed the converse of this relationship: resurgent partisanship and decreased ticket splitting as party labels and ideological positions have become more relevant to voters.

Voters have correctly perceived the widening ideological differences between the major parties in the United States. In addition, voters who perceive important differences between the parties are more likely to vote on the basis of party affiliation and ideological positions. As the ideological gulf between the parties in Congress has grown, mass partisanship has come to be defined more by ideology than in the past. The correlation between a voter's ideological position and party identification has increased substantially in the past twenty years (Knight and Erikson 1997; Levine, Carmines, and Huckfeldt 1997; Abramowitz and Saunders 1998). One result has been a decline in ticket splitting.

The fact that the 2000 and 2002 elections both produced unified government underscores the recent decline in split-ticket voting. The ubiquitous losses suffered by the president's party in midterm congressional elections (until recently) are often interpreted as a sign that voters prefer that the opposition party control Congress and serve as a check on the president (Alesina and Rosenthal 1995; Erikson 1988; Mebane and Sekhon 2002). In the midterm elections of 2002, voters had a chance to elect more Democrats to serve as a check on a Republican president, and yet Republicans actually gained seats in both the House and Senate. With very few exceptions, the Republican gains in the 2002 elections came in states and districts where George Bush had run well ahead of Al Gore in the 2000 election. Thus, recent elections have strengthened the correlation between presidential and congressional voting. In addition, since 1952 divided government has ensued after nine midterm elections and seven presidential elections, so the midterm-loss phenomenon does not adequately explain the prevalence of divided government in the past forty years.

In addition, an examination of the House incumbents who survived in districts that were carried by the other party's presidential candidate highlights the importance of ideological positions in elections. The list of these winning incumbents in recent elections is primarily a roster of moderate Republicans (such as Chris Shays, Wayne Gilchrest, Jim Leach, and Jack Quinn) and moderate Democrats (such as Ken Lucas, Charlie Stenholm, Colin Peterson, and Dennis Moore).[15] In the 107th Congress, the average DW-NOMINATE score for Democratic incumbents in districts carried by Bush is −.14, as compared to an average of −.45 for Democrats representing districts that Gore won. Similarly, the average DW-NOMINATE score for Republican incumbents in districts carried by Gore is .52, as compared to an average of .74 for Republicans representing districts that Bush won. Politically moderate incumbents obscure party differences, which helps them appeal to voters from the opposite party and survive in competitive districts. Even in cases where ticket splitting occurs, the salience of party labels and party positions is still important.

The rise and fall of ticket splitting can be understood in terms of a fall and rise in the salience of party labels. It is important to consider American voting behavior in light of the actions of the parties in government. In recent years, ideological disputes in Washington have highlighted the policy differences between the parties. As a result, voters have come to see government and candidates in a more partisan and ideological light, which increases the salience of party labels in the voting booth. Voters who see important differences between the parties rely more heavily on party and ideology and thus are less likely to cast split ballots. As a result, ticket splitting has declined during the past twenty years.

The extremely close competitive balance between the two major parties makes it difficult to predict the future of divided government in the United States. However, the ideological differences between the parties and the salience of party labels are important indicators to follow. The bipartisanship that prevailed in the capital immediately after September 11, 2001, obscured party differences on the major issues of the day. Had it continued, we would expect to have seen an increase in ticket splitting in the coming elections. However, national government has since returned to ideologically charged partisan disputes on a variety of issues, from tax cuts to judicial nominations. The continuing party polarization in American politics means that ticket splitting should continue to decline, even below the relatively low levels seen in the 2000 election.

METHODOLOGICAL APPENDIX

Summary of NES *Variable Codes*

Split-ticket voting: Coded as 1 for respondents who voted for presidential and House candidates of opposite parties, 0 for respondents who voted for candidates of the same party.

Party Identification: The standard seven-point party identification scale, ranging from strong Democrats (coded as −3) to strong Republicans (+3).

Strength of Partisanship: Coded 1 for pure independents, 2 for independent leaners, 3 for weak partisans, and 4 for strong partisans.

Ideology: Summary of a respondent's self-assessed ideology, coded as −1 for liberals, 0 for moderates, and +1 for conservatives. This summary measure preserves a lot of missing data that is lost when using the seven-point ideological self-placement.

Incumbency: Coded +1 for a Republican incumbent, 0 for an open seat, and −1 for a Democratic incumbent.

Presidential Candidate Affect: Based on open-ended questions about the presidential candidates, this variable is the sum of the number of likes for the Republican and dislikes for the Democrat minus the number of likes for the Democrat and dislikes for the Republican (up to five mentions each). Values range from −10 (extreme affect advantage for the Democrat) to +10 (extreme advantage for the Republican).

Important Party Differences: Coded as 1 if the respondent says there are "important differences" in what the two major parties stand for, 0 if the respondent says "no" or "don't know."

Care About Outcome: Coded as 1 if the respondent cares "a good deal" about who wins the presidential election, 0 if the respondent doesn't care very much or doesn't know.

South: Coded as 1 for resident of one of the eleven former Confederate states, 0 for all others.

Straight-Party Ballot Device: Coded 1 if the respondent resides in a state with a straight-party option on the ballot, 0 if not.

Place Self Between the Major Parties: Coded as 1 for those who place themselves to the left of the Democratic Party and to the right of the Republican Party on the seven-point ideology scale, and 0 otherwise (including those who fail to place themselves or both parties on the scale).

House Incumbent of Own Party: Coded 1 if the respondent resides in a congressional district where the incumbent is from the same party as the respondent's chosen presidential candidate, 0 otherwise.

House Incumbent of Opposite Party: Coded 1 if the respondent resides in a district where the incumbent is from the opposite party, 0 otherwise.

Recall Name of Own-Party House Candidate: Coded as 1 if the respondent accurately recalls the name of the House candidate from the same party as his chosen presidential candidate, 0 otherwise.

Recall Name of Opposite-Party House Candidate: Coded as 1 if the respondent accurately recalls the name of the House candidate from the opposite party, 0 otherwise.

Presidential Pull on Republicans: Coded as 1 if a Republican partisan rates the Democratic presidential candidate better than the Republican candidate on the presidential candidate affect scale, 0 otherwise. Leaners are treated as partisans.

Presidential Pull on Democrats: Coded as 1 if a Democratic partisan rates the Republican presidential candidate better than the Democratic candidate on the presidential candidate affect scale, 0 otherwise. Leaners are treated as partisans.

Summary of Aggregate Variables

Split Districts: The percentage of congressional districts with split outcomes (carried by presidential and House candidates of different parties) in on-year elections.

President-House Ticket Splitting: The percentage of NES respondents who report voting for presidential and House candidates of opposite major parties.

Split Senate Delegations: The percentage of states with U.S. senators of different parties after each on-year election.

Important Party Differences: The percentage of NES respondents who report that there are "important differences" in what the parties stand for.

Mean Distance Between Parties: The difference between the mean DW-NOMINATE score for House Democrats and the mean DW-NOMINATE score for House Republicans in the Congress preceding each presidential election.

President's Victory Margin: The difference (in percentage points) between the presidential candidate with the most popular votes and the second-place finisher.

Incumbency Advantage: Gelman-King measure of the House incumbency advantage in each on-year election.

10 The Half-Hearted Rise: Voter Turnout in the 2000 Election

STEVEN E. FINKEL AND PAUL FREEDMAN

In 1992, an independent Texas millionaire named H. Ross Perot shocked the political world by winning 19 percent of the presidential popular vote—more than any other third-party candidate since Teddy Roosevelt ran as the Progressive (Bull Moose) Party nominee in 1912. But Perot's impressive performance was only one of the surprises in the election of 1992. The other —and arguably more significant—development was the sudden reversal of a decades-long decline in voter turnout. Since 1960, when 63 percent of the voting age population made its way to the polls, turnout had declined in every presidential election but one, and by 1988 had reached a postwar low of 50 percent (see Figure 10.1).

In 1992, however, this trend changed dramatically, as voter turnout increased by five percentage points, to 55.1 percent. In one year, almost half of the three-decade decline had been erased. What could account for such a steep and sudden rise? Certainly Perot's presence on the ballot had something to do with it, but subsequent analysis has shown that the Perot factor could not explain all of the unexpected increase (Nichols and Beck 1995). Was 1992, then, the beginning of a new era of higher voter turnout?

This question appeared to be answered in 1996, when turnout fell below 50 percent for the first time since 1924. Hopes that the 1992 increase could be sustained and built upon were dashed. "In the absence of an interesting, competitive race and without a credible alternative to the major-party offerings," wrote Nichols, Kimball, and Beck, "turnout fell to 49 percent . . . over 8 million fewer votes were cast in 1996 than in 1992" (1999, 23–24). "Short of a dramatic reversal in the momentum of public cynicism," the authors concluded, "there is little reason to expect voter turnout to increase in the foreseeable future" (44).

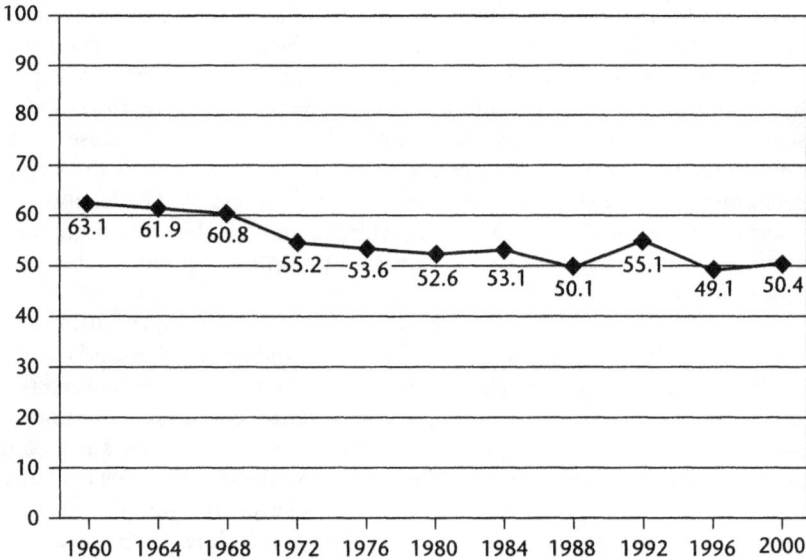

FIGURE **10.1**   Turnout in Presidential Elections, 1960–2000

Voter turnout, in short, was seen as having reached a new plateau: in any given election, about half of eligible voters would find their way to the polls; the rest would stay home. It came as little surprise to many, therefore, that voter turnout in the 2000 election came in right around 50 percent. By the end of Election Day, just about half of the voting-age population had cast a ballot. According to Federal Election Commission (FEC) statistics, the election of 2000 saw presidential turnout of 51.3 percent, an increase of two points over 1996, but still almost four points below 1992 levels. Even this apparent increase, however, is overstated. The FEC 2000 turnout estimate is based on early (July 2000) Census Bureau projections of the voting-age population. In this chapter we use actual 2000 Census data for the voting-age population in each state.[1] Doing so results in a national turnout rate of 50.4 percent, slightly lower—but we believe more accurate—than the FEC figure. Using either figure, the era of low voter turnout would appear to be still with us.

The story, however, is more complex. The real story of the 2000 election, we argue, is that conditions were in place for a far greater increase in turnout than was actually realized. Registration laws were less restrictive than in the past; party and campaign mobilization increased sharply. Moreover, a number of long-term attitudinal factors that were conducive to higher levels of turnout, such as political efficacy and civic duty, increased substantially. In addition, the overwhelming majority of the electorate perceived the race between Al Gore and George W. Bush to be close. In short, there was ample reason to suspect a significant rise in turnout over 1996 levels, perhaps recouping the entire slide from the 55 percent level of 1992. Other scholars have noticed this puzzle as well: "Given the sharp increase in the percentage who believed the election would be close, as well as the strong relationship between expectations about the closeness of the election and voter participation," note Abramson, Aldrich, and Rohde, "one might have expected a much greater increase in turnout than the 2-point rise between 1996 and 2000" (2002, 91).

Why, then, was there such a tepid increase in turnout in the 2000 election? The fault, we argue, lies primarily with candidates Al Gore and George W. Bush. Quite simply, the electorate was faced with a choice between two major-party candidates who failed to inspire either enthusiastic support or passionate opposition. Despite the frenetic pace of campaign advertising and mobilization efforts in one of the closest presidential elections in United States history, voters responded in decidedly lukewarm fashion toward the major-party standard-bearers themselves. As we will show, even the strongest partisans failed to rally behind their standard-bearers in 2000 to the extent that they had in previous years. Compared with Bill Clinton, George H. W. Bush, and Ross Perot in 1992—and even with Clinton and Bob Dole in 1996—Al Gore and George W. Bush failed to inspire the passion necessary to bring people to the polls. The rise in turnout in 2000, consequently, was only half-hearted.

We begin this chapter with a descriptive look at turnout at both the state and national levels in 2000. We then examine the correlates of voting over the past three elections, drawing on National Election Studies data for an individual-level portrait of turnout. Next, we estimate a more fully specified turnout model, drawing on pooled 1992, 1996, and 2000 National Election Studies data to estimate the effect of various factors in a multivariate context. We use these estimates to decompose the changes in turnout between 2000 and the two preceding presidential elections. The results both illustrate the unrealized potential for increased turnout in the 2000 election and inject some measure of optimism about the prospects for voter participation in the future.

U.S. Voter Turnout in Context

Electoral participation in the United States is notoriously low, especially when compared with other Western industrialized democracies (Powell 1986; Franklin 1996). During the 1990s, when turnout in the U.S. hovered at just above 50 percent of the voting-age population, more than three-quarters of the electorate on average turned out in the United Kingdom, the Netherlands, Norway, Germany, and Spain. Turnout was even higher in nations such as Austria, Denmark, Iceland, Italy, New Zealand, Sweden, and Turkey (not to mention both Liechtenstein *and* Luxembourg), where it averaged in the mid to high 80s. And in Australia and Belgium, turnout in the 1990s averaged higher than 90 percent of the voting-age population (International Institute for Democracy and Electoral Assistance 2001). Explanations for this cross-national variance—and the United States's poor performance in particular—have included the demobilizing nature of the party and electoral systems, electoral laws (e.g., although voter registration is automatic in some nations, the United States has a patchwork of relatively onerous registration requirements), and the sheer number of elections held in the United States (Brody 1978; Franklin 1996; Powell 1986; Jackman 1987).

However, if turnout in America is substantially lower than in other industrialized democracies, it has also experienced a decline over time. As we have already noted, the United States has seen a steady drop in voter turnout for much of the past forty years. In fact, turnout in the 1996 presidential election was the lowest since 1924. The story before 1960, however, is less clear. Voter turnout in the nineteenth and early twentieth centuries—as measured in terms of the voting-age population—was even more dismal than it was today, rarely rising above a third of the voting-age population. But, of course, for much of this period large portions of the voting-age population were, by virtue of gender, race, or place of birth, ineligible to cast a ballot. When one includes only the legally voting *eligible* population, estimates of turnout are considerably higher, often reaching as high as 80 percent or more of the eligible electorate through the 1880s. By the early twentieth century, however, voting levels began to taper off, falling to between 60 and 65 percent of the eligible electorate (Abramson, Aldrich, and Rohde 1999, 67).

For elections since 1920, when the Census Bureau began to release regular estimates of the voting-age population, turnout estimates are easier to calculate. Following the entrance of women into the electorate, turnout in the 1920s averaged in the mid-40-percent range. Turnout rose (with some ebbs and flows) over the next several decades, reaching a twentieth-century high in 1960, when 63.1 percent of the voting-age population went to the polls.[2] Since then, the falloff in turnout has been substantial and, until 1992, generally consistent from election to election (see Figure 10.1).

These declines are particularly vexing, given that rising levels of education and less restrictive voter registration procedures—two factors shown to be closely related to turnout—would have led one to expect an *increase* in turnout over time (Brody 1978; Rosenstone and Hansen 1993). Explanations for the secular decline in voter turnout are myriad. Declining turnout has been attributed to a decline in voter mobilization by candidates and parties (Rosenstone and Hansen 1993), to increases in residential mobility (Squire, Wolfinger, and Glass 1987), to an electorate disengaged and de-mobilized by the negative tone of political campaigns (Ansolabehere and Iyengar 1995; cf. Finkel and Geer 1998; Freedman and Goldstein 1999), to a rise in cynicism and distrust (Miller and Shanks 1996; Teixeira 1992), and to a decline in partisan attachments (Wattenberg 1998).

There is, in sum, no shortage of explanations for why voter turnout had been on the decline up until 1992. How, though, to account for the strange fluctuations in voter turnout over the past three presidential elections? In the analysis that follows, we show that many of the key variables implicated in these alternative explanations can also help illuminate recent patterns in turnout. We focus both on changes in the aggregate levels of these variables as well as their changing *effects*, in order to arrive at a more complete under-standing of voter turnout during this time period.

2000 Turnout at the State Level

Half of all voting-age Americans stayed home on Election Day in 2000, as voter turnout measured in terms of voting-age population (VAP) was 50.4 percent.[3] This figure masks a great deal of state-level variation. Eigh-teen states and the District of Columbia, for example, saw turnout rates of less than 50 percent, and in seven of these states less than 45 percent of the voting-age population turned out. States with the lowest rates of turnout included Texas, Nevada, Arizona, and Hawaii, all of which had rates be-tween 40 and 43 percent. In contrast, thirty-three states saw turnout rates of 50 percent or more as a share of VAP, and eight (Iowa, Montana, New Hampshire, Vermont, Wisconsin, Alaska, Maine, and Minnesota) had rates of at least 60 percent.

There was also significant variation in state-level *changes* in turnout since 1996. Turnout declined in thirteen states, including eight that saw a drop of at least a percentage point. By contrast, turnout increased in 2000 in thirty-seven states and the District of Columbia. (Turnout remained con-stant only in Indiana, at 48.8 percent.) Turnout rose by a percentage point or more in twenty-eight states, including thirteen that saw increases of at least three points. These included the presidential battleground states of Michigan (a 3.2-point increase), Pennsylvania (3.5 points), and Wisconsin (a 7.6-point rise).

What explains this variation in state-level turnout? The legal and politi-cal context that voters confront as Election Day approaches obviously var-ies from state to state, and these differences can have important implications for turnout. First and foremost, states differ in the registration requirements they impose on prospective voters. A handful of states currently provide for

Election Day registration (and one, North Dakota, has no registration requirements at all). By contrast, thirty-two states and the District of Columbia require citizens to register at least three weeks before Election Day.
In sixteen of these states, voters must be registered a full month in advance
(Federal Election Commission 2001). Voter turnout is strongly related to
these registration requirements (Wolfinger and Rosenstone 1980; Rosenstone and Hansen 1993). In 2000, as the length of the pre–Election Day
registration deadline increased, turnout declined significantly ($r = -.66$).
Mean turnout among states with Election Day (or no) registration was
62 percent, falling to 56 percent for states in which voters must be registered ten to twenty days in advance, and leveling off at around 50 percent
in states with deadlines greater than three weeks before Election Day. The
legal requirements in a given state, then, have a clear impact on state-level
turnout.

As we have suggested, the competitive environment of the presidential
race in a state also should affect the likelihood that citizens will turn out
to vote. We measured state-level competitiveness in several ways. First, we
found that turnout in 2000 was positively related to the closeness of the
presidential election, measured both by the final popular-vote margin and by
the last preelection poll in the state prior to November 7. As the presidential
race got closer (by either measure), turnout rose slightly. Second, turnout at
the state level was positively related to the presence of a governor's race and
the competitiveness of a state's senate race. More competitive Senate races
seem to have been associated with slightly higher turnout. All of these relationships, however, were modest, and none reached statistical significance.

We examined the competitiveness of the presidential race in a third way,
however, and found more substantial (and statistically significant) effects.
We looked at the resources invested by the campaigns and parties, using
the total number of general-election television advertisements aired in each
state's top media markets. These data, compiled by the Campaign Media
Analysis Group's ad-tracking system, provide comprehensive information
on every advertisement aired in the nation's top seventy-five media markets
(home to approximately 80 percent of the U.S. population), throughout the
2000 election (Freedman and Goldstein 1999; Goldstein and Freedman
2002). We aggregated these ad data to the state level to produce a measure
of general campaign activity in each state.[4]

Not surprisingly, the number of general-election ads broadcast in a state
is closely correlated with other measures of competition. In Texas, where a
Mason-Dixon poll a week before the election showed Governor Bush with
a 34-point advantage over Vice President Gore, the four largest media markets saw a grand total of thirteen general-election advertisements. Similarly,
in New York, where Gore led by fourteen points in the final week according to a Zogby poll, only eighty-one ads were broadcast. In stark contrast,

in Pennsylvania's markets there were close to twenty-nine thousand spots broadcast, Ohio saw twenty-eight thousand, and Florida was home to more than thirty-six thousand general-election ads. Needless to say, the presidential race in these states was significantly more competitive than in New York or Texas.

Among those jurisdictions with at least one top-75 media market, there is a modest but clear relationship between the number of ads broadcast and state-level turnout ($r = .21$). Turnout hovers at around 50 percent in those states that saw relatively small numbers of general-election ads. It climbs to 53 percent in states in which between five thousand and ten thousand spots were broadcast and to 56 percent in states whose media markets saw the highest levels of campaign advertising.[5] Moreover, the effects of campaign advertising remain even when registration law is controlled for in multivariate analysis. Campaign activity, therefore, is an important measure of competitiveness, and is associated with higher levels of turnout at the state level.

In sum, whether measured in terms of the voting-age population or the voting-eligible population, turnout at the state level can be understood as a function of the specific legal and electoral conditions facing citizens on Election Day. Both of these factors changed between 1996 and 2000 in ways that would lead one to expect higher levels of turnout. Seven states had Election Day registration in 2000, up from five in 1996, and between 1996 and 2000 registration deadlines grew more liberal in eight states but more strict in only four (and only slightly so in those states). In all, the average number of days before Election Day that a voter had to be registered by in order to vote declined by almost half a day between 1996 and 2000. At the same time, the volume of presidential-election advertising increased significantly during this period, from 166,028 to 245,165 spots aired (Goldstein and Freedman 2002). The puzzle, then, remains. Increased mobilization and campaign activity, a high degree of competition at the presidential level, and the increased ease of voter registration all should have contributed to a significant increase. Why did turnout in the aggregate fail to increase more dramatically? Answering this question requires us to move beyond state-level characteristics to explanations based on individual-level attributes and political attitudes.

Understanding Turnout at the Individual Level

To understand the individual-level correlates of turnout, we estimate a multivariate model, which we use to illuminate changes in turnout from 1992 to 2000. We rely on data from the National Election Studies (NES). As in the past, self-reported turnout in the 2000 NES exceeded estimates of actual turnout by a considerable amount.[6] Among all postelection respondents, 72.1 percent reported having voted on Election Day, compared with the actual turnout of 50.4 percent of the voting-age population. This compares to reported turnout of 71.8 in 1996 and 76.6 in 1992.[7] There were, however, two significant changes in the 2000 NES. First, the turnout question itself was changed to include additional response categories in an effort to provide more accurate (i.e., lower) reports of turnout. Unfortunately, since all respondents got the new version of the turnout question, it is impossible to gauge fully the impact of this shift. Second, there was a significant change in interview mode. For the first time, more than 40 percent of all preelection respondents were interviewed by phone rather than face to face. Although there were modest mode effects on reported turnout, the differences fortunately do not significantly affect the substantive conclusions we draw later in this chapter (see the methodological appendix at the end of this chapter for a more complete discussion).

Consistent with volumes of past research, turnout in recent elections has increased with the socioeconomic, attitudinal, and political resources that make voting less costly and more rewarding to citizens (Abramson, Aldrich, and Rohde 1999; Nichols and Beck 1995; Nichols, Kimball, and Beck 1999; Rosenstone and Hansen 1993; Verba, Schlozman, and Brady 1995). Table 10.1 reveals a series of familiar bivariate relationships between turnout and a host of socioeconomic, demographic, and attitudinal variables for the elections of 1992, 1996, and 2000. These patterns are also evident in the multivariate results reported in Table 10.2, which is based on our pooled data set combining NES data from all three years.[8]

Not surprisingly, turnout increases sharply with demographic factors like education, income, and age. People who are married and those who own their own homes were also more likely to vote in each of the last elections than those who are single or who rent. Similarly, women were 4.7 percentage points less likely to vote than men in 2000. This is a more pronounced gender gap than in 1996, when they were only 2.4 points less likely to vote, or in 1992, when the gap was a mere 0.8 points. By contrast, bivariate racial differences in turnout rates essentially disappeared in 2000. African Americans had been 8.8 percentage points less likely to vote than non–African Americans in 1996 and 6.9 points less likely in 1992, but were only 0.2 points less likely in 2000.[9] As Table 10.2 shows, nearly all of these relationships persist in our pooled model even after the effects of other variables have been controlled for. But although most of the effects in the multivariate model are in the same direction as in the bivariate analyses, women and African Americans are somewhat *more* likely to vote than men and white respondents once other factors have been taken into account.

Citizens who are more integrated into workplace or social networks are more likely to vote. This is partly because they are more likely to be contacted by political elites seeking to mobilize electoral participation (Rosenstone and Hansen 1993) and partly because of the skills and other resources they acquire through such social interaction (Verba, Schlozman, and Brady

TABLE **10.1**   1992–2000 individual-level correlates of voter turnout

	1992	1996	2000
Education			
Less than high school	50.4	49.4	48.5
High school graduate	73.1	66.6	65.8
Some college	85.2	78.6	76.1
College degree	90.6	88.1	91.8
More than college	95.2	92.2	94.3
Income			
Lowest quartile	59.8	55.5	55.8
Highest quartile	89.2	87.2	85.7
Age			
18–24	55.0	47.6	52.0
25–34	73.0	61.8	62.2
35–44	78.7	73.9	72.4
45–54	82.6	78.8	81.2
55–64	84.9	81.8	83.6
65–74	83.4	83.7	79.5
75+	80.0	84.0	79.8
Race			
African American	70.6	64.1	71.9
White and other	77.5	72.9	72.1
Gender			
Men	77.0	73.1	74.8
Women	76.2	70.7	70.1
Union Membership			
Union household	85.2	81.1	76.5
Nonunion household	74.7	69.6	71.2
Marital Status			
Married	81.5	80.3	79.3
Single/divorced	68.7	59.1	62.4
Homeownership			
Homeowner	82.5	78.3	79.9
Renter	65.8	57.5	55.1
Church Attendance			
Never attend religious services	69.3	58.7	59.6
Every week	82.2	84.3	82.6
Mobilization			
Contacted by candidate or party	92.3	88.6	90.6
Noncontacted	72.5	65.6	61.8
Civic Duty			
Happy to serve on jury	82.5	78.7	79.8
Rather not serve	67.1	63.2	60.7
Internal Efficacy			
Lowest	63.1	64.6	54.7
Highest	89.4	86.8	89.1
External Efficacy			
Lowest	57.7	58.6	49.1
Highest	86.6	82.1	87.0

(*continued*)

TABLE **10.1**   Continued

	1992	1996	2000
Political Trust			
Lowest	77.6	69.6	60.8
Highest	79.4	64.6	72.0
Strength of Partisanship			
Pure independent	57.0	41.3	47.8
Leaning	74.4	65.8	67.9
Weak partisan	76.2	69.7	71.8
Strong partisan	87.6	88.7	86.1
Perceived Closeness			
Close race	78.8	70.5	75.7
Not a close race	70.4	73.3	52.0
Weekly Newspaper Reading			
None	59.4	59.4	60.8
6–7 days	86.5	82.7	80.3
Political Information			
Lowest	38.3	34.2	51.4
Midpoint	83.0	65.8	84.5
Highest	96.5	93.3	97.9
Net Candidate Distance			
0–19 degrees	67.9	61.6	61.3
80–100 degrees	88.4	85.4	84.8
Candidate Likes			
None	56.3	49.5	53.3
1–5	79.7	76.2	77.2
6–10	91.8	90.9	84.8
Candidate Dislikes			
None	49.6	50.0	50.2
1–5	80.2	76.8	81.1
6–10	91.1	89.6	84.3

DATA SOURCE: *1992–2000 National Election Studies.*

1995). Union members, often prime targets for mobilization activity, are indeed more likely to vote than people in households without union members (although the difference in 2000—5.3 points—is less than half as large as the 11.5-point difference in 1996). Similarly, people who regularly attend church—where they are likely to encounter like-minded neighbors, join groups, and hear calls to political as well as spiritual action—are more likely to vote than those who never attend. And, of course, citizens who report having been contacted directly and asked to vote by a party or campaign are far more likely to vote than those who have not been mobilized. Those who were contacted in 2000 were 28.8 points more likely to vote than those who were not mobilized by a campaign or party, a wider gap than in 1996 or 1992.[10] When other variables are controlled for in our pooled model, individuals who were contacted by parties or campaigns were still

	Coefficient	Significance	Maximum Change in Probability	Centered Standard Deviation Change in Probability*
Registration closing date	−.010 (.005)	.072	−.06	−.02
Party or campaign contact	1.027 (.122)	.000	.14	.09
Long-Term Dispositions				
Strength of partisanship	.839 (.135)	.000	.12	.05
Political information	.216 (.032)	.000	.17	.07
Civic duty	.530 (.085)	.000	.09	
External efficacy	.164 (.040)	.000	.09	.04
Newspaper reading	.066 (.015)	.000	.08	.04
Short-Term Attitudes				
Care about outcome	.776 (.096)	.000	.12	
Perceived closeness of race	.186 (.096)	.054	.03	
Net candidate thermometer difference	.006 (.002)	.001	.10	.03
Candidate likes	.048 (.025)	.054	.08	.02
Candidate dislikes	.100 (.025)	.000	.14	.04
Socio-Demographic Attributes				
Length of time in community (Log)	.191 (.042)	.000	.13	.04
Married	.261 (.090)	.004	.05	
Homeowner	.393 (.095)	.000	.07	
Union member	.306 (.121)	.012	.05	
African American	.504 (.131)	.000	.08	
Male	−.276 (.087)	.001	−.06	
South	−.337 (.092)	.000	−.07	
Age	.010 (.003)	.001	.11	.03
Education	.309 (.036)	.000	.16	.09

(*continued*)

TABLE **10.2**   Continued

	Coefficient	Significance	Maximum Change in Probability	Centered Standard Deviation Change in Probability*
Income	.258	.057	.06	.02
	(.135)			
Church attendance	.597	.000	.09	.05
	(.112)			
1992 dummy variable	.200	.053		
	(.103)			
2000 dummy variable	.031	.779		
	(.109)			
Constant	−4.201	.000		
	(.306)			
Number of cases	4808			
Chi-Square	1674.32 (25 df)	p < .001		
Pseudo R^2	.45			
Percentage correctly classified	82.1%			
Percentage reported turnout	75.0%			

DATA SOURCE: *1992–2000 National Election Studies.*
*See note 11.

fourteen percentage points more likely to vote than individuals who were not, even after all other variables have been controlled (Table 10.2).[11]

Attitudes and perceptions of the political system and the citizen's place in it constitute another set of important factors that affect voting behavior. Citizens with a more pronounced sense of civic duty—measured in the NES (somewhat inadequately) by their willingness to serve on a jury—are far more likely to vote than those with a less-developed sense of civic responsibility. Similarly, citizens with a greater sense of political efficacy are more likely to vote. In particular, external efficacy—the sense that the political system is responsive to the opinions and interests of people like the respondent—leads to a greater likelihood of voting. Efficacy is measured by the respondent's agreement or disagreement with two statements: "People like me don't have any say about what the government does," and "I don't think public officials care much what people like me think." Respondents with the highest sense of efficacy were thirty-eight points more likely to vote in 2000 than were those scoring lowest on the scale. Even controlling for other variables, both civic duty and external efficacy increase the probability of voting by as much as nine points. (Internal efficacy, in contrast, has no impact once other variables are controlled for.) Finally, notwithstanding the attention it receives from political scientists and popular observers of politics, political trust is relatively unrelated to voter turnout (Hetherington 1999; Rosenstone and Hansen 1993). In 1996, the effect of trust (measured by a standard four-item scale) on turnout was actually slightly negative; in 2000 the relationship was essentially flat.[12]

Citizens who are more engaged with politics generally and engaged with a given election campaign in particular are, not surprisingly, more likely to vote than people who are less engaged, informed, and attentive. As Table 10.1 shows, people who say they care about the election outcome and those who follow politics closely in the news media are all much more likely to participate. In part, the effects of media consumption on turnout are due to the sheer information that citizens absorb. Politically relevant information is associated both with greater political engagement and higher levels of participation in political activities (Zaller 1992; Delli Carpini and Keeter 1996). Indeed, political information—measured by a standard battery of questions asking which office or position various political figures hold and which party controls each house of Congress—is one of the single best variables for distinguishing between voters and nonvoters. In 2000, citizens who scored highest on the NES political information quiz were a full 46.5 points more likely to vote than those who were unable to answer a single question correctly.[13] Even when other variables like education are controlled for in our pooled model, individuals who possess the highest levels of political knowledge in a given year are seventeen percentage points more likely to vote than individuals who possess the absolute lowest amount of political information.[14]

Turnout is also closely tied to strength of partisanship (Campbell et al. 1960). Strong partisans—whether Democrat or Republican—are more likely to vote than are weaker partisans, and independents are least likely to vote at all. In 1996, strong partisans were forty-seven points more likely to vote than pure independents. Strong partisans in 2000 were only thirty-eight points more likely to vote than independents, primarily because the latter group was somewhat more likely to vote in 2000 than in 1996 (47.8 versus 41.3 percent), a point we revisit later in this chapter. In our multivariate model, strong partisans are twelve percentage points more likely to vote than are independents.

Recognizing that a given vote contributes a bit more to the outcome in a close election than in a landslide, political scientists have long argued that turnout should be higher in close races. Indeed, as we reported earlier in this chapter, this was the case with state-level turnout in 2000. In recent years, however, individual-level perceptions of a close presidential election were at best only modestly related to turnout. In 1996 respondents who saw the Clinton-Dole race as a close one were actually *less* likely to vote than those who saw a less evenly matched contest (Nichols, Kimball, and Beck 1999). This changed dramatically in 2000. People who saw the race as close were twenty-four points more likely to turn out than those who did not. In part, this was because citizens who saw a close race were five points more likely to vote in 2000 than their counterparts in 1996. But the bulk of the effect was that those voters who saw the race as not being close were more than twenty points less likely to vote than in 1996 (52 versus 73.3). This shift may in part be due to the fact that the presidential election in 2000 was objectively and unambiguously a close one, unlike that of 1996. Consequently, citizens who failed to perceive a close race may likely have been less informed, less engaged, and in general less likely to vote for other reasons. Alternatively, perceptions of closeness may have mattered more in 2000, even controlling for citizen competence and political sophistication. We will explore these possibilities later in this chapter.

Finally, past research has shown that the extent of respondents' cognitive as well as emotional engagement with a candidate can affect the probability of participation (Marcus and MacKuen 1993; Holbrook et al. 2001). We looked at candidate assessments in two ways. First, we measured the net difference between preelection feeling thermometer ratings of the candidates. Our hypothesis is that turnout will rise as this difference increases, as citizens will be more motivated to vote when they favor one of the candidates by a wide margin. Conversely, they will be less motivated when they are indifferent about the candidates, either because they find them equally satisfactory or equally abhorrent (Weisberg and Grofman 1981). This is indeed the case. Turnout among respondents who saw little or no difference between Bush and Gore (a net difference of ten degrees or less on the one-hundred-degree feeling thermometer) was 60.3 percent. It rose to 84.7 percent among respondents who strongly favored one candidate over the other (a net difference of fifty-five degrees or more). A similar pattern is evident for ratings of Clinton and Gore in 1996 as well as for Clinton and the elder Bush in 1992. Relative candidate favorability ratings are thus strongly related to turnout: in our multivariate model they can mean as much as a ten-point difference in turnout.

A similar relationship is evident when we look at the number of reasons respondents are able to give for liking or disliking the candidates. As in past years, NES asked respondents in 2000 first whether there was anything in particular that they liked about each of the candidates. Up to five mentions were accepted for each candidate, including everything from past experience and leadership ability to physical appearance and other personal qualities. Respondents were then asked whether there were reasons to dislike each of the candidates. Again, up to five responses—ranging from comments about the candidate's character to criticisms of his policy positions—were accepted.

Both likes and dislikes are strongly related to voter turnout. Among respondents who are not able to offer a single reason for supporting either candidate, turnout in 2000 is only 53.3 percent. It rose to 77.2 percent for those who mention between one and five reasons and 84.8 for people mentioning six or more. Turnout rises just as sharply with respondents' ability to articulate reasons for *not* liking a candidate. Only half (50.2) of those who are unable to offer a single reason for disliking either candidate turn out to vote. This increases to 81.1 percent for those who offer one to five reasons and 84.3 percent of people who were able to articulate six or more reasons. Thus, although turnout rises in both cases with the number of mentions, sharp jumps are evident between people who are unable to offer a single positive or negative mention and those who can articulate at least one reason to support or oppose a candidate.

In our multivariate model it is clear that candidate likes and dislikes do not matter equally: disliking the candidates exerts nearly twice as large an effect on turnout as does liking them. Individuals, for example, who mention ten things they *dislike* about the major candidates are fourteen percentage points more likely to vote than individuals who do not mention any dislikes. The corresponding difference is only eight percentage points for mentioning ten things that an individual *likes*.

Explaining Change in Voter Turnout

Given these findings, how are we to make sense of the changes in voter turnout between the 1992, 1996, and 2000 elections? Most of the change in turnout from election to election can be attributed to changing *levels* of important independent variables, in particular, party contact, perceived closeness of the contest, and the individuals' likes and dislikes of the major-party candidates. Several variables, however, show differences in what can be called "salience," that is, different causal *effects* of the variable over time (Kaufmann and Petrocik 1999). We will show that these changes—notably in the effects of party identification—have also played important roles in the changes in turnout across the three elections.

"Level" Effects

The model presented in Table 10.2 shows the effects of each of the independent variables on the individual's decision to vote or abstain in a given election. With this information, we may easily explain the overall changes in turnout from one election to another by examining how the electorate as a whole may have moved in or out of "high turnout" categories over time. The mathematical calculations to determine the actual impact of each variable on overall change are relatively straightforward, and involve the product of the effect of the variable in a multiple-regression model and the change in the average value of the variable from one election to the next.[15]

TABLE **10.3**   The effects of changes in levels of independent variables on changing turnout, 1992–2000

	1992 Level	1996 Level	2000 Level	Impact on Change, 96–00	Impact on Change, 92–96
Perceived closeness	82%	54%	86%	.86	−.75
Party/campaign contact	21%	27%	36%	.82	.51
Education (1–7 scale)	3.93	3.91	4.00	.32	−.08
Civic duty	63%	56%	61%	.30	−.50
External efficacy (0–5 scale)	3.10	2.72	2.84	.23	−.72
South	30%	36%	31%	.22	−.28
Registration closing date (days)	25.47	24.74	23.34	.18	.09
Newspaper reading (days)	3.79	3.27	3.40	.08	−.32
Age (years)	44.08	44.68	45.06	.06	.10
Male	48%	45%	44%	.03	.12
Income (0–1 scale)	.57	.53	.54	.02	−.15
Black	12%	12%	12%	.02	−.04
Political information (normed, mean 0)	.00	.00	.00	.00	.00
Time in community (log)	2.69	2.66	2.64	−.03	−.07
Homeowner	69%	69%	68%	−.04	.01
Married	62%	61%	58%	−.08	−.05
Church attendance (0–1 scale)	.46	.46	.45	−.10	.02
Candidate likes (number)	2.77	2.48	2.26	−.14	−.19
Union member	18%	19%	16%	−.15	.07
Net thermometer diff.	34.75	36.96	33.28	−.23	.14
Care about outcome	78%	79%	77%	−.28	.22
Strength of partisanship (0–1 scale)	.60	.63	.59	−.40	.36
Candidate dislikes (number)	3.06	2.54	2.09	−.58	−.65
Total predicted change				1.09	−2.18
Actual turnout change (Reported)	.776	.729	.734	.49	−4.64

DATA SOURCE: *1992–2000 National Election Studies.*
NOTE: *Cell entries are percentages with the relevant characteristics, unless otherwise noted.*

Intuitively, these calculations provide an estimate of how turnout changed from the previous election compared to what it would have been if the levels of a particular independent variable had not changed at all. That is, they suggest how turnout in 2000 (or 1996) differed from what it would have been if each independent variable had remained at its 1996 (or 1992) level.

In Table 10.3 we show the impact of each independent variable on the changes in turnout between 1996 and 2000, and then between 1992 and 1996. The variables are listed in descending order of their effect on turnout change between 1996 and 2000. These figures readily explain why turnout increased only slightly in 2000, following the large drop between 1992 and 1996. As can be seen from the figures in the fourth column, the 2000 election possessed many characteristics that led to increased voter participation. Indeed, these are precisely the factors that led to the puzzle we posed at the outset of the chapter: why turnout in 2000 did not increase more dramatically. As noted earlier, the electorate accurately perceived the competitive nature of the 2000 election, in that a much greater proportion saw the contest as "very close." Despite the relatively weak influence of perceptions of closeness on turnout, noted in the previous section, this factor by itself contributed a rise in turnout over 1996 of nearly nine-tenths of a percentage point. The increased efforts of parties and campaigns in mobilizing the electorate in 2000 compared to 1996 had a similarly large effect on turnout. Over one-third of the electorate received some form of party or campaign contact, an increase from the 27 percent level of 1996. Moreover, this change contributed an increase in turnout of just over eight-tenths of a percentage point. These two factors—mobilization contact and perceived electoral closeness—were by far the largest influences on turnout change from the 1996 to 2000 period.

Several other features of the 2000 election context also produced a more participatory electorate. The long-term increase in the electorate's education level continued to have a positive effect on voter turnout, as did the long-term decline in state-level restrictions governing registration. Taken together, these two factors produced another half-percentage-point rise in turnout over 1996. Perhaps the most surprising feature of the 2000 election context, however, was the beginning of a reversal of the decades-long decline in political orientations such as external efficacy and civic duty. Both of these variables showed modest increases over their 1996 level, and taken together these changes produced an additional half-point increase in turnout.

The 2000 election, then, was perceived as more competitive, featured more party and campaign mobilization, less restrictive registration laws, and a more educated electorate with more favorable views concerning the political system and the individual's responsibilities for civic participation. Based on these changes alone, turnout in the 2000 election would have risen nearly 2.75 percentage points over 1996.

Why, then, did actual turnout rise only marginally from its 1996 level? The answer can be found on the negative side of the ledger in Table 10.3, by examining the factors that led turnout to decline over time. One factor was a decline in the overall strength of partisanship in the electorate since 1996. As we noted earlier, this produced a somewhat larger proportion of pure independents in 2000 than four years earlier. Although there was also a slightly higher proportion of strong partisans, overall partisanship declined in the electorate, and this contributed to a decrease in turnout of four-tenths of a percentage point.

The largest negative influences on turnout, however, were factors related to the candidates themselves. The electorate, as we noted earlier, was essentially unengaged with either major-party candidate compared to both 1996 and 1992. Although individuals mentioned on average 2.54 things they disliked about Bill Clinton and Bob Dole in 1996, they averaged only just over 2 dislikes in 2000. This diminished inventory of dislikes led to a decrease in turnout of nearly six-tenths of a percentage point. Similarly, the electorate mentioned fewer things they *liked* about the candidates than in 1996, yielding an additional 0.14–point decrease in turnout. Americans also rated the candidates more similarly on the feeling thermometer scale in 2000 than in 1996 (yielding a quarter-point drop in turnout), and they cared less about the outcome of the election (leading to an additional .25 percentage point decline in turnout). In short, voters appeared to be relatively indifferent toward the candidates and toward the electoral outcome compared to the previous election. These aspects of voter disengagement together produced a nearly 1.25-percentage-point decline in turnout in the 2000 election.

We may conclude, therefore, that the favorable electoral context for turnout was almost completely negated by the electorate's indifference toward the major-party candidates. The electorate was "satisfied" with the choices offered and rated them reasonably highly on the thermometer scales. However, they were not emotionally involved with either man. In fact, the total number of likes and dislikes that respondents mentioned in 2000 concerning the candidates was the lowest number since at least the 1964 election (Hughes and Conway 1997). Our explanation thus far is that a disengaged electorate responded only half-heartedly to the furious mobilization efforts made by the parties and campaigns in the closest election in modern American history.

Understanding 1996 versus 1992

The same kind of calculations provide important insights into changes in voter turnout between 1992 and 1996 and thus into the way changes in the electorate over the past decade have changed voter participation. In an election that witnessed a more than 4.5-percentage-point decrease in turnout, the only significant *mobilizing* element of the 1996 contest was the increase in party and campaign contact over the 1992 election. This increase contributed to a 0.51-point increase in turnout between 1992 and 1996. This, when coupled with the contribution of increased contact from 1996 to 2000, indicates that party mobilization has led to a total increase of approximately 1.33 percentage points since the 1992 election. Less-restrictive registration laws contributed only 0.09 percentage points to the increase between 1992 and 1996, or an increase of just under one third of a percentage point in total since 1992.

For nearly all other important variables, however, levels declined between 1992 and 1996. The long-term orientations of civic duty and external efficacy were lower in 1996 than four years earlier, as was newspaper reading and the perceived closeness of the contest. Taken together, these factors led to a drop of just over two percentage points in turnout by 1996. Moreover, the electorate's level of engagement with Bill Clinton and George

Bush in 1992 was significantly higher than its reaction to Clinton and Dole four years later. The mean number of candidate likes and dislikes was about one mention more in 1992 than in 1996, contributing to a 0.84-point decline in turnout in 1996 as well. In fact, the total number of likes and dislikes mentioned in 1992 was the highest since the 1964 election (Hughes and Conway 1997), and these calculations do not capture the additional engagement provided by the third-party candidate, Ross Perot.

In many ways, then, the election of 2000 differed markedly from 1992, though each witnessed a rise in turnout from the previous contest. The increased participation seen in the election of 1992 appears in retrospect to have been almost completely a candidate-driven phenomenon. Likes and dislikes of the major-party candidates were at their peak levels in thirty years, while party mobilization efforts in fact declined somewhat since 1988. Long-term political orientations such as efficacy, civic duty, and strength of party identification were all in decline as well (Hughes and Conway 1997). By contrast, the election of 2000 saw intensive (and successful) efforts at party mobilization as well as increases in long-term participatory attitudes such as efficacy and civic duty. At the same time, it featured major-party candidates who failed to capture the imagination, attention, or affection of the electorate. The result is that—notwithstanding 2000's half-hearted rise in turnout—the critical facilitative mobilization and attitudinal conditions are in place for larger increases in turnout in the future. Given more engaging and inspiring candidates who are able to forge more intense emotional bonds with the electorate than was the case in 2000, there is strong reason to expect higher turnout in the future.

"Salience" Effects

As we discussed earlier, changes in voter turnout between 1992, 1996, and 2000 may have been produced either by changing levels of important independent variables, by changes in the effects of these variables on the individual turnout decision, or by some combination of the two. For example, the proportion of individuals who cared about the outcome of the 1996 and 2000 elections may have been nearly identical, but the *effect* of caring about the outcome may have changed over time. We call this kind of effect on overall turnout levels a "salience" effect, that is, an effect produced by the different regression weights associated with independent variables over time (see Kaufmann and Petrocik 1999 for a similar approach).

In the analyses reported thus far, we assumed constant salience for each independent variable between 1992 and 2000. We also estimated the impact of changing levels of each variable on overall changes in turnout, given a common or pooled regression coefficient. To assess the extent to which sa-

TABLE **10.4**   Differences in effects of independent variables on turnout, 1992–2000

	Difference Between Turnout of High and Low Groups		
	1992	*1996*	*2000*
Perceived closeness of race	.02	.01	.07
Strength of partisanship	.08	.23	.06
Civic duty	.07	.06	.09
External efficacy	.07	.07	.12
Net thermometer difference	.09	.04	.09
Length of time in community	.15	.09	.11
Union member	.05	.06	−.02
Married	.02	.08	.02
African-American	.05	.04	.09
Age	.07	.15	.06
Education	.26	.24	.24

DATA SOURCE: *1992–2000 National Election Studies.*

lience, or the magnitude of the regression coefficients, changed over time, we estimated the turnout model separately for each election year. We then tested to determine whether differences between coefficients for 1996 and 2000, and then between 1992 and 1996, were statistically significant.

The effects of the explanatory variables in our pooled model were relatively stable. Out of twenty-four independent variables in our model, there were only eleven for which we found statistically significant differences between two or more elections, and many of these differences were of relatively small substantive magnitude. Thus, most independent variables had generally similar effects on turnout across the three elections. However, to the extent that salience differences did exist for these eleven variables, differences in turnout rates between individuals who were "high" and "low" on the variable in one election were not the same as the turnout difference between "high" and "low" respondents in another contest. In Table 10.4 we show the differences in turnout rates for the three elections for the eleven variables where *any* salience effects were found.

Table 10.4 shows the differences in estimated turnout rates between "high" and "low" respondents (using the same approach employed earlier), holding all other variables at their average value in the respective election. For example, the difference in turnout in 1992 and 1996 between individuals who thought the election would be "very close" and those who thought it would be not close was only 2 and 1 percent, respectively. In the 2000 contest, this figure rose to 7 percent. Thus, part of the explanation for the increase in turnout between 1996 and 2000 was not only that more individuals thought the election would be close, but also that perceived closeness *mattered* more for the vote decision in 2000 than in the previous election (consistent with the bivariate findings we reported earlier). Similarly, the salience of long-term dispositions such as civic duty and external efficacy also increased in 2000, with differences between high and low turnout groups increasing to over 9 and 12 percent, respectively, in 2000 compared to 6 and 7 percent in the previous election.

Among demographic variables, striking differences between the 2000 election and the two previous contests are evident in the vote propensities for union members and African Americans. Individuals who were union members (or who lived in a household with a union member) participated at about a 6 percent higher rate than nonmembers in both 1992 and 1996. This difference was completely wiped out in the 2000 election. For African Americans, the pattern is completely reversed; what was a 4-to-5-percent-higher probability of voting in 1992 and 1996, holding all other variables constant, grew to nearly a 10-point gap in 2000. Perhaps fittingly, given the closely contested nature of the 2000 election, these two processes cancelled one another out in terms of their effect on the outcome. Increased turnout among an intensely Democratic yet relatively small portion of the electorate (African Americans) was counterbalanced by *decreased* turnout among a moderately Democratic though somewhat larger bloc of voters (union households).

By far, the largest difference in salience across the three elections, however, is seen for party identification. Other things being equal, strong partisans had turnout rates that were twenty-three percentage points higher in 1996 than pure independents. This difference was eight percentage points in 1992 and only six percentage points in the 2000 contest. (These differences reflect a logistic-regression coefficient in 1996 for party identification on turnout that is over twice as large as its value in 1992, and over three times its value in 2000.) Thus, the 1996 electorate was the most partisan in its composition of any of the three contests, while differences between partisan groups in terms of turnout rates were more muted in the 1992 and 2000 contests.

A closer examination of this effect reveals several important additional findings. We generated an equation predicting voter turnout with all of the variables from Table 10.3, while separating the "strength-of-party-identification" variable into its seven constituent parts. We then estimated the probability of voting in each election for each of these groups, holding all other variables at their mean level. We show the results of this estimation in Figure 10.2.

The figure demonstrates significant differences between these groups that are both theoretically and electorally important. First, it can be seen that strong partisans were about eight points *less likely* to vote in 2000 than

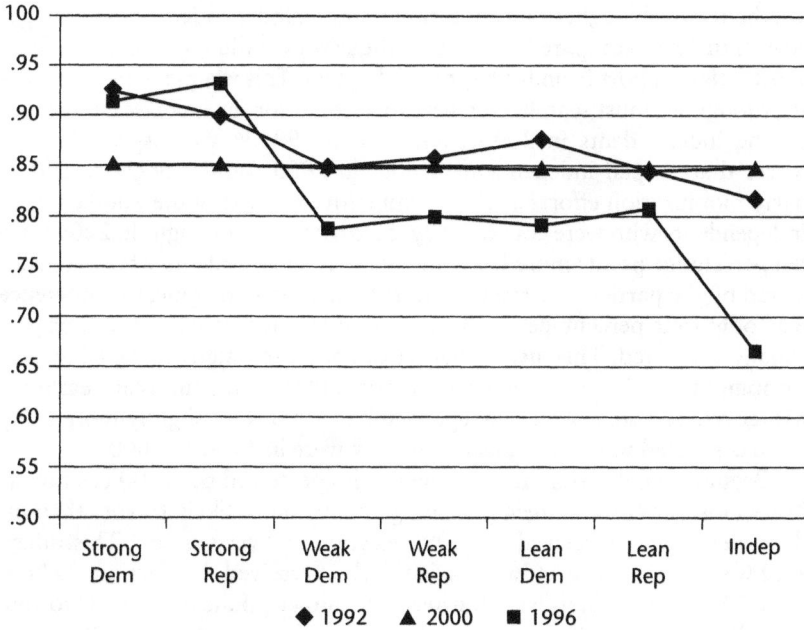

FIGURE 10.2   Estimated Turnout Probability by Party Identification, 1992–2000

in the two other contests. Strong Democrats were equally likely to vote in 1992 and 1996, while turnout among strong Republicans increased somewhat in support of Bob Dole compared to the Bush candidacy four years earlier. Interestingly, the decline in turnout among strong Democrats and strong Republicans between 1996 and 2000 was almost identical, as neither partisan group was as engaged with their candidate as they were four years before. Moreover, the decline in turnout among strong partisans—who comprise over 30 percent of the electorate and whose numbers *increased* somewhat in 2000—played a significant role in keeping turnout from rising more sharply. Had turnout rates among strong partisans been at their 1996 levels, we would have seen an additional 2.5-percentage-point increase in turnout in 2000 (i.e., an 8 percent higher turnout rate among 30 percent of the electorate). This relative lack of partisan interest, then, fits well into our overall description of the 2000 contest as one that reflected an electorate that was not emotionally engaged with the major-party candidates.

At the same time, independents turned out at a significantly higher rate in 2000 (and 1992) than in 1996 (an estimated difference of fourteen to eighteen percentage points). Nichols, Kimball, and Beck (1999, 38) attribute the relatively higher rates of turnout among independents (and younger voters) in 1992 compared to 1996 to the Perot candidacy, which attracted substantial support from both groups of voters. This is a plausible hypothesis, though we must search elsewhere to account for the increases in turnout among independents in 2000 compared to 1996.[16] We suspect that the forces that shaped independent turnout in 2000 were strongly related to party mobilization efforts and the competitive context of the 2000 contest. Independents who were contacted by the parties or campaigns in 2000 were ten percentage points more likely to vote than independents who were contacted by the parties or campaigns in 1996. At the same time, the difference was only four percentage points among independents who were not personally contacted. This means that parties and campaigns obtained greater turnout "yields" among independents in 2000 than four years earlier.[17] Moreover, as noted earlier, independents in 2000 were slightly more likely to be contacted in the first place than they were in 1996 or 2000.

Beyond mobilization, independents who perceived the 2000 election as "very close" were seventeen percentage points more likely to vote than independents who perceived the 1996 election as "very close." This difference was reversed among independents who perceived the elections as "not close." Such individuals were fourteen percentage points *more* likely to vote in 1996.

Thus, independents appear to have responded more strongly to mobilization efforts and the competitive context of the 2000 election than they did four years earlier. To this extent, since the number of independents in the electorate increased between 1996 and 2000, turnout would have declined even further if they had voted at the same rate. The fourteen-percentage-point increase in turnout among 13 percent of the electorate led to an approximately 1.8-percentage-point increase in overall turnout. This was not enough to offset the decline in turnout attributable to the decrease among strong partisans, but it prevented further declines on the basis of increased independence in the American electorate.

Conclusion

Understanding the puzzling half-hearted rise in turnout in the 2000 election requires understanding both the short-term forces contributing to low turnout, as well as those forces that should have increased turnout more substantially. In 2000, more citizens were contacted, more citizens thought the election would be close, and more citizens believed in the responsiveness of the system and the duty of the individual to take part in political life. These changes, however, were nearly, though not totally, offset by an increase in political independence and a sharp decrease in the affective engagement of the electorate with the candidates over time. These signs from 2000 indicate that, given the intensely competitive partisan balance and the slowing of the dealigning trend in the American electorate (Bartels 2000), it is altogether likely that the longer-term trends in turnout could be on a distinctly upward trajectory. At the same time, our emphasis on candidate-related influences on turnout suggests that participation in a given election will depend on the bonds generated between voters and candidates (see also Marcus and MacKuen 1993; Marcus, Neuman, and MacKuen 2000). Thus, if future elections produce candidates as uninspiring as George W. Bush and Al Gore, it is unlikely that turnout will rise considerably in the short term.

A significant additional part of the turnout story of these three elections is the difference in the relative *salience* of key variables over time. Certain demographic groups such as African Americans were more likely to vote in 2000 than in previous years, while groups such as union members, married people, and older individuals lost the edge in turnout that they had shown four (and eight) years before. The effect of long-term attitudinal factors such as civic duty and external efficacy increased in 2000 as well, and such changes also appear to augur well for future levels of turnout in presidential elections.

Finally, we found that turnout rates appear to change substantially for different partisan groups over time, in ways that reflect the appeal of the candidates as well as the mobilization and competitive aspects of the respective campaigns. Turnout changes, then, are a function not only of long-term attitudinal and demographic shifts in the electorate and short-term reactions to the candidates. They are also a function of the interaction between the electorate and the parties and campaigns that attempt to mobilize them to turn out and support a given candidate. Party and campaign contact yields voters more successfully in some contexts than others. This is perhaps another important way that campaigns "matter" in the individual vote decision and in the overall outcome of U.S. presidential elections.

METHODOLOGICAL APPENDIX
Question Wording and Mode in the 2000 NES Survey

Voter turnout as measured in the 2000 National Election Study is not strictly comparable to prior studies for two reasons. First, there was a change in question wording. As in the past, respondents were presented with the following statement:

In talking to people about elections, we often find that a lot of people were not able to vote because they weren't registered, they were sick, or they just didn't have time.

In past studies, there was a simple dichotomous follow-up: How about you—did you vote in the elections this November? In 2000, however, respondents were presented with an expanded set of response categories and were asked to select the statement that best described them:
- I did not vote [in the election this November];
- I thought about voting this time—but didn't;
- I usually vote, but didn't this time;
- I am sure I voted.

This expanded choice was an effort to reduce erroneous reports of turnout. According to the NES, "some people may remember having voted sometime in the past but confuse the source of that memory, accidentally misassigning it to the most recent election, when it actually derives from a prior election. We are therefore implementing a new item, with expanded response categories" (NES 2000 Codebook Introduction).

The second major change in the 2000 National Election Study was an increased reliance on telephone interviewing. Of the 1,807 preelection study respondents, 56 percent were interviewed face to face, and 44 percent were interviewed by phone. In the postelection study, approximately 20 percent of those originally interviewed in person were contacted by phone.

Consistent with past work in the literature, reported turnout is contingent on mode, with telephone interviewing leading to higher levels (Krosnick and Green 1999; Groves 1979; Groves and Kahn 1979; Wessel, Rahn, and Rudolph 2000). Respondents interviewed by telephone in both pre- and postelection waves were 6.4 points more likely to have reported voting than respondents interviewed in person in both waves (76.1 percent versus 69.7 percent; see table 10A.1). And respondents interviewed face to face in the first wave and by phone in the second reported intermediate levels of turnout (71.6 percent).

We estimated a version of the multivariate model that we report in this paper with an indicator for interview mode. The direct effect of having a postelection telephone interview (as opposed to a face-to-face interview) was approximately a 2.5-point increase in reported turnout. Importantly, this increase was relatively uniform. Including a series of interaction terms revealed no significant differences in mode effect by education, gender, race,

TABLE **10A.1**   Turnout by interview mode

Pre-/Post Mode	Reported Turnout
Face-to-Face / Face-to-Face	69.7
Face-to-Face / Phone	71.6
Phone / Phone	76.1

DATA SOURCE: *2000 National Election Study.*
Chi-square: 11.611, p < .003; phi: .086, p < .003.

partisanship, and most attitudinal attributes. There were, however, a handful of exceptions: The effect of being interviewed by telephone was somewhat greater among the least informed respondents, those with a low sense of civic duty, those who did not see the election as a close one, those whose thermometer ratings of the candidates were most similar, and to a lesser extent, those with lower levels of income. There was also a bivariate difference in turnout by race due to mode, with African Americans interviewed by phone ($N = 59$) being more likely to report having voted than non-African Americans. This difference is insignificant however, and disappears in multivariate analysis.

11   Minor Parties in the 2000 Presidential Election

BARRY C. BURDEN

Though neither Patrick Buchanan nor Ralph Nader garnered as many votes as some earlier minor-party candidates, they had the potential to affect the 2000 presidential election in ways that their predecessors could not. This is possible because of the sheer closeness of the major-party vote. The popular vote nearly rendered the presidential contest a tie, with Democrat Al Gore and Republican George W. Bush both winning about 48 percent of the vote. Moreover, the electoral college outcome, which depended on a contentious series of legal battles in Florida, gave Bush the majority by just one vote. Al Gore's 266 electoral votes are the most ever won by a losing candidate.[1] And 2000 was the first time in more than a century in which the winners of the popular and electoral votes were different. In an electoral context as balanced as this one, candidates from outside the two-party system who manage even meager showings can have remarkable effects on the election's outcome.

In this chapter I examine the roles that Reform Party nominee Buchanan and Green Party nominee Nader played in the 2000 presidential election. Using a variety of data from election returns, exit polls, and academic national surveys, I address two questions. First, how did minor-party voters reach their decisions given the great potential for sophisticated behavior in a close election? This requires that we determine the sources of minor-party support and the relationships between their electoral coalitions. Second, what effects did minor parties have on voter turnout and on who won the election? Answering this question requires us to analyze counterfactuals that estimate what would have happened had Buchanan and Nader not been running. The results expand the growing body of theoretical and empirical research on "major" minor parties in America generally as well as help us understand these parties' roles in the 2000 presidential election specifically.[2] The stark realities of this election are sure to force political scientists to rethink some of our conclusions about the dynamics of minor parties.

Minor parties have been of growing interest because their influence appears to have been increasing in recent years. In fact, five of the last nine presidential elections have seen strong minor-party showings. The most dramatic of these was Ross Perot's garnering of 19 percent of the popular vote in 1992 (Jelen 2001). There has also been substantial activity at the subpresidential level, most notably Jesse Ventura's Reform Party victory in the 1998 Minnesota gubernatorial election (Lacy and Monson 2002; Lentz 2001). But if the appearance of new academic work on the subject is an indicator, there appear to be broader forces at work that are conspiring to overcome the standard hurdles facing minor parties at all levels of government (Bibby and Maisel 2002; Herrnson and Green 2002; Sifry 2002). One purpose of this chapter is to explore the role of minor parties in the 2000 presidential election in the light of a burgeoning body of research.

My analysis begins by reexamining the election outcome in terms of social-choice analysis. A simple look at the preference rankings of candidates shows that, for the first time in the survey era, the winner of the presidential election was not the Condorcet winner, as explained in the next section. Moreover, almost no common voting method would have selected Bush as the winner. The analysis also shows than an unprecedented number of party supporters were strategic in 2000. The second section of this chapter analyzes Nader's standing in the polls dynamically by examining the patterns and determinants of his support over the final months of the campaign. Unlike nearly all minor-party candidates, Nader actually rose in the polls over time, even after controlling for the closeness of the major-party vote and support for other candidates. The third section turns to the effects that Buchanan and Nader had on voter participation and the major parties' vote shares. A larger number of minor-party voters would have abstained had their candidates not been in the race. Minor parties, most notably the Greens, increased turnout both directly by mobilizing votes for themselves and indirectly by adding interest to the campaign, for a total effect of around 2.5 percentage points. The next section of the chapter reexamines the possibility that Nader threw the election to Bush. It is clear that Florida almost certainly would have gone Democratic without Nader in the race. Yet it is at least possible that Bush would have won easily in the electoral college without Buchanan in the race. I then turn to examining the sources of minor-party support. Nader voters were more liberal, pro-choice, and educated than other voters on average. The factors that distinguished Nader from Gore in particular were primarily economic in nature. Nader voters disliked the administration's record and took their discontent out on Gore. Aggregate analysis shows that Nader did much better at drawing on his earlier support and Perot's base from 1996. Surprisingly, Buchanan and Nader both performed better where the major-party vote was closer. I conclude by suggesting how this multifaceted picture of results fits with existing work on minor parties in America.

A Perverse Social-Choice Function

Elections are a key mechanism for aggregating individual citizen preferences into collective decisions. The proper way to do this is a matter of great contention. A prominent line of research focuses on the rationality of voting rules and a society's social-choice function. Though no single method of aggregation is ideal, some appear more perverse than others because they violate common assumptions about how preferences ought to be represented. Arrow (1951) has argued that seemingly trivial characteristics such as transitivity and nondictatorship should be maintained, but he has also shown that no voting system can maintain several such characteristics simultaneously. This "impossibility result" confirms that no vote aggregation method is perfect. Plenty of examples can be generated that produce rather different social outcomes from the same individual preferences simply by altering the aggregation rules. At a minimum, one would hope that some basic principles of fairness are retained that at least make the process, and thus the outcome, appear legitimate to voters (see Hibbing and Theiss-Morse 1995).

Two common voting methods are majority and plurality rule. Majority rule would have failed in 2000 because no candidate won 50 percent of the popular vote. Plurality rule would have elected Gore since he won the popular vote. Neither majority nor plurality rule is more natural than or superior to more complicated methods. Indeed, the Founders purposely created the electoral college to avoid popular election. The question becomes whether this rather unique method of election selected the same winner that other aggregation schemes might have, or whether Bush's victory was an idiosyncratic result of the particular set of institutions and events that put him into office.[3]

One of the most stringent methods of selecting a candidate was proposed by the Marquis de Condorcet more than two hundred years ago. Condorcet argued that a winning alternative ought to be capable of defeating all other alternatives in head-to-head comparisons. That is, A should be the victor only if she beats both B and C in paired situations. Even if some voters choose strategically rather than sincerely—perhaps due to a combination of mechanical and psychological incentives (Duverger 1963)—the Condorcet winner should also be the election winner. The Condorcet criterion is an especially desirable method of choosing among multiple candidates because it sets the threshold of victory quite high. In many elections, a Condorcet winner does not even exist.

National Election Study (NES) data from 2000 make it possible to conduct a crude analysis of strategic voting. I follow a long line of research that uses rankings of the candidates on the NES "feeling thermometers" as estimates of the relative ordinal utilities each person has for each candidate. Thermometers are reasonable proxies for respondents' utilities for the candidates and tend to predict voting decisions well (Abramson et al. 1992, 1995, 2000; Brams and Fishburn 1983; Brams and Merrill 1994; Kiewiet 1979; Ordeshook and Zeng 1997; Palfrey and Poole 1987; Weisberg and Grofman 1981; Weisberg and Rusk 1970). Abramson and colleagues (1995) show that the winners of the popular and electoral vote in three notable third-party elections—1968, 1980, and 1992—were all Condorcet winners. In each of those years the electoral college victor also would have won the popular vote using Condorcet's standard of beating each of the other candidates in head-to-head comparisons. Clinton was easily the Condorcet winner in 1996 as well (Abramson, Aldrich, and Rohde 1998).

It is reassuring that different voting schemes—simple plurality rule, the electoral college, the Condorcet criterion, and perhaps even approval voting —all select the same candidate in each of the past four elections with significant minor parties (Brams and Fishburn 1983; Brams and Merrill 1994; Kiewiet 1979). It is more remarkable that every presidential election for which adequate survey data exist seems to have chosen the Condorcet winner, regardless of minor-party showings. This is satisfying because no voting method is ideal, and the Condorcet method is so stringent.

The 2000 election is not so tidy. Not only did George W. Bush not take the popular vote, but the data clearly show that he was not the Condorcet winner either. This is apparently the first time in the survey era that this has happened. Figure 11.1 shows the pairwise rankings of the four presidential candidates in graphical form.[4] The arrows point to the candidates who lose in each comparison. Pat Buchanan is the "Condorcet loser" because each of the other three candidates beat him in head-to-head comparisons. This is indicated by the three arrows pointing toward his name. Gore is the Condorcet winner, beating each of the other candidates (see also Abramson, Aldrich, and Rohde 2002). In between these two extremes, Nader is preferred to Buchanan but loses to both major-party nominees. Bush loses to Gore but defeats both minor-party candidates.

Several other voting methods would also choose Gore as the winner. Running through the list of voting methods that are commonly discussed in textbooks on the subject (e.g., Shepsle and Bonchek 1997), Gore wins whether one uses a plurality runoff, a sequential runoff, or approval voting procedures.[5] The 2000 election thus represents a highly unusual event in

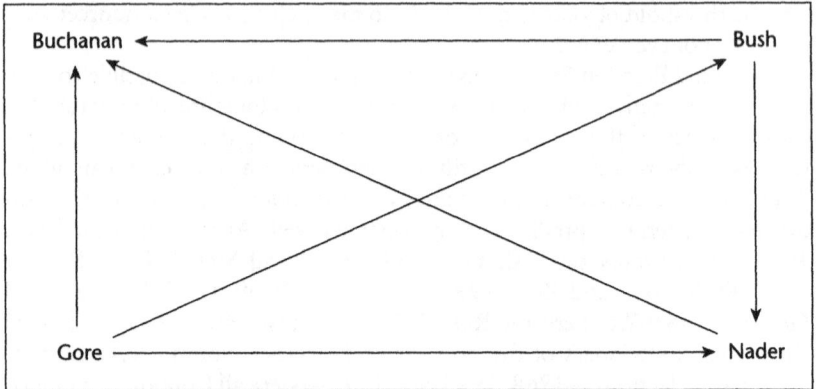

FIGURE 11.1   Pairwise Rankings of Presidential Candidates

modern U.S. politics, as the electoral college appears to be the *only* existing nondictatorial method that would result in George W. Bush's election.

The thermometer rankings also show an unprecedented degree of strategic voting. Other presidential elections where strong minor parties ran of course saw strategic voting, but the pivotal roles that Buchanan and Nader played in 2000 took strategic behavior to a new plateau. Table 11.1 demonstrates this by comparing respondents' candidate rankings along with their vote choice and turnout decisions. The data show that a large majority of those who rated Buchanan or Nader as their most preferred candidates before the election actually voted for someone else. Among voters, over 80 percent of people who rated Buchanan or Nader highest did not vote for them. Most of the Nader preferrers who voted chose Gore, with the remainder splitting between Bush and Nader.

This suggests that many voters were deciding which candidate from outside the current administration was worth their support rather than simply whose platform was nearest their ideal points (Cho 2000; Lacy and Burden 2002). It seems that Nader preferrers and Nader voters are two distinct groups. If the Nader camp was comprised mostly of traditional liberals interested in ideological purity, a strategic voter would have chosen Gore. Presumably, a leftist voter who prefers Nader but fears that his candidacy is not viable would turn to Gore as second choice. A sizable contingent of Nader preferrers appear to have felt that way but abstained. Although many Nader preferrers who voted did pick Gore, it remains counterintuitive that so many voted for Bush instead. Many of these voters must have been motivated not just by progressive ideals but by the desire to end the Clinton-Gore reign and decided that Republican Bush was most likely to do that.

Respondents who ranked Buchanan first were even more disloyal, but their strategic votes were cast more in Bush's direction than in Gore's. More interesting are the abstention rates for each of these groups. About one in five Bush preferrers abstained while one in four Gore supporters did. But more than a third of those who favored Nader abstained, and 42 percent of Buchanan's preferrers stayed home.

This is an unprecedented amount of strategic voting among minor-party supporters (see Abramson et al. 1995; Cho 2000; Ordeshook and Zeng 1997). Strategic considerations are even more widespread if strategic "voting" means more than just choosing a candidate who is not one's most preferred alternative. To the extent that abstention is a purposeful activity akin to choosing a candidate (Aldrich 1997; Lacy and Burden 1999, 2002), many Americans who preferred Buchanan or Nader found nonvoting a more satisfactory decision than either jumping to a minor-party candidate at the other end of the spectrum or stomaching one of the major-party standard-bearers.

It is noteworthy that abstention rates were highest among voters who preferred one of the minor-party candidates. This lack of participation does not necessarily imply lack of enthusiasm for the candidate, however. The strength of support for a chosen presidential candidate was weakest for Nader. Nader voters said they felt less enthusiastic about their choice than did people who voted for one of the other three candidates. The percentage of NES respondents saying they "felt strongly" was 74 percent for Gore, 79 percent for Bush, and even 83 percent for Buchanan, but only 64 percent for Nader. The fact that so many of those who ranked Nader first abstained suggests that they were not particularly fond of *any* of the candidates. Those who voted for Nader probably felt tepid toward all of the candidates running and were only willing to cast protest votes because the antiestablishment Greens happened to be on the ballot. This might explain why appar-

TABLE **11.1**   Candidate rankings, vote choice, and abstention

	Preferred Candidate			
	Bush	Gore	Nader	Buchanan
Presidential Vote Choice				
Bush	93.8	4.8	19.9	59.1
Gore	5.9	94.7	60.9	21.2
Nader	.3	.5	19.2	6.2
Buchanan	0	0	0	13.5
Abstain	19.0	25.6	34.5	42.4
N	333	312	112	21

DATA SOURCE: *2000 National Election Study (weighted).*
NOTE: *Ranking based on preelection feeling thermometers since postelection thermometers do not include Buchanan. Ties are omitted.*

ently not many Nader voters regret their decisions. Only one in ten Nader voters say they wish they could change their vote after knowing how close the election was (Jackman 2000). Given the perversity of the election result shown earlier, it is simply remarkable that 90 percent would pick Nader again even knowing that Bush—often their third- or fourth-ranked choice —would be elected president.

Campaign Dynamics

Some of the more interesting aspects of minor parties are the changes they induce in otherwise normal presidential campaigns (Rosenstone, Behr, and Lazarus 1996). Among other things, a threatening outsider causes the Democratic and Republican nominees to deal with new issues, distribute their resources differently, and assemble altered coalitions. Strong minor parties introduce a great deal of uncertainty into the campaign and force the major parties to begin foraging about for votes more strategically. As a zero-sum game, any support that goes to third-party candidates effectively reduces the pool of votes available to the major parties. At the same time, the possibility of increasing turnout makes the situation look more like a positive-sum game. However, new voters mobilized by a minor party are relatively unpredictable, which often leads the major parties to shore up their bases.

To examine some of these dynamics, I have gathered trial-heat and tracking polls conducted over the last two months of the campaign. Nader's support in the polls bucks historical trends in one important way: it rises rather than falls. As Rosenstone, Behr, and Lazarus (1996, 41) argue, "Third-party support fades as the election approaches. This pattern of declining support has been apparent since the advent of survey data."[6] Though Rosenstone, Behr, and Lazarus argue that voters are apparently willing to consider minor-party candidates when the stakes are low, the electorate abandons them when the stakes increase near Election Day. They show that this pattern holds for seven different candidacies ranging from Robert LaFollette in 1924 to John Anderson in 1980.

Figure 11.2 shows that this decline does not hold for Nader.[7] Though the raw data points are a bit lumpy due to rounding, Nader's support clearly rises. A spline fit to the data shows the upturn well. Despite the variation around the main trend line, there seems to be about a percentage-point increase over the last two months of the presidential campaign.

Nader's rise in the polls apparently defies history. Not only does minor-party support wane in most polls as the consequences of committing to a candidate rise, but the 2000 major-party race remained close enough that Nader votes could have swung the election. Because of the closeness, one might have expected Nader to fall even faster than minor parties running in

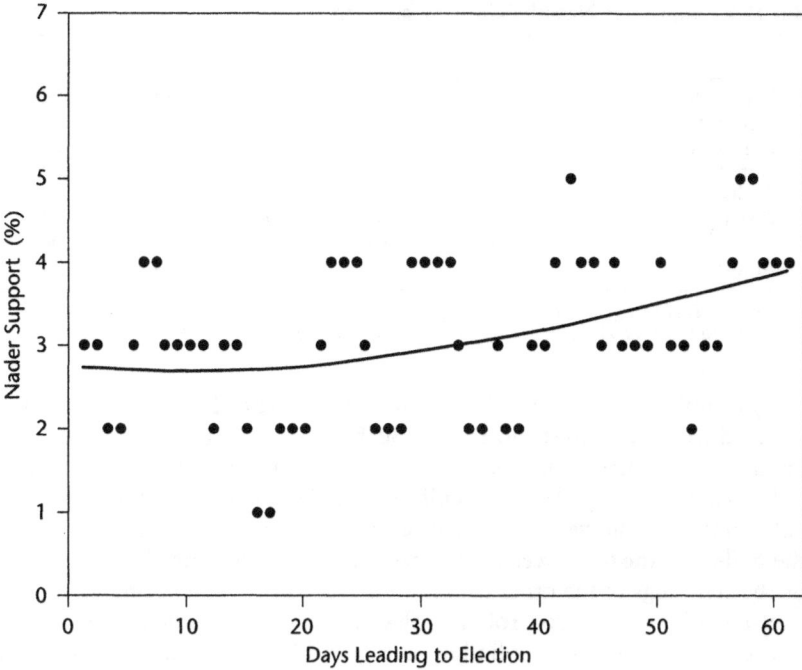

FIGURE **11.2**   Time Series of Nader Support in Gallup Tracking Polls

more lopsided elections. A "gut check" by Nader supporters late in the campaign should have caused them to waiver and throw their support, however weak, to Gore as the second best. If sophisticated maneuvering does not explain the rise in Nader support, what does?

Table 11.2 reports several simple time-series regression models of Nader support.[8] There are five columns, each of which introduces different independent variables to the analysis. The variables include a simple daily counter, Gore and Buchanan vote percentages, and a measure of the closeness of the race. Closeness is measured as the absolute difference between the Bush and Gore percentages, so higher values indicate a more lopsided race. This is done to be sure that the relationship between time and Nader's support is not spurious. It might be, for example, that Nader's support rises only because the race gets closer.

The first three columns of Table 11.2 examine the relationships between time, closeness, and Nader support. It appears—both independently and jointly—that Nader's standings rise later in the campaign and when the race is more lopsided. So Nader does better later in the campaign, even after showing that many of his supporters strategically left him when the major-

TABLE **11.2**   Explaining Nader's daily campaign support

	I	II	III	IV	V
Lopsidedness (Bush% – Gore%)	.12[+]		.12[+]	.12[+]	.08
Daily Counter		.02*	.03*	.03*	.02*
Gore %				.02	−.07
Buchanan %					.59*
Constant	3.63*	3.36*	2.88*	1.98	5.54
ρ	.48	.01	.15	.17	.06
Adjusted R^2	.21	.16	.15	.14	.24

DATA SOURCE: *Trial heat polls (see note 8).*
[+] *p < .10, * *p < .05, two-tailed test. Prais-Winston time series regression. N = 41.*

party campaign got tighter. The last two columns reveal how his support interacted with the nearest substitutes, Buchanan and Gore. It is perhaps surprising that Buchanan and Nader appear to do well or poorly together, as indicated by the positive and significant coefficient on the Buchanan variable. In the end, however, this analysis confirms that Nader's unique rise in the polls over the final weeks of the campaign is not due merely to closeness or the standings of the other candidates. The daily counter remains significant regardless of the control variables introduced. In addition, the size of the coefficient confirms the finding in Figure 11.2 that Nader rose about a point over the last two months of the campaign.

Turnout and Vote-Stealing Effects

Two of the most important effects a minor-party candidate can have are in increasing voter turnout and in altering the major-party vote split (Lacy and Burden 1999, 2002). Minor parties, of course, shake things up in a host of other interesting ways, from altering the campaign agenda to fracturing the major-party coalitions. In the end, however, it is enlightening to know how the election results would have been different without minor parties in the mix. Though one can never answer these counterfactual puzzles definitively by rerunning history (Asher 1995), they are ways of gaining insight on such questions using available data. We must make do by asking how things would have been different with Buchanan or Nader out of the race, assuming that everything else about the campaigns would have remained the same. This is an unrealistic but unavoidable assumption.

Exit polls asked voters about their choices in the hypothetical situation in which neither Buchanan nor Nader was running.[9] Table 11.3 presents a cross-tabulation of these hypothetical questions and self-reported votes. Because minor parties earned so few votes, the aggregate major-party split remains right at fifty-fifty even removing Buchanan, Nader, and the other minor-party nominees.

TABLE **11.3**   Self-reported effects of removing minor-party candidates

| | Actual Vote | | | | | | |
	Gore	Bush	Nader	Buchanan	Other	All	2-Party
Vote in 2-Way Race							
Gore	96.4	1.4	47.7	31.2	23.0	48.4	49.7
Bush	2.4	97.2	21.9	26.6	36.7	49.1	50.3
Abstain	1.2	1.4	30.5	42.2	40.3	2.5	
All	48.0	48.4	2.5	.5	.6		
2-Party	49.8	50.2					

DATA SOURCE: *2000 Voter News Service exit polls (weighted).*
NOTE: *Entries are column percentages.*

More intriguing is what individual voters would have done. Nearly all
Bush and Gore voters would have remained loyal in a two-way race, as one
might expect. This fits with the great consistency between ranking of and
voting for major parties shown earlier. In contrast, many minor-party voters would have abstained. Nearly 30 percent of Nader voters and more than
40 percent of Buchanan voters would have abstained without their candidates in the race. About half of Nader's votes would have gone to Gore, the
perceived next-best candidate. It might seem surprising that Buchanan's
brigade would have switched to Gore at least as strongly as it lined up behind
Bush, though I will provide some evidence later that Buchanan drew heavily
on the normally Democratic union vote. Regardless, this result should be
taken lightly since the number of Buchanan voters is too low (33) to reach
firm inferences. The point is merely that Buchanan's bloc would not have all
gone to Bush nor would all Nader votes have necessarily gone to Gore.

One can estimate the effects the candidates had on voter turnout by
multiplying their actual vote shares by the percentage who would have abstained in a two-way race. For example, 30.5 percent of Nader's 2.5 percent
of the popular vote—or 0.75 percent—would have stayed home if he had
not run. Taken together, minor parties boosted turnout directly by roughly
1.2 percentage points in 2000.

But candidates also have *indirect* effects on voter mobilization. Whereas
direct effects are caused by a candidate mobilizing his supporters in an immediate way, indirect effects occur when supporters of one's opponents are
mobilized by systemic changes in the campaign. Indirect effects are caused
by such things as increasing closeness, adding color and drama to the race,
introducing issues that mobilize new voters, and simply raising voter interest. The percentage of Bush and Gore voters who would have abstained in
a two-way race is suggestive of how large these indirect effects might have
been. These voters presumably turned out for one of the major-party candidates because a minor-party candidate reminded them about the importance of voting or threatened their candidates' victory. Without Buchanan

or Nader in the race to make things interesting, they would have abstained. The percentages of Bush and Gore voters who would have behaved this way are small since most would have voted in a two-way race as well, but they are many in number. Using the same method I used earlier, I estimate that turnout for Bush and Gore would have fallen by a similar 1.3 points, for a total (direct and indirect) turnout effect of about 2.5 points.[10]

These self-reported results are reasonable, but ought to be taken with a grain of salt given the small samples and known differences between opinions and behavior. If the results are reliable, they ought to be replicated in other data. To check this, I turn to aggregate election returns to help develop an understanding of the turnout consequences of minor-party voting in 2000. Because the electoral college operates on a winner-take-all basis within states, the first analysis relies on states as the units of analysis.

I begin with a regression model that predicts voter turnout in the states. Control variables are included to account for baseline turnout differences across states. Controls include such things as percentage college educated, per capita income, and population density. I hypothesize that the closeness of the race in the state as well as the vote shares for minor parties might each increase turnout. Closeness might boost turnout indirectly by convincing voters that their votes matter more or by simply making the campaign more interesting. Most importantly, the Buchanan, Nader, and other minor parties' vote shares are included to determine which of them managed to raise turnout directly. Because Buchanan and Nader were not listed on the ballot in a few states, I run the analysis both for all the states and for the forty-three states (and the District of Columbia) where both candidates appeared on the ballot. This enabled me to be sure that the results are not sensitive to effects caused by ballot-access restrictions.

The results are found in Table 11.4. The regression models suggest that state electorates with more whites, fewer cities, more education, and higher incomes all have higher turnout. These variables capture interstate differences sufficiently well that southern exceptionalism has disappeared. As expected, the closeness of the race seems to have a positive effect on turnout after controlling for minor-party showings. This could be because closeness per se encourages potential abstainers to turn out or because a closer race causes the candidates to engage in more voter mobilization (Cox and Munger 1989). Buchanan has a negligible effect on turnout, but Nader in contrast appears to have increased voter participation directly.

This state-level analysis, in conjunction with the survey data analyzed earlier, confirms that Nader had an indisputable effect on voter turnout. Many of his supporters were so committed to him—or dissatisfied enough with every other candidate—that they simply would have abstained had Nader not run. It is this inverse relationship between voters' enthusiasm and their candidate's vote shares that allows some of the poorest-performing minor parties to have some of the largest direct effects on voter turnout.

TABLE **11.4**   Explaining voter turnout by state

Variable	All States	B & N on Ballot
Nader %	1.02*	1.30*
Buchanan %	.70	1.36
Other Minor Parties %	−90.13	−188.44
Lopsidedness of Major-Party Race	−.14*	−.16 +
South	.83	1.49
Percentage Caucasian	.35*	.35*
Population Density	.001	−.001
Percentage College Educated	.26 +	.18
Per Capita Income	.00004	.0002
Constant	16.90*	14.23 +
Number of Cases	51	44
R^2	.77	.78

DATA SOURCE: *State data.*
NOTE: *Entries are OLS coefficients, weighted by the voting age population.*
$+ p < .10$, $* p < .05$, *two-tailed test using White/Huber robust standard errors.*

Though many would have chosen not to vote in a two-way race, the largest group of Nader voters would have gone to Gore. In fact, many journalists have speculated that the Florida fiasco could have been avoided if Nader had not run since Gore would have picked up enough net Nader supporters to defeat Bush there.

Throwing the Electoral College

The analysis presented so far indicates that the outcome of the 2000 election was perverse. Bush not only lost the popular vote but also failed to be the Condorcet winner. Nonetheless, these findings do not address whether Nader indirectly elected Bush by stealing votes disproportionately from Gore. Though many Nader voters said they would have voted for Gore in a hypothetical two-way race, it is difficult to know how well these responses would predict their actual behavior were that to occur. And the data presented so far are merely national averages that cannot reveal how minor parties affected the major-party vote in particular states.

Florida was the center of attention for over a month following the November 7 election. The razor-thin result there was subject to ballot recounts and a series of legal maneuvers by the parties aimed at starting, stopping, and controlling the recounts. Just a few hundred votes separated Bush from Gore, yet Nader received nearly 100,000 votes. If even a small fraction of his voters had chosen Gore instead, the Democrats would have won the presidency.[11] In fact, Buchanan and *six* even more obscure minor-party candidates each received more votes than Bush's margin of victory. Together, these extremely small minor parties account for 250 times the 537 votes that

TABLE **11.5**   Explaining Gore's vote by county

Variable	All Counties	Nader on Ballot
Nader 2000 %	−.18	−.36***
Nader 1996 %	.89***	.93***
Clinton 1996 %	.95***	.94***
South	−.39	−1.10
Percentage Caucasian	−.08***	−.07***
Population Density	.0001***	.0001***
Percentage College Educated	−.04	−.02
Per Capita Income	.0003***	.0003***
Constant	3.43	4.17
Number of Cases	3017	2453
R^2	.90	.90

DATA SOURCE: *County data.*
NOTE: *Entries are OLS coefficients, weighted by total votes cast.*
***$p < .001$, *two-tailed test using White/Huber robust standard errors.*

distinguished Bush from Gore in the end. Though Nader's absence might have given Gore a clear Florida win, the absence of a number of right-wing minor-party candidates from Buchanan to Hagelin to Browne might have allowed for a clear Bush victory.

Although issues of ballot design and election law are important, they have overshadowed the kingmaker effects that Nader and other minor-party nominees might have had beyond the butterfly ballot.[12] For a deeper look at this relationship, Table 11.5 shows the results of a regression model that explains the Gore vote. Here the dependent variable is Gore's vote share in each county, though the specification looks much like the state-turnout model in Table 11.4. Nader's support in 1996 and 2000 are included as independent variables to determine how the Gore and Nader fortunes covaried. In addition to a set of control variables, Clinton's share of the 1996 vote is included to measure general support for Democratic presidential candidates and the Clinton–Gore administration.

The results suggest that Gore and Nader were indeed viewed as near, though certainly not perfect, substitutes, as indicated by the negative sign on the variable for Nader's vote share in 2000. This suggests that although Nader drew some of his support from the Gore camp, a much larger share of it came from other sources. Potential abstainers appear to make up the lion's share of Nader's support. This corroborates the substantial turnout effects found in the state analysis (Table 11.4) and the self-reported estimates in which many Nader voters report that they would have abstained in a two-way election.

However, many Nader voters also stated that they would have supported Gore had their candidate not been running. If the dynamics in Florida were at all similar to this average effect, then it is evident that Al Gore would

TABLE **11.6**   States where Buchanan might have cost Bush electoral votes

State	Gore–Bush Difference (A)	Votes for Buchanan (B)	Ratio (A/B)	Electoral Votes
Iowa	4144	6400	.65	7
New Mexico	366	2762	.13	5
Oregon	6765	12210	.55	7
Wisconsin	5708	12825	.45	11

DATA SOURCE: *State data.*

be president today had it been a traditional two-candidate race. But was Ralph Nader able to drain away enough Democratic votes to cost Gore the presidency?

In the days following the election itself, the unsettled Florida outcome left the electoral college up for grabs. Gore held 266 electoral votes to Bush's 246. Since 270 are needed to win the presidency outright, the Florida outcome would determine the next president of the United States, as long as the other state outcomes remained fixed. At the same time, four other states were won by razor-thin margins that could have gone either way. Even conceding Florida to Gore, Bush could have won the presidency with moderate vote shifts in Iowa, New Mexico, Oregon, and Wisconsin. Collectively, they could have thrown the election to Bush.

As Table 11.6 shows, Gore beat Bush by a small number of votes in each of these four states. In all four states the Bush-Gore margin accounted for less than half a percent of the total votes cast (the same threshold below which Florida law requires a recount). Yet together these four states hold thirty electoral votes, five *more* than in Florida.[13]

Also, in each of these states Buchanan won more votes than the difference between Bush and Gore. Had Buchanan not been on the ballot, it is at least possible that Gore would have lost these states and Bush would have been elected regardless of the Florida outcome. It is difficult, however, to know for certain. All that would have been required was that enough Buchanan voters chose Bush rather than vote for Gore or abstain. Assuming for the moment that no Buchanan voters would have chosen Gore, "enough" is anywhere from a reasonable 13 percent in New Mexico to a less realistic 65 percent in Iowa. Since many Buchanan voters nationally would have picked Gore in a two-way race, the thresholds were higher than this in reality.

One cannot know for certain whether Bush would have won these four states without Buchanan in the race. It appears to be possible but perhaps not likely. National exit polls indicate that about one in four Buchanan voters would have chosen Bush, but the ratios probably vary depending on the state. Unfortunately, state exit polls included too few Buchanan voters to reach firm conclusions. Had Pat Buchanan not been running, it is at least plausible, though perhaps not likely, that Florida would have been subject to less scrutiny and that Bush would have been elected easily with as many as 301 electoral votes.

Sources of Minor-Party Support

According to exit polls, Nader's support came mostly from those who voted for Clinton in 1996 and, secondarily, from those who abstained in that election. Together, they made up 55 percent of the Nader coalition. This confirms the suspicion that he drew mostly from the left and from those less engaged with the system. As a share of previous voters, Nader drew mostly from the Perot camp, though it is only about a tenth of "Perotistas," and this smaller pool makes the total Perot contribution modest. More Perot voters broke for Bush in 2000 than for all of the others candidates combined (Rapoport and Stone 2001).

It is not yet clear what individual-level determinants drove citizens to vote for Buchanan and Nader. To address this question I estimate a vote-choice model using exit-poll data. These data have the benefit of large samples that make it possible analyze minor-party voting. Otherwise rich NES data simply have too few Buchanan and Nader voters to allow firm inferences. The primary drawback of exit polls is that the sample excludes abstainers, but this is an unavoidable trade-off.

I estimate a discrete-choice model that includes a set of explanatory variables generally suspected to influence vote choice. These variables fall into four broad categories. I begin with measures of general political orientation: party identification and ideology. Both are long-term attachments shown to have strong effects on voting behavior. Next are several economic evaluations. Economics and elections are deeply intertwined, and these variables allow for national and personal as well as retrospective and prospective judgments to influence vote choice. The third set of variables measures the sociocultural nature of contemporary American elections. I include a variable that measures attitudes on abortion, a measure of religious attendance, and a variable that weighs whether a person identifies with the religious right. Finally, I include a set of demographic control variables such as race, education, gender, and age. The wordings of the questions are given in the Measurement Appendix at the end of this chapter.

The estimates in Table 11.7 show how variables influenced the choices between each of the other candidates and Nader. Nader is chosen as the arbitrary baseline category since not all pairwise comparisons are simultaneously estimable. Using Nader as baseline allows one to examine the most interesting Gore-Nader and Buchanan-Nader comparisons. Positive coefficients indicate that higher values on the independent variables lead to a greater likelihood that voters support a candidate other than Nader. For ex-

TABLE **11.7**   A model of presidential vote choice

	Gore vs. Nader	Bush vs. Nader	Buchanan vs. Nader	Other Minor vs. Nader
General Orientations				
Democrat	1.85*	.14	1.92*	.47
Republican	.32	2.35*	1.20+	.37
Ideology	.43*	1.48*	.33	1.06*
Economic Evaluations				
National Prospections	−.22+	−.39*	−.33	−.06
National Retrospections	−.44*	.03	−.13	−.66+
Personal Retrospections	−.44*	−.01	.03	−.26
Cultural Politics				
Abortion Attitude	−.08	.40*	.88*	.44+
Church Attendance	.06	−.10	.28	.12
Religious Right	.50	.79+	1.85*	1.14+
Demographic Controls				
Married	.06	.10	1.97*	.31
Homosexual	.16	−.68	−1.04	−.01
Age	.22*	.14*	−.06	.03
Income	.05	.18*	−.09	−.11
Education	−.22*	−.29*	−.55*	−.02
Union Member	.14	−.35	1.02*	−.71
African American	2.01*	−.13	.87	.94
Latino	.01	−.39	−.85	−.48
Female	.50*	−.06	.06	−.43
Constant	3.04*	−.74	−5.24*	−2.38*
Number of Cases		5012		
Log Likelihood		−2323.0		

DATA SOURCE: *2000 Voter News Service exit polls (weighted).*
NOTE: *Cell entries are multinomial logit coefficients.*
$+p < .10$, $*p < .05$, *two-tailed test.*

ample, the significant coefficient of .50 on the female dummy variable reveals that women are significantly more likely to vote for Gore than Nader, all else held constant. But the variable's insignificance in the remaining columns indicates that women are no more likely to vote for another candidate relative to Nader. Some classes of variables affect all of the comparisons with Nader while others influence only one or two of the pairings.

The major factors separating Gore and Nader voters are economic evaluations. Economic variables fail to achieve statistical significance in most other cases, but all three measures are strongly related to the Gore-Nader vote. In all three cases those who are less content with the economy tend to choose Nader over Gore. This might reflect a failed strategy on Gore's part in not associating himself closely enough with strong economic performance during the Clinton years. This was difficult to do, of course, since Gore also wished to distance himself from Clinton the person. It might also be that

Nader voters misperceived the strong economy as weak or that they focused on different aspects of economic performance such as inequality. Although most Americans viewed the economy positively in 2000 (see Norpoth, Chapter 3 in this book), those who were dissatisfied with it clearly turned to Nader over Gore.

In accord with earlier work (Cho 2000; Lacy and Burden 1999, 2002), it seems that minor-party candidates owe much of their support to anti-incumbent sentiment. And the substantive effects of these variables are not trivial. For a voter who is undecided between Gore and Nader, viewing the current economy as "poor" rather than "excellent" increases his probability of picking Nader from .50 to .79, a change of nearly thirty percentage points. Though national retrospections turn out to matter more than national prospections and personal retrospections, all three clearly separated Gore and Nader voters in 2000.

Contrast the power that economics has to separate Gore and Nader voters with the weaker effects of the cultural variables. Attitude toward abortion and identification with the religious right have consistent effects on every comparison *aside* from Gore-Nader. Pro-choice voters are more likely to choose Nader than Bush, Buchanan, and other minor parties. Yet abortion attitudes do not distinguish between Gore and Nader. Again, assuming that a voter is initially torn between the candidates, the probability of voting for Nader rises by anywhere from .27 (Bush) to .43 (Buchanan) as we move from the pro-life voter to the pro-choice voter. For at least some voters abortion was definitive. The power of these variables to shape the voting decision fits with earlier work on the importance of abortion in modern electoral politics (Abramowitz 1995; Adams 1997). But other cultural issues matter too. Belonging to the religious right makes a person 19 to 36 percent more likely to vote against Nader. These effects are strongest for the Buchanan-Nader pairing, which makes sense given the socially conservative content of the Buchanan rhetoric. Consistent with this, married respondents are far more likely to pick Buchanan over Nader, though marriage has no impact otherwise. In contrast to the denominational differences that drive voting based on sociocultural issues, religiosity itself, as least as measured by frequency of church attendance, appears unrelated to vote choice in 2000 (cf., Gilbert et al. 1999).

Long-term political orientations such as partisanship, ideology, and demographic predispositions have strong effects on vote choice. As one might expect, liberals are almost always more likely to vote for Nader than an opponent, and partisans support their nominees in most cases. The one exception to this is that both Democrats and Republicans favor Buchanan over Nader. This might reflect the fact that Nader, unlike former Republican Buchanan, comes from outside of the conventional party system. This finding reinforces two themes. First, of all voters, Nader voters were the least enamored of the entire slate of candidates. Second, minor-party candidates differ from one another about as much as they differ from their major-party competitors.

Finally, though African Americans and to a lesser degree women favored Gore over Nader, age and education had more systematic effects on the Nader vote. All else remaining constant, younger voters and those with more education were more likely to vote for Nader. This fits with conventional views of party identification and minor-party voting in which the young are expected to support minor parties disproportionately. It is noteworthy that age does not distinguish Buchanan and Nader voters, as young people tend to support minor parties of all stripes. Though income and education are often assumed to run in the same direction because they contribute to a person's socioeconomic status, they sometimes work in opposite directions here. Nader occupied a niche that attracted those with higher educations and lower incomes. Although both Buchanan and Nader raised objections to free trade, union members were more likely to favor the Reform Party than the Green Party in 2000. Whereas Nader seems to have won votes on college campuses, Buchanan collected more in the union halls.

Many Americans knew they might be electing their third-most preferred candidate, so why did so many nonetheless vote for Buchanan and Nader? The vote-choice model revealed that Nader tended to win the votes of white, liberal yet nonpartisan voters who were discontented with the economy. These findings confirm earlier work that found that economic grievances, age, and strength of partisanship are all associated with minor-party support (Abramson et al. 1995, 2000; Alvarez and Nagler 1995, 1998; Gold 1995; Lacy and Burden 1999, 2002; Rosenstone, Behr, and Lazarus 1996). But in addition to understanding why individuals behave as they do, we should also wonder what contributes to minor-party showings at the aggregate level.

Table 11.8 addresses this issue by regressing the Buchanan and Nader county vote shares on a series of political and demographic variables. In addition to a common set of controls, I include measures of Nader's showing in 1996 to measure support specific to his candidacy. But I also wish to see the degree to which Buchanan and Nader drew from Perot's 1996 base and the votes of other minor parties that year. Rapoport and Stone (2001), for example, find that Republicans, not minor parties, were the main beneficiaries of the Perot movement's collapse. It is reasonable to hypothesize that minor parties drew support from the Perotistas as well. Finally, the closeness of the election is included to assess strategic voting.

The results indicate that Nader far exceeded Buchanan's ability to build on his earlier campaigns. Not only did Nader regain most of the votes earned

TABLE **11.8**   Explaining Nader and Buchanan county vote shares

	Nader	Buchanan
Nader's 1996 Percentage	1.04*	−2.49*
Perot's 1996 Percentage	.14*	−.10
Other Minor Parties' 1996 Percentage	.18⁺	.58
Lopsidedness of Major-Party Race in State	.18*	.48*
South	−.58*	4.41*
Percentage Caucasian	.004*	.36*
Population Density	−.00002	−.001*
Percentage College Educated	.12*	−.18*
Per Capita Income	−.00003*	.0001*
Constant	−.98*	20.71*
Number of Cases	2453	3015
R^2	.71	.42

DATA SOURCE: *County data for counties in which the candidate was on the ballot.*
NOTE: *Entries are OLS coefficients, weighted by the voting age population.*
⁺$p < .10$, *$p < .05$, two-tailed test using White/Huber robust standard errors.*

in his lackluster 1996 run for president, but it appears that he drew from the Perot camp as well. Nader took about 15 percent of the 1996 Perot vote while Buchanan apparently pulled in none.

Once again, the analysis shows that differences among minor parties make it difficult to generalize. Much of the literature looks for commonalities in voting for different minor parties across elections (Gold 1995; Gilbert et al. 1999; Herrnson and Green 2002; Lacy and Burden 2002; Rosenstone, Behr, and Lazarus 1996). However, researchers ought to acknowledge differences as well. Nader was more likely to win the votes of those living outside the South, with more education, and with lower incomes. Buchanan did better in the South and among those with less education and those with higher incomes. Buchanan and Nader appealed to quite different kinds of voters.

After including the 1996 minor-party vote shares and controlling for demographics like race, region, and education, the lopsidedness of the election is positively related to both the Buchanan and Nader votes. This confirms a finding repeated throughout this chapter: that minor-party voters were highly sensitive to the possibility of being pivotal in a close major-party contest. The "wasted vote" logic and sophisticated voting were apparently on many Buchanan and Nader supporters' minds.

Conclusion

The 2000 presidential election has done much to enlighten our understanding of minor parties in U.S. politics. At a practical level, 2000 added two fascinating observations to the growing number of cases available for study. In some ways, this research will reinforce earlier conclusions based primarily on Wallace, Anderson, and Perot. For instance, supporters of minor-party candidates are less partisan and less satisfied with the nation's economic performance than other voters. These are the same relationships that helped and hurt earlier minor parties.

At the same time, the Buchanan and Nader candidacies stand apart from their predecessors. Among other things, these candidates could have easily affected who won the election. Gore probably would have won without Nader in the picture, and Bush could have won more easily had Buchanan not been around. These minor-party candidates occupy an important slot at the end of a string of such candidacies. Indeed, five of the last nine presidential elections have witnessed significant minor parties. Nader rather than Buchanan managed to build on these successes by tapping into the bank of Perot's voters. Nader's candidacy is unique in that his standing rose during the final days of the campaign, an anomaly among minor-party presidential campaigns. And despite the closeness of the election, minor-party voters in 2000 were far more strategic than their predecessors. A larger share of Buchanan and Nader supporters would have rather abstained than vote for another candidate. These unusual dynamics led to one of the least satisfying social-choice outcomes of any presidential election.

One of the findings of this chapter is that Buchanan and Nader introduced an unprecedented amount of distortion into the aggregation of preferences. This was possible because of the extreme closeness of the major-party contest. Though eventually chosen the victor, Bush did not win the popular vote and would not have won using just about any other democratic voting method. Nader also made minor-party history by defying the strong tendency of such candidates to lose support in the final days of the campaign. It actually appears that Nader rose in the polls in the weeks preceding election day, this despite the possibility that his presence meant the election could be thrown to many of his supporters' third-choice candidate.

Building on earlier work, this chapter also showed that minor-party candidates have effects on both turnout and the major-party vote shares. Buchanan and Nader had surprisingly large turnout effects despite their small vote totals. This suggests that the most meager campaigns might actually raise turnout the most because they bring out diehard supporters who would otherwise abstain. Running as minor-party candidates in the same election, Buchanan and Nader remind us of the great, though often downplayed differences among such candidates. Nader drew support from young voters, the educated, liberals, and those upset with the economy; Buchanan won his votes in the South, from the religious right, and from the less educated. These differences warn against the development of a grand theory of minor-party coalitions.

MEASUREMENT APPENDIX

Exit-poll data were collected on Election Day 2000 by the Voter News Service. Pollsters collected self-administered questionnaires from more than thirteen thousand voters. In Table 11.3, the two-way race question is "If these were the only two presidential candidates on the ballot today, who would you have voted for? 1 Al Gore (Dem), 2 George W. Bush (Rep), 3 Would not have voted for president." The wording of the questions used in Table 11.7 are listed here. Note that several of them were recoded in the ways explained earlier in this chapter.

Democrat and *Republican*: "No matter how you voted today, do you usually think of yourself as a: 1 Democrat, 2 Republican, 3 independent, 4 Something else?"

Ideology: "On most political matters, do you consider yourself: 1 Liberal, 2 Moderate, 3 Conservative?"

National Prospections: "During the next year, do you think the nation's economy will: 1 Get better, 2 Get worse, 3 Stay about the same?"

National Retrospections: "Do you think the condition of the nation's economy is: 1 Excellent, 2 Good, 3 Not so good, 4 Poor?"

Personal Retrospections: "Compared to four years ago, is your family's financial situation: 1 Better today, 2 Worse today, 3 About the same?"

Abortion Attitude: "Which comes closest to your position? Abortion should be: 1 Legal in all cases, 2 Legal in most cases, 3 Illegal in most cases, 4 Illegal in all cases."

Church Attendance: "How often do you attend religious services? 1 More than once a week, 2 Once a week, 3 A few times a month, 4 A few times a year, 5 Never."

Religious Right: "Do you consider yourself part of the conservative Christian political movement, also known as the religious right? 1 Yes, 2 No."

Married: "Are you currently married? 1 Yes, 2 No."

Homosexual: "Are you gay, lesbian, or bisexual? 1 Yes, 2 No."

Age: "To which age group do you belong? 1 18–24, 2 25–29, 3 30–39, 4, 40–44, 5 45–49, 6 50–59, 7 60–64, 8 65–74, 9 75 or over."

Income: "1999 total family income: 1 Under $15,000, 2 $15,000–$29,999, 3 $30,000–49,999, 4 $50,000–$74,999, 5 $ 75,000–$99,999, 6, $100,000 or more?"

Education: "What was the last grade of school you completed? 1 Did not complete high school, 2 High school graduate, 3 Some college or associate degree, 4 College graduate, 5 Postgraduate study."

Union Member: "Do you or does someone in your household belong to a labor union? 1 Yes, I do, 2 Yes, someone else does, 3 Yes, I do and some-one else does, 4 No one does."

African American and *Latino*: "Are you: 1 White, 2 African American, 3 Hispanic/Latino, 4 Asian, 5 Other?"

Female: "Are you: 1 Male, 2 Female?"

Appendix: Chronology of the 2000 Presidential Campaign

BARRY C. BURDEN

1999

7 January   President Clinton's trial begins in the Senate after his impeachment in the House a month before on charges of perjury and obstruction of justice. Clinton becomes the second president ever to be tried on impeachment charges.

12 February   The Senate acquits President Clinton of impeachment charges. Though a majority of senators vote in favor of each count, they fall short of the 67 votes required by the Constitution to convict. Clinton's approval ratings remain near an all-time high, with most Americans agreeing that he should have been acquitted.

9 March   Former Gov. Lamar Alexander (R-TN) announces that he will run for president again.

16 March   Steve Forbes (R-NY) officially begins his second crusade for the Republican nomination. Forbes performed poorly in 1996 despite substantially outspending his opponents.

29 March   Conservative commentator Pat Buchanan announces his candidacy for the Republican nomination in New Hampshire, the site of his 1992 primary upset of George H. W. Bush.

12 June   Gov. George W. Bush (R-TX), son of former president George H. W. Bush, officially begins his presidential campaign. He quickly raises large sums of money and becomes the Republican establishment favorite.

16 June   Vice President Al Gore (D-TN) finally makes his expected presidential campaign announcement.

13 July   Conservative Sen. Bob Smith (R-NH), one of the Republicans seeking the nomination, leaves the Republican Party but continues his presidential quest as an independent. He later flirts with the U.S. Taxpayers Party and is eventually welcomed back into the Republican fold by his Washington colleagues.

14 July   Rep. John Kasich (R-OH) drops out of the presidential race and endorses Texas Governor Bush.

16 August   Lamar Alexander ends his brief presidential pursuit after a poor showing in an Iowa straw poll.

8 September   Having established a campaign committee months earlier, former professional basketball player Sen. Bill Bradley (D-NJ) announces that he will challenge Al Gore for the Democratic nomination.

9 September   Outgoing Sen. Daniel Patrick Moynihan (D-NY) endorses Bill Bradley for president, saying that Gore is "unelectable."

27 September   Former vice president Dan Quayle (R-IN), having strategically relocated to Arizona, surprises the political world by declaring that he will not continue his presidential candidacy. Former prisoner of war Sen. John McCain (R-AZ) makes his campaign official the same day. Campaign finance reform becomes a key component of his campaign message.

20 October   Elizabeth Dole (R-KS), an executive branch veteran and wife of former presidential candidate Robert Dole, suspends her presidential campaign before it is even formally begun. She offers no endorsements on the way out and points to fund-raising difficulties as the reason for her departure.

25 October   Buchanan leaves the Republican Party to seek the Reform Party nomination. New York developer and millionaire Donald Trump left the GOP for the Reform Party the day before.

27 October   A Democratic "town meeting" featuring Bradley and Gore is held in New Hampshire.

28 October   A Republican "town meeting" in New Hampshire features five candidates, but notably absent is frontrunner George W. Bush. At the same time, Bob Smith ends his independent bid for president in part because of the death of fellow Republican Sen. John Chafee (R-RI), which offers Smith a possible committee chair position.

16 December   Strange bedfellows Bradley and McCain pledge joint support across party lines for a ban on "soft-money" donations to political campaigns. They meet at the same site in Claremont, New Hampshire, where Bill Clinton and Newt Gingrich shook hands on a failed campaign finance reform agenda in 1995.

19 December   Bradley and Gore appear together on NBC's *Meet the Press*. Gore proposes that the candidates debate twice weekly and run no campaign advertisements, an idea rejected by underdog Bradley.

2000

4 January   Elizabeth Dole adds to Bush's long list of endorsements. By this point, of the original dozen contenders for the Republican nomination (alphabetically, Lamar Alexander, Gary Bauer, Pat Buchanan, George Bush, Elizabeth Dole, Steve Forbes, Orrin Hatch, John Kasich, Alan Keyes, John McCain, Dan Quayle, and Bob Smith), only Bauer, Bush, Forbes, Hatch, Keyes, and McCain remain to do battle in the 2000 caucuses and presidential primaries.

5 January   Sen. Ted Kennedy (D-MA) provides Gore with some liberal credentials by endorsing him rather than Bradley. This occurs on the first day of "Debate Week," which features four intraparty debates.

24 January   The first round of the Iowa Caucuses occurs, giving victories to the frontrunners Bush and Gore, though neither is a slam dunk. Gore takes 63 percent of the Democratic vote while Bush takes 41 percent of the Republican vote, followed close behind by Forbes's 30 percent.

26 January   After a pitiful showing in Iowa, Orrin Hatch (R-UT) ends a short-lived presidential campaign that never attracted much attention.

1 February   McCain pulls out an upset victory over Bush in the New Hampshire primary, thus turning the Republican nomination into a serious two-way race. He wins nearly half of the Republican vote to Bush's 31 percent and Forbes' 13 percent. Gore edges Bradley by just four percentage points in a surprisingly close Democratic race.

2 February   Just a day after his defeat in New Hampshire, Bush gives what would become a controversial address at anti-Catholic Bob Jones University in South Carolina.

4 February   Nearly unknown Republican candidate Gary Bauer, former head of the conservative Family Research Council, ends his campaign after earning just 1 percent of the New Hampshire vote. New polls show McCain with enough momentum to pull even with Bush in the upcoming South Carolina primary. Though his New Hampshire win was unexpected, a strong showing in the conservative South is even more surprising.

6 February   Hillary Clinton announces her campaign for the New York Senate seat held by Moynihan. She becomes the only First Lady to run for the U.S. Senate.

11 February   Forbes drops out of the race after finishing third behind McCain in Delaware, where McCain had not even campaigned but Forbes, in contrast, had spent a great deal of money.

14 February   Trump announces on the *Today Show* that he is out of the running. This occurs just days after Minnesota Gov. Jesse Ventura left what he called a "dysfunctional" Reform Party. Meanwhile, the Reform Party convention in Nashville is an incoherent mess.

16 February   Bauer endorses McCain following a three-way debate and just before the important South Carolina contest.

19 February   Bush stomps McCain by more than ten points in the South Carolina primary. Though Democrats and independents support McCain in the open primary, the Bush campaign turned out more of the conservative base.

23 February   Reviving his campaign after the South Carolina loss, McCain defeats Bush in the Michigan and Arizona primaries. His victories depend on the votes of crossover Democrats and independents since Bush still wins a majority of the base Republican vote.

29 February   Bush and Gore each sweep several primaries. Bush wins surprisingly large victories in Washington and Virginia, stemming in part from McCain's attack on the religious right.

7 March   Super Tuesday primaries held in over a dozen states confirm that Bush and Gore will win their parties' nominations. Bradley fails to win a single state this day, and McCain wins only in New England with the help of Democrats and independents. Bush appears not to suffer among Catholics despite the Bob Jones University controversy. The candidates, now nearly out of money, begin looking toward the general election.

9 March   Bradley and McCain suspend their presidential campaigns. Bradley endorses Gore while McCain merely wishes Bush well and confirms that he will remain a Republican.

14 March   Bush and Gore clinch their parties' nominations in southern state primaries, thus setting up the longest general election campaign in history.

22 April   Young Cuban refugee Elian Gonzales is forcibly removed from his temporary Miami home by INS agents. The long Florida drama eventually ends, but its repercussions will likely affect the presidential vote there. National polls show Bush with a continuing five- to ten-point lead over Gore.

10 May   McCain finally endorses Bush.

13 July   Following weeks of little campaign activity, Bradley throws his full support behind Gore by releasing his Democratic convention delegates.

26 July   Bush announces that Richard Cheney is his choice as vice-presidential running mate. Cheney, a Washington veteran who had been heading Governor Bush's search for a running mate, agrees to run only after some persuasion. Cheney brings experience, clout, and appeal among the party base. Meanwhile, African-American television commentator and former United Nations ambassador Alan Keyes becomes the last of Bush's eleven Republican opponents to bow out, endorsing the Bush-Cheney ticket.

31 July   The Republican National Convention begins in Philadelphia. Over the course of four days, a flawless and relatively moderate convention stresses education issues and inclusiveness. The right wing of the party, so prominent in earlier conventions, is nowhere to be seen, while uncontroversial figures like Laura Bush and Colin Powell are the key speakers. McCain is also on board, though his pet issue—campaign finance reform—gets no attention.

8 August   Gore announces in Connecticut that Sen. Joseph Lieberman (D-CT) will be his running mate. Lieberman is the first Jew, orthodox at that, on a major-party ticket. He differs from Gore on issues including school vouchers and Social Security. Notably, Lieberman was the first Democrat to criticize President Clinton after the Lewinsky scandal became public.

9 August   The Reform Party convention begins in Long Beach, California. Party founder Ross Perot is absent, while Buchanan and John Hagelin of the Natural Law Party battle for the nomination. The winner will inherit over $12 million in federal funds made available by Perot's showing in 1996.

11 August   Buchanan beats Hagelin two to one in mail-in Reform balloting. He announces that black activist Ezola Foster will be his running mate.

14 August   The Democratic National Convention begins in Los Angeles. The convention spotlights a number of party leaders, including Bradley, several Kennedys, Bill and Hillary Clinton, and a handful of celebrities. Gore tries to separate himself from the Clinton legacy by declaring that he is "his own man." His acceptance speech and the convention focus on policy specifics to contrast with the generality of the Republican image of a month earlier. The Democrats appear to have the momentum for once and pull ahead of Bush for the first time.

September   Polls show Bush and Gore in a dead heat, one of the closest presidential campaigns in decades.

3 October   The first presidential debate is held in Boston. Though veteran debater Gore is expected to dominate Bush, he appears arrogant while Bush exceeds his low expectations. The result is a close decision in which heavy discussion of issues such as tax cuts, prescription-drug coverage, and education predominate. Nader is excluded from the debate and later sues over it.

5 October   The only vice-presidential "debate" is held in Kentucky. The civil discussion between Cheney and Lieberman across a common desktop impresses viewers. Cheney had been becoming a liability to the GOP ticket because of poor performance on the campaign trail, but his sincerity and gravitas in the debate turn him into an asset.

11 October   The second presidential debate occurs at Wake Forest University. The format is a discussion with the candidates seated at desks, as in the vice-presidential meeting. The exchanges focus on foreign policy, and the moderator tries to find differences between the candidates. Gore seems subdued, while Bush holds his own and is perceived as the victor.

17 October   The final presidential debate is a "town hall"–style meeting in St. Louis on the heels of Mideast violence and the death of Missouri governor and Senate candidate Mel Carnahan. Gore performs better and is more aggressive, and the audience's questions center on such issues as affirmative action, the death penalty, health care, and education.

2 November   A Maine reporter reveals Bush's 1976 arrest for drunken driving in Kennebunkport. Bush quickly acknowledges the new information and expresses remorse. The news does not seem to cut Bush's lead. Meanwhile, Perot endorses Bush on *Larry King Live*, apparently without Bush's prior knowledge, though the drunken-driving news overshadows the endorsement.

7 November   A confusing election night leaves the presidential election unsettled. The electoral college vote is historically close, and the decision apparently depends on the outcome in Florida. Early in the evening it appears that Gore has won Florida, but the television networks then call the state for Bush several hours later. The networks declare him the election winner, but that declaration is then retracted. At one point, Gore concedes to Bush by phone, but then calls him back saying that Florida remains unsettled. It also appears that Republicans have lost several seats in both chambers of Congress. The Senate is likely to be split fifty–fifty if the Washington seat goes to Democrat Maria Cantwell, as expected. Close presidential votes in New Mexico, Oregon, and other states are to be scrutinized as well, but the Bush and Gore camps quickly dispatch teams to represent them in the Florida proceedings. Nader finishes with 2.6 percent of the national vote, far less than the 5 percent needed to secure federal matching funds in 2000. Buchanan barely registers with 0.4 percent of the popular vote. In addition to Florida irregularities, Buchanan and Nader each could have influenced who won as Bush won 48.0 percent of the vote to Gore's 48.3 percent.

8 November   The first complete counts in Florida show Bush beating Gore by 1,784 votes out of nearly 6 million cast. Florida law calls for an automatic recount. A number of voting irregularities in Florida are reported. Most noteworthy is the confusing "butterfly ballot" format used in Palm Beach County that caused some Gore supporters to vote mistakenly for Buchanan. Punch-card systems used in much of Florida are also suspect. Canvassing boards in Florida and the American public wrestle with how "hanging" and "pregnant" chad—the material removed by voters' incomplete punches—should be counted.

14 November   The Republican secretary of state for Florida, Katherine Harris, requires county elections officials to complete their recounts by 5:00 P.M. and the next day refuses to accept late totals. It remains unclear who won the presidential election, though by now it is apparent that Gore won the national popular vote.

15 November   Gore proposes that he meet with Bush personally and that he is open to the possibility of recounting all of the Florida ballots by hand. Bush declines.

16 November   The Florida Supreme Court allows counties to proceed with hand recounts of ballots.

21 November   The Florida Supreme Court rules that counties may continue their recounts until November 26. The recounts dominate the news over the Thanksgiving holiday.

22 November   Cheney experiences chest pains and is checked into the hospital.

26 November   Without including Palm Beach County recounts, Harris certifies Bush as the winner in Florida by a mere 537 votes. Bush claims victory with 271 electoral votes and begins an unofficial presidential transition.

4 December   The U.S. Supreme Court vacates the Florida Supreme Court's extension of the certification deadline, remanding the case to the Florida Supreme Court for reconsideration. A judge in Leon County, Florida, rules against Gore's call for hand counts of contested and rejected ballots in Miami-Dade County. Many suspect that Democratic votes were disproportionately undercounted and that a full hand count would benefit Gore. The only chance remaining for Gore is the Florida Supreme Court. Bush pushes onward with his unfunded transition, headed by Cheney, while the Florida legislature considers a special session to choose electors.

8 December   Providing a surprising shot in the arm for Democrats, the Florida Supreme Court rules 4–3 that all undervotes should be counted by hand.

12 December   The U.S. Supreme Court ends the legal wrangling over Florida by issuing a decision in *Bush v. Gore*. A 7–2 majority decides that the count ordered by the Florida Supreme Court violated the federal equal protection clause because of the lack of statewide recount standards. Rather than waiting for such statewide standards, the Court rules 5–4 in favor of Bush, arguing that there is not enough time to do a full hand count that meets "minimal constitutional standards."

13 December   The thirty-six days of legal and political maneuvering since the election comes to a formal conclusion. Gore offers a gracious concession speech and is followed soon after by Bush's acceptance speech, which emphasizes bipartisanship. Despite losing the popular vote by more than half a million votes over more than 100 million cast, Bush wins the presidency with 271 to Gore's 266 electoral votes (with one Democratic elector abstaining to protest the lack of representation in Congress for the District of Columbia). Gore's electoral vote total is the highest ever for a losing candidate, and 2000 becomes the first election in over a century in which the popular vote and electoral vote winners were different.

Reference Matter

Notes

Chapter 1

1. In fact, Gore had never actually claimed to have invented the Internet, but merely to have provided crucial support for the early research. In other cases, however, it was clear that Gore had exaggerated claims.

2. Ironically, one of the main results of the experiment with phone interviews in 2000 was a decision that the data they produced were not comparable enough to the NES time-series data dating back to the 1950s. As a result, the idea of switching entirely to a telephone operation was at least temporarily scrapped, leaving the 2000 NES data not fully comparable with either NES's preceding or subsequent studies.

3. As have several other studies in the past (e.g. Page and Jones 1979), Kanthak and Norrander actually use the difference in thermometer ratings of the two major-party candidates as their dependent variable in order to obtain a numeric dependent variable for regression analysis.

4. The lure of the counterfactual is strong because any single case can potentially be explained by so many factors. Some science-fiction writers imagine that social scientists could stand outside of history and manipulate variables to observe their effects. Yet the authors usually conclude that changing any single factor is likely to have unexpected consequences. See Wilcox (2000) for a review.

Chapter 2

We wish to thank Steve Mockabee, Clyde Wilcox, and Nancy Zingale for their comments on earlier versions of this paper.

1. The public's recollections of how the original Bush administration handled

the economy or other matters were likely to be unreliable by 2000 given that partisan biases affect memories. On the other hand, it was clear to people that Bush the father did not get caught in the type of moral scandals that plagued Clinton, so a restoration of the Bush administration was seen by some as a legacy battle between the economic successes of the Clinton years and the moral high ground of the Bush years.

2. Retrospective voting could certainly be defined more broadly to include nonissue matters, but the concept is identified with Fiorina (1981), which seems to restrict the term to issues and policies. For example, Fiorina writes, "Traditional retrospective voting can occur on any kind of issue" (9). The policy focus is clear in his listing of the premises of the traditional theory of retrospective voting: "Citizens use their votes to indicate confidence or lack of confidence in the incumbent administration. Support ratifies the package of incumbent policies and activities" (45). Fiorina differentiates two types of retrospective evaluations, both of which are issue based: simple ones (SRES), which include items such as personal financial situation and civil rights, and mediated retrospective evaluations (MRES), which include items such as presidential performance generally and management of the economy specifically. MRES are "mediated either externally, by a citizen's choice of information sources and opinion leaders, or internally, by prior predispositions" (80). Fiorina views questions on presidential performance and government performance on the economy as MRES because they contain a reference not only to past performance but also to a political entity (such as the president). Attitudes toward that political entity are affected by preconceptions such as the respondent's partisanship (106–7). However, even Fiorina's notion of MRES is not as broad in treating non-issue-based evaluations of the previous administration as we intend the term *succession effects* to be. In short, we view "succession effects" as broader than issue-based "retrospective voting."

3. We restrict ourselves to closed-ended questions out of our concern over the ability of people to verbalize the reasons behind their actions (Nisbett and Wilson 1977) and their assessments of political candidates (Rahn, Krosnick, and Bruening 1994). At the same time, we recognize that the open-ended material provides a useful perspective on people's perception of the election in its own right (see Kessel's chapter 4). See the dialogue over the usefulness of closed- versus open-ended questions by Kessel and Weisberg (1999).

4. Most pre-2000 values in the tables in this chapter are based on the 1948–1996 NES cumulative data file, using the poststratification weight variable (9a). We have adjusted the thermometer values in calculating means so that the 97 code is treated properly as a value of 100. We have also weighted the NES 2000 survey results in tables 2.1–2.3 and 2.5–2.7 by the poststratification weight variable (2). The logit equations use the unweighted data.

5. Although George Bush won the presidency after the U.S. Supreme Court ruled on the Florida case in such a way as to secure his victory in the electoral college, Al Gore won the popular vote and won the majority of votes among NES re-

spondents. This leads to interesting questions as to how to assess the accuracy of vote models. The standard we will employ here will be the one ordinarily used in logit analysis: the extent to which individual votes are correctly predicted. This means that a 100 percent correct prediction would predict a Gore victory of a slightly larger proportion than his actual popular vote lead. This is the standard that analysts customarily employ, without caring when the survey data are off one or two percentage points from the actual vote decision, though at least the prediction is usually in the right direction. But the unusual result of the 2000 election does add one additional way to examine the results. In addition to explaining why Gore won the votes of a majority of NES respondents, it is important to analyze why the election was as close as it was. Had the election been one-sided, we would not need to be concerned about the prediction problem. Given that it was so close, we need to examine what combination of factors made the winner's margin so razor thin.

6. See also Shanks and Strand (2002) for analysis of a survey that asked a broader set of issues.

7. Ideology was not included in the model because NES did a wording experiment on that question, so that only half of the respondents answered the traditional question.

8. The text terms effects as "marginal" when they are shown to be significant at the .10 level in the table, if they are in the expected direction, since this corresponds to a one-tailed test at the .05 level.

9. For comparison, the standard deviation of scores given to Bill Clinton was 29.7, so the dispersion on Gore was well under the value for a highly controversial figure.

10. This result mirrors the finding of Weisberg and Mockabee (1999) for the 1996 election, in which candidate integrity, empathy, and leadership are significant, but competence is not.

11. The two Clinton variables and party are all significant if they are used as the only predictors in a vote equation, yielding 89.0 percent predictive success without any variable involving either George Bush or Al Gore. Since the Clinton job approval is significant when the candidate differential is not included, the candidate differential must reflect the Clinton job approval. The other relevant baseline model is one in which only party identification and the candidate differential are predictors; both variables are significant in this model, with 91.6 percent predictive success.

12. The question on moral climate was worded similarly to this. The economy questions asked directly whether President Clinton made the nation's economy better or worse, while the security question asked whether the administration "made the United States more secure from its foreign enemies, less secure," and so on.

13. The succession models in table 2.8 have higher predictive success. However, that may be due to the need to use the candidate differential in them to bring

in a measure of the current election, a measure that is so close to the vote that Page and Jones (1979) use it as a surrogate for the vote.

14. The candidate differential is not included as a predictor in the final model, since it was included in equations 4 and 5 only to bring matters related to the 2000 election into succession models.

15. Ideology was omitted from this analysis because the NES asked noncomparable questions to different half-samples. The inclusion of ideology as a predictor in table 2.9 would cause some of the predictors to lose their significance, while ideology itself would not be significant (see also Chapter 6).

16. Obviously, the Clinton economy variable and the retrospective economy variable monitor similar reactions. However, retrospective economic evaluations would still not be significant if the Clinton economic evaluation were dropped from the model. Indeed, the model shown in table 2.9 is quite resilient to changes in the set of variables included. For example, abortion remains insignificant when the religiosity and evangelical variables are dropped.

17. Religiosity also is not significant in the full equation, probably because it affects reactions to Clinton's effects on the nation's moral climate and perhaps evaluations of Clinton more generally.

Chapter 3

For comments I am grateful to the participants of the conference on the 2000 election at Ohio State University, March 7–10, 2002 ("Assessing the Vitality of Electoral Democracy in the U.S.: The 2000 Elections") and of several professional meetings (sponsored by Public Choice and American Political Science Association 2001), especially Herb Asher, Paul Beck, Barry Burden, Chip Chappell, Harold Clarke, Han Dorussen, Mo Fiorina, Sunshine Hillygus, Kathleen Knight, Mike Lewis-Beck, Martin Paldam, Fritz Schneider, Herb Weisberg, and Clyde Wilcox.

1. NES data for the general population (including nonvoters) largely confirm the distribution of economic opinion reported by the VNS exit polls for Election Day voters, even though the question wordings differ. NES asks whether the "nation's economy over the last year" has gotten better, stayed the same, or gotten worse. In 1992, "worse" exceeded "better" by a 72–5 margin, whereas "better" exceeded "worse" by 38–17 in 1996, and by 39–17 in 2000. The NES question about personal finances (over the past year) also shows a negative balance for 1992, a positive one for 1996, and an even more positive one for 2000.

2. The Democratic lead in NES data is more pronounced than it is in the VNS exit polls, averaging ten percentage points in the presidential years 1992–2000. But this can be attributed to voting turnout, which reduces the advantage of Democrats and also depresses the share of independents among actual voters.

3. In the presidential elections of 1912 and 1924, third-party intrusions severely distort the vote shares of the major parties. To avoid problems with such outliers, the presidential vote is replaced with the vote for House candidates in 1912 and 1924.

4. The standard test for a random walk allows us to reject that hypothesis beyond a shred of doubt (Dickey-Fuller $t = -4.7$, $p < .01$).

5. It should be noted that such a process is by no means common among stationary phenomena. The presidential vote series, however, is a textbook case for an AR(2) process with opposite signs. The main diagnostic tool for identifying this process, the partial autocorrelation function, yields the following values: $+.32$ for lag one, and $-.36$ for lag two, each significant at the $.05$ level, given a standard error of $.15$. Also note that the parameter estimates of the AR(2) model are such that the stationarity conditions are met: (1) $\phi_2 + \phi_1 < 1$; (2) $\phi_2 - \phi_1 < 1$; (3) $-1 < \phi_2 < 1$.

6. I am grateful to Patrick Lynch (1999) for making available those data. For data since 1988, see the Bureau of Economic Analysis (BEA) web site, table 6, January 31, 2001.

7. To be precise, the overall mean was removed from each economic series (2.15 for GNP growth, and 2.86 for inflation), and the deviations from the mean were inverted (multiplied by –1) for the elections in which Republicans had control of the White House.

8. The index of economic performance (ECON) is defined as (Real GNP Growth —1.5Inflation). That combination produces the same fit for the vote as is the case with the two economic measures used separately.

9. Indeed, long before Election Day 2000, the two-term model of the presidential vote alone produced a forecast that came uncannily close to the final result. It predicted a 50.2–49.8 vote division in favor of the Republican candidate in the 2000 presidential election, albeit with a dangerously large margin of error. I first presented that forecast for the 2000 election at the Foreign Policy Association meeting, New York, October 19, 1999. Granted, I later issued a different forecast, incorporating primary election performance (table 3.1), that missed the result by a lot more even though the model from which it was derived has a much smaller standard error.

10. The set of elections where sitting presidents were not running omits the 1920 case. With a score of –27 on the economic index, the 1920 election is an extreme outlier nearly eight standard deviations (3.0) from the mean for this group (-1.6). At the same time, the set of elections in which sitting presidents were running for reelection contains several cases that appear to exert an undue influence on the relationship (1932, 1936, 1980). Tests show, however, that the estimates prove quite robust when each of those elections is excluded in turn.

11. The parameter for the economic index in the nonincumbent model was set to zero since the estimate turned out not to be significant.

Chapter 4

1. The measure he used for this was a standardized multiple regression coefficient since his analysis was done in the era before maximum likelihood estimation became popular.

2. In the search for these, I was guided not only by Stokes's work, but also by a model designed to compare voting patterns across states (Comparative State Election Project 1973); a model designed to compare presidential, senatorial, and gubernatorial voting (Hinckley, Hofstetter, and Kessel 1974); and comparisons between citizen attitudes and congressional and presidential behavior (Hofstetter 1976; Clausen 1973; Kessel 1974). In *The New American Voter* (Miller and Shanks 1996, 588), Warren Miller accepted the resultant model as "a direct extension of the . . . approach employed in *The American Voter*."

3. The complete set of the questions: "Is there anything in particular you like about the Democratic Party?"; "Is there anything in particular you don't like about the Democratic Party?"; "Is there anything in particular you like about the Republican Party?"; "Is there anything in particular you don't like about the Republican Party?"; "Is there anything in particular about Candidate A that might make you want to vote for him?"; "Is there anything in particular about Candidate A that might make you want to vote against him?"; "Is there anything in particular about Candidate B that might make you want to vote for him?"; and "Is there anything in particular about Candidate B that might make you want to vote against him?"

4. For a discussion of the differences between open-ended and closed-ended questions, see Kessel and Weisberg (1999).

5. The partisan valences used as independent variables in the subsequent probit analysis in tables 4.3 and 4.4 weight each variable by the number of comments made. They are: (positive Democratic comments + negative Republican comments)–(positive Republican comments + negative Democratic comments). This is equivalent to multiplying the valence value derived in the text by the total number of comments about that attitude object and dividing by fifty.

6. The candidate categories were chosen from attributes mentioned by enough respondents to sustain analysis, and the issue categories grew out of Aage Clausen's (1973) analysis of congressional voting and my (Kessel 1974) study of presidential State of the Union messages.

7. I included every code for which there were at least ten positive or negative first mentions. I also included substantively related items regardless of their direction. For example, a code favoring expansion of Social Security passed through the at-least-ten-mention screen. However, I also counted those comments that favored contraction of Social Security and those that mentioned Social Security without any indication of the direction of their views. Occasionally, I looked at responses that were substantively interesting regardless of their frequency, for example, references to Dick Cheney or Joe Lieberman.

8. Notice that comments about both candidates as family men were almost entirely positive. The pro-Democratic valence is due to there having been so many more such references to Gore.

9. For the record, there was a total of five responses concerning Joe Lieberman and four about Dick Cheney. The vice-presidential candidates did not figure in presidential voting decisions.

10. This model has been applied to choice between the major-party candidates, Bush and Gore. Pat Buchanan, Ralph Nader, and other minor candidates are excluded from this analysis.

11. The standardized components are particularly useful for comparing the importance of components across elections (see Kessel 1992, appendix 9.1). Also, they correct for differences in the variance of different components. For example, the unstandardized MLEs for parties and issues are .41 and .32. However, the variance for parties is a mere 1.7 while that for issues is 25.0. So the standardized MLEs are 1.07 and 3.16, respectively, adjusting for the fact that issue attitudes can vary across more units than party attitudes.

12. Vice President Gore's relation to President Clinton in the 2000 campaign was complex. Gore wanted to stay far away from Clinton's ethical problems and also took a policy stance to the left of the president's.

13. Their unstandardized MLEs are less than twice their standard errors, so they are not significant at the .05 level.

14. The finding about 1952 is important. That election is often categorized as a deviating election that is explained by Eisenhower's personal appeal. But here we see that party attitudes were more important and candidate attitudes were less important that year.

15. The exception was 1968 when international involvement was not significantly related to vote choice. This might seem anomalous since the war in Vietnam was raging, but Nixon and Humphrey advocated essentially the same policies on the war (Page and Brody 1972).

16. On the impact of foreign policy on voting choice, see Aldrich, Sullivan, and Borgida (1989).

17. In 1996, however, natural resources was not significantly related to vote.

18. These green attitudes in 2000 had nothing to do with Ralph Nader. The dependent variable in this model was the choice between Bush and Gore.

Chapter 5

We thank the Joyce Foundation for funding the 2000 American Politics Study. We thank Greg Caldeira, Jennifer Jerit, Susan Meyer, Jason Mycoff, Herb Weisberg, Clyde Wilcox, and anonymous reviewers for helpful comments and Andy Farrell for research assistance.

1. This postelection survey was conducted for the authors by the Center for Survey Research at The Ohio State University from November 13, 2000, through December 21, 2000. The sampling for this survey was done via random-digit dialing, making it possible to reach any household within the forty-eight contiguous states and Washington, D.C. Within each household, voting-age adults were randomly selected by the most-recent-birthday method. This nationally representative sample includes an oversample from the Great Lakes region (Illinois, Indiana, Michigan, Minnesota, Ohio, and Wisconsin). The final sample had 1,229 completions and a response rate of 42.1 percent.

2. We use the 2000 American Politics Survey because of the detailed information about the campaign finance issue, which is our focus. Although the NES does touch on the issue of campaign finance, it does not have the same level of detail about specific reform proposals studied here. See also Grant and Rudolph (2003) for more analysis of this survey.

3. The frequencies found are consistent with those of Francia et al. (2000), who surveyed congressional campaign contributors who gave over $200 during the 1996 election cycle.

4. Our factor analysis shows a striking resemblance to Webster et al.'s (2000) factor analysis of survey data from congressional campaign donors.

5. Without estimating the correlation parameter, one assumes that (after controlling for the variables in the model) there is no correlation. Thus, the model would be equivalent to two independent probit models: a probit model of turnout and one of candidate choice. In other words, if this correlation is zero, then after accounting for the variables in the model, the voters are assumed to be random draws from all respondents. If this correlation is *not* equal to zero, then there are additional variables not accounted for in the model that determine both turnout and candidate choice. These additional variables may be unmeasurable, such as the personalities of the candidates or lopsided local mobilization efforts by one of the parties.

6. In analysis not shown, we estimated a model of presidential vote that included only one type of reform attitude—regulatory reform. This variable was not statistically significant.

7. Although it does not include a general measure of ideology, our model does control for respondents' attitudes toward a number of policy issues over which liberals and conservatives traditionally disagree. The question of how much money the government should spend on services is a classic point of contention between liberals and conservatives. In addition to controlling for what might be termed *economic ideology*, our model also controls for social ideology by including respondents' attitudes toward the government's role in protecting traditional family values. Finally, by measuring whether respondents thought tax cuts should apply to the middle class only or to both the middle class and very wealthy individuals, our model controls for what was arguably the most prominent ideological issue in the 2000 campaign. In sum, we feel confident that these policy variables, along with partisanship, effectively account for the effects of ideology.

8. To facilitate comparisons across coefficients, all variables were scaled on a common 0 to 1 range.

9. Elsewhere we find that the effects of economic perceptions are strengthened considerably when they are accompanied by an attribution of responsibility to the Clinton administration (Rudolph and Grant 2002).

10. As with presidential vote, we estimated a model of congressional vote that included only regulatory reform; this variable was statistically insignificant.

11. Open races and races between two incumbents are excluded from the anal-

ysis. Attempts to model vote in open seat races failed to converge because of the small number of cases in the data set.

Chapter 6

Special thanks go to Saundra K. Schneider; this paper could not have been completed without her help. I would also like to thank the participants of the 2000 "Assessing the Vitality of Electoral Democracy" conference—particularly, Herbert B. Asher, J. Merrill Shanks, Herbert F. Weisberg, and Clyde Wilcox—for their comments and suggestions.

1. The 2000 National Election Study incorporated several new question formats for obtaining respondents' liberal-conservative placements. In the preelection wave of the study, one-half of the sample located themselves and the presidential candidates along the traditional seven-point scale, with labeled positions ranging from "extremely liberal" to "extremely conservative." The other half of the sample was presented with a series of branching questions. For respondents' self-placements, they were first asked, "When it comes to politics, do you usually think of yourself as a liberal, a conservative, a moderate, or haven't you thought much about this?" If respondents identified themselves as liberal (or conservative), they were then asked "Would you call yourself a strong liberal [conservative] or a not very strong liberal [conservative]?" Those who said they didn't think much about ideology were asked, "If you had to choose, would you consider yourself a liberal or a conservative?" The responses to these questions were then combined to create a seven-point scale. The branching format for the presidential candidates was slightly different. For each candidate, respondents were asked, "What about ___? Is ___ a liberal, a conservative, or a moderate?" Those who identified the candidate at a nonneutral position were then asked, "Would you call ___ a strong liberal [conservative] or a not very strong liberal [conservative]?" For each candidate, the responses to these questions were combined to place that candidate along a five-point scale. Ideological placements of the two major parties were only contained in the postelection wave of the NES, and they were obtained using the traditional seven-point scale. To facilitate comparisons of the item means, all of the ideological scales must be transformed to span a common range. Accordingly, the five-point scales are assigned integer values from one to five. All of the seven-point versions are also rescaled to produce equally spaced intervals from one to five. In every case, larger values indicate more conservative positions.

2. Liberal placements were the first two categories on the five-point scales and the first three categories of the seven-point scales. Similarly, conservative placements were the last two (or three) categories.

3. Respondents were asked which party had the most members in the House of Representatives and in the Senate prior to the 2000 election; the offices held by Trent Lott, William Rehnquist, Tony Blair, and Janet Reno; and the home states of George W. Bush, Al Gore, Dick Cheney, and Joseph Lieberman.

4. The multidimensional scaling analysis examines dissimilarities in the NES respondents' evaluations of eleven stimuli: Bill Clinton, Al Gore, George W. Bush, Dick Cheney, Joseph Lieberman, Ralph Nader, Bill Bradley, John McCain, Hillary Clinton, the Democratic Party, and the Republican Party. The 2000 NES interview schedule also included feeling thermometers for Pat Buchanan and the Reform Party. However, preliminary analyses indicated that public evaluations of these two stimuli were fundamentally different from the others (generally, more hostile). Therefore, they are excluded from the MDS.

5. A metric multidimensional scaling analysis is performed here because there are only eleven stimuli—too few for a stable solution with a nonmetric analysis. That being said, a nonmetric MDS of the same data produces nearly identical results. The stress value for the configuration is .18.

6. The point for Hillary Clinton is obviously separated from the other stimuli, but in the opposite direction from the other "outsider" points. This is almost certainly due to her completely unique status (i.e., simultaneous First Lady and senatorial candidate) during the 2000 election. Thus, it is very reasonable that her perceived position is somewhat distant from the stimuli that are associated more directly with *presidential* election politics.

7. For this part of the analysis, the ideological self-placement variable is used with its more traditional scoring scheme: The categories are assigned successive integer values from one to seven, with larger values indicating less liberal and more conservative positions.

8. The eight issues are: guaranteed jobs; government services and spending; defense spending; private versus government health insurance; government assistance for African Americans; women's role in society; environmental regulation; and environmental protection versus jobs. The reliability for this scale (Cronbach's alpha) is 0.68.

9. Respondents were asked how well each of the following traits described Bush and Gore: moral; really cares about people like you; knowledgeable; strong leader; dishonest; intelligent; out of touch. Responses were originally recorded on a four-point scale: from one, for "Describes the candidate extremely well," to four, for "Does not describe the candidate well at all." Responses were recoded as necessary so that larger values indicated more positive beliefs. Then, the scores for Gore were summed and subtracted from the summed scores for Bush. The reliability of the overall scale (Cronbach's alpha) is 0.84.

10. Respondents were asked whether the national economy had gotten better or worse over the previous year and whether unemployment had gotten better or worse over the previous year. Responses were recorded on a five-point scale, with larger values indicating more negative evaluations of economic performance. A summated rating scale was created from the two items, with a reliability (alpha) of 0.55.

11. Respondents indicated the degree to which Bill Clinton displayed each of the same five personality traits that were used to evaluate Bush and Gore. A sum-

mated rating scale of the Clinton evaluations was created, with a reliability (alpha) of 0.80.

Chapter 7

1. Party identification, or partisanship, has been measured regularly since 1952 by both commercial pollsters and academic researchers. The Gallup poll, for example, regularly reports proportions of Democrats, independents, and Republicans in *The Gallup Report*, available in most university libraries. In political science, there is a long history of research on the meaning and measure of partisanship, both in the United Sates and abroad. See, for example, recent discussions by Niemi and Weisberg (2001, chapter 17), Miller and Niemi (2002), Green, Palmquist, and Schickler (2002), Fiorina (2002), Bartels (2002), and Weisberg and Greene (2003). For the distribution of partisanship over time, see table 2.1 of this book and Stanley and Niemi (2001).

2. Logistic regression is an appropriate method when the dependent variable is dichotomous. As we explain later, both of our dependent variables (whether a respondent is Democratic or not and whether a respondent is Republican or not) are dichotomous, which makes logit analysis more appropriate than so-called ordinary least squares regression.

3. Ideally, we would have a single equation, one that assesses the contribution of every relevant group over the entire period under study. In fact, we need several models because the groups considered relevant change over time. Hispanics, for example, were not a large enough group to be considered politically significant before the 1980s. Religious fundamentalists were a large enough group, but they were not considered a coherent political force until the mid-1970s. As a result, survey questions that are needed to identify the appropriate groups have not been asked over the entire period. (In addition, how to measure the concept of fundamentalism has been debated widely—see, for example, Rothenberg and Newport 1984.) And, obviously, groups defined by recent birth dates—such as those born after 1958 or 1970—could not be defined early in the series.

4. The results reported here differ slightly from those in our earlier articles. In earlier analyses we included working class (i.e., self-reported social class) among the groups. That variable was not included in the 1996 or 1998 NES; we opted to exclude it from all earlier years rather than begin yet another new model. An examination of the models for all prior years with and without the class variable reveals very small differences for the coefficients of all other variables.

5. The survey question used by the National Election Studies to measure partisanship is: "Generally speaking, do you usually think of yourself as a Republican, a Democrat, an independent, or what?" Democrats and Republicans are asked if they are "strong" or "weak," and independents are asked if they lean toward the Democratic or the Republican Party. For our analysis, we use respondents' answers to the first question only, on the assumption that the core of the party is better represented by the avowedly partisan respondents. There is considerable

debate, however, over the meaning of the "leaner" category—whether leaners are truly "devoid of any psychological sense of belongingness or allegiance to a party" (Miller and Shanks 1996, 127) or are in fact partisans who answer "independent" for reasons of social desirability. See especially Keith et al. (1992) and Weisberg (1999).

6. The NES survey in 1998 did not include variables identifying where respondents grew up. Consequently, to include the 1998 survey and to enable comparison across the decade of the 1990s, the native southern white variable was replaced by a southern white variable in 1990 and later. Over the years, native southern whites have moved toward the partisan leanings of whites who have migrated into the South, making natives less distinctive in partisan terms. As expected, the southern white group is not only larger but also more Republican and less Democratic than native southern whites. In 2000, however, even among native southern whites, the incremental probability of identifying with Democrats was negative. This indicates that the result discussed later is not an artifact of having changed the definition from native to all southern whites.

7. One should not overinterpret fluctuations for relatively small groups, such as the Jewish population. Figures may change sharply simply because they are based on a small number of cases.

8. Comparable results for Republicans have a distorting mirror-image aspect. Given the general Democratic tendencies of the group ties, removing the group ties means that the group's share of Republican identifiers, perhaps tiny to begin with, often swells to greater than 100 percent of its former size.

Chapter 8

1. Bush won a plurality of men's votes in 1992, and Dole did the same in 1996.

2. The gender gap on the NES government guarantee of jobs question was always statistically significant from 1972 to 2000, when the seven-point scale option was used. Earlier versions of the question were used from 1956 to 1968, and a statistically significant gender gap occurred in four of the five surveys in which the question was asked.

3. This difference was mostly due to the very heavy allegiance of white southern men to the Democratic Party.

4. Slightly different questions were used in the 2000 NES for those respondents who were interviewed over the phone rather than in the traditional face-to-face method. To maintain as many cases as possible, the variables used in this analysis are those that combine answers from both the face-to-face and phone surveys.

5. Considerable missing data occurs in the 2000 NES. In the phone interviews, an unusually large number of respondents chose the "haven't thought much about this" option. For example, in response to the defense-spending question, 16 percent of those surveyed in person chose the "haven't thought much" option compared to 26 percent of those interviewed over the phone. With listwise deletion, two-thirds of the cases are lost, leaving only 592 respondents in the regression

analysis. Thus, we used mean substitution to handle missing values on the independent variables. Results from a listwise-deletion analysis are given in the appendix to this chapter (see Table 8A.1). In that analysis, significant interaction effects occurred for ideology and government services, but not for government jobs.

6. We also tested other formats for measuring the presence of female candidates. These included (1) dummy variables for female Republican candidates and female Democratic candidates and (2) a single female candidate variable that was scored as follows: −1 for any female Republican candidate, 1 for any female Democratic candidate, and 0 for no female candidate or a female candidate from both parties. Neither of these produced statistically significant interaction terms when combined with gender.

7. Missing data presented fewer problems for the congressional analysis. Using listwise deletion results in the loss of only thirty-nine additional cases. Nevertheless, results using listwise deletion are given in Table 8A.2.

Chapter 9

Thanks to Laura Arnold, Brady Baybeck, Barry Burden, Paul Goren, Tim Johnson, Bryan Marshall, and Rich Timpone for comments.

1. The split district figures for 1900–1996 come from Stanley and Niemi (2000). The split district calculation for 2000 is from Polidata® (2001). The ticket splitting estimates are calculated from NES surveys. Elections before 1900 are excluded because ticket splitting was extremely rare prior to the Australian ballot reforms just before the turn of the century (Rusk 1970). In addition, direct election of U.S. Senators was constitutionally mandated in 1913.

2. This has not always been the prevailing view. For example, Broder (1972) and Phillips (1975) argue that ticket splitting increased in the 1972 elections because voters did not perceive policy differences between the major parties.

3. To be fair, more recent studies have revised Fiorina's initial policy-balancing theory by focusing more specifically on voter expectations of election outcomes and subsequent government policies (Lacy and Paolino 1998; Smith, Brown, Bruce, and Overby 1999; Mebane 2000; Scheve and Tomz 1999; Mebane and Sekhon 2002). However, the revised balancing theories still depend on the existence of ideologically polarized parties as the central motivation for moderate voters to engage in strategic balancing behavior.

4. Indeed, Key advocated more distinctive issue-oriented party platforms (as well as stronger party organizations) as a way to revitalize partisan ties in the electorate (Epstein 1983).

5. There is no data point for 1956, when NES did not ask the "important differences" question.

6. Measures of presidential candidate positions were created by Zaller and Hunt (Zaller 1999).

7. Party identification is measured on a seven-point scale (−3 is a strong Democrat, +3 is a strong Republican). Ideology is measured using the three-point self-

placement summary (−1 is a liberal, 0 is a moderate, +1 is a conservative). Both variables are coded so that they should be positively correlated with the vote measures. The three-point ideology summary is used to minimize data lost in the seven-point ideology measure.

8. A complete description of each variable is included in the methodological appendix at the end of the chapter.

9. I follow the coding used by Mattei and Howes (2000) in creating the presidential cross-pressure variables.

10. Uncontested races afford the voter no choice between casting a split ticket or a straight ticket. Third- party votes are relatively rare and confound tests of policy balancing. The name-recall questions were not included in the NES battery before 1978. Otherwise, the variables used for this analysis go back to 1972.

11. The strength-of-partisanship variable is held constant at 1 (pure independent), and all other variables are held constant at 0. These are the median values for each variable except for strength of partisanship (median is 3, a weak partisan), important party differences, and care about outcome (where the median is 1, someone who does care about the outcome). These values were chosen to simulate a voter who is susceptible to many forces that produce ticket splitting.

12. Diagnostic tests indicate that 1920, 1984, and 2000 were influential observations in model 1, with Cook's d values being slightly larger than the critical value of .18 (Fox 1991). In model 2, none of the observations generated influence statistics that exceeded the critical value. The results for both models are the same when influential cases are dropped or when a robust regression method, which corrects for outliers and influential cases (Fox 1991), is used. See Brunell, Grofman, and Merrill (2001) for similar results. Brown and Wright (1992) examine the relationship between ticket splitting and state-level party polarization and also find an inverse relationship.

13. It is possible that moderate voters are more comfortable splitting their votes between two centrist parties rather than between two ideologically extreme parties. Voters may be less certain about the likely policy outcomes negotiated by elected officials who occupy opposite poles on the ideological spectrum (Lacy and Niou 1998). However, this argument subverts the basic motivation for policy balancing: the need to strike a balance between ideologically extreme parties and their elected officials.

14. An F test indicates that the coefficients for the interaction term and the main effect for victory margin are statistically different from one another at the .05 significance level.

15. Of the thirty-three conservative Blue Dog Democrats in the 107th House, twenty-two represented districts that Bush won in the 2000 election.

Chapter 10

The authors wish to thank Greg Smith for diligent research assistance, and Rich Timpone, Herb Weisberg, and Clyde Wilcox for valuable editorial comments.

1. Our source for state-level VAP data (the denominator in the turnout estimate) is the Census 2000 Summary File 1 (SC 1) 100–Percent Data, Tables P5 and P12. Our source for state-level number of votes cast for president (the numerator) is the Federal Election Commission report, Federal Elections 2000 (http://www.fec.gov/pubrec/fe2000/tcontents.htm).

2. This figure is based on data from the Federal Election Commission. Using a slightly higher estimate of the voting-age population, the *Statistical Abstract* reports 1960 turnout as 62.8 percent.

3. Of course, the voting-age population is itself only a rough estimate of the *eligible* electorate. Many people included in Census Bureau voting-age population figures are not in fact eligible to cast a ballot. Noncitizens, felons (in many states) and ex-felons (in some states), are all ineligible, as are individuals deemed mentally "incompetent." McDonald and Popkin (2001) argue that the universe of eligible voters has grown smaller relative to the VAP over time, leading to the erroneous conclusion that turnout has declined to a greater extent than it has since 1972. Following McDonald (2001), we estimated state-level "voting-eligible turnout" (VEP), adjusting VAP estimates with Census data on noncitizens and Department of Justice data on each state's prison, parole, and probation populations. The result is a VEP measure of turnout that is highly correlated ($r = .96$) with the traditional VAP measure. Average VEP state-level turnout is 55.1 percent, an increase of 1.3 points over 1996 VEP turnout. By comparison, traditional VAP turnout increased by 1.3 points, from 49.1 percent to 50.4 percent in 2000. Using either VAP or VEP in state-level analyses, moreover, leads to the same substantive conclusions regarding the nature and degree of changing turnout between the 1996 and 2000 elections.

4. Such a measure will, of course, be an imperfect one. We obviously leave out a wide range of campaign activity such as candidate visits, radio advertising, direct mail, and phone calls. Moreover, we have constructed a relatively blunt indicator of competition—aggregate number of ads broadcast—rather than indicating the relative intensity of advertising by the two campaigns. However, in 2000 the campaigns were rather evenly matched in their targeting (Goldstein and Freedman 2002). Finally, our measure will inevitably miss activity in states that do not have media markets that rank in the top seventy-five markets.

5. Once again, the same pattern is evident—albeit with slightly higher levels of turnout—if one uses the VEP measure rather than voting-age turnout.

6. The challenges in using survey data to estimate voter turnout are well known. Factors such as respondent misreporting, sampling biases, and even the stimulating effect of participating in a preelection wave lead even high-quality surveys like the NES consistently to overestimate aggregate turnout (Anderson and Silver 1986; Belli et al. 1999; Katosh and Traugott 1981; Traugott and Katosh 1979). As Burden (2000) has demonstrated, the disparity between the NES and official turnout figures for presidential elections has grown dramatically over the past four decades, from eleven points in 1952 to twenty-four points in 1996, a trend that Burden attributes to declining response rates and attendant response bias.

7. These figures are based on data weighted by the appropriate full-sample postelection weight for each year: v923008 (1992) v960005b (1996), and v000002a (2000). Analyses that use unweighted data or that use a different weight variable will report different levels of turnout. In particular, some analysts will choose a weight that is designed to make comparisons to pre-1992 data, a weight variable that would be inappropriate for our purposes. As a result, our figures may differ slightly from those appearing in other reports.

8. Table 10.2 displays logistic regression estimates, their associated standard errors, and significance levels for each independent variable in the pooled model for predicting turnout in the 1992–2000 period. We present only the variables that were statistically significant at the .10 level. These variables explain approximately 45 percent of the "variance" in the turnout decision. The model results in correct predictions of turnout in 82.1 percent of all cases across the three elections, a significant improvement over the 75 percent one would predict on the basis of reported turnout in the three elections combined.

9. This difference is in part an artifact of mode changes. African Americans interviewed in person were approximately four points less likely than non–African Americans to report having voted in 2000. Among respondents interviewed by phone ($N = 59$), however, African Americans were almost seven points *more* likely to report having cast a ballot. Even among in-person interviews, however, African Americans registered a two-percentage-point increase in turnout in 2000 over 1996, while non–African Americans registered a two-percentage-point decrease.

10. Interestingly, mobilization was effective in 2000 not because mobilized citizens were more likely to vote than their counterparts in earlier elections, but because unmobilized citizens were *less* likely to vote than they had been in the past. Only 61.8 percent of noncontacted citizens voted in 2000 versus 65.6 percent in 1996 (and 72.5 percent in 1992). Party and campaign contact, in effect, had to work harder to lift citizens up from this lower baseline.

11. We present the "change in probability" associated with having a "high" or a "low" value of each variable in the third column, which gives an indication of the relative influence of each factor in the turnout decision. We set the baseline turnout probability to be .75 and calculate the change in turnout probability based on having "high" or "low" values of each variable. For categorical variables such as party contact, marital status, home ownership, and perceived closeness of the race, a "low" value is 0 and a "high" value is 1. For variables that have more than two categories, we set the "low" and high" values to their minimum and maximum possible level. For example, we compare individuals who have less than a high school education to individuals with an education beyond the college degree, individuals in states with Election Day registration to individuals in states that require registration one month (thirty-one days) before the election, political independents to strong partisans, and individuals with no dislikes of the major-party candidates to those who express ten dislikes. It should be noted that all of

these calculations yield the *maximum* possible change in turnout for individuals at a given prior probability of voting. The actual changes in turnout attributed to many of the variables will be smaller, as there are, for example, very few individuals who record ten dislikes of the candidates. An alternative measure for non-dichotomous variables is the change in turnout probability for a baseline individual who is one-half of a standard deviation above the mean on a given variable, compared with the turnout probability for a baseline individual who is one-half of a standard deviation below the mean. These figures are presented in the last column of table 10.2.

12. The trust scale included the following four items: "How much of the time do you think you can trust the government in Washington to do what is right—just about always, most of the time or only some of the time?" "Would you say the government is pretty much run by a few big interests looking out for themselves or that it is run for the benefit of all the people?" "Do you think that people in the government waste a lot of money we pay in taxes, waste some of it, or don't waste very much of it?" and "Do you think that quite a few of the people running the government are crooked, not very many are, or do you think hardly any of them are crooked?"

13. In 2000, respondents were asked to identify the "job or office" held by William Rehnquist (8.9 percent correct), Trent Lott (7.1), Tony Blair (29.2), and Janet Reno (50.1), along with questions about partisan control of the House (49.9) and Senate (45.1).

14. Because different questions with different degrees of difficulty were used in each election year to gauge the respondent's level of information, it is impossible to compare the actual values across election years. Consequently, we subtracted the average number of correct responses in that year from each respondent's value, creating a normed index for each year with an average value of zero. Individuals with positive values are higher than the average respondent in that year, while individuals with negative values are below the sample's average.

15. Strictly speaking, these kinds of calculations are exact only in the context of a linear-regression model, not the nonlinear logistic specification of table 10.2. Consequently, we reestimated the effects of these variables though ordinary least-squares regression to obtain the estimates shown in table 10.3. All variables that were statistically significant in the logistic regression of table 10.2 were also significant in the OLS estimation. We also conducted similar analyses using the logistic-regression coefficients from table 10.2 (with a baseline probability of .73), and found a nearly identical pattern of effects as those we report in table 10.3. The most important factors that led to turnout increases in either analyses were party contact and increases in perceived closeness, education, civic duty, and external efficacy. The most important factors that led to turnout decreases were candidate thermometer ratings, caring about the outcome, strength of partisanship, and the number of dislikes of the candidates.

16. It is possible that the Ralph Nader candidacy stimulated turnout among

some independents in 2000. Based on the relatively few Nader voters in the NES data, and assuming that *every* Nader voter would have stayed home had Nader not run (cf. Burden in Chapter 11 of this book), we estimate that the Nader effect could account for *at most* 3.4 of the 6.9-point increase in turnout among independents.

17. It is also the case that "yield" differentials help to explain the disengagement of strong partisans in 2000. That is, strong partisans who were contacted in 2000 were as likely to vote in 2000 as in either of the other two election years, while strong partisans who were *not* contacted were eight percentage points less likely to turn out than in either 1992 or 1996. Thus, mobilization efforts compensated to some degree for the relative lack of engagement in 2000 with the major candidates among even strong partisans, and they compensated for the "normal" lack of engagement with the candidates found in 2000 among independents as well.

Chapter 11

I thank Rob Van Houweling, Jonathan Wand, and the ICPSR for supplying data and Dean Lacy, Phil Paolino, Rich Timpone, Herb Weisberg, Clyde Wilcox, and Gerald Wright for helpful comments.

1. Gore was eligible to win 267 electoral votes, but one Gore elector from the District of Columbia abstained as a protest.

2. As others have noted, the term *third party* is imprecise because there are often many minor-party candidates available to vote for (Gilbert et al. 1999; Herrnson and Green 2002). Earlier studies tended to limit analysis to those who received at least 5 percent of the popular vote (Cho 2000; Lacy and Burden 1999; Rosenstone, Behr, and Lazarus 1996) or examined less successful campaigns (Herrnson and Green 2002). I take the middle ground by examining Buchanan and Nader, neither of whom achieved 5 percent or any electoral votes but both of whom are thought to have affected the election outcome substantially.

3. These counterfactuals depend on the tenuous assumptions that candidate strategies and voters' preferences would have been the same even with different voting systems in place.

4. These results are unchanged if one uses unweighted rather than weighted data or analyze all respondents rather than just voters. They are close but not identical to Abramson, Aldrich, and Rohde (2002, table 6–1).

5. As Brams and Fishburn (1983), Brams and Merrill (1994), and Kiewiet (1979) argue, there are several ways in which approval votes might be computed from feeling thermometer rankings. For simplicity's sake, I take the simplest form —sincere approval voting—where ties are discarded and voting for a candidate is considered an approval vote.

6. This appears to be true in every presidential election where a viable minor party ran. The only exception might be Ross Perot in 1992 if one takes his reentry into the campaign rather than his initial public support as the baseline. Another, clearer exception is the 1998 gubernatorial election in Minnesota, where Reform

Party candidate Jesse Ventura rose from near obscurity to victory in the final weeks of the campaign (Lacy and Monson 2002; Lentz 2001).

7. Buchanan's support appears to follow the traditional pattern of minor-party decline, though it is difficult to know this with confidence. His support hovers around 1 percent, thus making rounding error huge and leaving little room for movement downward. Though rounding makes it difficult to be definitive, Gallup appears to have overestimated Buchanan's support by less than half a point and overestimated Nader's support by 1.5 points.

8. A collection of several dozen trial-heat polls is used here rather than the Gallup tracking polls shown in Figure 11.2. Tracking polls are adequate for analyzing the broad contours of campaigns, but they are problematic for time-series analysis because the observations are not independent. Though time-series models allow for autocorrelation, tracking polls are based on rolling three-day averages (and in Gallup's case, quotas on the third day to compensate for missed respondents on the first two days). Fortunately, Nader's rise in the polls is robust since it appears in both tracking polls and trial-heat polls, even after introducing control variables. Undecided voters have been removed so that candidates' percentages add up to 100.

9. "If these were the only two presidential candidates on the ballot today, who would you have voted for?" (Al Gore [Dem], George W. Bush [Rep], or Would not have voted for president).

10. Another way to get leverage on the turnout and vote-stealing effects is to estimate them based on predictions from regression models of vote choice and abstention (Lacy and Burden 1999, 2002). Only NES data will work, however, as exit polls by definition exclude abstainers. Unfortunately, the 2000 NES data includes only thirty-three Nader voters and three Buchanan voters.

11. Indeed, only about 1 percent of the Nader vote would have been needed to make up the final Bush-Gore difference. But one cannot say that 537 were all that were needed for Gore to win. Florida law requires a recount whenever the difference is less than 0.5 percent of the total votes cast. Gore would have needed to win by roughly thirty thousand votes initially to avoid an automatic recount or recanvass. Legal maneuvering might have developed differently if Gore was the leader in the initial count, leading to an unknown outcome. This kind of analysis also requires one to assume that turnout and the other minor parties' vote totals would remain constant.

12. For a careful analysis of voting irregularities in the 2000 presidential election, see the series of papers by Wand and colleagues at <http://elections.fas.harvard.edu>.

13. Under this scenario, Bush would have won even if he had given Gore New Hampshire. Bush won New Hampshire's four electoral votes by just 7, 211 popular votes.

References

Abramowitz, Alan I. 1981. "Choices and Echoes in the 1980 U.S. Senate Elections: A Research Note." *American Journal of Political Science* 25: 112–18.
———. 1995. "It's Abortion, Stupid: Policy Voting in the 1992 Presidential Election." *Journal of Politics* 57: 176–86.
———. 2001. "The Time for Change Model and the 2000 Election." *American Politics Research* 29: 279–82.
Abramowitz, Alan I., and Kyle L. Saunders. 1998. "Ideological Realignment in the U.S. Electorate." *Journal of Politics* 60: 634–52.
———. 2002. "Ideological Realignment and U.S. Congressional Election." In *Understanding Public Opinion*, 2d ed., ed. Barbara Norrander and Clyde Wilcox. Washington, D.C.: CQ Press.
Abramson, Paul R., John H. Aldrich, Phil Paolino, and David W. Rohde. 1992. "'Sophisticated' Voting in the 1988 Presidential Primaries." *American Political Science Review* 86: 55–69.
———. 1995. "Third-Party and Independent Candidates in American Politics: Wallace, Anderson, and Perot." *Political Science Quarterly* 110: 349–67.
———. 2000. "Challenges to the American Two-Party System: Evidence from the 1968, 1980, 1992, and 1996 Presidential Elections." *Political Research Quarterly* 53: 495–522.
Abramson, Paul R., John H. Aldrich, and David W. Rohde. 1998. *Change and Continuity in the 1996 Elections*. Washington, D.C.: CQ Press.
———. 1999. *Change and Continuity in the 1996 and 1998 Elections*. Washington, D.C.: CQ Press.
———. 2002. *Change and Continuity in the 2000 Elections*. Washington, D.C.: CQ Press.
Achen, Christopher H. 1982. *Interpreting and Using Regression*. Beverly Hills, Calif.: Sage.

Ackerman, Bruce. 1993. "Crediting the Voters: A New Beginning for Campaign Finance." *American Prospect* 13: 71–89.

Adamany, David W., and George E. Agree. 1975. *Political Money*. Baltimore, Md.: Johns Hopkins University Press.

Adams, Greg D. 1997. "Abortion: Evidence of an Issue Evolution." *American Journal of Political Science* 41: 718–37.

Aistrup, Joseph A. 1996. *The Southern Strategy Revisited*. Lexington: University of Kentucky Press.

Aldrich, John H. 1997. "Positive Theory and Voice and Equality." *American Political Science Review* 91: 421.

Aldrich, John H., John L. Sullivan, and Eugene Borgida. 1989. "Foreign Policy Voting in Presidential Elections: Are Candidates 'Waltzing before a Blind Audience?'" *American Political Science Review* 83: 123–41.

Alesina, Alberto, and Howard Rosenthal. 1995. *Partisan Politics, Divided Government, and the Economy*. New York: Cambridge University Press.

Alford, John R., Holly Teeters, Daniel S. Ward, and Rick K. Wilson. 1994. "Overdraft: The Political Cost of Congressional Malfeasance." *Journal of Politics* 56: 788–801.

Alvarez, R. Michael, and Jonathan Nagler. 1995. "Economics, Issues, and the Perot Candidacy: Voter Choice in the 1992 Presidential Election." *American Journal of Political Science* 39: 714–44.

———. 1998. "Economics, Entitlements and Social Issues: Voter Choice in the 1996 Presidential Election." *American Journal of Political Science* 42: 1349–63.

Alvarez, R. Michael, and Matthew M. Schousen. 1993. "Policy Moderation or Conflicting Expectations: Testing the Intentional Models of Split-Ticket Voting." *American Politics Quarterly* 21: 410–38.

Anderson, Barbara A., and Brian D. Silver. 1986. "Measurement and Mismeasurement of the Validity of the Self-Reported Vote." *American Journal of Political Science* 30: 771–85.

Andolina, Mary, and Clyde Wilcox. 2000. "Public Opinion: The Paradoxes of Clinton Popularity." In *The Clinton Scandal and the Future of American Government*, ed. Mark J. Rozell and Clyde Wilcox. Washington, D.C.: Georgetown University Press.

Ansolabehere, Stephen, Roy Behr, and Shanto Iyengar. 1993. *The Media Game*. New York: Macmillan.

Ansolabehere, Stephen, and Shanto Iyengar. 1995. *Going Negative: How Political Ads Shrink and Polarize the Electorate*. New York: Free Press.

Arrow, Kenneth J. 1951. *Social Choice and Individual Values*. New Haven, Conn.: Yale University Press.

Asher, Herbert B. 1988. *Presidential Elections and American Politics*. 4th ed. Chicago: Dorsey Press.

———. 1995. "The Perot Campaign." In *Democracy's Feast: Elections in America*, ed. Herbert F. Weisberg. Chatham, N.J.: Chatham House.

Bartels, Larry M. 2000. "Partisanship and Voting Behavior, 1952–1996." *American Journal of Political Science* 44: 35–50.

———. 2002. "Beyond the Running Tally: Partisan Bias in Political Perceptions." *Political Behavior* 24: 117–50.

Bartels, Larry M., and John Zaller. 2001. "Presidential Vote Models: A Recount." *PS: Political Science and Politics* 34: 9–20.

Beck, Paul Allen. 1986. "Model Choice in Political Science: The Case of Voting Behavior Research." In *Political Science: The Science of Politics*, ed. Herbert F. Weisberg. New York: Agathon.

Beck, Paul Allen, Lawrence Baum, Aage R. Clausen, and Charles E. Smith Jr. 1992. "Patterns and Sources of Ticket Splitting in Subpresidential Voting." *American Political Science Review* 86: 916–28.

Belli, Robert F., Michael W. Traugott, Margaret Young, and Katherine A. McGonagle. 1999. "Reducing Vote Overreporting in Surveys: Social Desirability, Memory Failure, and Source Monitoring." *Public Opinion Quarterly* 63: 90–108.

Belli, Robert F., Santa Traugott, and Steven J. Rosenstone. 1994. "Reducing Over-Reporting of Voter Turnout: An Experiment Using a Source Monitoring Framework." *National Election Studies Technical Report* #35.

Bibby, John F., and L. Sandy Maisel. 2002. *Two Parties—Or More? The American Party System.* Boulder, Colo.: Westview Press.

Bloom, Howard S., and H. Douglas Price. 1975. "Voter Response to Short-Run Economic Conditions: The Asymmetric Effect of Prosperity and Recession." *American Political Science Review* 69: 1240–54.

Bond, Jon R., and Richard Fleisher, eds. 2000. *Polarized Politics: Congress and the President in a Partisan Era.* Washington, D.C.: CQ Press.

Born, Richard. 1994. "Split-Ticket Voters, Divided Government, and Fiorina's Policy-Balancing Model." *Legislative Studies Quarterly* 19: 95–115.

———. 2000a. "Congressional Incumbency and the Rise of Split-Ticket Voting." *Legislative Studies Quarterly* 25: 365–87.

———. 2000b. "Policy-Balancing Models and the Split-Ticket Voter, 1972–1996." *American Politics Quarterly* 28: 131–62.

Box, George E. P., and Gwilym M. Jenkins. 1976. *Time Series Analysis: Forecasting and Control.* San Francisco: Holden-Day.

Box-Steffensmeier, Janet M. 1996. "A Dynamic Analysis of the Role of War Chests in Campaign Strategy." *American Journal of Political Science* 40: 352–71.

Brams, Steven J., and Peter C. Fishburn. 1983. *Approval Voting.* Boston, Mass.: Birkhäuser.

Brams, Steven J., and Samuel Merrill III. 1994. "Would Ross Perot Have Won the 1992 Presidential Election under Approval Voting?" *PS: Political Science and Politics* 27: 39–44.

Broder, David S. 1972. *The Party's Over: The Failure of Politics in America.* New York: Harper & Row.

Brody, Richard A. 1978. "The Puzzle of Political Participation in America." In *The New American Political System*, ed. Anthony King. Washington, D.C.: American Enterprise Institute.

Brody, Richard A., David W. Brady, and Valerie Heitshusen. 1994. "Accounting for Divided Government: Generational Effects on Party and Split-Ticket Voting." In *Elections at Home and Abroad*, ed. M. Kent Jennings and Thomas E. Mann. Ann Arbor: University of Michigan Press.

Brown, Clifford W., Lynda W. Powell, and Clyde Wilcox. 1995. *Serious Money: Fundraising and Contributing in Presidential Nomination Campaigns.* Cambridge, U.K.: Cambridge University Press.

Brown, Robert D., and Gerald C. Wright. 1992. "Elections and State Party Polarization." *American Politics Quarterly* 20: 411–26.

Brownstein, Ronald. 2000. "Men's Backing Help Power Bush Past Gore." *Los Angeles Times*, September 27.

Brunell, Thomas L., and Bernard N. Grofman. 1998. "Explaining Divided U.S. Senate Delegations, 1788–1996." *American Political Science Review* 92: 391–99.

Brunell, Thomas L., Bernard N. Grofman, and Samuel Merrill III. 2001. "Accounting for Changes in the Number of Districts with Split House-President Outcomes, 1900–1996." Paper presented at the annual meeting of the Public Choice Society, San Antonio, Texas.

Buckley v. Valeo, 424 US 1 (1976).

Burden, Barry C. 2000. "Voter Turnout and the National Election Studies." *Political Analysis* 8: 389–98.

Burden, Barry C., and David C. Kimball. 1998. "A New Approach to the Study of Ticket Splitting." *American Political Science Review* 92: 533–44.

———. 2002. *Why Americans Split Their Tickets: Campaigns, Competition, and Divided Government.* Ann Arbor: University of Michigan Press.

Campbell, Angus. 1960. "Surge and Decline: A Study of Electoral Change." *Public Opinion Quarterly* 24: 397–418.

Campbell, Angus, Philip E. Converse, Warren E. Miller, and Donald E. Stokes. 1960. *The American Voter.* New York: John Wiley.

Campbell, Angus, and Warren E. Miller. 1957. "The Motivational Basis of Straight and Split-Ticket Voting." *American Political Science Review* 51: 293–312.

Campbell, James E. 1987. "The Revised Theory of Surge and Decline." *American Journal of Political Science* 31: 965–79.

———. 1992. "Forecasting the Presidential Vote in the States." *American Journal of Political Science* 36: 386–407.

———. 2001. "The Referendum That Didn't Happen: The Forecasts of the 2000 Presidential Election." *PS: Political Science and Politics* 34: 33–38.

Campbell, James E., and James C. Garand, eds. 2000. *Before the Vote.* Thousand Oaks, Calif.: Sage.

Carmines, Edward G., and Geoffrey C. Layman. 1997. "Issue Evolution in Postwar American Politics." In *Present Discontents*, ed. Byron E. Shafer. Chatham, N.J.: Chatham House.

Ceaser, James W., and Andrew E. Busch. 2001. *The Perfect Tie: The True Story of the 2000 Presidential Election.* Lanham, Md.: Rowman & Littlefield.

Center for Responsive Politics. 1997. *Money and Politics Survey.* Princeton Survey Research Associates. Archived at the Roper Center, Storrs, Connecticut.

Chaney, Carole Kennedy, R. Michael Alvarez, and Jonathan Nagler. 1998. "Explaining the Gender Gap in U.S. Presidential Elections, 1980–1992." *Political Research Quarterly* 51: 311–39.

Chappell, Henry W., Jr., and William R. Keech. 1991. "Explaining Aggregate Evaluations of Economic Performance." In *Economics and Politics: The Calculus of Support*, ed. Helmut Norpoth, Michael Lewis-Beck, and Jean-Dominique Lafay. Ann Arbor: University of Michigan Press.

Cho, Sungdai. 2000. "Does Incumbency Matter? Strategic Vote Choice among Third-Party Supporters in U.S. Presidential Elections." Paper presented at the annual meeting of the Midwest Political Science Association, Chicago.

Citrin, Jack. 1996. "Affirmative Action in the People's Court." *The Public Interest* 122: 39–48.

Clarke, Harold D., Helmut Norpoth, and Paul Whiteley. 1998. "It's about Time: Modeling Political and Social Dynamics." In *Research Strategies in the Social Sciences*, ed. Elinor Scarbrough and Eric Tanenbaum. Oxford: Oxford University Press.

Clarke, Harold D., and Marianne C. Stewart. 1994. "Prospections, Retrospections and Rationality: The 'Bankers' Model of Presidential Approval Reconsidered." *American Journal of Political Science* 38: 1104–123.

Clausen, Aage R. 1973. *How Congressmen Decide: A Policy Focus.* New York: St. Martin's Press.

Clymer, Adam. 2000. "And the Winner Is Gore, If They Got the Math Right." *New York Times*, September 4.

Cobb, Kim. 2000. "Female Voters Study Candidates, Education; Undecided Women May Swing Election." *Houston Chronicle*, October 22.

Colorado Republican Federal Campaign Committee v. Federal Election Commission, 518 US 604 (1996).

Comparative State Election Project. 1973. *Explaining the Vote: Presidential Choices in the Nation and the States.* Chapel Hill, N.C.: Institute for Research in Social Science.

Conover, Pamela J., and Stanley Feldman. 1981. "The Origins and Meaning of Liberal/Conservative Self-Identifications." *American Journal of Political Science* 25: 617–45.

Converse, Philip E. 1964. "The Nature of Belief Systems in Mass Publics." In *Ideology and Discontent*, ed. David E. Apter. New York: Free Press.

Converse, Philip E., Angus Campbell, Warren E. Miller, and Donald E. Stokes.

1961. "Stability and Change in 1960: A Reinstating Election." *American Political Science Review* 55: 269–80.

Cook, Elizabeth Adell. 1998. "Voter Reaction to Women Candidates." In *Women and Elective Office: Past, Present, and Future*, ed. Sue Thomas and Clyde Wilcox. New York: Oxford University Press.

Cook, Elizabeth Adell, Ted G. Jelen, and Clyde Wilcox. 1992. *Between Two Absolutes: Public Opinion and the Politics of Abortion*. Boulder, Colo.: Westview Press.

Cook, Elizabeth Adell, and Clyde Wilcox. 1995. "Women Voters in the 'Year of the Woman.'" In *Democracy's Feast: Elections in America*, ed. Herbert F. Weisberg. Chatham, N.J.: Chatham House.

Cox, Gary W., and Mathew McCubbins. 1993. *Legislative Leviathan: Party Government in the House*. Berkeley: University of California Press.

Cox, Gary W., and Michael C. Munger. 1989. "Closeness, Expenditure, and Turnout: The 1982 U.S. House Elections." *American Political Science Review* 83: 217–32.

Delli Carpini, Michael X., and Scott Keeter. 1996. *What Americans Know about Politics and Why It Matters*. New Haven, Conn.: Yale University Press.

DiIulio, John J., Jr. 1997. "Conclusion: Valence Voters, Valence Victors." In *The Elections of 1996*, ed. Michael Nelson. Washington, D.C.: CQ Press.

Dimock, Michael A., and Gary C. Jacobson. 1995. "Checks and Choices: The House Bank Scandal's Impact on Voters in 1992." *Journal of Politics* 57: 1143–59.

Dolan, Kathleen. 1998. "Voting for Women in 'the Year of the Woman.'" *American Journal of Political Science* 42: 272–93.

Downs, Anthony. 1957. *An Economic Theory of Democracy*. New York: Harper and Row.

Dubin, Jeffrey A., and Douglas Rivers. 1989. "Selection Bias in Linear Regression, Logit, and Probit Models." *Sociological Methods and Research* 18: 360–90.

Duch, Raymond M., Harvey D. Palmer, and Christopher J. Anderson. 2000. "Heterogeneity in Perceptions of National Economic Conditions." *American Journal of Political Science* 44: 635–52.

Duverger, Maurice. 1963. *Political Parties: Their Organization and Activity in the Modern State*. Trans. Barbara North and Robert North. New York: John Wiley.

Eagan, Margery. 2000. "Campaign 2000: This Year, May the Best Ladies' Man Win." *Boston Herald*, October 3.

Edsall, Thomas B. 2000. "Wooing Working Men; Gore Makes Inroads in Key Constituency." *Washington Post*, September 11.

Epstein, Leon D. 1983. "The Scholarly Commitment to Parties." In *Political Science: The State of the Discipline*, ed. Ada Finifter. Washington, D.C.: American Political Science Association.

Erikson, Robert S. 1988. "The Puzzle of Midterm Losses." *Journal of Politics* 50: 1012–29.

———. 2001. "The 2000 Presidential Election in Historical Perspective." *Political Science Quarterly* 116: 29–52.

Eulau, Heinz. 1986. *Politics, Self, and Society: A Theme and Variations.* Cambridge: Harvard University Press.

Federal Election Commission. 2001. "Party Fundraising Escalates." http://www.fec.gov/press/051501congfinact/051501congfinact.html Accessed on September 9, 2001.

Federal Election Commission v. Colorado Republican Federal Campaign Committee, 213 F3d 1221 (2001).

Federal Election Commission v. National Conservative Political Action Committee, 470 US 480 (1985).

Finkel, Steven E., and John Geer. 1998. "A Spot Check: Casting Doubt on the Demobilizing Effect of Attack Advertising." *American Journal of Political Science* 42: 573–95.

Fiorina, Morris P. 1981. *Retrospective Voting in American National Elections.* New Haven, Conn.: Yale University Press.

———. 1988. "The Reagan Years: Turning to the Right or Groping toward the Middle?" In *The Resurgence of Conservatism in Anglo-American Democracies,* ed. Barry Cooper, Allan Kornberg, and William Mishler. Durham, N.C.: Duke University Press.

———. 1996. *Divided Government,* 2d ed. Boston: Allyn and Bacon.

———. 2002. "Parties and Partisanship: A 40-Year Retrospective." *Political Behavior* 24: 93–115.

Fiorina, Morris P., Samuel Abrams, and Jeremy Pope. 2003. "The 2000 Elections: Can Retrospective Voting Be Saved?" *British Journal of Political Science* 33: forthcoming.

Fiorina, Morris P., and Kenneth Shepsle. 1989. "Is Negative Voting an Artifact?" *American Journal of Political Science* 33: 423–39.

Fiss, Owen M. 1996. *The Irony of Free Speech.* Cambridge, Mass.: Harvard University Press.

Foley, Edward. 1994. "Equal-Dollars-per-Voter: A Constitutional Principle of Campaign Finance." *Columbia Law Review* 94: 1204–57.

Fox, John. 1991. *Regression Diagnostics.* Newbury Park, Calif.: Sage.

Francia, Peter, John C. Green, Paul S. Herrnson, Wesley Joe, Lynda Powell, and Clyde Wilcox. 2000. "Donor Dissent: Congressional Contributors Rethink Giving." *Public Perspective* July/August: 29–32.

Franklin, Charles H. 1991. "Eschewing Obfuscation? Campaigns and the Perceptions of Senate Incumbents." *American Political Science Review* 85: 1193–214.

Franklin, Mark. 1996. "Electoral Participation." In *Comparing Democracies: Elections and Voting in Global Perspective,* ed. Lawrence Leduc, Richard G. Niemi, and Pippa Norris. Thousand Oaks, Calif.: Sage.

Freedman, Paul, and Ken Goldstein. 1999. "Measuring Media Exposure and the Effects of Negative Campaign Ads." *American Journal of Political Science* 43: 1189–208.

Fritz, Sara, and Dwight Morris. 1992. *Handbook of Campaign Spending*. Washington, D.C.: CQ Press.

Frymer, Paul. 1994. "Ideological Consensus within Divided Party Government." *Political Science Quarterly* 109: 287–311.

Frymer, Paul, Thomas Paul Kim, and Terri S. Bines. 1997. "Party Elites, Ideological Voters, and Divided Party Government." *Legislative Studies Quarterly* 22: 195–216.

Funk, Carolyn L. 1996. "Understanding Trait Inferences in Candidate Images." *Research in Micropolitics* 5: 97–123.

———. 1999. "Bringing the Candidate into Models of Candidate Evaluation." *Journal of Politics* 61: 700–720.

Gais, Thomas. 1998. *Improper Influence: Campaign Finance Law, Political Interest Groups, and the Problem of Political Equality*. Ann Arbor: University of Michigan Press.

Gallup. 2001. "Polls and Trends: Campaign Finance." http://www.gallup.com/poll/indicators/indcamp_fin.asp. Accessed on September 10, 2001.

Garand, James C., and Marci Glascock Lichtl. 2000. "Explaining Divided Government in the United States: Testing an Intentional Model of Split-Ticket Voting." *British Journal of Political Science* 30: 173–91.

Gelman, Andrew, and Gary King. 1990. "Estimating Incumbency Advantage without Bias." *American Journal of Political Science* 34: 1142–64.

Gilbert, Christopher P., David A. M. Peterson, Timothy R. Johnson, and Paul A. Djupe. 1999. *Religious Institutions and Minor Parties in the United States*. Westport, Conn.: Praeger.

Gilbert, Craig, and Katherine M. Skiba. 2000. "Politics Gender Gap Is Here to Stay; Experts Tie Trend to Views of Government Role." *Milwaukee Journal Sentinel*, October 30.

Gilens, Martin. 1988. "Gender and Support for Reagan: A Comprehensive Model of Presidential Approval." *American Journal of Political Science* 32: 19–49.

Glastris, Paul. 1997. "Immigration Boomerang: Despite Clinton's Scandals, It's the GOP that Bought Itself Big Trouble." *U.S. News and World Report*, March 17, 24–25.

Gold, Howard J. 1995. "Third-Party Voting in Presidential Elections: A Study of Perot, Anderson, and Wallace." *Political Research Quarterly* 48: 751–73.

Goldenberg, Edie N., Michael W. Traugott, and Frank R. Baumgartner. 1986. "Preemptive and Reactive Spending in U.S. House Races." *Political Behavior* 8: 3–20.

Goldstein, Ken. 2002. "What Did They See and When Did They See It? Measuring the Volume, Tone, and Targeting of Television Advertising in the 2000 Presidential Election." Paper presented at the Conference on Assessing the Vitality of Electoral Democracy in the U.S., Columbus, Ohio, March 7–10.

Goldstein, Ken, and Paul Freedman. 2002. "Lessons Learned: Campaign Advertising in the 2000 Elections." *Political Communication* 19: 5–28.

Goodstein, Laurie. 2001. "Bush's Stem Cell Decision Opens a Rift in Anti-Abortion Movement." *International Herald Tribune Online,* http://www.iht.com/articles/29169.htm, August 13.

Gore, Al. 2000. "America 2000: The Democratic Convention. Al Gore's Acceptance Speech." http://www.pbs.org/newshour/election2000/demconvention/gore.html Accessed on September 6, 2001.

Grant, J. Tobin, and Thomas J. Rudolph. 2003. "Value Conflict, Group Affect, and the Issue of Campaign Finance." *American Journal of Political Science* 47: 453–69.

Green, Donald, Bradley Palmquist, and Eric Schickler. 2002. *Partisan Hearts and Minds: Political Parties and the Social Identities of Voters.* New Haven, Conn.: Yale University Press.

Green, John C., John S. Jackson, and Nancy L. Clayton. 1999. "Issue Networks and Party Elites in 1996." In *The State of the Parties,* ed. John C. Green and Daniel M. Shea. Lanham, Md.: Rowman & Littlefield.

Greene, William H. 1997. *Econometric Analysis,* 3d ed. Upper Saddle River, N.J.: Prentice Hall.

Grofman, Bernard, William Koetzle, Michael McDonald, and Thomas Brunell. 2000. "A New Look at Split-Ticket Outcomes for House and President: The Comparative Midpoints Model." *Journal of Politics* 62: 34–50.

Groseclose, Tim, and Keith Krehbiel. 1994. "Golden Parachutes, Rubber Checks, and Strategic Retirements from the 102nd House." *American Journal of Political Science* 38: 75–99.

Groves, Robert M. 1979. "Actors and Questions in Telephone and Personal Interview Surveys." *Public Opinion Quarterly* 43: 19–205.

Groves, Robert M., and Robert L. Kahn. 1979. *Surveys by Telephone: A National Comparison with Personal Interviews.* New York: Academic Press.

Haller, H. Brandon, and Helmut Norpoth. 1994. "Let the Good Times Roll: The Economic Expectations of American Voters." *American Journal of Political Science* 38: 625–50.

———. 1997. "Reality Bites: News Exposure and Economic Opinion." *Public Opinion Quarterly* 61: 555–75.

Hasen, Richard L. 1996. "Clipping Coupons for Democracy: An Egalitarian Public Choice Defense of Campaign Finance Vouchers." *California Law Review* 84: 1–60.

———. 1999. "Campaign Finance Laws and the Rupert Murdoch Problem." *Texas Law Review* 77: 1627–66.

Herrnson, Paul S., and John C. Green, eds. 2002. *Multiparty Politics in America,* 2d ed. Lanham, Md.: Rowman & Littlefield.

Hetherington, Marc J. 1999. "The Effect of Political Trust on the Presidential Vote, 1968–96." *American Political Science Review* 93: 311–26.

———. 2001. "Resurgent Mass Partisanship: The Role of Elite Polarization." *American Political Science Review* 95: 619–31.

Hibbing, John R., and Elizabeth Theiss-Morse. 1995. *Congress As Public Enemy: Public Attitudes toward American Political Institutions.* New York: Cambridge University Press.

Hillygus, D. Sunshine, and Simon Jackman. 2002. "Assessing Campaign Effects in Election 2000." Paper presented at the Conference on Assessing the Vitality of Electoral Democracy in the U.S., Columbus, Ohio, March 7–10.

Hinckley, Barbara, Richard Hofstetter, and John H. Kessel. 1974. "Information and the Vote: A Comparative Election Study." *American Politics Quarterly* 2: 135–58.

Hofstetter, Richard. 1976. *Bias in the News: Television Coverage of the 1972 Election Campaign.* Columbus: Ohio State University Press.

Holbrook, Allyson, L., Jon A. Krosnick, Penny S. Visser, Wendi L. Gardner, and John T. Cacioppo. 2001. "Attitudes toward Presidential Candidates and Political Parties: Initial Optimism, Inertial First Impressions, and a Focus on Flaws." *American Journal of Political Science* 45: 930–50.

Holbrook, Thomas E. 2001. "Forecasting with Mixed Economic Signals: A Cautionary Tale." *PS: Political Science and Politics* 34: 39–44.

Hughes, John E., and M. Margaret Conway. 1997. "Public Opinion and Political Participation," In *Understanding Public Opinion*, ed. Barbara Norrander and Clyde Wilcox. Washington, D.C.: CQ Press.

Ingberman, Daniel, and John Villani. 1993. "An Institutional Theory of Divided Government and Party Polarization." *American Journal of Political Science* 37: 429–71.

International Institute for Democracy and Electoral Assistance. 2001. "Voter Turnout from 1945 to Date: A Global Report on Political Participation." http://www.idea.int/Voter_turnout/index.html. Accessed on December 12, 2001.

Jackman, Robert W. 1987. "Political Institutions and Voter Turnout in Industrialized Democracies." *American Political Science Review* 81: 405–23.

Jackman, Simon. 2000. "Post-Election Survey." Report for Knowledge Networks. http://jackman.stanford.edu/papers/2610tabs.pdf.

Jacobson, Gary C. 1990. *The Electoral Origins of Divided Government.* Boulder, Colo.: Westview Press.

———. 2000. "Party Polarization in National Politics: The Electoral Connection." In *Polarized Politics: Congress and the President in a Partisan Era*, ed. Jon R. Bond and Richard Fleisher. Washington, D.C.: CQ Press.

———. 2001. *The Politics of Congressional Elections.* 5th ed. New York: Longman.

Jacobson, Gary C., and Michael A. Dimock. 1994. "Checking Out: The Effects of Bank Overdrafts on the 1992 House Elections." *American Journal of Political Science* 38: 601–24.

Jacoby, William G. 1988a. "The Impact of Party Identification on Issue Attitudes." *American Journal of Political Science* 32: 643–61.

———. 1988b. "The Sources of Liberal-Conservative Thinking." *Political Behavior* 10: 316–32.

———. 1991. "Ideological Identification and Issue Attitudes." *American Journal of Political Science* 35: 178–205.

———. 1995. "The Structure of Ideological Thinking in the American Electorate." *American Journal of Political Science* 39: 314–35.

———. 2002. "Liberal-Conservative Thinking in the American Electorate." In *Research in Micropolitics: Political Decision Making, Participation, and Deliberation, Volume 6*, ed. Michael X. Delli Carpini, Leonie Huddy, and Robert Y. Shapiro. Greenwich, Conn.: JAI Press.

Jelen, Ted G. 2001. *Ross for Boss: The Perot Phenomena and Beyond*. Albany, N.Y.: SUNY Press.

Jelen, Ted G., Sue Thomas, and Clyde Wilcox. 1994. "The Gender Gap in Comparative Perspective: Gender Differences in Abstract Ideology and Concrete Issues in Western Europe." *European Journal of Political Research* 25: 171–86.

Johnston, Richard, Michael G. Hagen, and Kathleen Hall Jamieson. 2002. "Dynamics of the 2000 Presidential Campaign: Evidence from the Annenberg Study." Paper presented at the Conference on Assessing the Vitality of Electoral Democracy in the U.S., Columbus, Ohio, March 7–10.

Kaiser, Robert. 2000. "And the Winner Will Be . . . : Al Gore, According to the Election Soothsayers' Nearly Foolproof Formulas." *Washington Post Weekly*, June 5.

Katona, George. 1975. *Psychological Economics*. New York: Elsevier.

Katosh, John P., and Michael W. Traugott. 1981. "The Consequences of Validated and Self-Reported Voting Measures." *Public Opinion Quarterly* 45: 519–35.

Kaufmann, Karen M., and John R. Petrocik. 1999. "The Changing Politics of American Men: Understanding the Sources of the Gender Gap." *American Journal of Political Science* 43: 864–87.

Keith, Bruce, David B. Magleby, Candice J. Nelson, Elizabeth Orr, Mark C. Westlye, and Raymond E. Wolfinger. 1992. *The Myth of the Independent Voter*. Berkeley: University of California Press.

Kessel, John H. 1974. "The Parameters of Presidential Politics." *Social Science Quarterly* 55: 8–24.

———. 1980. *Presidential Campaign Politics*. Homewood, Ill.: Dorsey.

———. 1992. *Presidential Campaign Politics*. 4th ed. Pacific Grove, Calif.: Brooks/Cole.

Kessel, John H., and Herbert F. Weisberg. 1999. "Comparing Models of the Vote: The Answers Depend on the Questions." In *Reelection 1996: How Americans Voted*, ed. Herbert F. Weisberg and Janet M. Box-Steffensmeier. New York: Chatham House.

Key, V. O., Jr. 1964. *Politics, Parties, and Pressure Groups*. 5th ed. New York: Thomas Y. Crowell.

———. 1966. *The Responsible Electorate*. Cambridge: Harvard University Press.

Kiewiet, D. Roderick. 1979. "Approval Voting: The Case of the 1968 Election." *Polity* 12: 170–81.

———. 1983. *Macroeconomics and Micropolitics*. Chicago: University of Chicago Press.

Kimball, David C. 1997. *The Divided Voter in American Politics*. Ph.D. diss., Ohio State University.

Kimball, David C., Chris T. Owens, and Matthew J. McLaughlin. 2002. "Straight Party Ballots in State Legislative Elections." *Spectrum: The Journal of State Government* 75: 26–28.

Kinder, Donald R. 1986. "Presidential Character Revisited." In *Political Cognition*, ed. Richard R. Lau and David O. Sears. Hillsdale, N.J.: Lawrence Erlbaum.

Knight, Kathleen, and Robert S. Erikson. 1997. "Ideology in the 1990s." In *Understanding Public Opinion*, ed. Barbara Norrander and Clyde Wilcox. Washington, D.C.: CQ Press.

Kramer, Gerald H. 1971. "Short-Term Fluctuations in U.S. Voting Behavior." *American Political Science Review* 65: 131–43.

Krosnick, Jon, Matthew Courser, Kenneth Mulligan, and LinChiat Chang. 2002. "Exploring the Causes of Vote Choice in the 2000 Presidential Election: Longitudinal Analyses to Document the Causal Determinants of Candidate Preferences." Paper presented at the Conference on Assessing the Vitality of Electoral Democracy in the U.S., Columbus, Ohio, March 7–10.

Krosnick, Jon A., and Melanie C. Green. 1999. "The Impact of Interview Mode on Data Quality in the National Election Studies." *National Election Studies Technical Report* #58.

Lacy, Dean, and Barry C. Burden. 1999. "The Vote-Stealing and Turnout Effects of Ross Perot in the 1992 U.S. Presidential Election." *American Journal of Political Science* 43: 233–55.

———. 2002. "The Vote-Stealing and Turnout Effects of Third-Party Candidates in U.S. Presidential Elections, 1968–1996." Unpublished manuscript.

Lacy, Dean, and J. Tobin Grant. 1999. "The Impact of the Economy on the 1996 Election: The Invisible Foot." In *Reelection 1996: How Americans Voted*, ed. Herbert F. Weisberg and Janet M. Box-Steffensmeier. Chappaqua, N.Y.: Chatham House.

Lacy, Dean, and Quin Monson. 2002. "The Origins and Impact of Electoral Support for Third-Party Candidates: A Case Study of the 1998 Minnesota Gubernatorial Election." *Political Research Quarterly* 55: 409–37.

Lacy, Dean, and Emerson M. S. Niou. 1998. "Elections in Double-Member Districts with Nonseparable Preferences." *Journal of Theoretical Politics* 10:89–110.

Lacy, Dean, and Philip Paolino. 1998. "Downsian Voting and the Separation of Powers." *American Journal of Political Science* 42: 1180–99.

Lang, Kurt, Gladys Engel Lang, and Irving Crespi. 1998. "Discerning the Mandate: Voter Intentions and Media Interpretations." Presented at the annual meeting of the American Political Science Association, Boston, September.

Lau, Richard R. 1985. "Two Explanations for Negativity Effects in Political Behavior." *American Journal of Political Science* 29: 119–38.

Lawrence, David. 1999. *America: The Politics of Diversity*. Belmont, Calif.: West/ Wadsworth.

Layman, Geoffrey C. 1997. "Religion and Political Behavior in the United States." *Public Opinion Quarterly* 61: 288–316.

Layman, Geoffrey C., and Thomas M. Carsey. 1998. "Why Do Party Activists Convert? An Analysis of Individual-Level Change on the Abortion Issue." *Political Research Quarterly* 51: 723–50.

Lentz, Jacob. 2001. *Electing Jesse Ventura: A Third-Party Success Story*. Boulder, Colo.: Lynne Rienner.

Levine, Jeffery, Edward G. Carmines, and Robert Huckfeldt. 1997. "The Rise of Ideology in the Post-New Deal Party System, 1972–1992." *American Politics Quarterly* 25: 19–34.

Lewis-Beck, Michael S. 1988. *Economics and Elections: The Major Western Democracies*. Ann Arbor: University of Michigan Press.

Lewis-Beck, Michael S., and Mary Stegmaier. 2000. "Economic Determinants of Electoral Outcomes." *Annual Review of Political Science* 3: 183–219.

Lewis-Beck, Michael S., and Charles Tien. 2001. "Modeling the Future: Lessons from the Gore Forecast." *PS: Political Science and Politics* 34: 21–23.

Lockerbie, Brad. 2001. "Forecast 2000: An Afterthought." *American Politics Research*, 29: 307–12.

Luskin, Robert C. 1987. "Measuring Political Sophistication." *American Journal of Political Science* 31: 856–99.

Lynch, G. Patrick. 1999. "Presidential Elections and the Economy 1872 to 1996: The Times They Are a Changin' or the Song Remains the Same?" *Political Research Quarterly* 52: 825–44.

MacKuen, Michael B., Robert S. Erikson, and James A. Stimson. 1992. "Peasants or Bankers? The American Electorate and the U.S. Economy." *American Political Science Review* 86: 597–611.

Magleby, David B., and Marianne Holt. 1999. "The Long Shadow of Soft Money and Issue Advocacy Ads." *Campaigns and Elections* 20: 22–27.

Magleby, David B., and Candice J. Nelson. 1990. *The Money Chase: Congressional Campaign Finance Reform*. Washington, D.C.: Brookings Institution.

Mansbridge, Jane. 1985. "Myth and Reality: The ERA and the Gender Gap in the 1980 Election." *Public Opinion Quarterly* 49: 164–78.

Marcus, George E., and Michael B. MacKuen. 1993. "Anxiety, Enthusiasm, and the Vote: The Emotional Underpinnings of Learning and Involvement during Presidential Campaigns." *American Political Science Review* 87: 672–85.

Marcus, George E., W. Russell Neuman, and Michael B. MacKuen. 2000. *Affective Intelligence and Political Judgment*. Chicago: University of Chicago Press.

Marinucci, Carla. 2000. "Famous Women Helping Gore, Nader: They Emphasize Abortion Rights, Health Care." *San Francisco Chronicle.* October 26.

Markus, Gregory B., and Philip E. Converse. 1979. "A Dynamic Simultaneous Equation Model of Electoral Choice." *American Political Science Review* 73: 1055–70.

Mattei, Franco, and John S. Howes. 2000. "Competing Explanations of Split-Ticket Voting in American National Elections." *American Politics Quarterly* 28: 379–407.

Mattei, Franco, and Herbert F. Weisberg. 1994. "Presidential Succession Effects in Voting." *British Journal of Political Science* 24: 269–90.

Mattei, Laura R. Winsky, and Franco Mattei. 1998. "If Men Stayed Home . . . The Gender Gap in Recent Congressional Elections." *Political Research Quarterly* 51: 411–36.

McAllister, Ian, and Robert Darcy. 1992. "Sources of Split-Ticket Voting in the 1988 American Elections." *Political Studies* 40: 695–712.

McConnell, Mitch. 2001. "In Defense of Soft Money." *New York Times,* April 1.

McDermott, Monika. 1997. "Voting Cues in Low-Information Elections: Candidate Gender As a Social Information Variable in Contemporary United States Elections." *American Journal of Political Science* 41: 270–83.

McDonald, Michael P. 2001. "The Turnout Rate among Eligible Voters for U.S. States, 1980–1998." Unpublished manuscript.

McDonald, Michael P., and Samuel L. Popkin. 2001. "The Myth of the Vanishing Voter." *American Political Science Review* 95: 963–74.

Mebane, Walter R., Jr. 2000. "Coordination, Moderation, and Institutional Balancing in American Presidential and House Elections." *American Political Science Review* 94: 37–57.

Mebane, Walter R., Jr., and Jasjeet S. Sekhon. 2002. "Coordination and Policy Moderation at Midterm." *American Political Science Review* 96: 141–57.

Meffert, Michael F., Helmut Norpoth, and Anirudh V. S. Ruhil. 2001. "Realignment and Macropartisanship. *American Political Science Review* 95: 953–62.

Midlarsky, Manus I. 1984. "Political Stability of Two-Party and Multiparty Systems: Probabilistic Bases for the Comparison of Party Systems." *American Political Science Review* 78: 929–51.

Miller, Arthur H., and Martin P. Wattenberg. 1985. "Throwing the Rascals Out: Policy and Performance Evaluations of Presidential Elections." *American Political Science Review* 79: 359–72.

Miller, Warren E. 1991. "Party Identification, Realignment, and Party Voting: Back to Basics." *American Political Science Review* 85: 557–68.

Miller, Warren E., Donald R. Kinder, Steven J. Rosenstone, and the staff of National Election Studies. 1999. National Election Studies, 1992: Pre-/Post-Election Study [dataset]. Ann Arbor: University of Michigan, Center for Political Studies [producer and distributor].

Miller, Warren E., and J. Merrill Shanks. 1996. *The New American Voter.* Cambridge, Mass.: Harvard University Press.

Miller, William, and Richard G. Niemi. 2002. "Voting: Choice, Conditioning, and Constraint." In *Comparing Democracies*, 2d ed., ed. Lawrence LeDuc, Richard G. Niemi, and Pippa Norris. London: Sage.

Mockabee, Stephen T. 2001. "Party Polarization in American Politics: Congressional Polarization and Public Attitudes." Presented at the annual meeting of the Midwest Political Science Association, Chicago, April.

Nadeau, Richard, and Michael S. Lewis-Beck. 2001. "National Economic Voting in U.S. Presidential Elections." *Journal of Politics* 63: 150–81.

National Election Studies, Center for Political Studies, University of Michigan. 1995–2000. *The NES Guide to Public Opinion and Electoral Behavior*. http://www.umich.edu/nes/nesguide/nesguide.htm. Ann Arbor: University of Michigan, Center for Political Studies [producer and distributor].

Nelson, Michael. 1997. "The Election: Turbulence and Tranquility in Contemporary American Politics." In *The Elections of 1996*, ed. Michael Nelson. Washington, D.C.: CQ Press.

Neuborne, Burt. 1999a. "Is Money Different?" *Texas Law Review* 77: 1609–26.

———. 1999b. "Toward a Democracy-Centered Reading of the First Amendment." *Northwestern University Law Review* 93: 1055–73.

Nichols, Stephen M., and Paul Allen Beck. 1995. "Reversing the Decline: Voter Turnout in the 1992 Election." In *Democracy's Feast: Elections in America*, ed. Herbert F. Weisberg. Chatham, N.J.: Chatham House.

Nichols, Stephen M., David C. Kimball, and Paul Allen Beck. 1999. "Voter Turnout in the 1996 Election: Resuming the Downward Spiral?" In *Reelection 1996: How Americans Voted*, ed. Herbert F. Weisberg and Janet M. Box-Steffensmeier. Chatham, N.J.: Chatham House.

Nie, Norman H., Sidney Verba, and John R. Petrocik. 1979. *The Changing American Voter (Enlarged Edition)*. Cambridge, Mass.: Harvard University Press.

Niemi, Richard G., and Herbert F. Weisberg. 1993. *Classics in Voting Behavior*. Washington, D.C.: CQ Press.

———. 2001. *Controversies in Voting Behavior*. 4th ed. Washington, D.C.: CQ Press.

Nisbett, Richard E., and Timothy D. Wilson. 1977. "Telling More Than We Can Know: Verbal Reports on Mental Processes." *Psychological Review* 84: 231–59.

Nixon v. Shrink Missouri Government PAC, 161 F3d 519 (2000).

Norpoth, Helmut. 1995. "Is Clinton Doomed? An Early Forecast for 1996." *PS: Political Science and Politics* 28: 201–7.

———. 1996a. "The Economy." In *Comparative Democratic Elections*, ed. Lawrence LeDuc, Richard Niemi, and Pippa Norris. Newbury Park, Calif.: Sage.

———. 1996b. "Presidents and the Prospective Voter." *Journal of Politics* 58: 776–92.

———. 2001. "Primary Colors: A Mixed Blessing for Al Gore." *PS: Political Science and Politics* 34: 45–48.

———. 2002. "On a Short Leash: Term Limits and the Economic Voter." In *Economic Voting*, ed. Han Dorussen and Michael Taylor. London: Routledge.

Norrander, Barbara. 1997. "Independence Gap and the Gender Gap." *Public Opinion Quarterly* 61: 464–76.

———. 1998. "Gender and Economic Voting." Paper presented at the Midwest Political Science Convention, Chicago, April 23–25.

———. 1999a. "Is the Gender Gap Growing?" In *Reelection 1996: How Americans Voted*, ed. Herbert Weisberg and Janet Box-Steffensmeier. Chatham, N.J.: Chatham House.

———. 1999b. "Evolution of the Gender Gap." *Public Opinion Quarterly* 63: 566–76.

Ordeshook, Peter C., and Langche Zeng. 1997. "Rational Voters and Strategic Voting: Evidence from the 1968, 1980, and 1992 Elections." *Journal of Theoretical Politics* 9: 167–87.

Page, Benjamin I. 1978. *Choices and Echoes in Presidential Elections*. Chicago: University of Chicago Press.

Page, Benjamin I., and Richard A. Brody. 1972. "Policy Voting and the Electoral Process: The Vietnam War Issue." *American Political Science Review* 66: 979–95.

Page, Benjamin I., and Calvin C. Jones. 1979. "Reciprocal Effects of Policy Preferences, Party Loyalties, and the Vote." *American Political Science Review* 73: 1071–90.

Palfrey, Thomas R., and Keith T. Poole. 1987. "The Relationship between Information, Ideology, and Voting Behavior." *American Journal of Political Science* 31: 511–30.

Patterson, Thomas E. 2001. *The American Democracy*. 5th ed. New York: McGraw-Hill.

———. 2002. *The Vanishing Voter*. New York: Knopf.

Peters, John G., and Susan Welch. 1980. "The Effects of Charges of Corruption on Voting Behavior in Congressional Elections." *American Political Science Review* 74: 697–708.

Petrocik, John R., and Joseph Doherty. 1996. "The Road to Divided Government: Paved without Intention." In *Divided Government*, ed. Peter F. Galderisi. Lanham, Md.: Rowman & Littlefield.

Phillips, Kevin P. 1975. *Mediacracy: American Parties and Politics in the Communications Age*. Garden City, N.Y.: Doubleday.

Polidata®. 2001. "Presidential Results by Congressional Districts." www.polidata.org/prcd. Accessed on March 17, 2001.

Poole, Keith T., and Howard Rosenthal. 1997. *Congress: A Political-Economic History of Roll Call Voting*. New York: Oxford University Press.

Popkin, Samuel L. 1991. *The Reasoning Voter: Communication and Persuasion in Presidential Campaigns*. Chicago: University of Chicago Press.

Potter, Trevor. 2001. "Time to Restore Trust in Our Campaign System." *Christian Science Monitor*. July 12.

Powell, G. Bingham, Jr. 1986. "American Voter Turnout in Comparative Perspective." *American Political Science Review* 80: 17–43.

Rabinowitz, George B. 1976. "A Procedure for Ordering Object Pairs Consistent with the Multidimensional Unfolding Model." *Psychometrika* 41: 349–73.

Rahn, Wendy M., John H. Aldrich, Eugene Borgida, and John L. Sullivan. 1990. "A Social-Cognitive Model of Candidate Appraisal." In *Information and Democratic Processes*, ed. John Ferejohn and James Kuklinski. Urbana-Champaign: University of Illinois Press.

Rahn, Wendy, Jon Krosnick, and Marijke Breuning. 1994. "Rationalization and Derivation Processes in Survey Studies of Political Candidate Evaluation." *American Journal of Political Science* 38: 582–600.

Rapoport, Ronald B., and Walter J. Stone. 2001. *Party Change in America: Ross Perot, Third Parties, and Major-Party Response*. Unpublished manuscript.

Raskin, Jamin, and Jon Bonifaz. 1993. "Equal Protection and the Wealth Primary." *Yale Law and Policy Review* 11: 273–332.

Roberts, Cokie, and Steve Roberts. 2000. "The Talented Ms. Karenna." *USA Today*, February 27.

Rohde, David W. 1991. *Parties and Leaders in the Postreform House*. Chicago: University of Chicago Press.

Romer, Daniel, Kate Kenski, Paul Waldman, Christopher Adasiewicz, and Kathleen Hall Jamieson. 2003. *Capturing Campaign Dynamics: The New National Annenberg Election Survey*. New York: Oxford University Press.

Rosenstone, Steven J., Roy L. Behr, and Edward H. Lazarus. 1996. *Third Parties in America: Citizen Response to Major Party Failure*. 2d ed. Princeton, N.J.: Princeton University Press.

Rosenstone, Steven J., and John Mark Hansen. 1993. *Mobilization, Participation, and Democracy in America*. New York: Macmillan.

Rosenstone, Steven J., Donald R. Kinder, Warren E. Miller, and the staff of National Election Studies. 1998. National Election Studies, 1996: Pre-/Post-Election Study [dataset]. 3d release. Ann Arbor: University of Michigan, Center for Political Studies [producer and distributor].

Rosenstone, Steven J., Margaret Petrella, and Donald R. Kinder. 1993. "The Consequences of Substituting Telephone for Face-to-Face Interviewing in the 1992 National Election Study." *National Election Studies Technical Report* #43.

Rothenberg, Stuart, and Frank Newport. 1984. *The Evangelical Voter*. Washington, D.C.: Free Congress Research & Education Foundation.

Rudolph, Thomas J., and J. Tobin Grant. 2002. "An Attributional Model of Economic Voting: Evidence from the 2000 Presidential Election." *Political Research Quarterly* 55: 805–23.

Rusk, Jerrold G. 1970. "The Effect of the Australian Ballot Reform on Split Ticket Voting: 1876–1908." *American Political Science Review* 64: 1220–38.

Sapiro, Virginia. 2002. "It's the Context, Situation, and Question, Stupid: The

Gender Basis of Public Opinion." In *Understanding Public Opinion*, 2d ed., ed. Barbara Norrander and Clyde Wilcox. Washington, D.C.: CQ Press.

Scheve, Kenneth, and Michael Tomz. 1999. "Electoral Surprise and the Midterm Loss in U.S. Congressional Elections." *British Journal of Political Science* 29: 507–21.

Schlozman, Kay, Nancy Burns, Sidney Verba, and Jesse Donahue. 1995. "Gender and Citizen Participation: Is There a Different Voice?" *American Journal of Political Science* 39: 267–93.

Schulman, Mark A., and Gerald M. Pomper. 1975. "Variability in Electoral Behavior: Longitudinal Perspectives from Causal Modeling." *American Journal of Political Science* 19: 1–18.

Sears, David O., Richard R. Lau, Tom R. Tyler, Harris M. Allen, Jr. 1980. "Self-Interest vs. Symbolic Politics in Policy Attitudes and Presidential Voting." *American Political Science Review* 74: 670–84.

Shanks, J. Merrill, and Douglas A. Strand. 2002. "The Electoral Relevance of Broad Policy-Related Domains and Specific Issues." Paper presented at the annual meeting of the American Political Science Association, Boston, August-September.

Shapiro, Robert Y., and Harpreet Mahajan. 1986. "Gender Differences in Policy Preferences: A Summary of Trends from the 1960s to the 1980s." *Public Opinion Quarterly* 50: 42–61.

Shepsle, Kenneth A., and Mark S. Bonchek. 1997. *Analyzing Politics: Rationality, Behavior, and Institutions.* New York: W.W. Norton.

Sifry, Micah L. 2002. *Spoiling for a Fight: Third-Party Politics in America.* New York: Routledge.

Sigelman, Lee, Paul J. Wahlbeck, and Emmett H. Buell, Jr. 1997. "Vote Choice and the Preference for Divided Government: Lessons of 1992." *American Journal of Political Science* 41: 879–94.

Smith, Bradley A. 1996. "Faulty Assumptions and Undemocratic Consequences of Campaign Finance Reform." *Yale Law Journal* 105: 1049–92.

———. 1997. "Money Talks: Speech, Corruption, Equality, and Campaign Finance." *Georgetown Law Journal* 86: 45–100.

———. 1998. "Soft Money, Hard Realities: The Constitutional Prohibition of a Soft Money Ban." *Journal of Legislation* 179: 179–200.

———. 1999. "The Sirens' Song: Campaign Finance Regulation and the First Amendment." *Journal of Law and Policy* 6: 1–44.

———. 2001. *Unfree Speech: The Folly of Campaign Finance Reform.* Princeton, N.J.: Princeton University Press.

Smith, Charles E., Jr., Robert D. Brown, John M. Bruce, and L. Marvin Overby. 1999. "Party Balancing and Voting for Congress in the 1996 National Election." *American Journal of Political Science* 43: 737–64.

Smith, Charles E., Jr., and John H. Kessel. 1995. "The Partisan Choice: George Bush or Bill Clinton?" In *Democracy's Feast: Elections in America*, ed. Herbert F. Weisberg. Chatham, N.J.: Chatham House.

Smith, Charles E., Jr., Peter M. Radcliffe, and John H. Kessel. 1999. "The Partisan Choice: Bill Clinton or Bob Dole?" In *Reelection 1996: How Americans Voted*, ed. Herbert F. Weisberg and Janet M. Box-Steffensmeier. New York: Chatham House.

Smith, Tom W. 1990. "Classifying Protestant Denominations." *Review of Religious Research* 31: 225–45.

Sniderman, Paul M., Richard A. Brody, and Philip E. Tetlock. 1991. *Reasoning and Choice: Explorations in Political Psychology*. New York: Cambridge University Press.

Sniderman, Paul M., Joseph F. Fletcher, Peter H. Russell, and Philip E. Tetlock. 1996. *The Clash of Rights: Liberty, Equality, and Legitimacy in Pluralist Democracy*. New Haven, Conn.: Yale University Press.

Sorauf, Frank J. 1992. *Inside Campaign Finance: Myths and Realities*. New Haven, Conn.: Yale University Press.

———. 1994. "Politics, Experience, and the First Amendment: The Case of American Campaign Finance." *Columbia Law Review* 94: 1348–68.

Soss, Joe, and David T. Canon. 1995. "Partisan Divisions and Voting Decisions: U.S. Senators, Governors, and the Rise of a Divided Federal Government." *Political Research Quarterly* 48: 253–74.

Squire, Peverill, Raymond E. Wolfinger, and David P. Glass. 1987. "Residential Mobility and Voter Turnout." *American Political Science Review* 81: 45–66.

Stanley, Harold W., and Richard G. Niemi. 1991. "Partisanship and Group Support, 1952–1988." *American Politics Quarterly* 19: 189–210.

———. 1995. "The Demise of the New Deal Coalition: Partisanship and Group Support, 1952–1992." In *Democracy's Feast*, ed. Herbert F. Weisberg. Chatham, N.J.: Chatham House.

———. 1999. "Party Coalitions in Transition: Partisanship and Group Support, 1952–1996." In *Reelection 1996: How Americans Voted*, ed. Herbert F. Weisberg and Janet Box-Steffensmeier. Chatham, N.J.: Chatham House.

———. 2000. *Vital Statistics on American Politics*. 7th ed. Washington, D.C.: CQ Press.

———. 2001. *Vital Statistics on American Politics, 2001–2002*. Washington, D.C.: CQ Press.

Stokes, Donald E., Angus Campbell, and Warren E. Miller. 1958. "Components of Electoral Decision." *American Political Science Review* 52: 367–87.

Stokes, Donald E., and Gudmund R. Iversen. 1966. "On the Existence of Forces Restoring Party Competition." In *Elections and the Political Order*, ed. Angus Campbell, Philip E. Converse, Warren E. Miller, and Donald E. Stokes. New York: John Wiley.

Sunstein, Cass R. 1993. *The Partial Constitution*. Cambridge, Mass.: Harvard University Press.

———. 1994. "Political Equality and Unintended Consequences." *Columbia Law Review* 94: 1390–414.

Teixeira, Ruy A. 1992. *The Disappearing American Voter*. Washington, D.C.: Brookings Institution.

Timpone, Richard J. 1998a. "Structure, Behavior, and Voter Turnout in the United States." *American Political Science Review* 92: 145–58.

———. 1998b. "Ties That Bind: Measurement, Demographics, and Social Connectedness," *Political Behavior* 20: 53–77.

Tolleson-Rinehart, Sue, and Mark Somma. 1997. "Tracking the Elusive Green Women: Sex, Environmentalism, and Feminism in the United States and Europe." *Political Research Quarterly* 50: 153–70.

Traugott, Michael W., and John P. Katosh. 1979. "Response Validity in Surveys of Voting Behavior." *Public Opinion Quarterly* 43: 359–77.

Verba, Sidney, Kay Lehman Schlozman, and Henry E. Brady. 1995. *Voice and Equality: Civic Voluntarism in American Politics*. Cambridge, Mass.: Harvard University Press.

Wattenberg, Martin P. 1991. *The Rise of Candidate-Centered Politics*. Cambridge, Mass.: Harvard University Press.

———. 1998. *The Decline of American Political Parties, 1952–1996*. Cambridge, Mass.: Harvard University Press.

Webster, Benjamin, Clyde Wilcox, Peter Francia, John C. Green, Paul S. Herrnson, and Lynda Powell. 2000. "Competing for Cash: Individual Financiers of Congressional Elections." In *Playing Hardball: Campaigning for the U.S. Congress*, ed. Paul S. Herrnson. New York: Prentice-Hall Publishers.

Weisberg, Herbert F. 1987. "The Demographics of a New Voting Gap: Marital Differences in American Voting." *Public Opinion Quarterly* 51: 335–43.

———. 1999. "Political Partisanship." In *Measures of Political Attitudes*, ed. John P. Robinson, Phillip R. Shaver, and Lawrence S. Wrightsman. San Diego: Academic Press.

———. 2000. "Another Look at the Structure of Attitudes toward Presidential Candidates." Paper given at the annual meeting of the Midwest Political Science Association, Chicago, April.

———. 2002a. "Partisanship and Incumbency in Presidential Elections." *Political Behavior* 25: 339–60.

———. 2002b. "The Party in the Electorate As a Basis for More Responsible Parties." In *Responsible Partisanship? The Evolution of American Political Parties since 1950*, ed. John C. Green and Paul S. Herrnson. Lawrence: University Press of Kansas.

Weisberg, Herbert F., and Janet Box-Steffensmeier, eds. 1999. *Reelection 1996: How Americans Voted*. Chappaqua, N.Y.: Chatham House.

Weisberg, Herbert F., and Steven Greene. 2003. "The Political Psychology of Party Identification." In *Electoral Democracy*. ed. Michael B. MacKuen and George Rabinowitz. Ann Arbor: University of Michigan Press.

Weisberg, Herbert F., and Bernard Grofman. 1981. "Candidate Evaluations and Turnout." *American Politics Quarterly* 9: 197–219.

Weisberg, Herbert F., and Stephen T. Mockabee. 1999. "Attitudinal Correlates of the 1996 Presidential Vote: The People Reelect a President." In *Reelection 1996: How Americans Voted*, ed. Herbert F. Weisberg and Janet M. Box-Steffensmeier. Chappaqua, N.Y.: Chatham House.

Weisberg, Herbert F., and Jerrold G. Rusk. 1970. "Dimensions of Candidate Evaluation." *American Political Science Review* 64: 1167–85.

Welch, Susan, and John Hibbing. 1992. "Financial Conditions, Gender and Voting in American National Elections." *Journal of Politics* 54: 197–213.

Wertheimer, Fred, and Susan Manes. 1994. "Campaign Finance Reform: A Key to Restoring the Health of Our Democracy." *Columbia Law Review* 94: 1126–59.

Wessel, Christina, Wendy Rahn, and Tom Rudolph. 2000. "An Analysis of the 1998 NES Mixed-Mode Design." *National Election Studies Technical Report* #57.

Wilcox, Clyde. 1996. *Onward Christian Soldiers? The Religious Right in American Politics*. Boulder, Colo.: Westview Press.

———. 2000. "Social Science in Space and Time." In *Space and Beyond: The Frontier Theme in Science Fiction*, ed. Gary Westfahl. Westport, Conn.: Greenwood.

———. 2002. "Wither the Christian Right?: The Elections and Beyond." In *The Election of the Century and What It Tells Us about the Future of American Politics*. Armonk: M.E. Sharpe.

Wlezien, Christopher. 2001. "On Forecasting the Presidential Vote." *PS: Political Science and Politics* 34: 24–31.

Wlezien, Christopher, and Robert S. Erikson. 2001. "After the Election: Our Forecast in Retrospect." *American Politics Research* 29: 320–28.

Wolfinger, Raymond, and Steven J. Rosenstone. 1980. *Who Votes?* New Haven, Conn.: Yale University Press.

"Women and Men: Is a Realignment under Way?" 1982. *Public Opinion* (April-May): 21–32.

Wright, Gerald C., Jr. 1978. "Candidate Policy Positions and Voting in Congressional Elections." *Legislative Studies Quarterly* 3: 445–64.

Wright, Gerald C., Jr., and Michael B. Berkman. 1986. "Candidates and Policy in United States Senate Elections." *American Political Science Review* 80: 567–88.

Wright, Matthew B. 1993. "Shirking and Political Support in the U.S. Senate, 1964–84." *Public Choice* 76: 103–23.

Zaller, John R. 1992. *The Nature and Origins of Mass Opinion*. Cambridge, U.K.: Cambridge University Press.

———. 1999. "Know Nothing Voters in U.S. Presidential Elections, 1948–1996." www.sscnet.ucla.edu/polisci/faculty/zaller/. Manuscript.

Index

Palmer, Harvey D., 113
Palmquist, Bradley, 249
Paolino, Phil, 164, 209, 211, 223, 251
Partisanship, *see* Party identification
Party coalitions, *see* Party identification
Party identification, 4, 8, 31–33;
124–25, 249–50; and gender gap,
143–45, 147–53, 157–58; and ideology, 8, 104–7, 116–18, 176; and
party coalitions, 126–40; and vote,
20, 41–46, 220–24; and voter
turnout, 200–203; over time, 8,
31–32
Party ideology, *see* Party identification
Party polarization, *see* Political parties: polarization of
Party realignment, *see* Political parties: realignment of
Party salience theory, 21; and ticket
splitting, 161–62, 165–77
Patterson, Thomas E., 11, 176
Perot, H. Ross, 233, 234, 256–57;
candidacy affecting 1992 voter
turnout, 180, 202; popular vote in
1992, 38, 207; supporters in 2000
election, 220, 223–25
Peters, John G., 29
Peterson, David A. M., 222, 224, 256
Petrocik, John R., 106, 143, 164, 194,
198
Phillips, Kevin P., 251
Political independence, *xi*, 31–33,
126, 143, 164, 196, 232, 250; and
split-ticket voting, 163, 170, 173;
and voter turnout, 192, 200–203,
242, 255–56
Political involvement: and voter
turnout, 94, 187–94
Political parties: differences between
165–74; polarization of, *xi*, 8, 21,
138–40, 144, 174–77; realignment
of, 53, 131, 143–44; voter attitudes
toward, 66–69, 71–72

Political sophistication: and ideology,
107–12; and voter turnout, 187–94
Pomper, Gerald M., 113
Poole, Keith T., 164, 167, 209
Pope, Jeremy, 23
Popkin, Samuel L., 113, 115, 253
Potency, 80–81
Potter, Trevor, 100
Powell, Colin, 233
Powell, G. Bingham, Jr., 182, 183
Powell, Lynda W., 87, 246
Presidential nominees: public images
of, 66–71, 76–78
Presidential primaries, 7, 51, 145,
231–32
Presidential term limits, 4–5, 58–60,
63–64
Price, H. Douglas, 54
Probit analysis, 13, 75, 93–94, 246.
See also Logistic regression
Protestantism: and party identification, 20, 31–33, 41–46. *See also*
Religion; Religious denomination

Quayle, Dan, 4, 230

Rabinowitz, George B., 108
Race: and party identification, 31–33,
41–46; and voter turnout, 187–94.
See also African Americans
Radcliffe, Peter M., 66
Rahn, Wendy M., 113, 204, 240
Rapoport, Ronald B., 220, 223
Raskin, Jamin, 87, 88
Rational choice models, 9, 10, 208
Reagan, Ronald, 3, 50, 54, 144; attitudes of women towards, 141; legacy of, 5, 27, 29–30; popularity of,
37–38
Reform Party: convention, 231, 233.
See also Pat Buchanan, H. Ross
Perot, Jesse Ventura
Region: and party identification, 31–
33

The authorized representative in the EU for product safety and compliance is:
Mare Nostrum Group
B.V Doelen 72
4831 GR Breda
The Netherlands

* 9 7 8 0 8 0 4 7 4 8 5 6 8 *